LITERATURE
of the
NORTH

LITERATURE of the NORTH

edited by

DAVID HEWITT and MICHAEL SPILLER

ABERDEEN UNIVERSITY PRESS

First published 1983
Aberdeen University Press
A member of the Pergamon Group

The publishers gratefully acknowledge the financial assistance of the Scottish Arts Council in the publication of this book.

British Library Cataloguing in Publication Data
Literature of the north
1. Literature
I. Hewitt, David II. Spiller, Michael
808.8 PN45

ISBN 0 08 028453 1
ISBN 0 08 028468 X Pbk

PRINTED IN GREAT BRITAIN
THE UNIVERSITY PRESS
ABERDEEN

Contents

Preface and Acknowledgements

In 1978, the University of Aberdeen held an Open Day, for which one of the editors of this volume set himself the apparently not too demanding task of preparing a literary map of the University's catchment area – the north and north-east parts of Scotland, including the Orkney and Shetland Islands, from which for centuries students have come in to what a university poet called 'the grey howe at the fit o' the Spital Brae.' Though the area is large, it is thinly populated; yet the map quickly grew dense with names and places, as the compiler and his colleagues discovered the astonishing number and variety of poets and novelists, literary historians and critics, and men and women of letters who belonged to the North, either by accident of birth or by the circumstances of their education and working lives. Even if we let go Lord Byron, on whom the North seems to have bestowed chiefly a terrifying Calvinist childhood, there remained some seventy men and women for whom any Dictionary of Scottish Literature would make room, whose native places dot the map from Lerwick to Montrose, from Lewis to Old Aberdeen itself. Such riches seemed to justify the boast of James Beattie, himself a nationally respected poet in the age of Johnson and Boswell, that

The Southland chiels indeed hae mettle,
And brawly at a sang can ettle;
Yet we right couthily might settle
    On this side Forth.
The devil pay them wi' a pettle,
    That slight the North!

And feeling that his boast has gained more substance in the two centuries since, past and present members of the Department of English (Language and Literature) in the University of Aberdeen have assembled this volume of essays. In choosing only poets and writers of fiction, we have left out some distinguished names: the autodidact

Hugh Miller and the great scholar and critic Herbert Grierson; the collectors of ballad and folk song, David Herd, Peter Buchan and Gavin Greig; the moralist and historian, Bishop Gilbert Burnet, and that prince of Scots lexicographers, David Murison. What remains includes literature from mediaeval times to the present day, and literature both well known and unfamiliar: we hope that the reader who is already an enthusiast for the poetry of Barbour's *Brus* or the fiction of George Mackay Brown will be delighted to discover the fantastic recesses of Sir Thomas Urquhart's prose or the vigorous country verse of Alexander Ross, the dominie of Lochlee. The writer of each essay has ended with suggestions for further reading, listing as far as possible books and articles that are available to the general reader.

For their permissions to reprint quotations from the works discussed in this volume, the editors are most grateful to: Jonathan Cape Ltd. and the Estate of Eric Linklater (*Private Angelo*, 1946); Curtis Brown Ltd., on behalf of the Estate of Lewis Grassic Gibbon (*A Scots Quair*, 1967); Faber and Faber Ltd. (W.H.Auden, *Collected Shorter Poems*, 1966, Neil Gunn, *The Silver Darlings*, 1941 and *The Collected Poems of Edwin Muir*, 1963); Victor Gollancz Ltd. (Iain Crichton Smith, *From Bourgeois Land*, 1969, *Selected Poems*, 1970, *Love Poems and Elegies*, 1972, *The Notebooks of Robinson Crusoe*, 1973 and *In The Middle*, 1977); Granada Publishing Ltd. (Eric Linklater, *Roll of Honour*, 1961); Dairmid Gunn (Neil Gunn, *Highland River*, 1937, *The Shadow*, 1948, and *The Atom of Delight*, 1956); Hogarth Press Ltd. and George Mackay Brown (*A Calendar of Love*, 1967, *A Time to Keep*, 1969, *Magnus*, 1973, *Hawkfall*, 1974 and *Witch and Other Stories*, 1977); Macdonald Publishers, Edinburgh (Iain Crichton Smith, *The Long River*, 1955 and *Hamlet in Autumn*, 1972); Mrs. Mary Macdonald (Fionn MacColla, 'Mein Bumpf', *At the Sign of the Clenched Fist*, 1967, *The Albannach*, 1971 and *Too Long in this Condition*, 1975); Macmillan, London and Basingstoke (Eric Linklater, *The Man on my Back*, 1941); A.D. Peters and Co. Ltd. (Eric Linklater, Magnus Merriman, 1934, *Ripeness is All*, 1935, *A Year of Space*, 1954 and *Fanfare for a Tin Hat*, 1970); Iain Crichton Smith (*New Poets 1959*, *Thistles and Roses*, 1961, *The Law and the Grace*, 1965 and *Orpheus and Other Poems*, 1974); and the Souvenir Press Ltd. (Neil Gunn, *Butcher's Broom*, 1934, *Young Art and Old Hector*, 1942 and *The Serpent*, 1943; Fionn MacColla, *And the Cock Crew*, 1977 and *The Minister*, 1979).

King's College
Aberdeen 1982

Michael Spiller
David Hewitt

THE NORTHERN INITIATIVE: JOHN OF FORDUN, JOHN BARBOUR and the author of the 'SAINTS' LEGENDS'

Matthew P. McDiarmid

To this day the visitor to Old Aberdeen, as he makes his way by the cobbled High Street past the mitred university chapel, where lie the remains of the founding bishop William Elphinstone, to the Dutch-looking Town House of 1788 and beyond it to the embattled-seeming Cathedral of St Machar, feels the demand of past achievement for due acknowledgement. In that walk he can easily imagine how the builders' sense of a living past might touch their work, not least when revolutionary events made them still more aware of that past.

In the second half of the fourteenth century, when the revolution in Scottish affairs effected by the long wars of independence was working painfully towards a settlement, and when authority confronted the new disturbances of ecclesiastical controversy and schism, the church at Aberdeen became the centre of what may well be termed a school of history-writing. The writers were motivated by loyalty to country and kirk, and their initiative was to prove of vital importance for the nation's culture; briefly, it set going Scottish 'history' and Scottish literature. The three authors concerned all held office in the Cathedral.

John of Fordun (in Kincardineshire), a chaplain at Aberdeen, completed versions of his Annals of Scotland in 1363 and 1385, about which year he died. His Latin work, which can only be passingly appreciated here, was the fruit of researches in Scottish, English and Irish libraries and was continued by a succession of writers: Andrew Wyntoun and Walter Bower, writing c. 1405-20 and 1441-49; John Mair, Hector Boece and George Buchanan publishing in 1521, 1526 and 1582. However credulously the Annals report the beginnings of the Scottish race and kingdom, they are still a valued source and their influence, direct or transmitted, is discernible through many generations of poets and prose-writers, from Barbour to Burns. Fordun gave a shape to Scotland's consciousness of its history, a voice to the principles by which it worked, and in so doing affected that history. John Barbour, archdeacon at Aberdeen, wrote his heroic poem *The Bruce* in the years 1376-1378, but like his Latin-writing friend had long travelled the land collecting material, accounts preserved in castle or abbey, still current lays, the faithful memories of old soldiers and their sons. The third of these writers was the author of religious Lives, lost ones that circulated, he assures us, 'in syndry placis' and the surviving ones now known as *The Scottish Saints' Legends*. We do not know for sure who he was, but references in these show him to have been a 'mynistere of haly kirk' very familiar with both Aberdeen and Elgin.

How was it that the initiative came from the north? The cathedral at Elgin, fired in 1390, was lamented then as the glory of the nation and an attraction to foreigners. That of Aberdeen was significantly different. The burgh had been burned by the troops of Edward III in 1336, and probably the church at the same time, for the Cathedral as we know it is the new structure commenced by Barbour's bishop, Alexander Kinninmund (1355-1380), about whom more hereafter. The challenge from the past to rebuild must have been daily with the cathedral's servants. They were doubtless also stirred by the improving economy of the region. The rebuilt port had restored its trade with the Baltic, and whatever losses the north had known it had not suffered the same degree of foreign spoliation as the south. Its connections with the reigning families were close. It was to Aberdeen that the young King, David Bruce, returned from his French refuge; his father's sister kept her castle at Kildrummy and his own sister lived and died in Aberdeen. His nephew and successor, Robert Stewart, liked to holiday and hold court at Braemar, and the determination of members of that king's family to establish themselves, however lawlessly, in the north is noticed in every account of the period. We should remember that Glasgow and Edinburgh (not yet a capital) did not have their later importance.

Whatever special promptings of circumstance the north may have known, it will be readily understood that it shared with the liberated nation a concern with the past – as with similarly fruitful effects did the no-longer-independent Scotland of 'Ossian' Macpherson, Lord Hailes, Burns and Scott. That concern was not only with the independent nation but also with the independent church and its traditions. It was the church that had given the most consistent and fervent support to the armies of Balliol, Wallace and Bruce, bringing to their cause a religious dimension. Like other bishops David of Moray had preached an anti-English crusade. The two dimensions, secular and spiritual, can be illustrated from a charter of 1360 issued by Alexander Kinninmund, under whom our three writers served. It refers to the request of a certain David Brown, now impoverished, that his land be held by a cousin. In granting the request the bishop chooses to remember the service done by David's grandfather Adam in fighting alongside Wallace at Falkirk 'for the freedom and rights of our kirk' (*pro libertate et jure ecclesiae nostrae*). The gratuitous allusion tells us much about Kinninmund and the sentiments that ruled his Chapter. They animated the verse of Barbour and, especially where Scottish saints were considered, that of his colleague, the author of the *Legends*. For Fordun too the traditions of church and nation go together.

Of course, there were Scottish poets before Barbour, but our knowledge of them is only fragmentary. Thus it is plain from Latinised tales and verses in Fordun and his vernacular imitator Wyntoun that there was a 'saga' of the deeds of Malcolm Canmore, in which his encounters with Macbeth and other treacherous Scots figured prominently. In the year 1286, fateful for Alexander III and Scotland, a Norwegian ambassador fetched from the Scottish court a romance which we now know only as a translated section of the *Karlamagnussaga*. It would seem that in the same last quarter of the thirteenth century Thomas Lermont of Ercildoune made a version of the Tristram story and a collection of prophetic sayings, then a popular *genre*. The *Sir Ferumbras* with which Bruce heartened his men at Loch Lomond was most likely not written in French. There was doubtless translation, sometimes poetic, of the more fanciful Latin narratives. Wyntoun mentions a Scots version of Honoré d'Autun's marvellous account of strange places and peoples, the *Imago Mundi*. But these are tantalising trivia, and in any case we can be sure that, for the most part, what was composed before the destructive wars showed only the conventional face of European romance and could not have been as vital and dramatic as the war-time lays preserved or reworked by Barbour, Wyntoun, and Hary in his epic *Wallace*. Naturally the country that produced figures of European importance like Duns Scotus and Michael Scott would also have had its Latin poets, and among them must be ranked Bruce's great chancellor, Bernard of Linton, who was not only responsible for the fine rhetoric of the Declaration of Arbroath in 1320 but also for a verse account of his master's career (partly 'prosified', partly quoted, by Walter Bower). It may have been read by Barbour at Aberdeen but he could never have got from it the vividly factual detail derived from the lays that enliven his description of the years of danger.

John Barbour properly figures in this review of early northern writing though there is good reason to think that he was not a native of the north. He received his first appointment, as a precentor at Dunkeld 1359, from bishop John Luce, whose name suggests an origin in the south-west. It is his poetical scenes in the south-west that are said to be personally known to him, and are most particularly described. Again the three witnesses that he cites belong to that area. The Irish war to which he gives such space, writing with such knowledge and interest, was almost exclusively an enterprise of the south-western lords. His language as evidenced in his rhyming sounds is much closer to northern English than is that of his poetical colleague, whose connection with the Scottish north is more evident.

None the less, it was in Old Aberdeen and doubtless also in the bishop's manse at Rayne that he composed the *Bruce* and his lost 'Genealogy of the Stewarts'. With his friend David of Mar, who was to be secretary to Joanna, David Bruce's Queen, he represented the northern bishops at the parliament that arranged the ransoming of King David from English captivity. On three occasions he visited Paris, once in the company of the Earl of Douglas whose apparent objective was the Baptist's shrine at Amiens, also visited by the author of the *Legends*. Like his fellow poet, also almost certainly a graduate of the Sorbonne, his reading from sources outside Scotland was entirely in French and Latin authors. (One has to regret the failure of modern Scottish universities to produce equally good Europeans, men and women whose further studies are not parochially confined to the English connection). His diocese was an extensive one and its inspection must have been arduous. Once extreme ill health brought, at King Robert's request, an indulgence from the Pope at Avignon excusing him from such duties.

The true encourager of Barbour's patriotic verse was doubtless his worthy Bishop, but he found a more exalted patron in the King. As an Auditor of the Exchequer – an office also filled in his day by Sir Hugh of Eglinton, who is surely the poet of that name and title mentioned by William Dunbar – he would be well known to Robert II, and it would appear from a record of the next reign that it was the presentation of a copy of the *Bruce*, most likely at Braemar, that secured for him a lifetime pension. The citizens of Aberdeen may not have appreciated the privilege of paying it from the burgh's water tolls, but there can be no doubt that in his day – he died in March 1395 – and long afterwards he was recognised as the national poet.

What is the first thing that needs to be said about his famous poem? It is that the 'fredome' in the great lines, 'A! fredome is a noble thing!/Fredome mayss man to haiff liking', has reference to more than a national loyalty, though without the nation Barbour cannot conceive the order and security that allow the ordinary affairs and relationships of life to be freely and happily conducted. It refers to natural rights, a concept very familiar to him as a student of civil law, and indeed the very basis of all those legal arguments that supported the Scottish case at Rome, and that were collected into a book by Alan of Montrose. There were rights conferred by old tradition, common acceptance, such as both nation and individual could claim, and there were rights inherent in the individual that natural and Christian reason had to recognise. Barbour can jest about a possible conflict between them – at a given moment, he asks, which has the more urgent priority, the debt of nature that a man owes to his wife, or the traditional service that he owes to his lord. But he does not jest when he asserts that free men fight best for freedom, citing the freeing of slaves in republican Rome so that they would defend the city more gladly against the enemy at the gates, Hannibal. In making that assertion he could not have failed to have in mind the fact that his Scotland, so much earlier than England or France, had done away with serfdom, a revolutionary consequence of the fight for survival. Whatever natural rights a man might possess they were all contained in the word 'justice', and what justice would there be when the judge was both a stranger to the tradition and the suppliant's foe? Of course, the chaos of acquisitive tyranny that was unleashed on Scotland had a response on the simplest level of feeling, but with 'clerks', educated men, such feeling was supported by an appeal to reason. Freedom was the law of nature, the way of reason.

Certainly the Scottish community did not see the issue as a mere conflict of kings –nor even as a conflict of native and alien baronages, for were the native barons not the well indoctrinated sons of the Church, which was committed to the independent tradition, and did the Church not have other humbler but similarly taught sons? In the Declaration and the 'Narrative of Bamborough' (this last discovered not long since in a Spanish lawyer's case-book), both naturally compiled by clerics, it is a very self-conscious entity that speaks: the Scots are an ancient and free people; their kings, such as Robert Bruce, are their chosen leaders and cannot undo the nation according to their will or convenience. As John Mair (1518) was later to say, 'A kingdom is not like a man's shirt, to dispose of as he pleases'. Fordun, obviously expressing more than his own viewpoint approves the deposition of native tyrants, just as George Buchanan was to do in Reformation times. When David Bruce, for very personal reasons, proposed an English heir to the throne parliament told him that such a choice was intolerable and not in his competence. The *Bruce* ends with a prayer that king and lords will be just what their ancestors were, good servants of the independent nation.

It has even been said that Barbour does no more than glorify aristocrats, yet he invents a speech for a Scottish exile at the court of Edward II in which the strength of Bruce's forces is said to be the men who farm the country, every one of them having become as worthy as any knight. He is happy to have the king and his three noble lieutenants for heroes, but he finds room for the achievements of lesser men such as the Forester who takes Forfar castle, Sym of Ledington whose invention of the rope ladder delivers Roxburgh to Douglas, the farmer Bunnok who captures the English supply-station at Linlithgow, John Thomasson who brought the Carrick men safely home from the Irish disaster. After all, not only did history require him to concentrate on the few leaders, but to do so was to give his narrative the necessary unity of interest. The intelligent reader must see that the spirit and social tendency of the *Bruce* do not belong in the feudal and chivalric world. Barbour is not as Scott imagined him, a Scottish Froissart.

He does share the Frenchman's appreciation of valour wherever found, as in the conduct of Sir Giles de Argente at Bannockburn, and he shows much more awareness of the human meaning of the actions that he describes. On the same field of Bannockburn Edward Bruce who had, arguably, done most to secure the victory, looks down at the body of his friend the Earl of Mar and wishes that 'the journey wer/Undone, than he swa ded had bene'. At Dundalk where Edward fought his last battle a Scots knight looking on the many dead stumbles dazed from the field. That Barbour chooses to dwell on a widow's willingness to give her two sons to the cause of a fugitive king, and on the same king's 'ful gret curtesy' in halting his little army at Limerick in order to allow a laundress to have her baby in safety, is to his credit as well as the king's. Bruce, who gives all an example of fortitude in the face of reversals and personal losses – his wife, daughter, a brother – is a man of tears when he meets friends who have suffered similarly.

Nor does the ultimate justice of their cause seduce Barbour into falsifying tradition by passing over what was blameworthy or repellent in the actions and characters of his heroes. The Bruce's impulsive killing of John Comyn in the church at Dumfries is understood but not condoned. His execution of Sir David Barclay, who had not participated in a plot against the king but failed to betray his treacherous friends by reporting it, is seen as needlessly harsh, and a voice of protest is allowed. Hunted in the fastness of Carrick and Galloway the king, we are told, would use women both as mistresses and spies. Nor is his brother Edward free of fault. He is accused (to this writer it would seem unfairly) of hot-headed folly, not counting the risk and cost of his astonishing exploits both in Scotland and Ireland. Though he led the victorious van at Bannockburn and is said to have been responsible for the battle being fought at all, the credit for the victory is given wholly to the skilful generalship of his elder brother. The attack on the English over-lordship of Ireland is attributed to personal ambition, its failure to the above-mentioned readiness to face impossible odds. Perhaps tradition in the west country which suffered most in the Irish adventure biased Barbour's judgements here, for it does not seem to have occurred to him that Edward was not likely to commit Scottish forces to either of these great undertakings without the king's full approval, and that the fatal decision to fight at Dundalk before a Scottish relief arrived may have been due more to necessity than wilfulness. Randolph's temporary defection from the national cause because of his disgust with the piece-meal methods of guerilla warfare favoured by the always cautious Bruce is not passed over in silence, and in one action at least Douglas is shown as something less than knightly.

Realism, 'suthfastnes' or truth to fact, is a sobering principle in a narrative that might easily have become a simple tale of achievements and glories conformable to the chivalric code and fashion. The king could be ruthless where there was resistance, as when he burned 'all Bowchane/Fra end till end and sparyt nane', so that in Barbour's day men could still lament the devastation. It was not only a De Bohun that felt his axe, but a Campbell for breaking the line of march in Ireland. 'The Douglas Lardnere' is a tale of horror as well as daring enterprise. the slain English garrison of the hero's briefly recaptured castle at Lanark are tossed into a dungeon to swim in a 'foule melee' with their supplies of food and drink. When Scottish divisions, with Douglas and the young Walter Stewart (father of Robert II) under Randolph's command, raid northern England as far as York they go 'birnand, slayand and distroyand'; nor are priests spared by the long Scottish spears, as the mockingly named encounter 'The Chapter of Mytton' illustrates. Barbour knows that it is war and what that meant in these days of fighting for survival as a nation that he has to describe. It tells us much about his approach to his subject that he is almost as full in his account of the audacious trickery by which the Scots at Wardale in Yorkshire, refusing to descend from their fastness and accept the challenge of a superior army under the young and romantic Edward III, leave great fires burning to mislead the enemy about their intentions and escape by night over the supposedly impassable marsh to their rear. If Barbour calls his heroic history a 'romans' it is generally with the simple meaning 'story', and specifically with the sense of his own words, a story

Off men that war in gret distress,
And assayit full gret hardynes
Or thai mycht cum till thair entent.

Neither the 'gret distress' nor the 'gret hardynes' turns him from an account of often terrible events.

None the less, the elements of pseudo-historical allusion and even of illustrative invention have to be noticed, for he was a poet and no plain historian, except in the substance of his narrative. Thus he rebukes John of Lorne for comparing Bruce's prowess in the rear-guard action to that of Gaul MacMorna, when he might 'mair manerlik' (that is, more 'French-like') have likened him to Gaudifer de Larys, a hero of the *Roman d' Alixandre*. The same romance is a quite unnecessary source for the king's order to forget the business of taking wealthy ransoms till the day is won. More interesting is his debt to classical writers – unless Abbot Bernard's Latin verses helped him here – for the idea and matter of those spirited speeches that Bruce makes in the moment of defeat or victory.

we for our lyvis
And for our childer and our wifis,
And for the fredome of our land,
Ar strenyeit [compelled] in battale for to stand,
And thai for thair mycht anerly [only].

And in one inspiring place he quite naturally remembers Herodotus's account of Thermopylae. Just as the exiled Spartan king Demaratus tells the overweening Xerxes that Leonidas's few men are not there to die submissively, so an exiled Scottish knight tells Edward II that the Scots at prayer do not seek mercy but prepare to fight to the death. It is the same traitor knight who is later used to praise the Scots peasants as the staple of Bruce's armies and to warn Edward against risking another campaign until the peasants have forgotten their fighting skills. Such touches to the historical picture, of course, do not falsify it, and serve only to lend language to the spirit of the Scottish resistance.

Most important to the poet and patriot in Barbour is, however, the ideal of leadership that Bruce exemplifies. He is more than the great warrior-king, he is the father of his people, 'the few folk of ane symple land'. A little thing illustrates this familial and clan concept at Bannockburn; as men arrive at the appointed time in small or large companies he welcomes them, 'Spekand gud wordis heir and thair', so that they feel him to be *their* worthy king and his 'honour' in *their* hands. The account of the lamentation about his death-bed (in the courtly Froissart only a tribute to royal valour) has the meaning that the nation had come to be embodied in his person. This is so because, where his people were concerned, he had integrity, kept faith, which is the virtue on which Aristotle bases all other virtues, and which suffices,

To mak a man sa gud that he
May symply gud man callyt be.
He wes in all his dedis lele [faithfully].

Although this is actually said of the loyal Douglas (just as a century later Hary speaks of 'Gud Wallace'), good King Robert is to be remembered in the same way.

The 'suthfastnes' that the poet invites his readers to enjoy refers to style as well as matter. A sense of the real is to be conveyed, and this satisfying realism will be enhanced, not diminished, by our being made aware of the ideal dimension to which persons and actions must be related; as he observes in his Prologue, 'Thus contrar thingis evirmar/Discoveryngis of the tothir ar'. There had been such two-dimensioned realism in literature before Barbour; it is the intensely simple aspect in which it shows itself, losing nothing of the dignity that belongs to a statement of universal import, that distinguishes it here. Barbour had established the value and manner that would characterise the classic utterances of Scottish poetry, those of Henryson, Burns, the ballads. If foreign influences were later to be accepted, for example, those of Chaucer or Pope, they would be superficial and not substantial.

The author of the Scottish *Legends of the Saints* presents himself as an old and infirm priest dictating to a scribe 'for falt of sycht'. In earlier years, as he tells us, he had written widely known Lives of Mary and Jesus, and still seeks to instruct 'lordis . . . that steris landis and haly kirke'. Though he can quote the French poet-historian Helinand and the treatise on courtly love called *Le Roman de la Rose*, and had travelled in more than one country (France and Italy presumably), it is impossible to think of him ever having written on any but religious themes or making any but the most conventional comment. He is utterly credulous and can be very tedious, yet the patient reader, as has been the case with the present writer, may gradually find himself responding to the unqualified piety that can accept so many and so absurd *incredibilia*, and to a homely mode of telling that rarely admits a variation in mood or style. A reluctant response to an admirably simple and sincere man, but it is memorably evoked in one tale that sets off his quality to full advantage.

Before that particular appreciation is reached, however, one or two odd assertions of modern scholars have to be dismissed. He is not John Barbour, as his editor, Carl Horstmann, supposed. Marked differences from the *Bruce* in style and rhyming sounds make that impossible of belief. Nor, as other critics have maintained, is he only the partial author of the *Legends*, the Lives of St. Machar and St. Ninian being the work of another hand. Both these Lives have autobiographic data consistent with that given elsewhere, and they contain the formulaic signature repeated in all but two or three of the other tales, 'but schame, det, and dedly syne'. Though, for the most part, he is concerned to translate the *Aurea Legenda*, or Golden Legend, of Jacopo de Voragine, he is not the slavish translator that his editor W.M. Metcalfe declares him to be; on the contrary, he adds from his reading in many other sources, inserts his own comments, some of these autobiographic.

His northern connection, implied in the differences from the speech of the probably Lowland Barbour, is confirmed in the Legends of the above-mentioned Scottish saints, which have a local colouring entirely absent from his 'Life of St. Andrew'. The places in Old Aberdeen and the country about where St. Machar worked his miracles are well known to him: he observes that the promptly discovered well water with which the saint satisfied the thirsts of the workmen busy on his church 'servis yet til al the toune', and that men may yet see in a garden the stone into which he transformed a marauding boar with a blow of his staff. The Legends of the patron saints of Banchory-Ternan and Banchory-Devenick (even that of St. Columba who recognises in him his spiritual superior) are subordinated to the fame of the 'hye patron' of Aberdeen. St. Devenick, the missionary to Caithness, had asked for burial in a church of St. Machar, so the latter meets the coffin-bearers on the hill 'Creskane' (Hill of Corskie?) and sees that his promise is duly honoured. That church is called 'Banchory Dewynick till this day'. The poet is surprised that so great a saint should be so little known outside northern Scotland; and the reader may well share his surprise, since St. Machar is said to have succeeded to the charge of Martin of Tours, been buried at his side, and visited at his death by Jesus, the twelve apostles, St. Martin and St. Columba. A propagandist zeal inspires the Legend, and whether or not the author has a Latin Life before him it is clear that for a time at least he was a servant of the cathedral.

In the Ninian Legend connections with both Aberdeen and Elgin appear. 'In my tyme', says the poet, when David Bruce was King (1329-1371), one misty morning in Galloway the saint warned Sir Fergus Makdowel who commanded there (c. 1350) that an English force was on its way to seize him. At that moment Jak Trumpoure, 'ane gud burdowre', a merry fellow, blew his trumpet and was mistaken by the English for a Scottish ambush. The enemy fled through the mist and duly Sir Fergus gave substantial thanks at the saint's shrine at Whithorn. The source of information seems to have been Trumpoure who had a house in the Castlegate of Aberdeen in 1351 (witnessed by a charter in the University). Another witness to St.

Ninian's kindness, in this case the curing of inflammation in knee and leg after a journey to Whithorn, is named: 'a gudman in Murrefe borne,/in Elgyne, and his kine beforne . . . I kend hyme weile mony day./Johne Balormy wes his name'. It is John's son Thomas who figures in the *Register of Moray* under the year 1414.

Considering the feeling that attaches to them, these local references indicate, if they do not prove, the writer's northern origin. His identity is unknown but it seems worth noting that the records allow us to connect only one priest with both cathedral towns. He is William of Spynie who studied at Paris 1351–1363, was Precentor at Elgin 1372–1373, Precentor and then Dean at Aberdeen 1373–1397, and Bishop of Moray 1397–1406. These dates agree well with the period of the poet's reminiscences.

But it is time to say something of the strange Legend that transcends the ordinary scope of pious narrative. The tale of Mary the Egyptian is told in many languages. Of the versions that I have looked at none make the peculiarly convincing impact of the Scots one, convincing because the old monk Zozymas who listens to Mary's story convinces. On the one day in the year that he can leave the monastery to which his extreme piety has led him he prays in the desert. Over him falls the shadow of Mary; he looks up and sees a long-haired, naked woman, sun-blackened and with wrinkled face. She flees for shame of her nakedness but he must know who she is, and she stops for his despairing cry. They kneel, asking each other's blessing, a scene that recalls the meetings of St. Theresa and John of the Cross, Lear and Cordelia. At first she fears that the truth he seeks will drive him away,

> thou sal flee sone away, allace,
> as quha dois befor the face
> of ane edir [adder] that wald hym stang

but passionately he persists in his demand.

She has been seventeen years in the desert, for the first eight living on the two loaves that she brought there, then on 'gress'. As a girl she had sought lovers where they could be found, for lechery was all life meant to her, and still the old desires come back. To see Jerusalem she had given herself to a ship's crew but on arrival had oddly found herself unable to enter the temple. She had prayed, and a voice had bidden her bathe in the Jordan river and enter the desert. Since then her life had been one of solitary worship. As she makes her confession Zozymas wonders that she knows his name, and though she has never read or heard of the New Testament utters the sayings of Jesus. There are moments when she forgets to walk and her feet do not touch the sands. The wonder-struck monk knows that despite her past way of life he is in the presence of great holiness. It is the excited humility and urgency with which the old man listens and questions that involves the reader and gives to Mary's narrative a strange authority. Her one desire is to be given communion, and the following year, though troubled by his unworthiness, he gives it. But the next painfully awaited time of reunion he finds her dead. Writing that had stayed firm in the sand beside her body tells him that she had died after receiving communion. As Zozymas grieves that he wants the means to bury her a lion appears, with his great claws digs her grave, and goes off. The monk returns to his monastery and tells the story that she had forbidden him to tell while she lived. In his hundredth year he dies and, as he had so long wanted to be, is with Mary the Egyptian in heaven.

At first seeming a monkish tale of naively told marvels, the Legend comes to hold the serious imagination. This may be partly for the reason given by the author himself, the contrasting extremes of saint and sinner, partly because the relationship of Mary and Zozymas has overtones of spiritual romance, partly the agreement of the desert scene with the extremes of expressed aspiration and belief, and largely because in Zozymas the poet saw the same great simplicity and innocence of life that he genuinely desired for himself – 'Out of this lyfe that we may twyne/but schame, det, and dedly syne'. It is all these things together but mostly the last that makes 'Mary the Egipciane' rank above other verse Legends, certainly above such a pious confection as Chaucer's *Prioress's Tale*.

The *Legends* is one among other poetical works of early times that survived in a single manuscript. What was lost when the Wolf of Badenoch fired Elgin Cathedral? The Wolf was a product of the habit of violence bequeathed by the English wars, yet, as the writers noticed here illustrate, freedom is indeed 'a noble thing', since creative. In the next century three universities, including that of Aberdeen, were founded, and brilliant poets flourished: not the least of these a young Orkneyman writing in Moray (1446), Richard Holland, who could conceive and picture Europe as a family of nations freely and happily accepting the common rule of Nature and Reason. The fact that such a creative impulse in Scotland was first felt in the north should have its remembrance.

Suggestions for further reading:

In the absence of reliable and available modern critical studies of John of Fordun, Barbour and the author of the *Saints' Legends*, the reader should consult the following: *Legends of the Saints in the*

Scottish Dialect of the Fourteenth Century, ed. W.M. Metcalfe, Scottish Text Society, 3 vols. (Edinburgh, 1896); *The Buik of Alexander*, ed. Graeme Ritchie, Scottish Text Society, New Series, 4 vols. (Edinburgh, 1925), Introduction to vol. 1; with this should be read the comments and corrections by Matthew P. McDiarmid in the forthcoming first volume of *Barbour's Bruce*, ed. Matthew P. McDiarmid and J. Stevenson, Scottish Text Society, 4th Series, 3 vols. (Edinburgh, 1983, 1980, 1982); *Hary's Wallace*, ed. Matthew P. McDiarmid, Scottish Text Society, 4th Series, 2 vols. (Edinburgh and London, 1968–9), Introduction and Notes; G.W. Barrow, *Robert Bruce and the Community of the Realm of Scotland*, second edition (Edinburgh, 1976). Richard Holland's *Buke of the Howlat* is discussed in Flora Alexander's article in this volume; for a treatment of the poem's political and theological vision of Europe, and in particular for its main reference to the Councils of the Church in the first half of the fifteenth century, see my article, 'Richard Holland's *Buke of the Howlat*: an Interpretation' in *Medium Aevum*, 38 (1969), 277–290.

RICHARD HOLLAND'S 'BUKE OF THE HOWLAT'

Flora Alexander

At the Castle of Darnaway, near Forres, in 1450 or perhaps a few years earlier, Richard Holland wrote *The Buke of the Howlat* (The Book of the Owl). The contents of this poem demonstrate that here in the north was an audience with a sophisticated awareness of moral and political ideas. The poetic form used, an intricate stanza which links words within the line by alliteration, as well as linking lines to each other by the intensive use of rhyme, shows that Holland was technically highly competent, and would suggest that his audience appreciated such dexterity.

Little is known about Holland's life, but when we view the poem in the context of those pieces of information that are available to us, we become aware of a grim contrast between, on the one hand, the idyllic setting of the poem and the secure vision of harmony contained in it, and on the other hand the violence which engulfed his patrons, the Earl and Countess of Moray, and changed the course of his own life. Archibald, Earl of Moray was one of the powerful Black Douglases, a brother of William the 8th Earl of Douglas, and of James the 9th Earl. Holland's poem is in part a celebration of the greatness and faithfulness of the House of Douglas, yet within a few years of the writing of it Earl William had been stabbed to death in a quarrel by King James II, and the rest of the family was destroyed or fled the country.

Holland was a priest 'of Caithness' (i.e. ordained in that diocese), and, at the time of writing the poem, secretary to the Earl and precentor at Elgin Cathedral. The killing of Earl William, in 1452, was the result of a rivalry that reached deadly proportions between the King and the most powerful of the noble families in his kingdom. The struggle continued between King James and the remaining Douglas brothers, and in 1455 there was a battle at Arkinholm in the Borders in which the family were defeated. Moray was killed in that battle, and only weeks after his death his Countess, the 'dove of Dunbar' mentioned in Holland's poem, was married to one of her late husband's enemies, and the King's supporter, the Master of Huntly. This marriage appears to have been negotiated in order to preserve the Moray estates, and the marriage document contains a provision that Huntly should protect Holland, and others of 'the said ladyis men', from the wrath of the King. Thereafter Holland held clerical offices in Orkney and Shetland (it has been suggested that he may have been an Orcadian, since the uncommon surname Holland is found in Orkney records of the 15th and 16th centuries[1]), but he seems to have continued to involve himself with the Douglas interest. Earl James had fled to England after the defeat of 1455, and was giving support, in this time of the Wars of the Roses, to the House of York. In a secret treaty signed in 1462, the Earl of Ross and the Lord of the Isles pledged themselves to give aid to the King of England, in return for the prospect that if Edward IV were to gain Scotland, these two lords together with Earl James would hold the lands north of the Forth as his vassals. Holland's connection with Douglas apparently brought him to England at some point, because he was sent by the English King to Scotland in 1480. This was presumably in connection with some sort of espionage, and a Scottish Act of Parliament of 1482 excludes him by name, along with James Douglas and a few other 'sic like tratouris', from a pardon issued by James III. It is clear enough that by this time Douglas's behaviour towards the King of Scots can only be described as treasonable. But it is right to point out that in the early stages of the hostility between the Crown and the Black Douglases, the actions of James II were plainly aggressive, and, as at least one recent historian has suggested, the evil of the Douglases consisted in defending themselves when attacked.[2] The poet Holland was by one definition a traitor, but his treachery arose out of his continuing loyalty to a losing cause.

The poem is a re-telling of a fable in which the owl complains to the Pope, and ultimately to Nature, of his ugly appearance. He is made beautiful with the help of gifts of feathers from the other birds, whereupon he grows proud, and is punished by having the borrowed plumes removed. The owl's case is heard before an assembly of birds representing both the spiritual and the secular estates, and through the presentation of the secular dignitaries Holland finds a way to focus on the great virtues of the Douglas family. In this connection he tells the story, already recorded in Barbour's *Bruce*, of the 14th century Sir James Douglas, who displayed conspicuous loyalty by taking the heart of Robert the Bruce, suitably preserved, on an expedition to the Holy Land which Bruce himself had hoped to undertake, and who thereby lost his own life.

Critics of *The Buke of the Howlat* have had difficulty in understanding the connection between the bird-allegory and the Douglas story. Some have responded to 'the stirring account of the last days of Good Sir James'[3], but have found the owl fable trite and tedious, while others have dismissed the Douglas material as an intrusion in the poem, inserted to please Holland's patrons. David Laing performed a valuable service by publishing the poem in the Bannatyne Club series in 1823, but in his introduction he says that it has been regarded, 'without much injustice, as a prolix and very uncouth performance'. In particular he finds 'a singular lack of propriety . . . in the construction'[4]. Recently Thorlac Turville-Petre, writing in *The Alliterative Revival* (1977), concedes that there is good incidental writing, but is not persuaded that the work has great merit. He sees it as 'a clumsily-constructed eulogy of the House of Douglas'[5]. However Matthew P. McDiarmid, in a most enlightening piece of criticism in *Medium Aevum* 38 (1969), demonstrates convincingly that the poem is an integrated whole, and that the owl is put forward as a bad example, and a picture of everything that the current Earl of Douglas was not, constituting 'a kind of flattery by opposites, and at the same time a reminder, since even a Douglas was human, of the dangers of high position'[6]. Mr. McDiarmid shows that although to a modern way of thinking the connections between different parts of the poem are sometimes unexpected, they are nevertheless always perceptible, and the poem is very far from lacking coherence.

Indeed, while ranging widely over theological, moral, and political ideas, Holland is skilful in integrating these areas of interest. If we assume that his starting-point is the theological insight which emerges clearly from his Latin source[7], that all things come from God and that man therefore has no cause for pride, we can see that both moral and political ideas develop from this basis. Morals and politics inevitably overlap. The Douglases are celebrated because they do what is right for them in their appointed place in society, thus becoming 'of Scotland the wer wall [rampart]', and hence Holland places them next in honour to the King. When the owl in his arrogance thinks himself the equal of the Pope, a general moral point is made, and also there is a specific reference to ecclesiastical politics, in the indecorous Papal schisms of previous decades. (The Douglas family had during the 1440s given support to the schismatic Pope Felix V, although by 1450 there was once more an agreed Pope, and Scottish church life was 'restored to as much harmony as could be expected'[8].) Most of the thought in the poem is connected in some way with the idea that God, or his representative Nature, has created things rightly, and that the duty of His creatures is to inhabit harmoniously the position that has been allotted to them. In the third stanza Holland establishes the role of Nature in supporting a creation beneficial to man. The related idea of God's Providence is traced explicitly, later in the poem, in the history of the Douglas family, when Holland explains how an earlier Archibald Douglas had acquired by marriage the lands of Moray of Bothwell:

> And sa throw Goddis forsicht
> The Dowglass succedis. (ll. 558-9)

Further to Mr. McDiarmid's argument that Holland's work is more unified than has usually been realised, I wish to suggest that if we consider it in its context, as part of a literary tradition, the apparently odd juxtaposition of the owl fable and the Douglas material without explanation of the connection between them is in fact perfectly natural and acceptable. It can be shown that there are precedents for this mode of construction in English 14th-century poetry generally (and Scottish poets of the 15th century were well aware of what had been done by their English predecessors). In particular, this approach to structure has been recognised as being particularly favoured by poets of the English and Scottish alliterative tradition to which Holland belongs. Also there are significant resemblances between Holland's procedures and the methods used in a medieval tradition of visionary poetry.

J.A. Burrow has observed, in *Ricardian Poetry*, that it is common for English poetry of the 14th century to have a sharply articulated structure, with the constituent parts marked off, but with the relationship between these parts being left for the reader to discover.[9] Chaucer's *Parlement of Foules* [Fowls], which is a major source for Holland's poem, is put together in this way, as indeed are a number of Chaucer's works. This principle of construction should not present great difficulty to 20th-century readers, since it is not unlike the method of suppressing connecting and explanatory material which is a feature of much modern poetry.

The 14th- and 15th-century alliterative poets use extensively the procedure by which relationships are implied rather than overtly stated. Larry D. Benson, writing on *Sir Gawain and the Green Knight,* observes that every good alliterative poem in existence has at one time or another been judged to be badly constructed and poorly unified.[10] This is because critics have approached them with an inappropriate concept of structure. Benson cites as examples of poems similar in method to *Sir Gawain and the Green Knight*, two poems which are written in the same unusual and peculiarly demanding rhyming alliterative stanza as *The Buke of the Howlat*. These are *The Awntyrs of Arthur*, composed in northern England about 50 years before Holland's poem, and *Golagros and Gawain*, the work of a Scottish poet in the later 15th century. Each of these poems consists of two episodes, a shorter and a longer, which were once thought to be inadequately linked, but can now be seen to illuminate each other and create a total meaning which the alert reader can perceive for himself. *The Buke of the Howlat* is different from these two poems (although like *Sir Gawain and the Green Knight*) in that one of the two units frames the other, but the method of combining two pieces of material to explore a basic idea is common to the three stanzaic poems.

The literary tradition of the dream-vision may throw further light on Holland's poetic intentions. His model, Chaucer's *The Parlement of Foules*, belongs to this type of poem. Holland's own poem is not, strictly speaking, a dream-vision, because the narrator does not fall asleep before describing the assembly of birds and the resulting actions. But it follows the conventions of the dream-vision in a number of respects, and it may be appropriate to consider the abrupt transitions within the poem as being akin to transitions taking place within the consciousness of dreamers, which for that reason appear thoroughly naturalistic. Examples can be found in *The Parlement of Foules*, and, some fifty years after Holland's own work, in William Dunbar's *The Goldyn Targe*. In Dunbar's poem a blast of wind makes a whole cast of allegorical characters disappear back into their ship 'in twinkling of ane eye'. Holland's rapid switch from the antics of bird-jesters to the descent and judgement of Dame Nature is more startling only because we have not been told that the narrator is dreaming.

A.C. Spearing has remarked, in *Medieval Dream-Poetry*, that the dream-poem is not a clear-cut genre, in that there are related poems, such as Gower's *Confessio Amantis* and the 15th-century *The Flower and the Leaf*, which include many of the features associated with dream-poetry, but are not set in a dream. The essential tradition that lies behind both dream-poems and related literature is the tradition of visions which make possible spiritual adventure. As Spearing remarks, although the literature of spiritual exploration has for centuries in Western literature been overshadowed by the literature of action in the outer, physical world, there has been another, long-standing tradition of visionary literature, including many parts of Scripture, in which a narrator has some kind of truth revealed to him.[11] *The Buke of the Howlat* has in common with works in this tradition that it is concerned primarily with the world of the mind, rather than with external action. The moral and theological argument is put into the form of a fable, and the working out of the fable involves the narrator in observing while a message is sent from the Pope, situated in the forest of Darnaway (which is depicted in terms conventionally used to portray the Earthly Paradise), to the Emperor in Constantinople. There is time for the Emperor to make his way to Darnaway, and on his arrival a palace appears where, by implication, no palace is normally situated. All of this is the stuff of dream-visions, and if it were presented to us as a dream no-one would thinking of finding fault with it. If Holland has made a mistake, it is that he omitted to make his narrator close his eyes in stanza 3, and open them again at the end of the poem. He does in fact use words which suggest something akin to a visionary experience. The narrator falls in fear of a 'ferly [marvel]' (l.46), and in the last stanza the action is referred to as something which 'happinnit Holland [befell Holland]', as if it had affected him rather than simply been observed by him.

The construction of the poem, far from being inept, is in a way extremely impressive. The account of Douglas's mission with the heart of Bruce is placed with deliberate care at the centre of the work, occupying stanzas 35-41 (out of a total of 77 stanzas). This section is framed by two passages of almost equal length (5 stanzas preceding, and 6 following) which explain the significance of various of the Douglas family's armorial bearings, and in particular describe the 'bludy hert', the heart gules on argent, which the family bore in recognition of the service done to Bruce. Still working outwards from the middle of the poem, 17 stanzas in the first half devoted to the assembling of the spiritual and secular birds correspond to 17 in the second half dealing with the birds' feasting and entertainment. And at the extremities of the poem we find 12 stanzas at the beginning, which provide the setting and present the Howlat's lament and appeal to the Pope to be made beautiful, mirrored by an equal number at the end in which Nature offers her solution, the owl is punished for his pride, and Holland adds the moral and dedication of the poem. The structure is almost perfectly symmetrical, and displays the same concern for form that is also seen in the use of the highly elaborate stanza. As is frequently the case in medieval poems, the total length has a numerical significance. There are 1001 lines, and this number, like 101, signifies completion of a cycle followed by a new beginning; the author of *Sir Gawain and the Green Knight* arranges that poem and *Pearl* in 101 stanzas in order to convey this meaning. It seems highly probable that Holland's 1001 lines are arrived at with the same thought in mind, and it may be relevant that the total number of stanzas is 77, since this number is sometimes taken to signify the remission of sins after penitence.[12] After the owl expresses his new awareness that pride goes before a fall, it is appropriate for the poet to incorporate through number symbolism a reference to remission of sin and the possibility of new beginnings.

One of the reasons why Holland's poem has been little known and appreciated is that fable is not now a mode of writing which finds favour with adults. It is important to approach medieval fables without condescension, remembering that they were written by mature and sophisticated people, for adult audiences, and were widely enjoyed. We are inclined to resist the clear-cut moral significance of fables, and it is tempting to concentrate on the charmingly comic effects of anthropomorphism, and to feel some embarrassment over the solemn moral discourse that is an essential of the genre. Holland creates many delightful moments out of the conjunction of the human and the avian, which we legitimately enjoy, but it is vital that we see them in the context of the controlling moral theme. The illustration which forms the frontispiece to Laing's most handsome edition of the poem, is actually quite inappropriate because it makes the owl rather lovable. What we must not overlook is that in the middle ages the owl was commonly regarded as rather a sinister bird, whose preference for night over day was unnatural and morally symbolic. To us the owl's dissatisfaction with his appearance, and wish for improvement, may be entirely understandable, but we must not regard it as we would regard the urge to self-improvement in a present-day context. Holland's assumption is that Nature, and therefore God, makes things as they are for good reason, and that to try to alter fundamentals is both foolish and wrong. This is made perfectly clear early in the poem, when the owl in his complaint repeatedly blames Nature for his ugly appearance, and the Pope, to whom he is presenting his case, replies, 'apon Natur to pleyne (complain), it is perrell' (1.119). The owl is characterised as 'vilest in vice' (1.88), and there can be little doubt that when the poet depicts the owl's fear and distress at his own reflection, 'He grat [wept] grisly grim, and gaif a gret yowle' (1.53), the reader's reaction is expected to be amused disapproval rather than pity. We have to remind ourselves that the owl is an allegorical figure, not an individual bird, and he has to be seen not as a 'character', but as an embodiment of unreasonable and corrupt attitudes. If we sympathise with him we are lending support to disruptive desires. Holland leaves us in no doubt that the owl's pride is evil, to be avoided and feared, when he relates that the beautified bird hastened to adopt the teachings of Lucifer (1.905). Nature, when she reproves and punishes him, makes use of a comparison with the usurper Satan, and adds to it the idea taken from the Magnificat that the mighty shall be cast down:

> 'Thy pride,' quod the Princes[s], 'approchis our hie [too high]
> Like Lucifer in estaite;
> And sen [since] thow art so elate [proud],
> As the Evangelist wrait,
> Thow sall lawe be'. (11.932-6)

The owl can only win our approval at the end of the poem, when he shows that he has acquired a new understanding, and grasps the truth that he has been rightly punished for the sin of pride.

Holland's interest in bird-allegory is not confined to the narrative of the owl's rise and fall. To this basic plot he adds the idea of the assembly of the birds, ranging from the peacock Pope and the eagle Emperor down to the humble robin redbreast who rides as a henchman and the 'litill we[e] wran' who has the role of the dwarf. His principal source for this is, of course, Chaucer's assembly in *The Parlement of Foules*, but he uses the idea somewhat differently. He devotes more attention to the musterings of the birds than Chaucer does, and once they are assembled he gives them very little part to play in the story of the owl, which is compressed into a very few stanzas. In fact the proportions of Holland's poem are surprising. The reader might well suspect that he so much enjoyed working out ingenious correspondences between the human and bird worlds that he allowed himself to develop them more extensively than was necessary or advisable. But Holland's bird-society has a relevance to the essential theme which justifies the extensive treatment.

The basic method in the first part of the poem, in which the birds are assembled, is to build up a series of parallels between species of birds and areas of human society. These are frequently founded on visual features, e.g. cranes are cardinals because they have red hats, and the curlew is a clerk, because his long bill is an ideal instrument for writing with:

> For he couth write wonder fair,
> With his neb for mistar [instrument],
> Apon the se sand. (11.206-8)

Another major group of parallels makes use of comic, and sometimes satirical observations on human behaviour (usually clerical). The raven is a rural dean, unbending as a rake, who is especially inclined to go visiting country clergy when his larder is empty. The dove, because he whispers, is well suited to be a curate and hear confessions, and the crows and jackdaws are poor friars who

> Will cum to the corne yard
> At evin and at morn. (11.194-5)

By means of this detailed picture Holland establishes the idea that creatures are fitted by their nature to fulfil a particular role in society. The treatment in the first half of the poem is static, but in the later stages the birds take part in something more than a simple procession. After the Pope and the Emperor have greeted each other, the Pope entertains the secular estate to a feast, and this offers an occasion for various kinds of activity. The song-birds, mavis, merle, nightingale (whose origins must be in literature rather than in observation), and others, sing a hymn to the Virgin in which through the use of figures chosen from a common stock of devotional rhetoric Holland draws attention to the significant parallels between Old Testament and New, and builds up the idea of a divinely ordained harmony governing man's situation:

Haile ordanit or [before] Adam, and ay till indur!
Haile alterar of Eva in ave [into 'Ave Maria'] but ure
[without doubt]!

The singing is followed by episodes in which the jay, a juggler, and the rook, an Irish bard speaking partly in a rough-and-ready approximation to Gaelic, offer what is probably pure entertainment (although one critic has seen in the Irish bard a political reference to John, Lord of the Isles [13]). The celebrations move to a climax with a vigorous but ultimately good-humoured set-to between the teuchat (lapwing) and the gowk (cuckoo). This fight in which the teuchat pulls off the gowk's tail, and the gowk takes the teuchat and 'Flang him flat in the fire, fetheris and all' (1.838), is written to amuse, but there is also thematic importance in the fact that after striking their blows they kiss and make up their quarrel. The reconciliation is an aspect of that harmony which is envisaged earlier in the poem at a much more comprehensive level:

So that the Spirituale staite,
And the secular consait [opinion],
Mycht all gang in a gait,
Tender and trewe. (11.283-6)

It is probably fair to say that in determining the proportions of his story Holland has devoted too much attention to the comprehensive portrayal of the birds, by comparison with the very concise treatment of the owl. Perhaps his obviously strong sense of the importance of form induced him to force the material into a symmetrical shape, at the price of truncating the crisis of the owl-narrative so that it occupies the same amount of space as the opening treatment of the owl's problem, while containing more material. It does at least appear that the proportions are eccentric by design, and not through incompetence.

By creating a society of birds which forms a parallel to human society, Holland gains the means to write about the sin of pride with a light touch, and to make his point in bold, general terms which can be widely applied. To deal with the Douglas subject in the centre of the poem he makes use of a different symbolic language, that of heraldry, in which precise and vivid shapes and colours allow him to make moral and political points in a simple, economical fashion. The red heart is depicted on silver which 'is cleir corage in armes' (l.435), and the lion on the King's arms is 'richt rampand as roye (king)' (l.368). Heraldry was of course a practical art which was very widely understood. Within this poem it offers Holland unambiguous symbols by means of which he can comment on the importance of moral qualities, and on the position of the Douglas family in the kingdom, as well as on international relationships in the passage describing the arms of the Pope, the Emperor, and the Kings of France and Scotland. We may perhaps understand better the effectiveness of this as a means of communication with Holland's contemporary audience, if we reflect on Bishop Gavin Dunbar's use some seventy years later of a series of armorial bearings, to decorate the ceiling of the nave of St. Machar's Cathedral in Aberdeen. There 48 Shields of Pope, Bishops, Emperor, Kings, and Scottish nobles are placed so as to show visually relationships between powers within Scotland and without. Holland unites fable and heraldry, and thereby adds to the coherence of the poem, by placing the shields he is interested in on the tabard of the wood-pecker, who is in the bird-allegory a herald riding in attendance on the Emperor. This device of the significantly-decorated garment is one which he has adapted from the work of earlier writers: several examples are known, e.g. the robe of Nature ornamented with birds and animals.[14]

Although Holland's method is consistently to explore reality through the use of poetic fiction and symbol, he shows from time to time a strong impulse to establish links back to the direct discussion of moral issues. The celebration of Douglas virtues is done not only through the language of heraldry, but also in plain statement, occasionally so fervent that it verges on the embarrassing, e.g. of the name of Douglas,

> That word is so wonder warme, and ever yit was,
> It sinkis sone in all part
> Of a trewe Scottis hart,
> Rejosing us inwart
> To heir of Dowglas. (11.386-90)

Similarly, the truths learned by the owl, after he has received his punishment, are expounded through him most straightforwardly:

> Ye princis . . .
> That pullis [harass] the pure [poor] ay,
> Ye sall sing as I say,
> All your welth will away,
> Thus I warn you. (11.91-5)

Holland the servant of the Douglases, and Holland the cleric, are to be recognised in such passages. They are to be regarded not as lapses from the artistic level of the rest of the poem, but rather as valuable links between the poetic artifice and the ordinary, external world that the poetry is conceived to illumine. The delicate balance he achieves between the particular and the general, and between instruction and entertainment, makes the experience of reading *The Buke of the Howlat* a peculiarly satisfying one.

Suggestions for further reading:

The most recent edition of the poem is in *Scottish Alliterative Poems*, ed. F.J. Amours, Scottish Text Society 27, 38 (Edinburgh, 1892-7). Scattered references to it are found in books and articles on Scottish literature, but there is hardly any extended discussion. M.P. McDiarmid, 'Richard Holland's *Buke of the Howlat*: An Interpretation', *Medium Aevum*, 38 (1969), 277-90, is outstandingly good. Also useful are two more historically-angled articles. 'Holland of the *Howlat', Innes Review*, 23 (1972), 3-15, and 'Holland's *Howlat* and the Fall of the Livingstones', *Innes Review*, 36 (1975), 67-79, both by Marion Stewart. 'Structure and Style in Richard Holland's *Buke of the Howlat*', by Margaret A. Mackay, in *Proceedings of the Third International Conference on Scottish Language and Literature (Medieval and Renaissance)*, (Stirling, 1982) appeared after this chapter had been completed.

Notes:

1. M. Stewart, 'Holland of the *Howlat', Innes Review*, 23 (1972), 10-11.
2. R. Nicholson, *Scotland, the Later Middle Ages* (Edinburgh, 1974), 371.
3. F.J. Amours, *Scottish Alliterative Poems*, Scottish Text Society 27, 38 (Edinburgh, 1892-7), xxxiii.
4. D. Laing, *The Buke of the Howlat*, Bannantyne Club, (Edinburgh, 1823), i.
5. T. Turville-Petre, *The Alliterative Revival* (Cambridge, 1977), 115.
6. M.P. McDiarmid, 'Richard Holland's *Buke of the Howlat*: An Interpretation', *Medium Aevum*, 38 (1969), 277-90.
7. In the *Fabulae* of Odo of Cherington.
8. R. Nicholson, *op. cit.*, 335-8.
9. J.A. Burrow, *Ricardian Poetry* (London, 1971), 63.

10. L.D. Benson, *Art and Tradition in Sir Gawain and the Green Knight* (New Brunswick, N.J., 1965), 158-63.
11. A.C. Spearing, *Medieval Dream-Poetry* (Cambridge, 1976), 1-24.
12. H.N. Davies, 'The Structure of Shadwell's *A Song for St. Cecilia's Day, 1690*', in *Silent Poetry*, ed. A. Fowler (London, 1970), 232.
13. M. Stewart, 'Holland's *Howlat* and the Fall of the Livingstones', *Innes Review*, 36 (1975), 77.
14. In Alanus de Insulis, *De Planctu Naturae*.

All quotations from *The Buke of the Howlat* are taken from Amours's edition. In quotations I have modified spelling, to make Middle Scots words look more familiar to the modern reader, by consistently changing y to i and w to v, where i and v are used in the equivalent modern words.

PIONEERS OF PROSE: SIR THOMAS URQUHART and SIR GEORGE MACKENZIE

Michael Spiller

He hurried therefore upon them so redely, without crying gare or beware, that he overthrew them like hogs, tumbled them over like swine, striking athwart and alongst, and by one means or other laid so about him, after the old fashion of fencing, that to some he beat out their braines, to others he crushed their armes, battered their legs, and bethwacked their sides till their ribs cracked with it; to others again he unjoynted the spondyles or knuckles of the neck, disfigured their chaps, gashed their faces, made their cheeks hang flapping on their chin, and so swinged and belammed them, that they fell down before him like hay before a Mower: to some others he spoiled the frame of their kidneys, marred their backs, broke their thigh-bones, pash't in their noses, poached out their eyes, cleft their mandibules, tore their jaws, dung in their teeth into their throat, shook asunder their omoplates or shoulder-blade, sphacelated their shins, mortified their shanks, inflamed their ankles, heaved off of the hinges their ishies, their sciatica or hip-gout, dislocated the joints of their knees, squattered into pieces the boughts or pestles of their thighs, and so thumped, mawled and belaboured them every where, that never was corne so thick and threefold thresh't upon by Plowmens flailes, as were the pitifully disjoynted members of their mangled bodies, under the mercilesse baton of the crosse. If any offered to hide himself amongst the thickest of the Vines, he laid him squat as a flounder, bruised the ridge of his back and dash't his reines like a dog. If any thought by flight to escape, he made his head to flie in pieces by the Lambdoidal commissure, which is a seame in the hinder part of the scull. If anyone did scramble up into a tree, thinking there to be safe, he rent up his perinee, and impaled him at the fundament. If any of his old acquaintances happened to cry out, Ha Fryar Jhon my friend, Fryar Jhon, quarter, quarter, I yield myself to you, to you I render my self: So thou shalt (said he,) and must

> whether thou wouldst or no, and withal render and yield up thy soul to all the devils in hell, then suddenly gave them Dronos, that is, so many knocks, thumps, raps, dints, thwacks and bangs, as sufficed to warne Pluto of their coming, and dispatch them a going: if any was so rash and full of temerity as to resist him to his face, then it was he did shew the strength of his muscles, for without more ado he did transpierce him by running him in at the breast, through the mediastine and the heart. Others again, he so quashed and bebumped, that with a sound bounce under the hollow of their short ribs. he overtuned their stomachs so that they died immediately; to some with a smart souse on the Epigaster, he would make their midriff swag, then redoubling the blow, gave them such a homepush on the navel, that he made their puddings to gush out. To others through their ballocks he pierced their bum-gut, and left not bowel, tripe nor intral in their body, that had not felt the impetuosity, fiercenesse and fury of his violence. Beleeve that it was the most horrible spectacle that ever one saw.
> (*Gargantua and Pantagruel*, Book 1, ch. 27)

The massacre of the troops of Picrochole, King of Lerné, by the redoubtable Friar John of the Funnels, in the close of the Abbey of Seuilly, is one of the most famous events to have happened in the realm of Great Nonsense; a country which, considering the amount of small or everyday nonsense that is poured out by the human race, has been visited rather seldom by the masters of literature. Jonathan Swift's Gulliver and Lewis Carroll's Alice knew that country well; Cyrano de Bergerac went there himself, where his classical masters Aristophanes and Lucian had been before; and there are small outposts of it, such as Shandy Hall or Cold Comfort Farm, which the reader fatigued with too much sanity may visit and pass through refreshed. But the most glorious and sustained exploration of Great Nonsense is the source of my opening quotation, the five volume work of François Rabelais, *Gargantua and Pantagruel*, published in French between 1552 and 1564, and turned (in part) into English for us by a fantastically minded and frenziedly energetic knight of Cromarty in the North of Scotland, Sir Thomas Urquhart. That Sir Thomas was in all the British Isles probably the one man for the task, is suggested by his career and other writings; for the moment, since he immortalised himself through another man's work, something must be said of what he translated.

Great Nonsense, as I am using the term, is not sense destroyed, but rather sense countered, or opposed: 'contrasense' might be a better word. If we grant that the great instrument of human progress is reason, then reason is embodied in the use of words, and two chief manifestations of words are (both in their broadest sense) Catalogue and Logic. By the catalogue men name, list and arrange facts, to transmit knowledge and power: the witches in *Macbeth*, chanting their unsettling ingredients into the cauldron, are in the midst of an activity that stretches from the book of the generations of Adam (*Genesis* v) to our own Greater London Telephone Directory. To catalogue is to control: when chaos threatens, we sit down and make a list; whereas by logic we arrange not our external world but our thoughts: it is that discipline of concept and discourse which should be a counterpart of the discipline of an ordered society.

But lest this process, desirable for the most part, go too far, and wither us all to what Yeats called 'old, learned, respectable bald heads, forgetful of their sins', it has always been thought good that from time to time the forces of disorder should have their say or fling, in carnivals, saturnalia, Feasts of Fools and students' Rag Weeks, releasing the natural and irrational energies of mankind for too much eating, drinking or sex, for brawling, mocking and generally turning the world wrong side up. So too literature has its saturnalia of words, books of Great Nonsense, where logic and catalogue are ridiculed and parodied, words set free of all discipline ('When *I* use a word,' Humpty Dumpty said, 'it means just what I choose it to mean – neither more nor less.') and invention is liberated from things as they are, to make jabberwocks and Gargantuas. It follows, too, that the heroes of that literature should be the followers of extravagance, passion and absurdity: the brawlers, wenchers, drinkers, fools and madmen, rogues and freaks; and its villains and dupes, the heroes of the world of reason and logic: pedants, scholars, clerks, philosophers and lawyers.

So François Rabelais, scholar, learned doctor of medicine and rather half-hearted cleric, begins his epic of contrasense with a dedication to all 'most noble and illustrious drinkers, and you thrice precious pockified blades' and ends it with the Oracle of the Bottle, which is 'Trinc – a Panomphean word, that is, a word understood, us'd and celebrated by all Nations, and signifies – Drink.' And in between comes a vast, sprawling mockery of history and travel, learning and wit, which tells the stories of the giants Grangousier, Gargantua and Pantagruel, grandsire, father and son, all benevolent, tolerant and hugely curious, careering through the world of sixteenth century France and over the face of the globe with wild words, satire, fantasy and much good cheer. So large a work composed over a long time could be by no means even; the earlier books show a marked fondness for simple, coarse fun, and the later a preference for more philosophical jest in earnest, as if Chaucer's *Miller's Tale* gradually turned into

Gulliver's Travels. The progress of the work (if that is the word for it) is a reminder that, humanist and scholar as he was, Rabelais believed that knowledge leads to virtuous action, and Gargantuan folly is licensed to correct the excesses of the reason, not to destroy it. So the young Gargantua begins indeed with a beastly and hoggish 'education':

> Then did he study some paltry half-houre with his eyes fixed upon his book; but (as the Comick saith) his minde was in the Kitchin. Pissing then a full Urinal, he sate down at table; and because he was naturally flegmatick, he began his meale with some dozens of gammons, dried neats tongues, hard rowes of mullet called Botargos, Andouilles or sauciges, and such other forerunners of wine; in the mean while, foure of his folks did cast into his mouth one after another continually mustard by whole shovels full. Immediately after that, he drank a horrible draught of white-wine for the ease of his kidneys. When that was done, he ate according to the season meat agreeable to his appetite, and left off eating when his belly began to strout, and was like to cracke for fulnesse; as for his drinking, he had in that neither end nor rule; for he was wont to say that the limits and bounds of drinking were, when the cork of the shoes of him that drinketh swelleth up half a foot high. (Book 1, ch. 21)

But within two chapters, he is a reformed character, and Rabelais outlines the ideal education of a Renaissance princeling like any utopian philosopher. Likewise the ferocious Friar John of the Funnels has his dearest wish granted when Gargantua founds for him the Abbey of Thélème, whose motto is *Fay ce que vouldras* – 'Do what thou wilt' – but this is no den of orgiasts, but an aristocratic community of virtue and learning and high-minded recreation, because, as Rabelais seriously explains, 'men that are free, well-borne, well bred and conversant in honest companies, have naturally an instinct and spurre that prompteth them unto vertuous actions, and withdraws them from vice.' (Book 1, ch. 57) Amid all the boisterous homage to gut and gullet, Rabelais preserves the Renaissance enthusiasm for

> Our souls, whose faculties can comprehend
> The wondrous architecture of the world

and for the great servant of those faculties, discourse.

It was an enthusiasm fully, not to say wildly, shared by his translator. Having inherited ruinously managed estates, Sir Thomas Urquhart of Cromarty careered in the spirit of Carroll's White Knight through a life full of travel, fighting, litigation and imprisonments, with his mental saddlebags stuffed full of his own inventions to transform the world, writing and publishing enormous prefaces to proclaim that he would certainly have been

> a Maecenas to the scholar, a pattern to the soldier, a favourer of the merchant, a protector of the tradesman, an upholder of the yeoman, had not the impetuosity of the usurer overthrown my resolutions, and blasted my aims in the bud.
> (*Logopandecteision*, Book 6, 36)[1]

He suffered not only from usurers and creditors. having elected to ride in support of Charles II to the Battle of Worcester with about three thousand sheets of manuscript in his trunk (it is wholly characteristic of Urquhart that he measures this for us as 'six hundred and forty two quinternions') he had to suffer the indignity of seeing his priceless visions blown in the mud of Worcester streets, after the Protectorate soldiery plundered his lodgings. He was, it would seem, a vain, pedantic and fantastical man; and yet, he set himself to translate one of the greatest satires upon vanity, pedantry and folly, and though he accomplished only three books of Rabelais' five, produced a version which actually improves upon the original, and makes him, as Professor Saintsbury has said, 'the last and greatest of the great translators of the larger Elizabethan period.'

His exterior life is easily described; the life of that extravagant and wordy mind will take a little longer. He was born in 1611 – no one knows exactly where – as the eldest child of Sir Thomas Urquhart of Cromarty, who was a good and worthy man, but imprudent in his benevolence, and with a genius for tangling and mismanaging his prosperous estate, the property of the Urquhart Family since the mid-fourteenth century. (It was no doubt in the course of some particularly trying family embarrassment that in 1636 the younger Sir Thomas and his brother locked their hapless parent in an upstairs bedroom in the Castle of Cromarty 'fra the Mononday to the Fryday in the efter none', and were nearly prosecuted for it.) The younger Sir Thomas – let us now call him simply Urquhart, to avoid confusion – entered Aberdeen University in 1622 at the age of eleven, a practice not unusual in those days, and gracefully left on record the impression that 'for honesty, good fashions and learning, Aberdeen surpasseth . . . all other cities and towns in Scotland.' [2] There is no record of his having graduated, but while still young he went abroad, to France, Spain and Italy, and was by his own account fluent in the languages of all three, whence he returned about 1635 with a fair collection of books to grace the shelves of the family home. He then threw himself into the gathering storm of the Civil War and in 1639, rode out on May 13th to take part in the Trot of Turriff, in which the first blood of the War was shed. Urquhart was a staunch Royalist, and after the Covenanters took Aberdeen, ten days later, he made his way to England. Charles I knighted him at Whitehall on April 7th, 1641, and he remained furth of Scotland for three years, returning briefly only once in 1642 when his father died. But in 1645 he came back to his ruined estates, hopelessly burdened with what he called 'solicitudinary and luctiferous discouragements' – in plain English, pressing claims and debts. He invited further trouble by taking part in the razing of the walls of Inverness, and had in consequence to sue for pardon to the Commission of the General Assembly in 1650. The crowning of Charles II at Scone on January 1st, 1651 involved him in action to support the new monarch, and he joined in the march into England (manuscripts and all) which ended when Cromwell scythed through the Royalists at Worcester on September 3rd. Taken prisoner as Sir Thomas Orquaint (the English, as always, having trouble with Scots gutturals), he was first confined in the Tower, then at Windsor, and then paroled. For a few months he was back in Scotland, before surrendering to his parole to the Council of State in 1653. That was his *annus mirabilis*, the year of the publication of the first two books of Rabelais; after that, he recedes into the shadows. We hear of him briefly at Middelburg in Holland in 1658; and a late source in the eighteenth century tells us that he died in 1660, still overseas.

Rabelais was his last venture: before that, he had published, conventionally enough, three books of *Epigrams: Divine and Moral* in 1641, and then, in a splendid cascade of polysyllables, *The Trissotetras* (1645), *Pantochronochanon* (1652), *Ekskubalauron* (1652) and *Logopandecteision* (1653). Such titles might well have turned up in the 'stately and magnifick' Library of St. Victor which Pantagruel visited, shelved along with *Tartaretus de Modo Cacandi, Smutchudlamenta Scoti* and *Blockheadodus de Vita et Honestate Bragadochiorum*; and yet in fairness to Urquhart, it must be pointed out that as Latin ceased to be the universal language for all learned works, it was convenient often to give a portmanteau Greek or Latin title to a book in one's native tongue, as Milton did in his *Areopagitica*: scholars from Cracow to Cordova would know that *Logopandecteision* was 'a demonstration of a universal language'. *Pantochronochanon* is 'an utterance concerning the whole of Time', but it must be admitted that the other two give little enough away: *The Trissotetras* is, obscurely 'Three/Four' and *Ekskubalauron* yields us 'gold from a dunghill.'[3]

The Trissotetras, the first of his prose works, is a treatise on trigonometry, of which Urquhart evidently had, for his day, a considerable understanding (it will be remembered that when Samuel Pepys became a senior civil servant at the Navy Office, he had to engage a seaman to teach him simple arithmetic). What rendered *The Trissotetras* impenetrable and useless was Urquhart's fascination, even at this stage, with cataloguing: he attempted to devise a method of abbreviating all trigonometrical theorems into a mnemonic code, following the logarithmic procedures of his fellow Scotsman Napier. It has never been reprinted, apart from the Maitland Club edition of Urquhart's *Works* in 1834, and the reader of the first edition, helpfully told that 'the Disergetick Loxogonosphericals are grounded in four Axioms, viz. 1. Nabadprosver 2. Naverprortes [3.] Siubprortab and [4.] Niubprodnesver' (42) will readily see why. But that Urquhart should have used Napier's work, and mastered trigonometry even sufficiently to be able to bury it under a system of his own inimitable devising, is a tribute to the modernity of his intelligence. From trigonometry to genealogy: *Pantochronochanon: a Peculiar Promptuary of Time* is a genealogy of the Urquhart family from 1652 back to Adam and Eve. In an age which still generally accepted that the world was created in 4004 B.C. and relied heavily on the historicity of the genealogies of the Bible, the attempt was by no means lunatic: one of the treasures of Hatfield House to this day is a pedigree tracing Queen Elizabeth I's ancestry back to Adam; but by the mid 17th century, Urquhart's uninterrupted catalogue of his 152 ancestors would have raised doubts in any competent historian.

Other writers on Urquhart have remarked that in the Second Book of *Gargantua* Rabelais himself gives a mock genealogy of Pantagruel in a Biblical parody very like Urquhart's, and that by this date Urquhart had certainly read and translated it: it is difficult to imagine, therefore, that he could have taken his own 153 generations entirely seriously. At this time (1651-2) he was of course in prison in England; and it seems likely that the extravaganza of the *Pantochronochanon* was an attention-getting device, to show the Council of State that they were holding a man of more than ordinarily good family. But in deriving his surname from the Greek οὐροχαρτος (*ourochartos*: 'fortunate and well loved), he probably wrote with complete seriousness.

If that is a sample of his linguistic competence, it is probably as well that *Logopandecteision, an Introduction to the Universal Language* did not perform the promise of its title page. After an introductory account of the principles of the new language, the work turns into a huge polemic against his creditors in a further five books, alternating vitriolic attacks on their rapacity with boasts of what he might have accomplished had they let him alone. Its aim seems again to have been to recommend himself to his captors. The modern reader will find more delights in *Ekskubalauron*, a strange medley of all Urquhart's intellectual concerns, containing, as he himself might have said, portions both pantochronochanonic and logopandectic, as well as what the title page calls an attempt 'to frontal a Vindication of the honour of Scotland, from the Infamy whereinto the Rigid Presbyterian party of that Nation . . . hath involved it.' After an introductory epistle, Urquhart supplies a condensed version of his family genealogy, and then a long introduction to his universal language, clearer and better than that in *Logopandecteision*. His *Trissotetras* was really an attempt to construct a universal trigonometrical lexicon, as of signallers' code words; and similarly in *Ekskubalauron* he proposes a language of polysyllables (of which he was gluttonously fond) in which each single syllable would mean a concept or a quality, each added syllable being a restriction of the area covered by the one before. The idea is ingenious, and though properly speaking he proposes a universal *code* (e.g. shorthand) rather than a universal *language* (e.g. Esperanto), quite workable, as was shown nine years later when his fellow countryman, George Dalgarno of Aberdeen, published *Ars Signorum, or A Universal Character and Philosophical Language* (1661) using a concept-based syllabary just as Urquhart had proposed. Unfortunately, Urquhart's fatal leaning towards elaboration ruined his own scheme: he proposed joyously to invest, or infect, his language with such a battery of cases, genders and numbers as would have defeated Holofernes himself – and seems to have baffled even its inventor, for he never reached the stage of producing a grammar of the language at all. Instead, *Ekskubalauron* swings away into a catalogue of eminent Scotsmen, the last of whom is himself; and in so doing it gave posterity the most famous of all his writings, the account of the Admirable Crichton, his paragon and idol (James Crichton, 1560 - 1583?). The story of the life and death of this Scots precursor of Sir Philip Sidney shows Urquart at his narrative best; the reader will find it reprinted in its entirety in Richard Boston's excellent anthology of Urquhart's writings.

At the end of *Ekskubalauron*, as if regretting that he had written so much sense, he reflects that he might have composed more ornately:

> I could have introduced, in case of obscurity, synonymal, exargastick, and palilogetick elucidations; for sweetness of phrase, antimetathetick commutations of epithets; for vehement excitation of a matter, exclamations in the front, and epiphonemas in the rear. I could have used, for the promptlier stirring up of passion, apostrophal and prosopopaeil diversions: and for the appeasing and settling of them, some epanorthotick revocations, and aposiopetick restraints.

> I could have inserted dialogisms, displaying their interrogatory part with communicatively-pysmatick and sustentative flourishes; or proleptically, with the refutative schemes of anticipation and subjection: and that part which concerns the responsory, with the figures of permissions and concession.
>
> Speeches extending a matter beyond what it is, auxetically, digressively, transititiously, by ratiocination, aetiology, circumlocution, and other ways I could have made use of: as like wise with words diminishing the worth of a thing, tapinotically, periphrastically, by rejection, translation, and other means, I could have served myself.
>
> (*Tracts*, 167 - 8)

This logorrhea, this barely checked flux of words, is a symptom of Urquhart's ruling passion, an obsession with the infinite variety of things about him. In sterner souls, this produces the great taxonomies of Renaissance and scientific enlightenment: the *Chronologia* of Archbishop Ussher, the *Lexicon* of Hesychius, the *Adagia* of Erasmus, the *Historia Plantarum* of John Ray; in Urquhart, a delighted rattling off of strings of names and facts and dates: he cannot think of a word, but he must give you four synonyms for it as well; he cannot name a country without reciting half a dozen neighbouring ones; he cannot use a figure of speech without telling you there are six more he might have chosen instead. His most casual sentences betray this: describing Charles II, he writes that he was:

> for comliness of person, valour, affability, mercy, piety, closeness of counsel, veracity, foresight, knowledge and other virtues both moral and intellectual, in nothing inferior to any of his hundred and ten predecessors (*Tracts*, 126)

– where any other mortal would give four or five virtues, Urquhart gives nine; and the lunatic precision of that 'hundred and ten' is wholly his. Yet freakish though this seems in him, the instinct is bedded deep in the humanism of his age: the delight in the richness of human vocabulary is part of the Renaissance of learning, as we see in Shakespeare:

> So did this horse excel a common one
> In shape, in courage, colour, pace and bone;
> Round hoof'd, short jointed, fetlocks shag and long,
> Broad breast, full eye, small head and nostrils wide,
> High crest, short ears, straight legs, and passing strong,
> Thin mane, thick tail, broad buttock, tender hide:
> Look what a horse should have, he did not lack
> Save a proud rider on so proud a back.
>
> (*Venus and Adonis*, 11.293-300)

Even Macbeth, at one of his grimmer moments, has a touch of it:

> Ay, in the catalogue ye go for men,
> As hounds and grey hound, mongrels, spaniels, curs,
> Shoughs, water-rugs and demi-wolves are clept
> All by the name of dogs . . . (III.i)

Now had Sir Thomas, whose words come not single spies but in battalions, attempted an original piece of prose fiction, then reading the first Scottish novel would have been like dodging across a battlefield. But happily for himself, he submitted his genius to the control of Rabelais (and thereby left the first Scottish novel instead to Sir George Mackenzie, of whom more shortly), producing a translation that allows him to give of his best. The gusto of Rabelais is so continuous that Urquhart's love of amplifying is always appropriate, and often actually an improvement: the reader who has savoured the passage with which this chapter began may be surprised to discover that of the thirty or so acts of destruction that Friar John committed in the first 24 lines, Rabelais mentions only fifteen. Under his master's guidance, Urquhart discovered what, after Mozart, one might call the Leporello Principle: that anything may be comic and even made delightful to hear if one simply catalogues it for long enough (*Madamina, il catalogo è questo . . .*). Most adults would turn away contemptuously from a mention of methods of wiping the fundament; yet I defy the reader not to become first interested, then disarmed and finally admiring by Urquhart's rendering of Gargantua's invention of a Torchecul:

> I have (answered Gargantua) by a long and curious experience, found out a meanes to wipe my bum, the most lordly, the most excellent, and the most convenient that ever was seen? What is that (said Grangousier), how is it? I will tell you by and by (said Gargantua), once I did wipe me with a Gentlewomans Velvet-mask, and found it to be good; for the softness of the silk was very voluptuous and pleasant to my fundament. Another time with one of their Hoods, and in like manner that was comfortable. At another time with a Ladies Neck-kerchief, and after that I wiped me with some earpieces of hers made of Crimson sattin, but there such a number of golden spangles in them (turdie round things, a pox take them) that they fetched away all the skin of my taile with a vengeance. Now I wish St. Anthonies fire burn the bum-gut of the Goldsmith that made hem, and of her that wore them: This hurt I cured by wiping myself with a Pages çap, garnished with a feather after the Switzers fashion.
>
> Afterwards, in dunging behind a bush, I found a March-

Cat, and with it wiped my breech, but her clawes were so sharped that I scratched and exulcerated all my perinee; of this I recovered the next morning thereafter, by wiping myself with my mother's gloves, of a most excellent perfume and scent of the Arabian Benin. After that I wiped me with sage, with fennil, with anet, with marjoram, with roses, with ground-leaves, with beets, with colewort, with leaves of the vine-tree, with mallowes, wool-blade (which is a tail-scarlet), with latice and with spinage leaves. All this did very great good to my leg. Then with Mercurie, with pursley, with nettles, with comfrey, but that gave me the bloody flux of Lumbardie, which I healed by wiping me with my braguette; then I wiped my taile in the sheets, in the coverlet, in the curtains, with a cushion, with Arras hangings, with a green carpet, a table cloth, with a napkin, with a handkerchief, with a combing cloth, in all which I found more pleasure than do the mangie dogs when you rub them. Yeas, but (said Grangousier), which torchecul didst thou find to be the best? I was coming to it, (said Gargantua) . . . Afterwards I wiped my bum with a kerchief, with a pillow, with a pantoufle, with a pouch, with a pannier, but that was a wicked and unpleasant torchecul; then with a hat, of hats note that some are shorne, and others shaggie, some velveted, others covered with taffities, and others with sattin, the best of all these is the shaggie hat, for it makes a very neat abstersion of the fecal matter.

Afterwards I wiped my taile with a hen, with a cock, with a pullet, with a calves skin, with a hare, with a pigeon, with a cormorant, with an Atturneys bag, with a montero, with a coife, with a faulconers lure; but to conclude, I say and maintaine, that of all the torcheculs, arsewisps, bumfodders, tail napkins, bunghole cleansers and wipebreeches, there is none in the world comparable to the neck of a goose that is well downed, if you hold her head betwixt your legs; and beleeve me therein upon mine honour, for you will thereby feele in your nockhole a most wonderful pleasure, both in regard of the softnesse of the said downe, and of the temperate heat of the goose, which is communicated to the bum-gut, and the rest of the inwards, insofarre as to come to the regions of the heart and braines; and think not, that the felicity of the heroes in the Elysian fileds consisteth either in their Asphodel, Ambrosia or Nectar, as our old women here used to say; but in this (according to my judgement), that they wipe their tailes with the neck of a goose, holding her head betwixt their legs, and such is the opinion of Master John of Scotland, alias Scotus.

(*Gargantua*, Book 1, ch. 13)

The great catalogues are bravura pieces, cadenzas in the music of nonsense; but Urquhart, because of his continually restless mind and pen, is equally adept at the rattle of Rabelaisian conversation, with its tangents, parentheses, inconsequentialities and heedlessness. A long time was to pass before the novel learnt to render ordinary conversation with fidelity; but among satirists, and particularly by Urquhart, the chaos of human babble is skilfully caught.

Of Rabelais' five books, Urquhart published two, and left the third in manuscript to be printed in 1693 by Pierre-Antoine Motteux, who also translated Books Four and Five – competently, but without the perpetual vibration of light frenzy that is a keynote of Urquhart's work and personality. The editor of the 1774 reprint of Urquhart's *Tracts* is our only authority for the story that Urquhart died as oddly as he had written:

> This Sir Thomas, the third of that name . . . was a man of great learning and merit, and was a steady loyalist, on which account he suffered many hardships. He fought on the King's side at the Battle of Worcester, where he was taken prisoner, and was confined for several years in the Tower of London; from whence he made his escape, and went beyond the seas, where he died suddenly in a fit of excessive laughter, on being informed by his servant that the King was restored. (*Tracts*, 37)

Si non è vero, è ben trovato – if it is not true, it ought to be.

* * * * *

A death of a less merry kind is associated with Sir George Mackenzie of Rosehaugh (1636-1691), who published the first Scottish novel in the supposed year of Urquhart's death, 1660. History tells us that Mackenzie died peacefully in London; readers of Scott's *Redgauntlet* will remember the later apparition deep in the wood of Pitmurkie, with 'the fierce Middleton, and the dissolute Rothes and the crafty Lauderdale and . . . Claverhouse, as beautiful as when he lived', of 'the Bluidy Advocate MacKenyie, who, for his worldly wit and wisdom, had been to the rest as a god' (Letter xi). And in the century after his death, Robert Chalmers tells us, schoolboys going home across the Greyfriars Churchyard in Edinburgh (as they still do), would dart away from the front of Mackenzie's vault, shouting:

> 'Bluidy Mackingie, come oot if ye daur,
> Lift the sneck and draw the bar!'

Scholars remember him more kindly as they pass his coat-of-arms in the great staircase window of the Scottish National Library, for the founding of its forerunner, the Library of the Faculty of Advocates. The circumstances of his life and later writings are available to readers in Andrew Lang's still unsuperseded biography, *Sir George Mackenzie, His Life and Times* (1909); it is with his very youthful novel, *Aretina, or, the Serious Romance* (1660) that we are concerned here.

Mackenzie was born, probably in 1638, the eldest son of Simon Mackenzie of Lochslin in Rosshire, and thus nephew to the second Earl of Seaforth, George Mackenzie (d. 1651). He entered Aberdeen University in 1650, but moved to St. Andrews to graduate, and then proceeded to study law at Bourges. He was called to the Scottish Bar in 1659, and after the upheavals of the restoration of Charles II, was readmitted in 1661, to begin his legal career spectacularly with the defence of the Marquis of Argyll at his trial for high treason. But before he could have known that a settled career was to be possible, he had evidently hoped to make his name as a literary figure, and embarked on the first part of a long romance. *Aretina* was published in Edinburgh by Robert Broun 'at the sign of the *Sun*, on the North-side of the High Street', and is one of the rarest Scottish books: only three copies survive, one in the Scottish National Library, as is appropriate, one in the library of Edinburgh University, and one in the British Library. It is an octavo of 447 pages, containing a dedication 'To all the Ladies of this Nation', an 'Apologie for Romances', two royalist poems by Mackenzie, and a narrative of about 100,000 words. It has never been reprinted, and receives only a paragraph's attention in histories of Scottish Literature, if it is mentioned at all.

The word 'romance' has the two meanings of 'a tale of idealised adventure' (*The Prisoner of Zenda*) and 'a tale of idealised love' (*Pride and Prejudice*). Fifteen centuries ago, the Greek writer Heliodorus combined these in one classic structure, a narrative shape so profoundly satisfying that it formed the structure of countless later narratives, Mackenzie's included, down to the bookstall romances of our own day, and even now influences our expectations of real life itself. *Theagenes and Chariclea* is the story of two lovers who, after discovering their mutual love, are kept from consummating it by a series of coincidences, misadventures, dangers, escapes and pursuits until they are united in marriage at the end; the constancy of the lovers gives unity, and the succession of adventures gives variety. However unlike life, the formula has proved irresistible, and the only significant change that has been made in its European course is that from about 1700 or so the obstacle to the lovers' union became less and less external – kidnapping, malice of relatives, and so forth –

and more and more internal – misunderstanding, doubt, lack of knowledge, so that in a modern romance, the reader recognises that the hero and heroine are destined for each other, while they themselves do not, and the plot concerns itself with the closing of the gap between the reader's knowledge and the protagonists' (Shakespeare's *Much Ado About Nothing* is a transitional romance, having one pair of lovers of the classical kind – Hero and Claudio – and the other of the more modern kind, Beatrice and Benedick).

Mackenzie's *Aretina* is firmly in the classical tradition, and proceeds by subjecting two sets of lovers, Philarites and Aretina and Megistus and Agapeta, to various separations which postpone the consummation of their loves. However, in taking over this classical structure, the Renaissance added to it a preoccupation with discourse: the fascination with the Word as an instrument of moral and scientific systematising leads the Renaissance romancer to introduce into his novel set speeches at various points, speeches not only from the main characters, and not only about love: anyone may contribute a discourse on any moral or civil subject, such as justice, government, honour, taxation, warfare and so forth; we, who are used to discourse directed either by narrative (as in John Buchan) or by psychology (as in Henry James) feel that much of the discourse in, say, Sir Philip Sidney's *Arcadia* is oddly unrelated to the story. In practice, the developed Renaissance romance was rather closer to a one volume encyclopaedia than we now expect fiction to come, but the reader of Walter Scott, for example, can see there is still a touch of that moral and informative habit which Mackenzie, for one, thought normal.

As his predecessors, Mackenzie acknowledges Sir Philip Sidney's *Arcadia* (1593), a huge French romance by Mlle. de Scudery, *Clélie*, which was coming out in the years 1654 to 1660, and was to be translated by John Davies of Kidwelly as *Clelia: an excellent new Romance* (1665-61); and a strange romance in Latin by John Barclay, *Argenis* (1621). This last is *not* the first Scottish novel only because John Barclay was half-French, and never set foot in Scotland; his father, the Aberdeen jurist William Barclay, had emigrated in 1571. However, it supplied Mackenzie with the idea for the third book of his *Aretina*: the first, second and fourth books pursue the vicissitudes of the four lovers, but the third, in the frame of an inserted tale told by one of them, gives a coded account of the Scottish Civil Wars. Barclay's *Argenis*, though set romantically in classical Sicily, is a history of the French religious wars, each character representing a politician or soldier, very often by an anagrammatised name. This idea was not original with Barclay, but *Argenis* made it popular. Under the guise, then, of an account of troubles in Athens and Lacedaemon, under their kings Sophus (James VI and I), Anaxagius (Charles I), and Theopemptus (Charles II), and the usurper Autarchus (Cromwell), Mackenzie gives a close account of the Scots Civil Wars up to the rejoicings which marked the Restoration of Charles II in Edinburgh on June 19th, 1660. Even at so young an age, Mackenzie was a staunch royalist and bitter opponent of religious fanaticism and popular unrest, though not blind to the faults of James VI and I and his son. As the very first Scots account of the Scots Wars, and suggesting in places a knowledge of sources now lost to us, Mackenzie's Third Book is of considerable interest, even in its classical dress, and one could wish that he had given us less of his thoughts on high-minded love and honour, and more analysis of the affairs of his country.

Aretina has its incidental pleasures too, such as an early version of the Sawney Bean legend, some forty years before it first appeared in print. The promised second part – for Mackenzie offers the first only as 'a swatch of what I intend, reserving the web, till I see how the stuff pleases' – never appeared, perhaps because romances were less popular after the Restoration, and because Mackenzie himself was involved in graver matters. But the first account of the Scots Civil Wars is his, and his too is the distinction of the first piece of prose fiction to come out of Scotland.

Suggestions for further reading:

The best introduction to Sir Thomas Urquhart is Richard Boston's *The Admirable Urquhart* (London, 1975), giving a lightly written but informative introduction to generous extracts from *Logopandecteision* and *Gargantua and Pantagruel*; also still in print is the Saltire Society's *Selections from Sir Thomas Urquhart* (Edinburgh, 1942). John Willcock's biography, *Sir Thomas Urquhart of Cromartie, Knight* (1899), is the only book-length account, but though a pleasant read is whimsical and unmethodical. Hard facts, properly documented, are given in Henrietta Tayler's *History of the Family of Urquhart* (Aberdeen University Press, 1946), which devotes two chapters to Sir Thomas. His translation of Rabelais is in print in editions by Dent (Everyman Library) and Gordon Fraser Galleries; Aberdeen University has first editions of all of Sir Thomas's works except *Ekskubalauron*. There is only one book on Sir George Mackenzie, Andrew Lang's *Sir George Mackenzie, his Life and Times* (1909), and none of Mackenzie's works is available outside library collections. In the absence of any other critical work, I must refer the reader to my own articles, 'The Country House Poem in Scotland: Sir George Mackenzie's *Celia's Country House and Closet*' in *Studies in Scottish Literature* 12 (1974), 110-130; and 'The First Scots Novel: Sir George Mackenzie's *Aretina* (1660)' in *Scottish Literary Journal*, Supplement 11 (1979), 1-20.

Notes:

1. The first edition of Urquhart's *Logopandecteision* (1653) was printed, as Urquhart says on the last page, 'in scribled sheets and half sheets, before the Ink was oftentimes well dry, given out to two several printers', and so has two sets of page numbers, 1 to [80] covering Books 1 to 4, and 1 to [66] covering Books 5 and 6.
2. *Logopandecteision*, Book 6, 33.
3. Quotations from *Ekskubalauron* (or, as it is usually called, *The Jewel*) are taken from its reprint in *Tracts of the Learned and Celebrated Antiquarian, Sir Thomas Urquhart of Cromarty* (Edinburgh, 1774), referred to as *Tracts.*
4. Robert Chambers, *Traditions of Edinburgh* (new edition, 1869), 245.

THE BALLAD WORLD AND ALEXANDER ROSS

David Hewitt

North-east balladry constitutes the richest regional tradition in Britain. More ballad stories and more ballad versions have been recorded in the North-east of Scotland than elsewhere. The best versions have been recorded here: in the collection of Francis James Child, the greatest of ballad collectors, almost one-third of the A-texts came from Aberdeenshire. The region has produced the best singers – Jeannie Robertson in the modern period, for example and Anna Brown in the eighteenth century. Of the latter, Child wrote: 'No Scottish ballads are superior in kind to those recited . . . by Mrs. Brown, of Falkland'.[1] She was known as Mrs. Brown of Falkland, for that was where she was 'discovered' by collectors in the south of Scotland in the late eighteenth century; but she was born and brought up Anna Gordon, in Humanity Manse in Old Aberdeen, learned her ballads in upper Deeside, and is buried in Old Machar churchyard.[2]

In the late seventeenth century in the North-east of Scotland, the ballad was unquestionably the pre-eminent 'literary' form (although oral, not written), but sometime early in the eighteenth century, in the course of the transition from a primarily oral to a literate culture, the ballad lost that status. The tradition remained alive, however; in the bothy ballads of the nineteenth century farms labourers formulated and released their feelings about living and working conditions on farms. In the twentieth century, it was found that travelling folk and farm labourers in the North-east still sung orally-transmitted ballads, and the recordings made by Hamish Henderson for the School of Scottish Studies, particularly of Jeannie Robertson, have had no small influence on the contemporary re-emergence of folksong as a major literary kind, sung in social groups, used as a vehicle for political protest, performed on stage.

North-east balladry is thus a rich and living tradition; it has also had a considerable influence on Scottish *literature*. For instance, Sir Walter Scott's *Minstrelsy of the Scottish Border* (1802-3) includes as many North-eastern ballad versions as Border ones – he had access to North-east ballad texts recorded from Anna Brown, the 'Old Lady', and various correspondents in the area, and was indebted to the MSS of David Herd, who came from Kincardineshire and who included several North-east ballad texts in his *Ancient and Modern Scottish Songs, Heroic Ballads &c.* (1769). Scott's *Minstrelsy* was undoubtedly the most inspiring of all ballad collections, and in many cases it is Scott's (and thus North-east) ballad texts that have become the established form of a ballad in literature. *Thomas Rymer* (Child 37) still tends to be thought of as 'Thomas the Rymer', which was Scott's title, and it is Scott's composite text ('given from a copy obtained from a lady, residing not far from Erceldoune, corrected and enlarged by one in Mrs. Brown's MS'[3]) that is popularly known. But not only has North-eastern oral tradition entered and enriched Scottish literature as a whole, it has also been a continuous source of literary inspiration. Scott's imagination is permeated by the ballad: the impersonality of his lyrics, the use of ballad-like narratives as the plots of *The Heart of Midlothian* and *The Bride of Lammermoor*, the recurrence of romance forms in his long poems and fiction, his sense of the violence of Scottish history and of continuous friction between England and Scotland, his awareness of the supernatural – these are all evidence of the influence of the ballad upon him and his work. A later instance would be the bothy ballads, for their use of common speech to represent the outlook and attitudes of a particular social group, inspired Charles Murray to write his more richly perceived, more varied and more ironic poetry about the people of the North-east.

In general, the fertilising and vivifying influence of the ballad upon Scottish literature is well known; it is ironic, therefore, that when the richest regional tradition is that of the North-east, the poet who actually *wrote* a fine poem about the ballad world, Alexander Ross from Deeside, should be virtually unknown.

Ross, the son of a farmer, was born in the parish of Kincardine O'Neil in 1699. After attending the local school, he went to Marischal College, Aberdeen, from where he graduated in 1718. He was appointed tutor to the family of Sir William Forbes of Craigievar, then schoolmaster first in Aboyne and subsequently in Laurencekirk, where he became friendly with the father of James Beattie. In 1732 he went to Lochlee, at the head of Glenesk in Angus, and remained there as schoolmaster, session clerk and notary for the rest of his life. For years his poems circulated in manuscript, initially in his own circle in Lochlee, before James Beattie made a selection of his poetry, including his principal work *Helenore*, that was published in 1768. He died in 1784.

In *The Ballad and the Folk*, David Buchan argues, convincingly, that the ballads of Anna Brown belong to oral tradition, in other words that they are the songs of a non-literate culture. Anna Brown probably learned her ballads in the seventeen-fifties. Ballads collected in the North-east early in the nineteenth century are usually markedly inferior to Anna Brown's, and David Buchan maintains that the deterioration was due to the transition from a primarily oral to a primarily literate culture, and to the infection of oral methods of controlling and organising thought by literate. He says, for instance:

> . . . the attainment of widespread literacy altered substantially the old oral culture. First, it changed the modes of thought, and consequently slackened people's adherence to traditional belief and custom. Second, it reduced the importance of the oral community's arts and entertainments – proverbs, riddling sessions, tale-telling . . .[4]

David Buchan's analysis seems to imply that the change was largely loss. But I would wish to argue that for a period at least the advent of widespread literacy enriched traditional culture, and that Alexander Ross's poetry exemplifies this view. He must have been writing *Helenore* at about the same time as Anna Brown was learning her ballad stories; he translates her ballad world into a different literary form and in so doing he makes obvious many of the ballads' underlying concerns. He enriches traditional culture by making it conscious of itself.

From Anna Brown's ballads we get an impression of a world of conflict – between families and relatives over love, marriage and property, and, beyond the familial conflicts, between feuding clans, and between the Highlands and the Lowlands. Often conflict is exacerbated by the supernatural. It must be assumed that the ballads bear some relationship to the circumstances of life known by their creators, but the treatment of these circumstances is in no way naturalistic, and the real issues are frequently implied rather than stated. For instance, in her version of *The Baron of Brackley* (Child 203C) Inverey comes down Deeside to drive off the cattle of the Baron of Brackley. Brackley, who has only his brother to support him, thinks it prudent to remain indoors but is driven to defend his own by the taunts of his lady. At odds of 34 to 2, Brackley is inevitably killed; but it turns out to have been a plot, for Brackley's widow feasts Inverey, and detains him overnight before telling him the best way to escape. The ballad concentrates upon the clash of two men over property and a woman, and upon the woman's sexual treachery. It does not make explicit the wider cultural and political motives for the conflict: Inverey was a Farquharson and a Highlander, and Brackley was a Gordon and a Lowlander. The ballad was founded upon a real incident in 1666, but it ignores all the legal complexities that were involved: it seems that Brackley had first taken Inverey's cattle in payment of a fine imposed on the latter for salmon fishing out of season, and had refused a negotiated settlement. Thus an endemic Scottish probelm – the imposition of lowland law and order upon semi-autonomous highland clans – is also at issue but totally ignored by the balladist.

Anna Brown's romantic ballads are largely concerned with the opposition that lovers must overcome in order to achieve their union. Unlike the historical ballads, they are usually unlocalised but like those they emphasise action and ignore the complexities of human motivation. In *Young Bicham* (Child 53A) the hero is imprisoned by a Moor; in return for a promise of marriage, the Moor's daughter Shusy Pye helps him to escape. When he gets home he conveniently forgets his promise and is about to marry another when Shusy Pye turns up to claim him. Her mere arrival is enough to win back Young Bicham's love, even although it is his wedding day. There is no psychological description; Bicham acts on his recognition of his first love as though he were just waking up:

> Then up it started Young Bicham,
> An sware so loud by Our Lady,
> 'It can be nane but Shusy Pye,
> That has come oer the sea to me.'
>
> O quickly ran he down the stair,
> O fifteen steps he has made but three;
> He's tane his bonny love in his arms,
> An a wot he kissd her tenderly. (st. 18-19)

Anna Brown's ballads of the marvellous for the most part share the same dominant theme. In *Gil Brenton* (Child 5A) a mother tests her new daughter-in-law's virginity by magic. When she is found to be pregnant, the mother attacks the girl who tells the story of her seduction. The mother then perceives that the seducer was her own son and forces a confession from him. Once again the ballad does not make explicit what is going on. Magic is an active agent that only implies all sorts of tension between mother and daughter-in-law without making clear either the issue or the 'hang-up'; it does force a confrontation between mother and daughter-in-law, however, and through that the listener or reader perceives the conflict between mother and son about the suitability of his marriage partner, the mother's victory in enforcing a politically advantageous marriage and the son's ultimate victory over his mother in finding that his wife is also his love. In *King Henry*

(Child 32) an ugly woman is transformed into a beautiful one by the king's love and in *Allison Gross* (Child 35) the man is turned into a worm for refusing his favours to a witch and is only rescued by the intervention of the fairy queen: the ballads stress action, not its implications.

Such ballads may have their basis in the life that the people of the North-east knew, and simultaneously express their way of seeing and apprehending that life. But neither the apprehension nor its expression is at all naturalistic. Complex human situations are presented in terms of the disruption of a loving relationship between two people by a third. Natural psychological forces are expressed, without warning, in action or in the operation of magic; indeed, the repeated use of the magic numbers three, seven and nine, and of the fairy colour green almost implies that the action of the ballads has a supra-natural necessity. The balladists' responsiveness to wealth and finery indicates naive imaginings rather than experience:

> You coudna see her yallow hair
> For gold and pearle that were so rare.
>
> You coudna see her middle sma
> For gouden girdle that was sae braw.
>
> *The Twa Sisters* (Child 10B, st. 20-21)

In addition, the structure of the ballads, that elaborate patterning of balanced and paralleled phrases, stanzas and groups of stanzas (so well and so thoroughly analysed by David Buchan in *The Ballad and the Folk*), at once impresses one with the complex organisation of oral poetry and also enhances one's awareness that the ballad is a highly stylised art form.

In *Helenore* Alexander Ross deals with the matter of the ballads, but in a different verse form (the couplet) and a different poetic kind (the realistic pastoral). He brings to the ballad world a more literary and critical mind and the result is a poem that may not be more exciting than the ballads, but is unquestionably richer in historical, sociological and psychological detail. Ross, I submit, enriches traditional culture by making it aware of itself, before general literacy changed it fundamentally.

The action of *Helenore* or, *The Fortunate Shepherdess*, a poem of some 4000 lines in heroic couplets, takes place in and around the district of Flaviana. The heroine, Helenore, who is usually known as Nory, is the daughter of Colen and Jean and is more or less brought up with their neighbour's son, Lindy. Inevitably they think they are in love and promised in marriage to each other. One day, as Lindy is tending the herds, Flaviana is raided by a band of kettrin (caterans), who steal the cattle, tie Lindy up and abandon him. When news is brought back to Flaviana, Nory runs into the hills to find him, but goes in the wrong direction and gets lost. She is eventually found by a squire, who falls in love with her on the spot. The squire himself is alienated from his home by his father's determination that he should marry a rich but ugly woman. In Flaviana, Colen and Jean find that Nory is missing, and Colen goes to look for her; he assumes that she will have gone after the kettrin, so he follows them and gets caught. Meanwhile Lindy frees himself and goes home to find that both Colen and Nory are missing, so he too follows the kettrin and is captured. A kettrin girl called Bydby, who looks after Colen and Lindy, falls in love with Lindy, and offers to let them both escape provided Lindy promises to marry her. He agrees; they are freed but they give Bydby the slip and make off home. Bydby follows them, but she too gets lost and eventually lands up at the same place as Nory, whom she meets. Both girls return to Flaviana. There is then a long period of negotiation in which Bydby claims the reluctant Lindy, in which the squire claims Nory and is accepted by her, and in which Lindy eventually agrees to marry Bydby. The double marriage takes place; the kettrin arrive to retrieve Bydby, but are eventually converted from their predatory ways by the marriages and the accompanying festivities.

Such a summary makes *Helenore* sound like a poem of almost Spenserian artificiality. The names reinforce the impression – characters called Colen, Helenore, Lindy, and local names such as Flaviana, which is raided by 'Saevitians', Ross's 'proper name' for the kettrin. But these indications are misleading. Apart from Ross's extraordinarily original handling of language, which will be dealt with later, the poem actually unites a series of ballad stories into one action: it brings together narratives of the cattle raid in which the hero is lost (as in *The Baron of Brackley*); the ugly woman transformed into a beautiful bride (as in *King Henry*); parental opposition leading to the union of lovers in the green wood (*Gil Brenton*); the hero who escapes imprisonment with the assistance of a girl whom he rewards with a promise of marriage but whom he attempts to betray in favour of another (*Young Bicham*); the girl of low degree who marries the squire (*Child Waters*).

These are stock ballad situations, but Ross tends to interpret them realistically. Thus the transformation of an ugly woman into a beautiful one is achieved not by magic, but through the squire's rejection of one and discovery of the other. In *Young Bicham*, Shusy Pye's arrival is enough to win Young Bicham back. The situation in *Helenore* is not exactly parallel but Ross recognises that such human situations are not susceptible to the simple monetary solution of the ballad:

'Take back your daughter, madam,' he says,
'An a double dowry I'll gie her wi.' (st. 22)

In *Helenore* there is a lot of discussion and a lot of persuading. The nature of the bargain that Lindy made with Bydby is debated:

'She pleads a promise, and it's very true;
But he had naething but a jamphing view:
But she in gnapping earnest taks it a'.' (2746-8)

Among other issues they consider the pressure exerted on them by the Highlanders' ability and willingness to use force, on which Lindy feelingly remarks:

'Sir this is unko hard
This gate we have nae chance against a kaird;
Gin but she say she likes ane, that's enough,
As lang's they'll ca', to gar us had the pleugh.' (3284-7)

In a similar way dreams are not supernatural instruments as they tend to be in the ballads, but they achieve the same effect by predisposing the dreamer to certain courses of action. Thus Nory's dream, in which she and Lindy are drowning and in which she is rescued by an unknown man and Lindy by an unknown girl (1120-1145), prepares her for her ultimate rejection of Lindy and acceptance of the squire.

Ross places his ballad situations in a realistic geographic, historical and social environment. He is vague about the precise locale of his poem, but it is impossible not to conclude that he has Glenesk and the surrounding area in mind. Flaviana is Lochlee, or Tarfside; when the kettrin strike, Lindy is looking after herds of black cattle in one of the subsidiary glens – Glenmark, or Glenlee – which were the summer pasturage, according to the first *Statistical Account*. When Nory gets lost she wanders north-east into Feughside; Colen and Lindy follows the kettrin west to Glenmuick. The descriptions of the terrain suggest exactly that broken, rough and boggy ground that walkers still encounter:

Ay hading eastlins, as the ground did fa',
An' frae the height strove ay to had awa'.
But yet nae cuintray in her sight appears
But dens an' burns an' bare an' langsome moors. (1680-3)

As Nory wanders, she is afflicted by midges:

Now very sair the sun began to beat,
An' she was almaist scunfest with the heat;
The summer couts were dancing here an' there,
An' clouds of midges reeling in the air. (582-5)

The history implied by *Helenore* is consistent with the conditions Ross must have known. Glenesk is a lowland valley; there is no evidence of Gaelic being talked there in the eighteenth century. But the Lowlands faded into the Highlands somewhere between Crathie and Braemar and so Ross's poem is placed in a border country, where kettrin raids could be expected, and where there were indeed raids right into the eighteenth century. The system of land tenure and use described by Ross reflects that known by him in Lochlee:

Now Flaviana was the country's name
That ay this bony water-side did claim,
Frae yellow sands, that trindl'd down the same.
The fouks were wealthy, store was a' their stock;
With this, but little siller, did they trock.
Frae mang the stock his honour gat his fa',
An' got but little cunzie, or nane awa' . . .
The green was even, gowany and fair;
With easy sklent, on every side the braes
To a good height, wi' scatter'd busses raise;
Wi' goats an' sheep aboon, an' cows below,
These bonny braes all in a swarm did go.
No property these honest shepherds pled;
All kept alike, an' all in common fed. (403-21)

The last two lines sound indealistic; in fact they are a proper description of the real situation. None of the shepherds possess any land themselves, and the cattle, sheep and goats are communally tended on the common grazing. Theirs is not a cash-economy; they pay rent in kind to an absentee landlord – 'Frae mang the stock his honour gat his fa' '. And indeed this was the case. There had long been no resident proprietor. (The estate was formerly owned by that branch of the Lindsay family who lived in Edzell from the sixteenth century, and was sold to the Earl of Panmure in 1714. It was forfeited for his part in the Jacobite rising of 1715.) And even at the end of the eighteenth century, according to the *Statistical Account*, the heritors exacted service rather than money.

Ross's treatment of folk beliefs and practices provides a further measure of the effcet of his translation of the ballad world into literature. The ballads are permeated by the people's knowledge of fairies; this knowledge is so much a part of common understanding that fairies never need to be explained and slight and casual reference to them can be made in passing. Ross brings to his subject a more literal mind, and an eighteenth century awareness of the value of detail. Yet he describes folk practices fully, without any hint whatsoever of the amused, half-believing antiquarian interest shown by Burns in *Hallowe'en*. As a result we get a fuller picture of what people actually did than we ever get from a ballad, and we recognise from the unselfconsciousness of his descriptions that their practices were not quaint, half-invented survivals as in *Hallowe'en* but a natural part of living. This may be seen in the description of the rites following Nory's birth:

> Gryt was the care an' tut'ry that was ha'en,
> Baith night an' day, about the bony wean.
> The jizzen-bed [cradle] wi' rantree leaves was sain'd
> An' sicklike craft as the auld grandys kend;
> Jean's paps wi' sa't and water washen clean,
> For fear her milk gat wrang fan it was green;
> Then the first hippen [nappy] to the green was flung,
> And unko words thereat baith said an' sung;
> A burning coal with the hett tangs was ta'en
> Frae out the ingle mids, well brunt an' clean.
> An' thro' the corsy-belly [infant's vest] letten fa',
> For fear the wean should be ta'en awa'.
> Dowing an' growing was the dayly prayer,
> An' Nory tented was wi' unko care. (94-107)

The most important of all Ross's innovations in his treatment of the ballad world is his use of the language of the people about whom he writes. Instead of the specialised, poetic language of the ballads, or the cultivated English poetic diction of his friend James Beattie, Ross writes *Helenore* in a representation of the common speech of the North-east. In consequence, it is a poem that is rich not in metaphor but in experience. When Lindy in his search for Nory blunders upon the kettrin, he is set on by three of them who

> round about him bicker'd a' at anes,
> As they were playing at the penny-stanes. (1298-9)

The dialogue is entertaining. When Lindy states his case against marrying Bydby, he manages to express succinctly and vividly both his resentment that he should be held to a bargain concluded under duress and his moral outrage at Bydby's flagrant behaviour (implying that it might be acceptable in other social classes but not in his):

> Quo he: 'I'se warrant sickan words hae been,
> An't like your honor, her an' me between;
> "To lat you gae," gin she said, "what'll ye gimme?"
> I've aiblins said, "Indeed, I's tak you wi' me."
> Cud that be grounds so fast a grip to hadd,
> Or gee a lass a tittle till a lad?
> I wonder that she thinks na burning shame
> On sick an errand to have come frae hame.
> We that's poor fouks like at some pains to be
> To court our lasses their consent to gee,

An' think them light that hastily consent,
Afore some time an' pains on them be spent;
But to seek us, afore their pulse we try,
We count them scimp of shame an' modesty. (3146-59)

There is a tendency to cast speech into a proverbial form; in this Ross simultaneously reflects the traditional speech habits and modes of thought of his audience, and exploits the couplet's potential for pithy and aphoristic expression. Ross, talking to his Muse, encourages himself to write in spite of the example of Ramsay –

But I's be willing as ye bid me write –
Blind horse, they say, ride hardy to the fight,
And by good hap may come awa' but scorn:
They are na kempers a' that shear the corn. (33-6)

Colen tells his neighbour how lightly he and Lindy agreed to the bargain with Bydby:

At first I thought but little o' the thing,
But mischief frae a midge's wing may spring. (2731-2)

Helenore is a splendid poem – it entertains and is rich in human observation. It is also extremely interesting for it raises many issues concerning the transition from a primarily oral to a primarily literate culture. As I have already observed, David Buchan's analysis of that transition implies that the change was largely loss. These losses are paralleled by the consequences of political and economic developments and were repeatedly lamented in the course of the eighteenth century. Of course the very desire to record ballads shows an awareness of the decay of oral tradition, but equally that awareness stimulated Ramsay, Herd, Burns and the ballad collectors to record the culture that was passing. It is at least arguable that in the eighteenth and early nineteenth centuries all the collecting actually created a more general awareness of the total riches of oral tradition, and that oral tradition itself was richer as a result, for songs and ballads undoubtedly left the printed page and re-entered oral and verbal culture. Furthermore, the collecting of songs stimulated invention, and many new or reworked pieces went into the general repertoire.[5]

The argument is relevant to Ross. The finest ballads are superb; they can be mysterious and they can be stirring. Nothing in *Helenore* can equal the poetic excitement generated by *Thomas Rymer*. But their view of the experience they transmit is restricted by the limitations of the ballad genre, form and diction, and no ballad shows an understanding of the ballad world equal to Ross's. His knowledge of literature did not falsify his presentation of 'folk' experience, but provided him with a poetic vehicle and poetic models better adapted to the complexity of experience. In the eighteenth century the couplet was 'geared' to the discussion and analysis of social issues. Through *The Gentle Shepherd* Allan Ramsay showed Ross the possibilities of the realistic pastoral; Ross applied the form (as his mentor never did) to the description of a real world. He describes not just the social organisation and history of Flaviana, but also the people's habits and attitudes of mind. He thus makes explicit the politics, sociology and psychology underlying many of the ballads. I would maintain that he must have made his original audience in Lochlee aware of their own traditional culture. Of course such consciousness would ultimately be destructive of traditional culture, but in the transitional period at least it was possible both to know and to see.

Above all, Ross's use of local dialect must have made his first audience conscious of themselves as traditional song could never do. It was a revolutionary step and Ross knew it, although, like many revolutionaries, he presents his innovation as an attempt to recapture a lost past; his Muse tells him:

> Speak my ain leed, 'tis gueed auld Scots I mean;
> Your Southern gnaps I count not worth a preen.
> We've words a fouth, that we can ca' our ain,
> Tho' frae them now my childer sair refrain,
> An' are to my gueed auld proverb confeerin –
> Neither gueed fish nor flesh, nor yet sa't herrin. (56-61)

At first glance, Ross's target would seem to be English; in fact it is Allan Ramsay. Ramsay did not write in a local dialect; he created something like a standard poetic Scots – a highly rhetorical verse medium in which different social levels are reflected in different orthographic representations of the language. There is a tendency for more thoughtful characters (including narrators) to be represented in something like English, regardless of what the speaker may have sounded like, and for more earthy characters to speak a more rigorous Scots. Ramsay's example was followed by most Scots poets of the eighteenth century, including Burns, and by Scott and the novelists who suceeded him – an unhappy discrimination that exacerbated the linguistic problems of later Scots writers, as Derrick McClure and Colin Milton point out in their essays later in this volume. Ross rejects this, motivated in part by local patriotism as was James Beattie in his *Epistle to Alexander Ross* that prefaces the second and subsequent editions of *Helenore*:

> The Southland chiels indeed hae mettle,
> And brawly at a sang can ettle;
> Yet we right couthily might settle
> On this side Forth.

The devil pay them wi'a pettle,
That slight the north. (37-42)

Ross is also motivated by a sense of linguistic purity when he rejects Ramsay's language as 'neither gueed fish nor flesh, nor yet sa't herrin'. So Ross uses a single dialect. He interprets the life that he knew in the language of the people that he knew. No doubt he was more intelligent than most, but he writes not as a superior intellect explaining quaint country customs, but as one of the people about whom he writes.

Alexander Ross is the author of the first truly local poem, and he discovered the particular power of the local poem: in reflecting a people it makes them aware of themselves. But Ross is nowadays virtually unknown – a situation that reflects our ignorance rather than his merits. Perhaps his use of a north-eastern dialect accounts for his neglect. But his example must have been influential, and may have been one factor in the emergence of the 'doric' as a poetic language in the late nineteenth century. There were 18 editions of *Helenore* in the 100 years following its first publication, and of these 13 were published in Aberdeen and one in Brechin, the last in 1874. It is a local poem and was enjoyed locally, so does it not seem probable that Charles Murray knew *Helenore*?

Suggestions for further reading:

There is no readily available edition of *Helenore*. The standard text is in *The Scottish Works of Alexander Ross, M.A.*, ed. Margaret Wattie, Scottish Text Society, Third Series, 9, (Edinburgh and London, 1938). Nor is there any criticism on Ross. On the other hand, literature on the ballads is extensive. The great collection is, of course, Francis James Child's *The English and Scottish Popular Ballads*, 5 vols. (1882-98). The ballads of Anna Brown discussed in this essay may be more conveniently read in *A Scottish Ballad Book*, ed. David Buchan, (London and Boston, 1973), an anthology designed to accompany his important study of the ballads of the North-east, *The Ballad and the Folk* (London and Boston, 1972).

Notes:

1. F.J. Child, *The English and Scottish Popular Ballads*, vol. I part I (1882), vii.
2. See David Buchan, *The Ballad and the Folk* (London, 1972), 4-5. For the purposes of this essay I largely accept Buchan's

arguments about ballads and oral culture.

3. Scott, *Minstrelsy of the Scottish Border* (Kelso, 1802), vol. 2, 250.
4. Buchan, 199.
5. See Thomas Crawford, *Society and the Lyric* (Edinburgh, 1979).

JAMES BEATTIE: A FRIEND TO ALL

Joan H. Pittock

Of the figures of the Scottish Enlightenment whose achievements compelled the attention of civilised Europe the single influential poetic talent was that of James Beattie, Professor of Moral Philosophy and Logic in Marischal College from 1760 until the end of the century. It is true that James Macpherson, the progenitor of Ossian as we know him, was born in Badenoch and died at Kingussie, studied at both King's and Marischal, and was a contemporary of Beattie, but he was never known for the speculative philosophical concern with man, society and moral principles which grouped together the members of the Aberdeen Wise Club and their counterparts in Edinburgh and Glasgow.

Aberdeen had already produced Arbuthnot, friend of Swift and Pope and physician to Queen Anne; the Blackwells, father and son, both principals of Marischal, the younger of whom, investigating the influence of the environment of ancient Greece on Homer's inspiration, was a pioneer in primitivist thought; Alexander Gerard, the aesthetician and educationalist; as well as Reid and Campbell of 'commonsense' fame, and Beattie himself, who provided a highly popular counterblast to Hume's scepticism in his *Essay on Truth* (1770). In the realms of imagination as distinct from those of moral philosophy it is Beattie alone whose name appears in the numerous popular collections of poets issued by publishers for the expanding taste-concious public of the late eighteenth and nineteenth centuries. His poetry is found in the company of that of Collins, Gray, Akenside, Goldsmith, Cowper, Johnson, Blair, Falconer and others now forgotten. The variety of woodcuts and engravings which embellished his most famous poem, *The Ministrel* and even the attempts to finish it (for it was apparently left incomplete) indicate the strength of the imaginative stimulus to be found in his work.

It is the kind of stimulus offered by other names at that time whose magic held and may still hold the reader in an intimation of an enduring dream, nostalgia or delight in detachment from everyday strains and bustle. The cadences and imagery of Gray's *Elegy*, Goldsmith's *Deserted Village*, Chatterton's *Minstrell's Song* (from *Aella*), Macpherson's *Fingal* and Beattie's *Minstrel* catch in varying degrees, and with a fluctuating and intermittent appeal, an element of mystery and necessity in man's awareness of and his *rapport* with nature.

The influence of Beattie's poems on poets of the Romantic generations has been frequently noted, and has recently received closer attention in Everard King's *James Beattie* (Twayne, 1977). It is appropriate, too, in view of Beattie's international appeal, that Bernhard Fabian has established a comprehensive collection of Beattie material and transcripts at the Institutum Erasmianum at Münster. Most important, however, are the manuscript collections of Beattie material in Aberdeen University Library[1]. Though much of what is interesting has already been published, it is here that one gains an overwhelming impression of Beattie's generous and many-sided activities as friend, literary adviser, critic, creative talent and moral guide.

But a question whether Beattie has any relevance for the modern reader and indeed why he has mattered to others cannot be answered by categorising him and labelling him in the context of literary history and scholarship. We know that he became a bastion of the anti-sceptic groups when he attacked Hume in his *Essay on Truth* (1770), a work more remunerative in his life-time than either his poetry or even his chair, for it gained him a pension from the King and a place in the friendship and affections of many of his distinguished contemporaries, including Dr. Johnson and Mrs. Montagu. He is commemorated as its author in the allegorical portrait painted by Sir Joshua Reynolds, now in the Court Room of Marischal College, Aberdeen, which immortalises the rout of Hume and Voltaire by Beattie and the angels. We know that to write about minstrels, and hermits, and melancholy, as Beattie did, was to associate himself with Percy and Gray in the category which disposes of so many and such varied talents under the label 'Pre-Romantic'. It is easy enough to proceed from this to relate the influence of Beattie's *Minstrel* to the design of *The Prelude*; to realise that the figure of Edwin (Beattie's minstrel) might be part of the world of *Michael*; that Keats's *St. Agnes' Eve* is concerned with Beattie's kind of inspiration,

> Numerous as the shadows haunting fairily
> The brain, new stuff'd, in youth, with triumphs gay
> Of old romance ...

and that Scott not only writes of Beattie and his biographer in the introductory lines to canto 4 of *Marmion*,

Scarce had lamented Forbes paid
The tribute to his Minstrel's shade;
The tale of friendship scarce was told,
Ere the narrator's heart was cold -

but that *The Lay of the Last Minstrel* and *Rokeby* also echo Beattie. Perhaps even the evocative landscaping of Tennyson's *Oenone* owes something to Beattie's *Judgement of Paris* (1765). Such is Beattie's demonstrable relevance in the history of poetry. Is this enough to prove his relevance to a contemporary reader? If the answer can merely be affirmed in terms of the somewhat negative contexts of conventional literary history we are further daunted by Beattie's attitude to the Scottish language, current at his time but far from acceptable now, displayed in his pamphlet against Scotticisms (1779). He would seem, too, to play a paltry part in intellectual history by reason of his opposition to Hume in a spirit of what might be construed a kind of confident ignorance and complacency, an attitude which emboldened him to parody Voltaire in his *Castle of Scepticism* (1767), [2] one of his few imaginative prose works.

In this volume it is appropriate to take rather a different viewpoint. Beattie's life is bound to that of the north east peculiarly closely. Born near Laurencekirk in 1735, Beattie passed the whole of his professional life in Aberdeen, spending most of his summers at the spa in Peterhead. After graduating in 1753 he spent a few years schoolmastering at Fordoun, moving to Aberdeen Grammar School in 1758, and succeeding Alexander Gerard in the Chair of Moral Philosophy and Logic in 1760. During his lifetime Aberdeen was associated with a wide range of creative talent, especially in poetry and music. Several literary societies and a music society flourished in the town, and, as in Edinburgh, groups of professional men spent convivial hours in clubbable mood. The most celebrated of these is the Wise Club, or Philosophical Society of Aberdeen, founded in 1758 which Beattie (having been nominated by Gerard) joined on February 10, 1761. while Thomas Reid was President. The first topic on which he chose to speak was 'to enquire what is peculiar to the operations of the human mind of which we can form no ideas' (AUL MS 539).

About the same time Beattie, who had already published several poems in the *Scots Magazine* and had issued proposals in 1760 for printing a volume of poems and translations (which appeared in February 1761) wrote with his friends Arbuthnot and Mercer an ode describing the membership of yet another club to which he belonged, 'The Lemon Tree Club'. Its activities seem to have been rather more varied than those of the Wise Club, as the following stanzas suggest:

O mighty Genius, whereso'er
At whatsoever period seen,
At Delphi or at Durrideer,
At Athens, or at Aberdeen.

Thou Spirit of the sounding Mortar,
Apothecary Leslie, come,
And thou shalt have thy Mug of Porter,
And eke thy nipperkin of Rum,

O Moir look not upon us so,
Nor play with us the Critic Bully,
But smile as thou were wont to do,
And shut the musty pages of Tully ...

On banks of Don sits love-lorn Kattie,
Oh! listen to her tale of woe,
And prithee tell Professor Beattie
To speak with me before he go ...

O Beattie, with thy Muse Pindaric,
Resume once more thine ancient Lyre
And we shall mouth like David Garrick
And celebrate Miss Betty Byre. (AUL MS 3017/10/23/21)

Beattie's social forte was his good humour, versatility and generosity in exercising his musical and literary talents on behalf of his friends, from playing his violincello at Slains or Gordon Castle to interesting the Duchess of Gordon and Mrs. Montagu in the lack of fortune of his other humbler acquaintances. His furthering the fortunes of Alexander Ross is well known. To assist the sale of Ross's work he wrote his only acknowledged piece of vernacular poetry:

O Ross, thou wale of hearty cocks,
Sae crouse and canty wi' thy jokes!
Thy hamely auldwarld muse provokes
Me, for a while,
To ape our guid plain countra' folks
In verse and stile.

Sure never carle was haff sae gabby,
E're since the winsome days of Habby.
O mayst thou ne'er gang clung or shabby,
Nor miss thy snaker!
Or I'll ca' Fortune, Nasty Drabby,
And say, Pox take her.[3]

This second stanza is praised for its 'unusual elegance and vigour' in volume VIII of the *Oxford History of English Literature*, *The Mid-Eighteenth Century* (152); but of rather more interest is Beattie's attitude to Scottish poets and poetry in the same poem:

Since Allan's death, naebody car'd
For anes to speer how Scota far'd;
Nor plack nor thristled turner war'd,
To quench her drouth;
For, frae the cottar to the laird,
We a' rin South ....

It's true, we norlans manna fa'
To eat sae nice, or gang sae bra',
As they that come frae far awa';
Yet sma's our skaith:
We've peace (and that's well worth it a')
And meat and claith ....

.... Scotland wants na sons enew
To do her honour.

I here might gie a screed of names,
Dawties of Heliconian Dames!
The foremost place Gawin Douglas claims,
That canty priest.
And wha can match the fifth King James
For sang or jest?

Montgomery grave, and Ramsay gay,
Dunbar, Scot, Hawthornden, and mae
Than I can tell, for o' my fae,
I maun brak aff;
'Twould tak a live-lang summer-day
To name the haff.

The saucy chiels – I think they ca' them
Criticks – the muckle sorrow claw them,
(For mense or manners ne'er could awe them
Frae their presumption)
They need na try thy jokes to fathom,
They want rumgumption.

But ilka Mearns and Angus bairn
Thy tales and sangs by heart shall learn;
And chiels shall come frae yont the Cairn –
  amounth, right vousty,
If Ross will be so kind as share in
  Their pint at Drousty.[4]

This was not Beattie's only venture into vernacular poetry. however. In George Eyre-Todd's *Scottish poets of the Eighteenth Century* (2 vols., 1896) which with William Walker's *The Bards of Bon-Accord* (1887), presents the work of a considerable number of poets of Aberdeen and the North-east at this period, it is noted that John Skinner, the author of *Tullochgorum*, finished a pastoral piece begun by Beattie. Eyre-Todd attributes only the first three lines to Beattie, which in the four-line stanza form is unlikely. Another version of the poem exists among the Aberdeen University Library manuscripts (AUL MS 3017/10/23/18), in which the four concluding stanzas of the printed version are missing. The simplicity and directness of this piece (*The Ewie wi' the Crookit Horn*) shows Beattie's appreciation of the effectiveness of the vernacular in conveying the quality of everyday experience. There is a footnote to the Skinner anecdote, however, for about the year 1790 Skinner wrote a poem on Beattie. A note on it in AUL MS 3017/10/23 runs 'This burlesque poem, to the Scots tune of *Tullochgorum*, was written by the Rev. Mr. Skinner, Episcopal Minister of Langside in Buchan – and addressed to Dr. Beattie of Marischal College, whom the author had heard say of him, that he was a wretched Balladmaker'. Each stanza indicates cleverly enough a facet of Beattie's reputation, and the second is a fair sample of the whole:

Laus sane tibi Maxima
Debetur nunc et gloria
Et dabitur per secula
Ad finem seculorum
Nam tali stylo scribere
Tali stylo, tali stylo,
Tali stylo scribere
Argute tam at lepide
Quis potuisset praeter te
Doctissime doctorum?

(Which, in the spirit of *Tullochgorum*, we might translate:

They a' sall praise thee in the hicht,
And glorify wi' main and micht,
And never cease to praise thy slicht,
  Tho' centuries gae o'er 'em;
Siccan screivins, siccan screivins,

Siccan screivins sae polite,
Wha but thysel could e'er endite?
'Tis thou maun be the shining light
  O' a' our learned quorum!)

As teacher, poet and moralist Beattie was alarmed at the current modishness of scepticism, an inclination to barren speculation fashionable in Scottish philosophising. As a teacher he was particularly concerned with the problem of writing well and attractively. These preoccupations are illustrated in the themes and style of his poetry. One aspect of his own versatility as a poet emerges in his setting verses to well-known tunes – *The Hermit* (1776) was written to be sung to 'Pentland Hills' –

At the close of the day, when the hamlet is still,
And mortals the sweets of forgetfulness prove,
When nought but the torrent is heard on the hill,
And nought but the nightingale's song in the grove ...

(AUL MS 30/1/14)

Or there is the familiar epistolary tone of his verse letter of 1 August 1766 to Charles Boyd, where deftness of versification is amusingly harnessed to a deliberate heterogeneity of imagery:

I wish for wings or winds to speed my course,
Since Burnet and the fates refuse a horse.
Where now the Pegasus of ancient time,
And Hyppogripho famed in modern rhyme?
Where now that wooden steed, whose every leg
Like lightning flew, obsequious to the peg?
O where the wings by Dedalus design'd,
And China-waggons wafted by the wind?
A Spaniard reached the moon, upborn by geese;
(Then first 'twas known that she is made of cheese).
A fidler on a fish through waves advanced,
He thrum'd his catgut, and the dolphin danced;
Hags ride on broomsticks, heathern-gods on clouds,
Ladies on rams and bulls have dared the floods:
Much fam'd the shoes Jack Giant-Killer wore,
And Fortunatus' hat is fam'd much more.
Such vehicles were common once, I ween,
As broken-winded hacks are now at Aberdeen.
Bur modern Bards (alas!) must trudge on foot,
Or doze at home, expectant of the gout ...

(AUL MS 30/1/8a)

Appropriately enough, it was in satire that Beattie first voiced his moral indignation at current scepticism. In 1765 he published anonymously *Verses Occasion'd by the Death of the Revd Mr Charles Churchill, written by a native of Britain*. It has a rollicking patriotic quality which ensured its popularity. That it was borne of conviction is clear from Beattie's contemporary correspondence; it begins on a hectic note:

Churchill begone! with thee may discord's sire,
That hatch'd thy salamander-flame, expire!
Fame, dirty idol of the blameless crowd,
What half-made mooncalf can mistake for good?
Since shar'd by knaves of high and low degree,
Cromwell and Catiline, Guido Fawkes and thee.
By nature uninspired, untaught by art,
With not one thought that breathes the feeling heart,
With not one offering vow'd to Virtue's shrine,
With not one pure unprostituted line;
The hireling slave of faction and of spite,
His country's nuisance, and a Wilkes' delight. (ll. 1-12)

The concluding lines have a surprisingly almost vicious force:

But when a ruffian, whose portentous crimes,
Like plagues and earthquakes, terrify the times,
Triumphs thro' life, from legal judgement free,
For hell may hatch what law could ne'er foresee:
Sacred from vengeance shall his memory rest? –
Judas, tho' dead, th' damn'd, we still detest. (ll. 141-6)

He did not acknowledge the verses until the following year when they were reprinted to oppose the proposal to set up a memorial to Churchill in Westminster Abbey and re-titled *Verses on the Report of a Monument to be erected in Westminster Abbey, to the Memory of a late Author*. Nearer the main stream of Beattie's inspiration is *Retirement* (1761), in which writers on Beattie have identified the landscape of Fordoun and the glen near his house where he spent many leisure hours. It is fairly characteristic of this kind of poetry that 'A pensive Youth of placid mien' should be a kind of agent for the reader, and that Gray's influence should be seen in the opposition between Ambition and Solitude. The poem is a kind of forerunner of *The Minstrel* (1771) not only in these respects, but also in the way Beattie constructs the development of the poem in terms of the mental conditions contingent on each of the personifications. This involves an evocation of precisely those features of the landscape which soothe and refresh the mind, and the contrasting elements of mental activity which augment the fret of Ambition. The melancholy tone is not in overall control with wry and whimsical undertones, as in Gray's work, but shows a firmer moral awareness less skilfully and imaginatively deployed perhaps, but giving an individualised note. But this early experience was interrupted:

> . . . Ah why did Fate his steps decoy
> In stormy paths to roam,
> Remote from all congenial joy! –
> O take the wanderer home.
> Thy shades, thy silence, now be mine,
> Thy charms my only theme;
> My haunt the hollow cliff, whose pine
> Waves o'er the gloomy stream,
> Whence the scared owl on pinions grey
> Breaks from the rustling boughs,
> And down the lone vale sails sway
> To more profound repose . . . (St. 7)

Retirement was one of the few poems published in the 1761 volume to be retained by Beattie in subsequent collections of his work. As his old student, Chalmers, notes in the Life of Beattie prefixed to the last corrected and revised volume of his poems issued in 1811, 'Beattie was so dissatisfied with the first collection that he destroyed every copy he could procure'. Such was Beattie's pursuit of clarity and ease in style, his abandoning of the ornate for the clear and direct in the interest both of moral and emotional truth. His success was recognised by Wordsworth, who in a letter to R.P. Gillies dated 14 February 1815 compared the 'classical model' of Beattie favourably with 'the unsupportable slovenliness' of Hogg and Scott.[5] His early odes, rescued by Sir William Forbes for posterity,[6] demonstrate his inferiority to both Gray and Collins. He is unable to explore the various qualities of the personifications which are his themes to achieve any structured unity or cohesion. The tone is consequently hectic, the imagery appears arbitrary, the development of the sentiments banal. There is another influence, however, which may have afforded more help than has been recognised: in Beattie's *Elegy* (1761), the opening lines echo Johnson and carry some of his strength:

> Still shall unthinking man substantial deem
> The forms that fleet through life's deceitful dream?
> On clouds, where Fancy's beam amusive plays,
> Shall heedless hope the towering fabric raise?
> Till at Death's touch the fairy visions fly,
> And real scenes rush dismal on the eye;
> And, from Elysium's balmy slumber torn,
> The startled soul awakes, to think and mourn.

The moral element in Beattie's poetry has a positive strength in the development of each poem, whether it be in the fable of 'The Hares' (1761), begun in a light, wry narrative vein:

Yes, Yes, I grant the sons of earth
Are doom'd to trouble from their birth.
We all of sorrows have our share;
But say, is yours without compare
Look round the world; perhaps you'll find
Each individual of our kind
Press'd with an equal load of ill,
Equal at least. Look further still,
And own your lamentable case
Is little short of happiness. (ll. 1–10)

or in the development of the *Judgment of Paris* (1765), the *Ode to Hope* and *The Triumph of Melancholy* (1761). On 30 August 1765 Beattie wrote a letter introducing himself to Thomas Gray, then on a visit to the Earl of Strathmore. It is a letter from a disciple to a master, and it inaugurated a curious and fruitful acquaintance. Gray's subjects and themes had for years been most congenial to Beattie, and Gray for his part was eager to learn more about Scottish superstitions as material for poetry. In this correspondence Beattie explores his problems in finding an appropriate style: 'It is a fault common to almost all our Scotch authors, that they are too metaphysical: I wish they would learn to speak more to the heart, and less to the understanding.'[7] Beattie considered that the Scots were hamstrung in achieving an easy style by learning English as a dead language. In embarking on the verses he wrote to gain support for Ross's poems, Beattie laments the barrenness of the Scotch tongue for anything but low humour: 'Furthermore the Scottish dialect is different in almost every province. The common people of Aberdeen speak a language that would scarce be understood in Fife . . . I have attended so much to this matter, that I think I could know by his speech a native of Banffshire, Buchan, Aberdeen, Dee-side, Mearns, Angus, Lothian and Fife, as well as of Ross-shire and Inverness'.[8]

Beattie wished to instruct and guide his students in a plain, easy and attractive style, as well as to appeal to the hearts of his readers and as wide a public as possible: this he achieved with remarkable success in the opinion, for example, of no less a judge than Cowper. Writing to William Unwin on 5 April 1784 Cowper describes Beattie as

> . . . the most winning and amiable author I have ever met with . . . the only Author I have seen whose critical and philosophical researches are diversified and embellished by a poetical imagination that make even the driest subject and the leanest, a feast for an epicure in books. He is so much at ease too that his own character appears in every page and, which is very rare, we see not only the writer but the man. And that man so gentle, so well-temper'd, so happy in his

> religion, and so humane in his philosophy, that it is necessary to love him if one has the least sense of what is lovely. If you have not his poem called the Minstrel, and cannot borrow it I must beg you to buy it for me though I cannot afford to deal largely in so expensive a commodity as books, I *must* afford at least to purchase the poetical works of Beattie.[9]

The first book of *The Minstrel* was published in 1770, the second in 1774. *The Essay on Truth* was published in 1770. Beattie explains his reasons for writing the *Essay* to Gray in his letter of 1 May 1770:

> The principles of modern moral and metaphysical writers . . . as well as their method of investigation seemed to me to be equally unfavourable to Science virtue and good taste. I saw with concern, that the Publick in general, and the people of this country in particular, were every day growing more and more attached to them; and I also saw, or thought I saw, that those who admired them most, understood them the least . . .[10]

The Minstrel he describes as 'a moral and descriptive poem written in the manner of Spenser'. The development of the hero's sensibility is nurtured as he experiences nature in her different aspects.

> And oft he traced the uplands, to survey,
> When o'er the sky advanced the kindling dawn,
> The crimson cloud, blue main, and mountain grey,
> And lake, dim-gleaming on the smoky lawn:
> Far to the west the long long vale withdrawn,
> Where twilight loves to linger for a while;
> And now he faintly kens the bounding fawn,
> And villager abroad at early toil.
> But lo! the Sun appears! and heaven, earth, ocean smile.
> (St. 20)

The development of such sensibility, 'exquisitely keen' (as in Rousseau) is regarded objectively by the narrator:

> In truth he was a strange and wayward wight,
> Fond of each gentle and each dreadful scene,
> In darkness and in storm he found delight;
> Nor less than when on ocean-wave serene
> The southern Sun diffused his dazzling shene.
> Even sad vicissitude amused his soul:
> And if a sigh would sometimes intervene,
> And down his cheek a tear of pity roll,
> A sigh, a tear, so sweet, he wished not to control. (St. 22)

The changes wrought by the seasons on natural beauty –

> . . . the unsightly slime, and sluggish pool,
> Have all the solitary vale embrown'd . . . (St. 24)

are themselves intimations of mortality

> Borne of the swift, though silent wings of Time,
> Old age comes on apace to ravage all the clime. (St. 25)

Taught by his parents a morality identical to that of *The Cottar's Saturday Night* and educated by Nature in the ways of beauty and necessity, Edwin indulges in Fancy and dreams in his rural solitude. The point of the Spenserian stanza is felt in the description of the threats to his well-being:

> Hence! ye who snare and stupify the mind,
> Sophists of beauty, virtue, joy, the bane!
> Greedy and fell, though impotent and blind,
> Who spread your filthy nets in Truth's fair fane,
> And ever ply your venom's fangs amain!
> Hence to dark Error's den, whose rankling slime
> First gave you form! . . . (St. 41)

In songs of romance and fancy, in the songs of the minstrels, the mind regains its security of imagination and feeling:

> But hail, ye mighty masters of the lay,
> Nature's true sons, the friends of man and truth,
> Whose songs, sublimely sweet, serenely gay,
> Amused my childhood, and inform'd my youth.
> O let your spirit still my bosom soothe,
> Inspire my dreams, and my wild wanderings guide!
> Your voice each rugged path of life can smooth,
> For well I know wherever ye reside,
> There harmony, and peace, and innocence abide. (St. 42)

This is not merely a description of the growth of a poet's imagination; the experience is not one reserved to bard or minstrel, but to the innocence and happiness of a delicate sensibility not subjected to the buffets of society and its antagonisms – 'greetings where no kindness is' in Wordsworth's phrase. Edwin at least sees as he grows to manhood that

> One part, one little part, we dimly scan
> Through the dark medium of life's feverish dream . . . (St. 50)

His growth in wisdom and sensitivity in Book 1 of the poem is advanced by his encounter with the hermit in the second book to a recognition that Virtue can only exist where there is freedom to choose a course of action –

> Ambition's slippery verge shall mortals tread,
> Where ruin's gulf unfathom'd yawns beneath! . . .
> (Book 2, St. 34)

A philosophical awareness (in the fullest educational sense) of life's possibilities is therefore necessary:

> And Reason now, through number, time, and space,
>
> Darts the keen lustre of her serious eye,
> And learns, from facts compared, the laws to trace,
> Whose long progression leads to deity . . . (Book 2, st. 47)
>
> . . . lo, the shadows fly
> From Nature's face; confusion disappears,
> And order charms the eye, and harmony the ears! (ibid.)

So the Minstrel acquires skill and the conscious power to direct his art 'to soothe, to triumph, to complain'. At this point the development of Edwin's career ceases with the lament for the death of Beattie's mentor, Dr. Gregory, which (perhaps fittingly) ends the poem.

The success of *The Minstrel* for its readers lay primarily in its delineation of the moods of nature, and the responsiveness of man. As Hazlitt points out in his essay on Thomson and Cowper (*Lectures on the English Poets*, 1818) it is the identification of the source of our deepest awareness of our identity and as such a relief from the social encounters on which we embark with uncertainty and at risk:

> Every individual he meets is a blow to his personal identity. Every new face is a teazing unanswered riddle . . . But it is otherwise with respect to nature . . .
>
> The heart reposes in greater security on the immensity of nature's works, 'expatiates freely there', and finds breathing space . . . If we have once enjoyed the cool shade of a tree, and been lulled into a deep repose by the sound of a brook running at its foot, we are sure that wherever we can find a shady stream, we can enjoy the same pleasure again; so that when we imagine these objects, we can easily form a mystic personification of the friendly power that inhabits them.

In Beattie's *Minstrel* love of nature is a test of even religious truth.

> Oh, how canst thou renounce the boundless store
> Of charms which Nature to her votary yields!
> The warbling woodland, the resounding shore,
> The pomp of groves, and garniture of fields;
> All that the genial ray of morning gilds,
> And all that echoes to the song of even;
> All that the mountain's sheltering bosom shields –
> And all the dread magnificence of heaven,
> Oh, how canst thou renounce, and hope to be forgiven?
> (Book 1, st.9)

The Minstrel offers an account of the growth of an awareness at once romantic and moral. It acknowledges the need for enlightenment whilst enacting the experience of an isolated sensibility in swiftly changing landscapes, but landscapes associated with childhood and security. In an age where piety and devotion were practical substitutes for spirituality the sentiments it propounds have a direct appeal.

In the various roles that Beattie filled there is a distinctive quality that gives a peculiar fitness to Cowper's description of him: 'He is so much at ease too that his own character appears in every page, and, which is very rare, we see not only the writer but the man'. The growing mental disorder of his wife which prevented his accepting promotion to Edinburgh and deprived him of domestic comfort and family life did not diminish his concern for his friends, his students, or lastly, for his children. Even his comment on their deaths – 'How could I have borne to see their elegant minds mangled with madness!' – opens to the reader the nervous awareness of an almost marked vulnerability to as well as a refined appreciation of life which only a settled piety could control.

With such a disposition it is remarkable that he so thoroughly deserved the epitaph he composed for himself:

Forgive my frailties, thou art also frail;
  Forgive my lapses, for thyself may'st fall;
Nor read, unmov'd, my artless tale,
  I was a friend, O man! to thee, to all. (1760)

Suggestions for further reading:

1. Alexander Chalmers, *The Works of the English Poets*, 21 vols. (London, 1810), vol. 18, 515-533.
2. Margaret Forbes, *Beattie and his Friends* (London, 1904).
3. Everard H. King, *James Beattie* (Twayne, 1977).

Notes:

1. The Beattie Collection in Aberdeen University Library contains over four hundred letters and fragments written by Beattie and twice as many received by him, including letters to Beattie from Johnson and Gray. Manuscripts from this collection are referred to in this article as AUL MS (number). I am grateful to the Librarian of the University of Aberdeen for permission to transcribe the MS material in this chapter, and to Dr. Dorothy Johnston for her assistance in sifting the MSS. Mr. M.R.G. Spiller provided the vernacular translation of Skinner's poem.

2. See Ernest Campbell Mossner, 'Beattie's *The Castle of Scepticism*: An Unpublished Allegory against Hume, Voltaire and Hobbes,' *University of Texas Studies in English*, 27 (June, 1948).
3. The whole poem is printed in the *Penguin Book of Scottish Verse*, 279-82, but from a bad 19th century text. The extracts given here are from the text which Beattie had privately printed, upon his sending a letter and the poem to the Aberdeen Journal (June 6, 1768), and which is preserved at the end of Aberdeen University Library's copy of Alexander Ross's *The Fortunate Shepherdess* (Aberdeen, 1768), apparently a present sent by Beattie to Dr. Thomas Blacklock of Edinburgh.
4. 'Drousty' – an alehouse in Lochlee, where Alexander Ross lived.
5. *The Letters of William and Dorothy Wordsworth*, 3, *The Middle Years*, ed. E. de Selincourt, revised by Mary Moorman and Alan G. Hill (Oxford, 1970), 196.
6. In his *Account of the Life and Writings of James Beattie*, LL.D. (2 vols., London, 1806, 2nd ed. 1824), Sir William Forbes prints *Ode to Peace, Triumph of Melancholy, Epitaph* (on himself) and *Epitaph on Two Brothers* in an Appendix (vol. 1, 41-2) to rescue them from the oblivion to which Beattie would have consigned them.
7. *Correspondence of Thomas Gray*, ed. Paget Toynbee and Leonard Whibley, (3 vols, Oxford, 1935), vol. 3, 953-4.
8. *Ib.*
9. *The Letters and Prose Writings of William Cowper*, ed. James King and Charles Ryskamp, (2 vols., Oxford, 1981), vol. 2, 231.
10. *Op. cit.*, vol. 3, 1131.

THE FICTION OF GEORGE MACDONALD

David S. Robb

In his day, George MacDonald was thought of as a poet, as an apologist for a boldly unorthodox religious viewpoint, and as a best-selling novelist. Now, he is remembered mainly because of some stories for children, and as the author of two strikingly original fantasy novels which still bob in and out of print in the wake of Tolkien's popularity. The works by which he was most widely known, over two dozen novels set in more familiar Scottish or English landscapes, have almost completely passed from public awareness – almost as completely as they have passed from critical esteem. Yet it seems strange to believe that such clear originality manifested itself in only the smaller fragments of a lifetime's work, or that the author who has pleased so many generations of children is unreadable outside that incidental aspect of his large output. Study of his Scottish novels, especially, suggests to me that his area of achievement is wider than many recent commentators would have us believe, and that in George MacDonald, North-east Scotland produced not merely a Victorian eccentric, but a writer whose works constitute a real and valuable contribution to the Scottish novel as a whole.

Born into a nonconformist family in Huntly in 1824, MacDonald spent all his adult life either in England or abroad, though he never lost touch with his North-east roots. Having graduated from Aberdeen University in 1845 with a degree concentrating on modern languages and literature, he spent nearly a decade in what were, for him, false starts: he was in turn a private tutor then a Congregational minister. He and his Arundel congregation parted company in 1853. Whatever the precise circumstances of this event, the essential difficulty must have been caused by the incompatibility of the congregation's doctrinal conservatism and MacDonald's growing boldness in throwing off the church's teachings on such matters as election, predestination and eternal damnation. MacDonald was one of a small but growing number of Victorians for whom such teachings implied an immoral divinity – a contradiction so inconceivable that the doctrines had to be rejected. MacDonald preached universal salvation, and made it his business to attack orthodox thinking wherever he could. At first, after he had abandoned his pulpit, his audience merely comprised small gatherings in meeting-houses in Manchester, but he turned to literature (as no doubt he had long desired) and began to make a name as a writer of bold speculation, of profound optimism, and of a vigorous imagination. The rest of his long life was spent writing, preaching and teaching, trying to feed a large family (financial aid was always needed from his numerous well-wishers), wintering abroad for the sake of his precarious lungs, and tirelessly serving his twin passions for literature and for religious truth. From the 1850s, the writings appear in a steady flood. The astonishingly innovative *Phantastes* appeared in 1858, but the first Scottish novel, *David Elginbrod*, was not published until 1863. Thereafter, novels, poems, fairy-stories, sermons, translations and editions followed each other until 1897. He died in 1905.

MacDonald regarded poetry as the highest form of literary expression, and often regretted that he had so little time for it. Similarly, his fairy and fantasy writing grew more scarce once he established himself as a popular novelist. The novels, however, span his entire writing career, and they are more varied in their effects, and even in their meanings, than most accounts of them imply. What is more, they are less distant from the fantasy writing than is commonly believed. It is understandable that readers should tend to regard the two modes as entirely separate, as fictions in which MacDonald was attempting very different things. Nevertheless, I believe that a better understanding of MacDonald will see them as intimately related. At the beginning of this century, critics would praise the Scottish novels and dismiss the fantasies as unintelligible. Nowadays, the critical evaluation is reversed, on the assumption that a realistic art medium such as the novel is fundamentally ill-suited to express a transcendental religious vision. MacDonald, we are told, was forced by economic necessity to produce the sort of fiction which would sell: he was either blind to, or ignored, the aesthetic difficulties involved. I think that the truth was quite different, and that what seem, at first glance, to be realistic novels are designed as subversive attempts to alter our sense of reality, and of ourselves.

The essence of MacDonald's Christianity was his steadfast sense that God is our heavenly father, and that we are his children. Thanks to his own father's loving approachability, MacDonald (unlike many other Victorians) equated fatherhood with love. Wrath and punishment are part of fatherhood, but always subordinate to love. A god who could predestine the majority of his creatures to everlasting hell-fire would be a god of wrath; MacDonald's god of love is one with whom all his children will some day be reunited. Christ was important to MacDonald not because he took man's sins on himself and turned away God's wrath but because, through him, God made himself visible to men, and showed them how they could most fully realise themselves as the creatures God originally created. Christ is our goal, in the double but related sense that he is the God with whom we shall one day be reunited, and in that he is the highest human potential. We journey to him in the effort to become better, while we also approach him in journeying towards death. The fact that eventual reunion with him is inevitable does not remove from men the responsibility to strive for perfection.

It is on such a foundation of belief as this that all MacDonald's fiction is based. It is as if two biblical texts lay at the heart of his writing: 'Our days on the earth are as a shadow, and there is none abiding' (I Chronicles 29.15) and 'Except ye be converted, and become as little children, ye shall not enter into the kingdom of heaven' (Matthew 18.3).

To MacDonald, the world revealed by the senses, and the life men lead in it, are not real. There is a more real world, an eternal dimension of reality which is the reality of God; this earth will pass away. His aim in his writing, therefore, is to persuade his readers that this is so, and to encourage them to regard the world of the senses as but an ephemeral part of a vaster, more mysterious, totality. In a way, it is all a question of vision; he wishes to substitute for the eye's function (as materially understood) a creative, imaginative vision. God's reality is there all about us, glorious and unchanging. It is our perception of it which is at fault. It is often said that in his fantasy writing he is imagining alternative worlds to the familiar one; in his essay on 'The Fantastic Imagination' he himself discusses fairy stories on the assumption that they are alternative domains. Superficially, this is clearly a helpful way of thinking of them, but I believe it to be more accurate to see his fantasy works as still portraying the world men inhabit, only viewed differently. In these works, he offers us the world as it really is (from his point of view) – that is, more wonderful and magical, more terrible and dangerous, more animate and more evanescent, than we normally assume.

At one point in *Phantastes*, the hero, Anodos, is startled, as he journeys through fairyland, by the sudden transformation in the appearance of a little girl, whom he has just attempted to kiss, and who momentarily turns monstrous:

> I soon found that the same undefinable law of change operated between me and all the other villagers; and that, to feel I

> was in pleasant company, it was absolutely necessary for me to discover and observe the right focal distance between myself and each one with whom I had to do. This done, all went pleasantly enough.
>
> (*Phantastes*, ch.9)[1]

The photographic metaphor was possibly picked up from Charles Dodgson, whose intimacy with the MacDonalds dated from about the time of the writing of *Phantastes*. The metaphor neatly conveys the relativity of perception, and its use suggests that it is primarily moral perception with which MacDonald is concerned.

The beautiful scene in the second chapter of *Phantastes*, in which Anodos enters fairyland, illustrates the point further. As Stephen Prickett has noted, Anodos's Victorian bedroom is ornately decorated with the elements of nature in any case: fabrics and furniture depict intricate leaves and branches, while the wash-basin is of green marble. Anodos's morning dream about his bedroom becoming animate becomes the reality of the book: the life within the familiar is suddenly perceived. Similarly, in *Lilith* (1895), a raven becomes a little old librarian, a sexton in charge of a vast graveyard, and finally Adam himself. The dream-like mode of these works is, in part, a structural model to justify their lack of any obvious or familiar type of unity, but also a metaphor for the world as MacDonald believed it to be. He gives new vitality to the Romantic cliche that in dream or reverie mankind has access to eternal reality.

When Christians and philosophers insist that this is a world of shadows, they are normally urging us to see it as valueless. MacDonald, too, is opposed to materialism in all its forms, but his position is complicated by his seemingly opposite tendency to revel in the beauty and variety, the very evanescence, of the thing to be despised. Dreams are a way of seeing which reconciles this dichotomy; the outlook of the child is another. For it is not just the New Testament injunction to become like a child once again which hangs over MacDonald's fiction; it is the Romantic prizing of the child's way of seeing, as well. To MacDonald, the child combined innocence and imagination, and he had Wordsworth's word for it that

> . . . trailing clouds of glory do we come
> From God, who is our home.

A childlike imagination is far from a thing to be despised, MacDonald thought; it could be a means to truth and salvation. His writing is full of children, from the heroes and heroines of his fairy-stories and novels, to the grandest of the supernatural beings whom the children in his short story, 'The Golden Key', encounter on their journey to the country from which the shadows come. In the very depths of the earth, the heroine meets the Old Man of the Fire:

> The next moment she descried, in a corner of the cave, a little naked child, sitting on the moss. He was playing with balls of various colours and sizes, which he disposed in strange figures on the floor beside him. And now Tangle felt that there was something in her knowledge which was not in her understanding. For she knew there must be an infinite meaning in the change and sequence and individual forms into which the child arranged the balls, as well as in the varied harmonies of their colours, but what it all meant she could not tell ...
>
> 'Where is the Old Man of the Fire?' she said.
>
> 'Here I am,' answered the child, rising ...

But the child's way of seeing is not confined, by MacDonald, to his characters alone; he offers it to his readers, in the way he writes his books. He attempts to make us see ourselves as children of the heavenly father by appealing to the childlike in us, and he presents experience as perceived by a child – that is, as a journey of increasing knowledge. The world is evanescent because we are children growing in it, changing in it, and passing through it.

* * *

Children themselves, therefore, were less of a specialised audience, as far as MacDonald was concerned, than they are for most other writers, and it is partly to this that his most famous books for children owe their enduring appeal. Their success is not due, as one might have thought, to an avoidance of writing down to children; *At the Back of the North Wind* (1871), especially, is occasionally marred by precisely this fault. Yet this book, along with *The Princess and the Goblin* (1872) and *The Princess and Curdie* (1883) are allowed to benefit from the full wealth of MacDonald's symbolic imagination, and from the moral urgency which is one of his permanent strengths. For MacDonald's greatness as a writer of fantasy is not due merely to a knack of invention, a facility in cobbling together elements from his life, his dreams, and his reading so as to fashion enchantingly escapist domains. His inventiveness is at the service of the truth, and what he invents impresses by virtue of its suggestion of a vast underlying coherence which demands much from the individual if he is even to begin to understand it.

Thus, for example, in the great scene in which Diamond enters the land at the back of the North Wind, one's experience of the passage only begins with one's delighted, surprised response to the majestic spectacle which confronts the little boy in the icy wastes – the great figure of the frozen woman set in the face of the ridge of ice. The real power of the passage lies in the drama of the terrible, impossible demand made of Diamond, and his astonishingly faithful response:

> 'I want to go into the country at your back.'
> 'Then you must go through me.'
> 'I don't know what you mean.'
> 'I mean just what I say. You must walk on as if I were an open door, and go right through me.'
> 'But that will hurt you.'
> 'Not in the least. It will hurt you, though.'
> 'I don't mind that, if you tell me to do it.'
> 'Do it,' said North Wind.
> Diamond walked towards her instantly. When he reached her knees, he put out his hand to lay it on her, but nothing was there save an intense cold. He walked on. Then all grew white about him; and the cold stung him like a fire. He walked on still, groping through the whiteness. It thickened about him. At last, it got into his heart, and he lost all sense.
> (*At the Back of the North Wind*, ch. 9)

The reader finds himself confronting an allegory, not just of an individual's close brush with death, but of the demand for trusting self-abnegation which was, as MacDonald saw it, Christ's challenge to man. The passage is not just about fearlessly approaching physical death, but also about the death of self, as a wide reading in MacDonald, for whom this is a perennial theme, will confirm. MacDonald has the facility to use symbols in a way which is neither limitingly one-to-one (allegory, in the now habitually pejorative sense) nor hopelessly vague or merely teasingly suggestive. His symbols usually pull together meanings from different levels of implication, meanings which can be clearly spelled out, but whose relationships with each other are most satisfactorily uttered by the unifying image itself.

With its haunting title, *At the Back of the North Wind* is perhaps the best-known of MacDonald's books. In its juxtaposition of the worlds of Victorian London and of Diamond's nocturnal adventures with the North Wind, it illustrates especially clearly MacDonald's vision of a reality alternative to, but over-lapping with, the mundane. It also clearly shows how MacDonald sees the alternative as a dream-reality, and a child's reality. In the two Curdie books, he opts for a completely fairy-tale medium, although, once again, the socially stratified Victorian world – the worlds of nursery and of the artisan – are visible under only a thin veneer. *The Princess and the Goblin* is perhaps the best of his books for children: it is neither too sentimental nor too doctrinaire, and contains some of the finest symbols, notably the cave-dwelling goblins (comic and threatening in a well-judged balance) and Princess Irene's grandmother, mysteriously accesssible to the eyes of innocence and faith. The sequel of the next decade, *The Princess and Curdie*, marks a darkening of MacDonald's optimism. Evil is a more successful usurper, and more terrible measures must be taken to thwart it. It threatens the king himself, and even after it has been checkmated, MacDonald turns away from the expected happy-ever-after conclusion, by foretelling the eventual downfall of the city in generations to come. Once again, however, the book is blessed with scenes and symbols of uncomfortable and memorable power.

The two full-length adult fantasies, *Phantastes* (1858) and *Lilith* (1895), illustrate even more clearly the contrast of mood between MacDonald's earlier and later writings. In theological terms, he remains an optimist, in the sense that he retains a belief in the paramountcy of God's love, and in universal salvation. But his early stress on man's essential goodness gives way to a preoccupation with evil, and God's love increasingly takes the form of punishing the sinner into goodness – naughty children, it seems, must be whipped after all. These two fantasies, also, demonstrate especially clearly MacDonald's sense of reality as evanescent, and his instinct to place his reader in the role of the child. Thus, in *Phantastes*, the hero Anodos ('the pathless one') is an adult of exactly twenty-one years when he encounters the gorgeous being who claims to be his grandmother and who instils in him the desire (satisfied in the second chapter) to enter fairyland. Yet all through the book, Anodos strikes us a different times as being different ages, from the merest boy to the grown man, according to the circumstances and to his behaviour. The evanescence of fairyland is vigorously suggested, by the fanciful invention with which MacDonald has created it, by the constant parallel with dream, and by the patchy, episodic structure of the book from which a moral concern only gradually emerges. Anodos is without a path for much of the book not only in the simple sense that he has no predetermined route through this surprising landscape, but also in that he has for long no moral aim. Indeed, the process the book portrays is perhaps best seen as the growth of the realisation in Anodos that a path is needed. It is not a tightly organised book, but this conventional weakness is justified here in that it embodies MacDonald's vision of life in which a sense of direction only gradually becomes apparent, as it had done in his own case.

On first tackling the book, many readers allow their delight in the invention to be swamped by an anxious concern about meaning. This is unfortunate, though understandable, as they rightly perceive that they have to do with a network of symbols. To some readers, Freud and Jung come to offer help in symbolic explication but, on the whole, the offer is best gratefully declined. A wider reading in MacDonald himself is likely to be of more help, as well as a knowledge of the literary sources of his imaginative effects. The most important of these can be swiftly listed as the New Testament, Romantic poets and writers in English and German, and English literature of the sixteenth and seventeenth centuries, especially the religious poets, and allegorists like Spenser and Bunyan.

Almost his last work, *Lilith* combines, as *The Princess and Curdie* did, an optimistic message with a pessimistic mood. Superficially like *Phantastes* in landscape and in being based on a journey, the later fantasy is more directly concerned with the struggle to counter evil. The imagery is bleaker, more macabre, sometimes comically, often powerfully, as in the vision of Adam's eternal graveyard, or in the battle of the dead in the Evil Wood. Structurally, too, it is more complex, and better controlled than its predecessor. It has its weaknesses: MacDonald is no more secure from sentimentality than many another Victorian writer when he uses children as important carriers of his positive values. Furthermore, the bones of allegory are more clearly visible under the surface and they prevent the recreation of the youthful Romantic freshness which is one of the charms of *Phantastes*. Nevertheless, the allegory is a sign of purpose and control, structural strengths which are in satisfying accord with the moral firmness of the writer's outlook here. *Lilith* is a fine achievement; from an old writer whose imagination in other books seemed to have been thinning out, it is astonishing.

Fairy-tales and fantasy are clearly modes in which the evanescence of reality can readily be implied and in which MacDonald can directly appeal to the child in the reader. That the same generalisation can be made about MacDonald's Scottish novels is far less obvious. Indeed, most commentators dealing with these works see their only strength to be in the solidly realistic portrayal of Scottish place and manners which is, indeed, one of their great appeals. MacDonald not only draws on the kind of life he knew as a boy; he very often precisely locates his fiction in actual places, recognisable despite invented names. His early novels, especially *Alec Forbes of Howglen* (1865) and *Robert Falconer* (1868), contain detailed recreations of Huntly and its surrounding countryside, while they also draw heavily on his memories of student life at King's College, Aberdeen. For *Malcolm* (1875), he made special visits north to Cullen to check on details for its fictional counterpart, Portlossie. *Sir Gibbie* (1879) is set in

Aberdeen once again (in both the respectable and unrespectable parts of the town) and on upper Deeside. Later novels still are less precisely located in the North-east countryside which becomes, in his memory and imagination, an archetypal landscape of farm and moor and mountain, of castle and clachan, of paradisal summers and arctic winters, yet the Cabrach, for example, is still recognisable in *Castle Warlock* (1882) and *Heather and Snow* (1893).

The satisfactions of geographical precision are matched by his precise renderings of the people of the region. His reproduction of North-east speech is masterly. The occupations of farming and fishing are only fleetingly focussed upon, but the social life they support is fully there. Church life and school life are vividly done when narrative demands, but there is none of the dewy-eyed reverence for such things that is among the tell-tale signs of a 'Kailyard' treatment: MacDonald has bigger thematic fish to fry than to dwell in a bliss of sentimental memories. And anyway, his accounts of the life of the region have, at their best, a fullness and a documentary precision alien to Barrie and 'Ian Maclaren'. Similarly, his abundant humour is not designed to elicit from the reader an attitude of patronising affection towards the characters. Occasionally, indeed, it has a sharply satiric function (MacDonald is, at heart, simply too pugnacious to be a 'Kailyard' writer) but usually it is present, one feels, because it is present in the life he is evoking. One illustration must suffice. Alec Forbes and his friends have been stimulated by the winter snow to new heights of mischief:

> 'I never saw sic widdiefows!', chimed in a farmer's wife who was standing in the shop. 'They had a tow across the Wast Wynd i' the snaw, an' doon I cam o' my niz, as sure's your name's Charles Chapman – and mair o' my legs oot o' my coats, I doobt, than was a' thegither to my credit.'
> 'I'm sure ye can hae no rizzon to tak' shame o' your legs, gude wife,' was the gallant rejoinder; to which their owner replied, with a laugh:
> 'They warna made for public inspection, ony gait.'
> 'Hoot! hoot! Naebody saw them. I s' warran' ye didna lie lang! But thae loons – they're jist past a'! Heard ye hoo they saired Rob Bruce?'
> 'Fegs! they tell me they a' but buried him alive.'
> 'Ow! ay.'
>
> (*Alec Forbes of Howglen*, ch. 20)

Nevertheless, realism of the familiar sort is not the goal with which MacDonald is finally concerned, and he attempts to make of his familiar and convincing scenes a fantasy world – or, at least, a world tinged with fantasy. His central characters are always young, children or adolescent, for at least the bulk of the books in which they appear. As readers, we are induced to take an imaginative interest in their experiences and so, to that extent, become children and adolescents ourselves. As in the fairy writing, too, characters suddenly loom into prominence and play decisive and unexpected roles, for good or ill, in the moral drama of the hero's growth to Christlikenesss. MacDonald's young people are surrounded by characters of great individuality and who, like their fairy-tale counterparts, frequently contain elements of mystery and paradox. Indeed, it is in their sharing of recurring character-types that the two modes of MacDonald's fiction are most swiftly recognisable as intimately related. Yet, in the novels, the characterisation is firmly based on an experienced Scottish reality. What happens is that MacDonald offers his readers the Scotland of his own youth as a distanced, only half-familiar landscape which functions as an allegorical setting equivalent to fairyland. The greater his precision in detailing characteristics of speech and behaviour, the more effectively his Scottish scene performs this imaginative role. The balance between the real and the fairy-like is well maintained in the novels of the 1860s and 1870s. Thereafter, Scotland becomes, in his work, a place primarily of open land, farm and castle: it becomes more obviously a fairy-tale landscape, a place of the imagination.

Just like a fantasy landscape, the commonplace world portrayed by MacDonald is a moral assault course full of traps and threats for the innocent, but also full of unexpected help. His Scottish novels are, in the main, long and episodic, and usually based on narrative structures so simple that, as we read, we have only the slightest sense of long-term momentum. What would be counted a weakness in another novelist becomes a strength in the context of a MacDonald novel. As one of his later heroes says, speaking of his own life which has formed the substance of the novel as a whole: 'It's like going on and on in a dream, wondering what's coming next!' (*Castle Warlock*, ch. 53). Not only does MacDonald's imagination, at its best, manage a measure of reconciliation between the worlds of dream and everyday life, thereby giving scope for an astonishing array of types of character, situation, and fictional modes, but MacDonald is also able to suggest a dream-like quality of coherence underlying the variety of event, and to instil into his reader some of the trusting acceptance which characterises a dreamer. The dreamer's refusal to be surprised becomes a model for the experience of faith itself.

The familiar complaint against these novels, that they try to use a realistic form to express an optimistic Christian vision (that is, an unrealistic one) so that MacDonald is forced to spoil them with excessive authorial intrusion (direct preaching, and artificially happy endings) is thus an oversimplified account. MacDonald was alive to the formal difficulties confronting him in his attempts to give fictional form to his enlarged sense of the real, and developed a wide variety of devices to overcome them, of which his infusing of the novel with the colouring of dreams, of fairy-stories, and of children's fiction are among the most important. Nor is the Christian optimism imposed on the action: the narratives are permeated with echoes of the New Testament and the beliefs MacDonald based upon it. Just as much as the fairy writings, MacDonald's Scottish novels are symbolic narratives – allegories, in fact – and must be approached with the same expectations and willingness to interpret an only superficially familiar surface. This is not to say that, even in their own terms, these works are entirely successful: only two seem to me to approach that state, *Alec Forbes* and *Malcolm*. Nevertheless, most of the Scottish novels will offer, to the reader attuned to their method, far more than mere historical interest or the occasional glimpse of regional reality.

Suggestions for further reading:

The key work in any further reading on MacDonald is the biography by his son Greville MacDonald, *George MacDonald and his Wife* (London, 1924): despite holding his father in awe and reverence, Greville produced a vivid and full account of his subject's life, personality and friendships, an account which will probably never be entirely replaced. To date, there are two monographs in English on MacDonald's fiction, Robert Lee Wolff's *The Golden Key: A Study of the Fiction of George MacDonald* (New Haven, 1961) and Richard H. Reis's *George MacDonald* (New York, 1972). Wolff's is a seminal work, despite its heavy emphasis on the fantasy writing, and its irritating Freudian dogmatism; it is lively and memorable, if also critically weak. Richard Reis is merely critically weak. For criticism of a totally different order of sensitivity, the reader should turn to Stephen Prickett's material on the fantasies in his *Romanticism and Religion: The Tradition of Coleridge and Wordsworth in the Victorian Church* (Cambridge, 1976) and *Victorian Fantasy* (Hassocks, 1979), and also to Colin Manlove's chapter on MacDonald in his *Modern Fantasy: Five Studies* (Cambridge, 1975). Dr Manlove also provides one of the few substantial comments on the Scottish novels in his essay 'George MacDonald's Early Scottish Novels', to be found in Ian Campbell's anthology *Nineteenth-Century Scottish Fiction: Critical Essays* (Manchester, 1979): this is a sophisticated modern version of the traditional complaints against them. More favourable to the Scottish novels are Francis Russell Hart's few pages in his valuable *The Scottish Novel: A*

Critical Survey (London, 1978), but further discussion of the Scottish fiction is badly needed.

Note:

1. There is no standard edition of MacDonald's fiction, and libraries and bookshops are liable to offer a bewildering range of editions of individual works. Under these circumstances, it seems best to locate quotations by means of title and chapter, in the hope this will prove most widely convenient.

FROM CHARLES MURRAY TO HUGH MacDIARMID VERNACULAR REVIVAL AND SCOTTISH RENAISSANCE

Colin Milton

The pioneering part played by the dialect poets of the North-east in the modern revival of vernacular verse largely associated with Hugh MacDiarmid (C.M. Grieve) has been generally, if not always generously, recognised by recent historians of Scottish literature. There has been a tendency among some critics and literary historians to play down the substantial contribution to the vernacular movement made by poets like Mary Symon, Charles Murray, Violet Jacob, Marion Angus and Helen Cruickshank so as to add extra lustre to MacDiarmid's achievement and to see their poetry as interesting only to the extent that it anticipates his. This is hardly surprising, since most of those who have written on Scottish literature since the nineteen twenties have been sympathetic to the radical, modernist programme of MacDiarmid and his renaissance allies; but in making his aims the measure by which his predecessors are judged such critics do less than justice to earlier vernacular poets. Of course, even if different and perhaps fairer criteria were employed in evaluating their work none of the North-east poets referred to above would even approach MacDiarmid's stature, but I want to suggest two important qualifications to the conventional 'placing' of these writers. The first is that the aims MacDiarmid set himself as a poet are not necessarily relevant to poets whose conception of their art was very different: Nan Shepherd's comment on Charles Murray is revealing in this respect – 'Towards intellectual and symbolic poetry he was wary'[1] she says, making clear Murray's suspicion of two major elements in the modernist conception of poetry. Secondly, it can be argued that these older poets, in their best work at least, were more exciting, more innovative, more 'modern' than they are usually given credit for.

But why, in the first place, should there have been a general revival of interest in the writing of Scots in the last decades of the nineteenth century, and why was so much of the vernacular poetry produced between then and MacDiarmid's conversion to Scots in the early nineteen twenties written by North-east Scots?

The answer to the first of these questions lies in the fact that from the eighteen fifties onward, but particularly in the sixties and seventies, an old, regionally-based, orally transmitted culture was felt to be under grave threat from a number of powerful forces, particularly from the spread of education to those groups in society which had till then largely escaped it. It was among these groups, particularly among the peasantry, that traditional culture and local dialects were best preserved, so that their exposure to the modernising influence of late-Victorian schooling threatened not just their integrity but their very survival. The crisis was not just a Scottish one; it aroused anxiety in all parts of Britain among those who valued local and regional traditions. In the third chapter of *Tess of the D'Urbervilles*, Hardy comments on the differences between Tess and Mrs. Durbeyfield:

> Between the mother, with her fast-perishing lumber of superstitions, folklore, dialect and orally-transmitted ballads, and the daughter, with her trained National teachings and Standard knowledge under an infinitely revised code, there was a gap of two hundred years as ordinarily understood. When they were together the Jacobean and Victorian ages were juxtaposed.

Hardy makes it clear that his heroine's education has done more than replace outmoded Jacobean 'superstition' with sound, up-to-date Victorian 'knowledge'; it has also, to a large extent, substituted a uniform national culture for one with its roots in local circumstances and a standardised national speech for the dialect which is the medium of a distinctively local culture – 'national' in this context meaning, as it usually does, 'London-based' because we are told that Tess's teacher is 'London trained'.

At the time the story is set – Hardy's satiric reference to the controversial Revised Code of 1862 suggests the sixties – the process was not yet complete. Tess speaks 'proper' English 'abroad and to persons of quality' but still uses the dialect at home 'more or less'; even when she does employ dialect she handles it less surely than does her mother who uses it all the time. Her command of the local speech is less certain because it has been contaminated by the kind of English she has been taught at school. The contrast between Tess and Mrs. Durbeyfield in speech and in outlook demonstrates the enormous changes brought about in the space of a single generation by regular schooling, and accounts for the widespread fear in the last part of the nineteenth century that whatever remained of traditional culture would be swept away within, at most, a couple of generations.

The threat became increasingly serious in the eighteen fifties and eighteen sixties as education became a national issue, and the 1870

Education Act, which consolidated and extended existing voluntary provision in a rate-supported, universal and compulsory school system was only the culmination of tendencies towards rationalisation and central direction which had been building up in the previous two decades and which have already put a cultural distance of 'two hundred years as ordinarily understood' between Tess and her mother. The peasantry, to which the Durbeyfields belong, is the last repository of a locally-based, orally transmitted culture; increasingly, in the second half of the nineteenth century, its members are being drawn into schools and exposed to the influence of a nationally directed education system serving the ends of contemporary industrial society. Like many of his contemporaries, Hardy feared that the idiosyncratic and the local might vanish as a result of this process and be replaced by a monotonous linguistic and cultural uniformity.

Although not an uncritical admirer of traditional folk culture or of the past in general, Hardy was more aware than most of his literary contemporaries of the nature and value of what was threatened, simply because he himself was in important ways a product of it; his father and uncle were folk musicians, several of his relatives rural labourers or servants. But because he belonged to the skilled and prosperous section of the rural community – his father was a builder and mason – Hardy also had access, through education, to the literary culture of the cultivated middle classes. At the same time, because the later stages of his education were practical and vocational he was not drawn completely into the world of polite letters, something which might well have happened if he had been given a conventional literary education at university and which would have been to the detriment of his art.

Several of the North-east dialect poets involved in the first phase of the vernacular revival came from similar circumstances: Mary Symon's father was a saddler who had prospered sufficiently to become Provost of Dufftown and purchase the local estate of Pittyvaich; Charles Murray's father was a country carpenter who became a land steward while Helen Cruickshank's father was also a carpenter. Murray's early circumstances resemble Hardy's in two other important ways: he too grew up in close touch with the folk tradition because his father, Peter Murray, was both a composer and skilled reciter of vernacular verse: his obituary records that 'His rhymes in the vernacular, though they never appeared in print, were very readable and droll in sentiment. He took great delight in reciting poetry, and his famous son undoubtedly owes a good deal to his father's command of the vernacular.'[2] And Murray had a practical training as a surveyor and civil engineer rather than an academic education. Coming from such a background, these Scottish writers were, like Hardy, in close touch with folk culture, but because better off and more widely educated than the rural peasantry, not wholly identified with it. In them, the folk tradition becomes conscious and serves as the basis for art of a conventionally 'higher' kind; the largely oral world of dialect song and story appears in print through writers with one foot in the traditional culture of their local communities and one in the middle class culture of the time.

In Scotland, as in England, the fifties and sixties were decades of educational change, and continuing pressure for reform in the schools found legislative expression in the Education (Scotland) Act of 1872, which created 'one of the most centrally organised school systems in the world', [3] particularly after 1878 when all Scottish education came under the control of the Scottish Education Department. Consequently, the pressure for linguistic and cultural conformity exerted through the schools was even stronger than in the more devolved English system and the threat to all forms of regional identity even greater. But, more serious than this, the standards which Scottish schools were encouraged to adopt – particularly in matters of language – by the powerful schools inspectorate were not Scottish ones; the pressure was towards anglicisation, as inspectors' reports of the nineties clearly show. So, in Scotland, educational reform not only threatened regional distinctiveness but also, more fundamentally, national identity as well. As Alexander Mackie put it, in his introduction to one of the many editions of the North-east dialect classic, *Johnny Gibb o' Gushetneuk:*

> The Doric is here at its raciest, caught just in time before the Education Act of 1872 began to take effect. The dialect will not die yet awhile, but there is little doubt that under a compulsory English education its purity and breadth of vocabulary are already on the wane. [4]

Many observers thought that the dialect and traditional culture of the region were on the wane well before 1872: in his Preface to the first edition of *Johnny Gibb*, William Alexander described it as comprising 'illustrations of real life, mainly of an old-fashioned sort, and of a local dialect, which is getting gradually pushed into the background, or divested of some of its more characteristic forms.' The story is set in 1843, before the social and educational changes of the fifties and sixties began to alter the life of the community it describes. One sign that the vernacular was indeed being 'pushed into the background' when the book came to be written is the fact that the narrative framework of the story is almost entirely in English, although there are numerous and dense passages of dialect. At the same time, the circumstances under which Alexander's newspaper sketches came to appear in book form suggest a considerable though, to the author at least, unexpected degree of interest in vernacular writing among a newspaper reading public consisting largely of readers who were literate but not literary. The Preface explains that:

> As originally printed, the sketches met with a wider acceptance than had been looked for; and this, coupled with the direct request of various persons whose judgement the writer felt bound to respect, accounts for their now appearing in collected form. [5]

The unexpected amount of interest aroused by the appearance of *Johnny Gibb* in its original form indicates that anxiety about the survival of regional dialects and local traditions created by the educational reforms of the late nineteenth century also had positive effects. It increased people's consciousness of what was distinctive in the life and speech of their own area and it gave them an impetus not just to record things that were inevitably doomed, but to work actively to keep them alive according to the principle memorably summarized by the Friar in *Much Ado About Nothing*:

> . . . . for it so falls out
> That what we have we prize not to the worth
> Whiles we enjoy it, but being lack'd and lost,
> Why then we rack the value, then we find
> The virtue that possession would not show us
> Whiles it was ours.

It was because it reflected contemporary anxieties, particularly strong in Scotland, about the threat modern education posed to the traditional culture of the folk, that Charles Murray's poem 'The Whistle' caught the popular imagination early in the century. Appearing first in *Chamber's Journal* in 1906, [6] it was included in the greatly expanded *Hamewith* which Constable brought out in 1909 and almost immediately became Murray's best known and most anthologised poem. But despite being given the *imprimatur* in C.M. Grieve's otherwise venomous survey of Murray's poetry – it is, Grieve claims 'immeasurably better than anything else he has written' [7] – *The Whistle* is by no means Murray's best poem and the explanation for its popularity lies elsewhere than in its strictly literary qualities.

The poem begins with the 'wee herd' making a whistle for himself out of a 'sappy sucker' – making, in fact, the original folk instrument, the nineteenth century North-east equivalent of the pastoral oaten flute. And the tunes he plays on it, marches, springs, schottisches, reels, strathspeys and jigs, are *traditional* tunes picked up, as folk music tends to be, by ear and depending on innate and native musical-ity rather than on formal training. In his modest way the boy is part of a long process of cultural transmission of a traditional sort and has a kind of symbolic quality, standing for the culture of the folk, or for one aspect of it. It is clear from the poem that those involved in this transmission process are not wholly aware of what they are communicating; the music embodies the life of the folk and is linked to the personality of the 'artist' less than more conscious kinds of art:

> He tried a spring for wooers, though he wistna what it meant,
> But the kitchen-lass was lauchin' an' he thocht she maybe kent

Like all folk performers, the herd speaks not for himself, out of his own experience, but acts as a kind of mouthpiece for the accumulated experience of the community embodied in its traditional music. But in this case the process of transmission is cut short; the wee herd is the last link in this particular chain. When he goes back to school with the coming of the cold weather, his whistle is confiscated and destroyed by the schoolmaster. Common sense may tell us that the boy can easily make another whistle and perhaps conceal it more effectively from the dominie, but the fact that the poem ends with the burning of the whistle gives an unmistakeable sense of finality to the master's action:

> He couldna sough the catechis nor pipe the rule o' three,
> He was keepit in an' lickit when the ither loons got free;
> But he aften played the truant – 'twas the only thing he played,
> For the maister brunt the whistle that the wee herd made!

The conclusion suggests that in the clash between modern education and traditional culture the latter will inevitably be destroyed. The master, on his side, represents an educational ethos which has no place for – indeed which does not even recognise – the boy's talent, and which insists that he spend his time instead trying to master the elements of an 'official' culture for which he has no aptitude. The poem is, in other words, a kind of cultural parable through which certain powerful contemporary fears were expressed.

Hardy's belief that there had been a revolutionary cultural change in the space of a single generation was widely shared in the last decades of the century and fears for the survival of local culture and local speech were intensified by the fact that education, if the most powerful, was by no means the only standardising force at work. The decade in which *Tess of the D'Urbervilles* is set was one of the great periods of railway expansion in Britain, with substantial increases in both mileage and passenger receipts which were particularly marked in Scotland. It was during this decade too that a cheap and frequent local press began to develop as a result of the repeal of advertisement duty (in 1853), stamp duty (in 1855) and paper duty (in 1861): by the eighteen seventies inexpensive morning dailies were appearing in the major Scottish cities. The significance of these newspapers for the health of local culture was ambiguous. They regularly published material on local history and local customs, and at a time when newspapers and magazines were more important outlets for the imaginative writer than now, they were hospitable towards work which was in dialect or which otherwise reflected the life of their region. Alexander originally wrote *Johnny Gibb* as a series of sketches for *The Aberdeen Free Press* (a tradition maintained in the 'Donovan Smith' sketches of local urban life in the present-day *Press and Journal*). Of the poets mentioned earlier, Mary Symon first became widely known with the publication in the local press of some of her poems about the Great War; one of Charles Murray's best known poems, 'There's Aye a Something', first appeared in *The Press and Journal* and, of course, the first two Scots poems by Scotland's greatest twentieth century poet, Hugh MacDiarmid are to be found in the pages of *The Dunfermline Press* for September 30, 1922. At the same time, though local newspapers flourished, their focus became less exclusively local, particularly after 1870 when the government takeover of the telegraph service made national and international news more readily accessible.

For all these reasons, the eighteen sixties and eighteen seventies were decisive decades in the development of a movement to resist the standardising, rationalising pressures of the age and in favour of the local, the idiosyncratic, the dialectal: the period saw the foundation of the English Dialect Society in 1873 and the Folklore Society in 1878; while in Scotland,

> Local historians appear by the dozen . . . all aware of the fast-changing nature of the social life and the physical environment of their home parishes, and keen to record the historical evolution of the locality before it altered out of all recognition.[8]

A growing sense of the worth of local culture led in the North-east to a revaluation of a vernacular verse traditon which had remained strong in the region. For most of the century, the composing of dialect poetry had been regarded as a pastime without any real 'literary' importance, 'literature' implying something altogether more dignified:

> The art of writing verse in the vernacular has always been popular in our 'corner', but for a long period it was considered rather 'vulgar', and, with a few exceptions, unliterary. Only a small portion of it ever reached the status of book

form.[9]

Perhaps the main reason why vernacular verse produced in the North-east and other parts of Scotland before the end of the century was not considered to be 'literature' was the fact that the language it was written in derived from *spoken* regional dialects rather than from a consistent written Scots – that had died out in the eighteenth century. The reappearance of Scots as a literary medium late in the following century is not strictly a revival of written Scots but a reinvention of it on the basis of contemporary local speech, more or less phonetically rendered. The idiom of *Johnny Gibb* is manufactured. It was because this kind of written Scots was so close to the spoken language that Alexander decided to write his narrative in English, feeling that dialect could not be made to serve the purposes of an extended literary narrative. Nevertheless, *Johnny Gibb* is important for the way in which it developed and displayed the literary possibilities of a written Scots based on a spoken regional dialect and because its enthusiastic reception demonstrated that there was a wide public for vernacular writing. This combination of factors helps to explain the pre-eminence of the North-east in the revival of vernacular literature which took place around the turn of the century, even though it was in poetry rather than prose that the pre-eminence was displayed.

Part of the explanation for the change of direction lies in the difficulties which faced the contemporary writer of prose in attempting to combine an English narrative with Scots dialogue. Given the social and educational associations of Scots as against English, or indeed of any regional or class-based 'dialect' compared with the 'standard', it is difficult for the author who employs both in the same work not to seem patronising (at best) towards his 'rustic' or 'provincial' or 'common' dialect speaking characters. And this is particularly true if in his English narrative he employs the omniscient, authoritative narrative voice of the nineteenth century novelist. Consequently, the reader may find it difficult or impossible to accept the experience of dialect speaking characters as really serious or important. But while it was difficult for the regional novelist to avoid juxtaposing 'standard' and 'dialect', invoking thereby literary associations which subverted his intentions, the dialect poet had less of a problem. It was only with the work of Lewis Grassic Gibbon (J. Leslie Mitchell) in the nineteen thirties that the problem of finding an answerable style for vernacular narrative found a solution. Committed to writing as a career in a way that most of his vernacular predecessors were not, Grassic Gibbon was correspondingly more self-conscious about theoretical issues and more ambitious in his literary aims. He wanted to treat the life of his native region with a fullness only possible in the novel, but first had to solve what he called 'the old problem of dialect or no dialect'. The writer, he says, must opt for one of three courses:

> The first is to write in Scots, synthetic Scots for preference – everything in the book . . . The second way is to write in English – so that, names apart, the story might as well take place in Cornwall. The third method is what I myself employ: writing everything, descriptive matter and all, in the twists of Scottish idiom but not in the actual dialect except for such words as have a fine vigour and vulgarity and no exact English equivalent. [10]

Later, writing of the narrative technique he employed in *A Scots Quair*, he says that he wanted to mould the English language into 'the rhythms and cadences of Scots spoken speech, and to inject into the English vocabulary such minimum number of words from Braid Scots as that remodelling requires'.[11] Here the usually invidious contrast between English narrative voice and Scots dialogue has been eliminated, and *spoken* Scots has become the basis for everything in the novel. As with David Toulmin's novels which employ a similar technique, the effect is of a story told rather than a story written, and of a voice which generally expresses a consciousness closely linked with, though usually more alert and aware than that of the community as a whole.

The contribution of the North-east to the modern vernacular revival was in poetry rather than prose for another reason: as Bulloch suggests, there was a strong dialect verse tradition in the region long before anything which could be called a literary movement came into being. This tradition ultimately had its roots in the old oral song and ballad culture, which survived longer and more vigorously in the North-east than in the rest of Scotland because of the relative cultural stability of the area. In spite of significant changes in patterns of landholding, settlement and agricultural activity in the late eighteenth century and the beginning of the nineteenth, the North-east was less affected than most of lowland Scotland by the major industrial changes and associated population movements of the first half of the nineteenth century. Though there was considerable movement within the region, particularly from the land to the country towns, this had little effect on cultural patterns or on local speech. Geographical isolation also helped to preserve the distinctiveness of the region: although communications within the North-east and with the south improved substantially in the late eighteenth century it was the coming of the railway and the spanning of the great firths in Victorian times that made the North-east easily accessible from the South.

Traditionally, too, many of its strongest economic links had been with the foreign cultures of Scandinavia and northern Europe rather than with England or even southern Scotland.

As a result, the North-east was affected later and more gradually than most of the lowlands by modernising, standardising influences from the south. Again, general literacy reached the area late, probably in the last half of the eighteenth century, so that the standardising influence of print was hardly felt in the area till then. Even by the middle of the following century 'English had made very little invasion of the colloquial speech of the landward folk'[12] in areas like Strathdon, the birthplace of Charles Murray. Local dialect and local culture remained strong, and folk-song and popular balladry continued to flourish in the region, so that 'North-east balladry constitutes the richest regional tradition in Britain.'[13] This rich, thriving local culture was the soil out of which the modern vernacular literature of the North-east grew.

Nearly all the creators of that literature were born in a single decade – Violet Jacob and Mary Symon in 1863, Charles Murray in 1864, Marion Angus in 1866; and a number of other major figures in the vernacular movement who were not imaginative writers were also born in the sixties. All, in other words, belonged to the first generation of Scots to be exposed to the full weight of the standardising and anglicising pressures of the reformed school system. Their careers demonstrate, however, that these pressures were in some ways as much a stimulus as a threat to vernacular culture. A schooling conducted largely in English – or Scottish English – seems to have had the effect of making dialect speakers more conscious (and self-conscious) about linguistic matters in a way which often stimulated literary activity.

If the local success of dialect works like *Johnny Gibb* and the strength of the vernacular poetic tradition were important in encouraging young writers from the North-east to try their hands at poetry in dialect, they were also encouraged by the success of nationally known literary figures in exploiting dialect material. In 1887 Robert Louis Stevenson, already established as a successful prose writer, brought out a volume of verse entitled *Underwoods*, containing a substantial number of Scots poems. Stevenson did not see himself as initiating a revival of vernacular poetry: on the contrary, in his note to the poems in Scots he says that 'The day draws near when this illustrious and malleable tongue will be forgotten', adding that he will be among the last 'native Makers' in a 'dying language'. But his example helped to preserve Scots and encourage its use as a medium for verse, particularly since *Underwoods*, which also contained English poems, was directed not at a parochial market for local verse but at the general poetry-reading public. It was Stevenson above all who made vernacular verse a literary rather than a sub-literary genre:

> Verse in the vernacular received the benison of book shape only now and again, and then mostly as a harmless and subsidised hobby. As a literary and successful venture it did not reach the outside world till Stevenson took it in hand: since when it has been cultivated to good purpose by many men, not least by the author of *Hamewith.*[14]

Unlike Murray's Scots, however, which is close to being a transcription of the speech of his native Donside, Stevenson's vernacular is an eclectic and more literary idiom; although like all modern written Scots it has its roots in spoken dialect – Stevenson said that he read his own verse 'in the drawling Lothian voice' he learned as a boy – in vocabulary it is 'synthetic', drawing its lexical resources from different regional dialects in a way which partly anticipates MacDiarmid's more strenuous efforts to create a 'synthetic' Scots thirty years later. But when *Underwoods* first appeared, such an approach to extending and reinvigorating written Scots was likely to have less general appeal than the impulse to affirm regional identity against the forces threatening it by writing in a regional dialect. Indeed, in his note to the Scottish poems in the volume, Stevenson seems to anticipate criticism for the 'impurity' of his Scots:

> I note again, that among our new dialectitians, the local habitat of every dialect is given to the square mile. I could not emulate this nicety if I desired, for I simply wrote my Scots as well as I was able, not caring if it hailed from Lauderdale or Angus, from the Mearns or Galloway; if I had ever heard a good word, I used it without shame.

Another poet whose success encouraged the writing of dialect verse in the last two decades of the nineteenth century was James Logie Robertson, whose versions of Horace in Scots began to appear in *The Scotsman* in 1881 and were collected as *Horace in Homespun* in 1886. They consisted, according to the preface, of 'Sketches of Scottish Life and Character among the Ochils' and are put in the mouth of 'Hugh Haliburton', shepherd of that region. Logie Robertson's Scots is more distinctively local than Stevenson's, in keeping with his rustic persona and his use of a real and specific locality, but it is still a fairly dilute and literary language compared with the authentically regional, strongly flavoured idiom of Murray's vernacular verse.

In his 1926 survey 'Scottish Poetry of Today', Robert Bain looked back at Murray's enormous and instantaneous success with the 1900 *Hamewith* and attributed it largely to the fact that he had 'brought a new province into Scottish poetry – Buchan', while 'the fascination of a comparatively unknown dialect considerably helped the vogue of the poet'.[15] In fact, Murray did more than bring a new province and new dialect into Scots poetry – he was the poet in the literary tradition who established the language of a particular region of Scotland as a vehicle for poetry of real distinction and more than local circulation, and his example had a powerful influence on the vernacular poets who followed him. So, when Violet Jacob published her first volume of Scots verse in 1915, her title, *Songs of Angus*, made it clear that she was using the dialect of a particular region, and in his preface to the collection, John Buchan praised the linguistic integrity of her work, contrasting it with Stevenson's eclecticism:

> . . . above all it is a living speech, with the accent of the natural voice, and not a skilful mosaic of robust words, which, as in sundry poems of Stevenson, for all the wit and skill remains a mosaic.

And in his note to his own 1917 collection *Poems in Scots and English*, Buchan emphasised that the vernacular he himself used was both genuinely local and a spoken rather than a literary idiom:

> . . . the Scots pieces in this little collection are written in the vernacular which is spoken in the hill country of the Lowlands, from the Cheviots to Galloway. Scots has never been to me a book tongue; I could always speak it more easily than I could write it.

Many, perhaps most vernacular enthusiasts involved in the early years of the vernacular revival assumed that a strong and pure Scots was synonymous with a rural Scots. City-dwellers were more subject to modernising pressures and cities were also places where different local traditions met, mingled and lost their separate identities; urban Scots was generally thought to be weak and corrupt, a mongrel idiom beneath the writer's attention. And just as Doric had survived best in rural communities, so too had other native values and traditions. For a modernist like the young C.M. Grieve, on the other hand, the future lay with urban and industrial life, and the vernacular poet seemed imprisoned behind the kailyard wall, nostalgically celebrating a dying rural order, confining himself to kinds of experiences which had less and less to do with the lives of the majority of Scots. Later, Grieve was to argue that a poetry both modern and able to address the full range of poetic purpose *was* possible in Scots but only if, instead of working with limited local dialects, the *disjecta membra* of the full national language of the past, writers set about creating a more comprehensive literary vernacular. In this enterprise, the very quality of local dialect literature after 1900 came to seem an obstacle to Grieve and his supporters, since it drew attention and effort away from the one thing needful, the creation (or recreation) of a genuinely *national* language. In the mid-twenties when Grieve was developing these ideas, he was particularly hostile to the dialect of the North-east primarily, one suspects, because at the time it seemed, in literary terms, by far the most vigorous of Scotland's regional dialects. So, while the bulk of the vernacular verse in the three volumes of *Northern Numbers* which he edited[16] had been contributed by writers from the North-east, by 1925, in his article on Murray, Grieve was asserting the North-east dialect 'is perhaps the poorest of them all and certainly the least capable of being used to genuine poetic purpose.' His main evidence was the absence of any significant contribution from the region to the 'high' literary tradition of the vernacular. It is characteristic of the intransigent cultural elitism of the modernist that Grieve should either dismiss as insignificant or be ignorant of the extraordinary richness of the folk literature of the region.

The alleged literary barrenness of the North-east was no accident as far as Grieve was concerned. The local dialect was, apparently, a degenerate one, and taking up Andrew Lang's description of the language of *Hamewith* as 'pure' and 'rich',[17] Grieve puts his own ironic construction on the terms:

> Aberdeenshire Scots is certainly the reverse of 'pure': anything further from the conceivable norm – anything more corrupt – it would be difficult to find in any dialect of any tongue. And as to 'rich' – yes, as the 'haggis' is, in the sense in which Lang refers to the 'haggis' in that criticism of Burns: but the very reverse of rich in beauty-creating powers, in intellectual resource, in technical accomplishment.[18]

In the correspondence which (naturally) followed, Grieve developed this claim, accepting a suggestion in a letter from R.L. Cassie that the distinctive character of North-east dialect was due to its extensive assimilation of Norse and Gaelic elements. To many this might seem a strength, for Grieve it was a weakness:

> 'It was, indeed, the largeness of that accession that led me to declare that Aberdeenshire Scots is furthest from any conceivable norm of Scots.'[19]

The notion implicit in all this that a dialect is somehow 'corrupted' by 'foreign' influences, strongly suggests contemporary doctrines of racial and cultural purity and reminds the reader that in 1925 Grieve had not yet completed the transformation from national to international socialist.

Cassie had argued that the demonstrable vitality of North-east Scots ought to make it the 'nucleus and mainspring of the reviving

Scots language', but for Grieve its 'impurity' together with its largely rural origins made it an inhospitable medium for the 'significant intellection' which he thought vernacular poetry needed to raise it above its present 'narrow and dismal rut'.

From the eighteen seventies to the turn of the century, the tendency had been to regard Scots, as Stevenson had done, as almost certainly doomed to extinction within a very short time, but by the eighteen nineties the movement for its preservation and for the defence of Scots culture in general, had made considerable headway. Even in this period, the North-east seems to have been at the forefront of interest in the vernacular: when Grierson was appointed to the first Chair of English at Aberdeen in 1894, his first programme for the new course included the vernacular literature of lowland Scotland. Later, he contrasted the situation in Aberdeen with that in Edinburgh, which he moved to in 1915:

> The Chair which I occupied in Aberdeen was described expressly as a Chair of English, including Scottish literature; and I lectured regularly on the Scottish poets of the fifteenth and sixteenth centuries . . . and on the revival of Scottish literature in the eighteenth century. Coming to Edinburgh I found myself in a rather different position. Scottish literature was not a definitely prescribed portion of the work of the Chair.[20]

Just after the turn of the century, even the Scottish Education Department seemed to have have had a change of heart: writing in 1907, John Buchan recorded that 'The Scotch Education Department have issued a Memorandum on the teaching of English, in which teachers are urged not to treat Lowland Scots as a provincial dialect, but to encourage its use among children'.[21] How much effect this had in the classroom is difficult to assess, but it is important to be aware that changes were taking place in the cultural climate long before Grieve's 'renaissance' campaigning began.

One of the vehicles of the early phase of the revival in the eighteen nineties was the Edinburgh-based *Scots Observer* edited by W.E. Henley, and it was in the *Observer* that Charles Murray's first published poem, 'The Antiquary', appeared in December 1889. Murray's association with the *Observer* continued after the magazine moved to London and was renamed the *National Observer*. Throughout its brief life – from 1888[22] to 1894 – he contributed regularly, and the connection is a significant one, because despite his Tory imperialism in politics, Henley had catholic and generally progressive literary tastes and was a great encourager of young writers. As a result the *Observer* appealed most strongly to the young and to those in sympathy with literary innovation, and its original links with the wave of cultural nationalism in Scotland in the nineties reflect the extent to which the assertion of regional or national identity against the standardising forces of late Victorian society was one of the forward-looking impulses of the period. In his biography of Kipling, Charles Carrington sums up the *Observer's* connection with nationalism and with a literary adventurousness which appealed to the young:

> some of Henley's associates in Edinburgh set him up as the editor of a weekly magazine which was intended as a contribution to the Scottish literary revival. The *Scots Observer* first came out in 1889 . . . and within a few months it captivated the taste of the younger set.[23]

Murray's involvement with the *Observer* and with Henley and his group (which included Stevenson, Logie Robertson, Yeats and Kipling) hardly supports the idea that Murray was 'backward-looking', an 'establishment' figure fixed in outmoded attitudes until the massive trauma of the Great War transformed him into a pallid forerunner of MacDiarmid.[24] It suggests instead that, by the standards of the nineties, Murray was a literary progressive, involved in the contemporary rejection of Victorian assumptions about the language and subject matter proper to poetry.

In the nineties re-emerged that recurrent impulse in literary history to move away from a specifically 'poetic' diction, and bring the language of poetry closer to the 'real language of men'. Linked with it was the idea that the subject matter of poetry should be drawn, not from some special area of feelings but from ordinary experience and contemporary life. So, in the course of the decade Yeats began to move away from the elaborate idiom of his early poems towards a more direct, concrete, colloquial style. At about the same time he advised Synge to leave the precious atmosphere of Paris and go to 'the Aran Islands and find a life that had never been expressed in literature, instead of a life where all had been expressed'.[25] There Synge found a vigorous and distinctive spoken idiom uncontaminated by literary associations, which was the ideal antidote to the abstracting and idealising tendency of the literary language of the time and which became the basis for his own mature style. For Yeats and Synge the fact that life on the Aran Islands had never found expression made it the ideal stimulus for the contemporary writer, striving to escape Victorian 'eloquence', while for Grieve, writing thirty or so years later and with little understanding of the literary climate of the eighteen nineties it was largely because Charles Murray, in chronicling the life of the North-east, had not 'a single forerunner of the slightest consequence' that he failed as a poet.

The problems of the patriotic Scots writer at the end of the century were similar to those of the patriotic Irish writer of the same period. Both wanted – as did spokesmen for other distinctive regional traditions, like Hardy – to assert the importance of the local against the centralising tendencies of the age, but neither had a readymade literary idiom to hand. The Anglo-Irish writer lived in a culture dominated by literary imports from England, in which even native writing in English was powerfully influenced by the prestige of the mainstream literary tradition and its language. In the Irish literary revival, an authentically Irish literary language had to be created largely from the resources offered by the distinctive forms of English spoken in Ireland, just as in Scotland, a modern written Scots for literary purposes had to be created on the basis of spoken dialect. However, in contrast to the situation in Ireland, a distinctive written Scots had existed and a variety of it even survived and was employed well into the nineteenth century, although by then it was no longer the vigorous and versatile idiom it had been but an Augustan semi-Scots, deriving from the anglicised side of Burns's work. Even more than the literary English of the late-Victorian period, it was a generalising, abstracting and idealising kind of language, uncongenial to the forward-looking poet of the nineties because its characteristics made it unsuitable for presenting the individual and local, major preoccupations of the younger writers of the time. In choosing instead a 'strong' dialect Scots as the medium for their poetry, vernacular poets like Murray and Mary Symon were rejecting a generalising literary language, and the outlook of a leisured literary intelligensia which lay behind it, in favour of an idiom which grew out of the experience of ordinary unliterary people. And tired of the philosophical pretensions of much late nineteenth century poetry, these poets might also have been attracted by another advantage of writing in dialect, mischievously pointed out in Hardy's essay on Barnes:

> Dialect . . . offered him another advantage as the writer . . . Even if he often used the dramatic form of peasant speakers as a pretext for the expression of his own mind and experiences – which cannot be doubted – yet he did not always do this, and the assumed character of the husbandman or hamleteer enabled him to elude in his verse those dreams and speculations that cannot leave alone the mystery of things, – possibly an unworthy mystery and disappointing if solved, though one that has a harrowing fascination for many poets.[26]

The literary idiom available to the Scots poet in the nineteenth century is exemplified in the *Whistle Binkie* collection which went through many editions around the middle of the century. Alexander Rodger's 'Come to the Banks of the Clyde' is a reasonably typical piece although, to be fair, a stronger Scots is found in some of the verse. A single stanza gives the flavour –

Come to the banks of Clyde
Where health and joy invite us;
Spring now, in virgin pride,
There waiteth to delight us:
Enrobed in green, she smiles serene –
Each eye enraptured views her;
A brighter dye o'erspreads the sky,
And every creature woos her.

Rodger presents a generalised landscape, a literary terrain rather than a real place, and nothing in the language or the way in which the scene is described would allow us to identify it as the banks of Clyde or, indeed, as anywhere in particular, were it not for the title and the name of the river in the text. In contrast, when Charles Murray presents a landscape – in 'Spring in the Howe O' Alford' for example, or 'The Hint O' Hairst' (both early poems) – there is an abundance of particulars described in the distinctive dialect of the area. An impression of the natural scene is created quite different from than seen by Rodger's literary tourist: Murray's countryside is a countryman's one, alive with the kind of detail which comes from a countryman's inside knowledge of rural life. Above all, it is a landscape filled with *activity*, made by human beings, rather than a wholly natural scene offering a serene and generalised beauty for contemplation. Such a landscape can only be described in the language of the community which has made it:

There's burstin' buds on the larick now,
A' the birds are pair'd an' biggin';
Saft soughin' win's dry the dubby howe,
An' the eildit puir are thiggin'.

The whip-the-cat's aff fae hoose to hoose,
Wi' his oxtered lap-buird lampin',
An' hard ahint, wi' the shears an' goose,
His wee, pechin' 'prentice trampin'.

The Laird's approach gets a coat o' san',
When the grieve can spare a yokin';
On the market stance there's a tinker clan,
An' the guidwife's hens are clockin'.

The Mason's harp is set up on en',

He's harlin' the fire-hoose gable.
The sheep are aff to the hills again
As hard as the lambs are able.

('Spring in the Howe O' Alford')

Murray creates a vivid sense of the bustle which spring brings and the excitement it generates by moving rapidly from one scene or activity to the next, a technique of juxtaposition without linking commentary or attempt to draw significance from what is being described which is recognisably 'modern'. It links Murray's practice with the literary 'impressionism' of the turn of the century and even with the more radical ideas of the Imagists about 'the language of common speech' and 'rendering particulars exactly'.[27] In two later poems entitled 'Spring' and 'Winter', from *In the Country Places*, Murray pushes economy even further, and because the form is less traditional than the quatrains of 'Spring in the Howe O' Alford', the effect is even more modern. These poems create a vivid impression – not so much of the season, but of how people experience it – in only eight lines, a feat reminiscent of the attempts made by Pound and the Imagists to emulate the extreme brevity of some Oriental poetry. 'Spring' and 'Winter' are, so to speak, North-east *haiku* in which 'a whole way of life, at a given time and place, in a given society, is crystallised':[28]

Noo that cauldrife winter's here
There's a pig in ilka bed,
Kindlin's scarce an' coals is dear;
Noo that cauldrife winter's here
Doddy mittens we maun wear,
Butter skites an' winna spread;
Noo that cauldrife winter's here
There's a pig in ilka bed.

('Winter')

It is not only the kind of language he uses or the way in which he sometimes treats his subject matter which links Murray with the beginnings of the modern movement in poetry; it is also the subject matter itself, particularly in the extent to which his poetry deals with work and with working people – subjects regarded as unsuitable for verse by critics who believed that poetry was 'beautiful' in proportion to its remoteness from everyday life. In many of his portraits of countryfolk, Murray focusses on the work that they do, so that in *Hamewith* we have 'The Packman', 'The Lettergae', 'The Miller', 'Skeely Kirsty' (an old woman skilled in traditional healing) and the old gravedigger in 'A Green Yule' – and in his poems about landscapes or about the seasons there is the same interest in work, in the varied activities going on in that place or at that time of year. This is hardly surprising because in choosing to write largely about ordinary, non-intellectual country people, Murray was choosing to write about people who were active rather than introspective and likely to express themselves as fully and individually in what they did as in what they thought or said. Many of them are, of course, capable of vigorous and individual utterance, but words are proportionally less important to them than to the intellectual.

Murray's interest in work links him with the best known of the contributors to Henley's reviews, the young, but already celebrated, Rudyard Kipling, whose 'Barrack-Room Ballads' began to appear in *The Scots Observer* in February 1890 and created an immediate sensation because of their novelty of both style and content. Kipling's fascination with slang and cant, technical language, regional and class dialects – and his success in exploiting these – offered powerful encouragement to other contemporary poets interested in exploring similar areas of language. And with his interest in non-standard language went an interest in areas of society and kinds of experience hitherto largely excluded from the high literary tradition. Kipling was, 'first and foremost the poet of work', a subject which 'poetry and fiction before his time had avoided'[29] – in the high literary tradition, at least, although in the popular tradition, one of the sources of his inspiration, work was a frequent subject. In his exploration of this area of life Kipling was, in a way, part of the contemporary return to folk and popular experience, although, unlike most of the poets involved in that movement, it was largely city life and urban speech that interested him.

Murray's 'The Antiquary' appeared in *The Scots Observer* before the first of the 'Barrack-Room Ballads', but Kipling was senior to the Scots poet in literary reputation and exactly the sort of writer to have an influence on him – he was, after all the chronicler and celebrater of the practical professional men like Murray who were consolidating the empire. Kipling's influence is at its most direct and obvious in 'The Alien', a poem from the expanded 1909 *Hamewith*, which deals with the longing for home felt by a European exile in colonial Africa. In it Murray employs a Kiplingesque stanza form and (unhappily) borrows Kipling's characteristic tricks of spelling to convey the Scots-accented English of the speaker. But Kipling's real influence on Murray lies elsewhere: in the encouragement his success gave to the exploration of dialect and to the treatment of kinds of experience – notably work – rarely treated in serious poetry.

Murray is also, like Kipling, an ambiguous figure, belonging partly to an older moralising and rhetorical manner and partly to a more modern kind of poetry. This ambiguity is one of the things which makes it difficult to find appropriate criteria for judging the work of either poet. In the admiring introduction T.S. Eliot wrote for his selection of Kipling's verse, he uses Arnold's distinction between 'verse' and 'poetry' to argue that Kipling was essentially a writer of verse who sometimes almost by accident produced poetry. Grieve employs the same distinction in his attack on Murray, maintaining that the difference between 'J.B. Selkirk's' work and Murray's is 'the difference between Scottish poetry and Scottish verse.' Whatever motive lies behind its use, the distinction is an invidious one, suggesting a difference in kind where what is really involved is a difference in degree. Eliot's essay does, however, suggest a juster basis for judging the kind of poetry Kipling – and Murray – wrote. The key, Eliot suggests, lies in the intimate dependence of this kind of writing on the spoken language and on recitation; Kipling's poems, he says, 'are best when read aloud, and the ear requires no training to follow them easily'.

Like Kipling's poetry, that of Charles Murray is almost always inseparable from the speaking voice – even when not obviously dramatic. It works best when spoken aloud to an audience rather than read silently and was written with recitation in mind, something which is hardly surprising when one considers that the language in which it is written is, in effect, a transcription of spoken dialect. Like Kipling's poems, which were being recited at smoking concerts and in music-halls before the end of the century, Murray's verse tended to be performed orally, and to the same kind of popular and non-literary audience. Describing his boyhood on an Aberdeenshire farm between the wars, Jack Webster recollects how family, farmhands and neighbours made their own entertainment:

> . . . the general disorder was brought to a halt as my grandfather intoned from his favourite corner of the fire-side: 'Weel lads, fit aboot 'Stumpy'?' And away they went, a full-blooded orchestra cramped into the parlour of a farmhouse, swinging into strathspeys and reels and old-fashioned waltzes . . . One tune followed another, interpolated with the songs of Robbie Burns (we never called him Rabbie) or a more recent recitation from the North-east poet called 'Hamewith', whose real name was Charles Murray from Alford.[30]

Recent critics have recognised the oral and popular character of Murray's work, but generally in a patronising way; largely dismissing Murray, George Kitchin says of his verse, 'For recitation at soiree or smoker there was nothing like it', and he concludes by echoing Grieve's judgement that '*Hamewith* hardly counts as poetry'.[31]

The dependence of the vernacular poetry of the nineties and the early part of the century on spoken regional dialect was an inescapable consequence of the disappearance of a standard written Scots. But the early vernacular poets were also writing at a time when recitation and rote memorisation of verse were more important in school, family circle and various kinds of entertainment than now. Such 'recital' verse was, naturally, a 'popular' poetry, not necessarily in the sense of a poetry of the labouring classes, but rather as a kind of poetry appreciated by those who were 'intelligent and educated without having what we would now call literary tastes, who liked poetry without in any way finding it a necessity'.[32]

Such verse is likely to have more in common with song than with more intellectual or literary kinds of poetry; it will be clear and straightforward in meaning, rhythmically regular and will tend to exploit a limited range of easily understood and shared emotions – humour, pathos, patriotism (local or national), terror and so on. If such poetry does have an intellectual element, it will not be the challenging 'significant intellection' demanded by Grieve but the traditional wisdom of the proverb or old saying. Such poems are 'a kind of rhyming proverb' recording in memorable form 'some emotion which every human being can share'[33] rather than – in the way of modernist art – challenging and disturbing their audience. The unexamined cultural progressivism of much Scottish literary history endorses the modernist stance while condemning writers who respect traditional values. So Charles Murray is criticized for his 'backward-looking'[34] attitudes while a poet who allied himself with such forces as Mussolini's blackshirts and Stalin's Cheka is praised as forward-looking and progressive.

In fact, Murray's attitude to the past and to the rural life he sprang from is more complicated than the usual references to 'rural nostalgia' or 'kailyard attitudes' suggest; he has more in common with Hardy than with Ian Maclaren. In *The Mayor of Casterbridge* we are reminded of the virtues of a traditional way of life which is rapidly vanishing but also of the barbarism, cruelty and violence of the past. The Roman amphitheatre, the bear-baiting stake, the pool in which unwanted infants were drowned, all survive and remind us of these things – and the skimmity-ride shows that, among some parts of the community at least, atavistic impulses survive. While Hardy also presents the attractive things about the past, its leisurely pace and lack of regimentation, its stronger and more spontaneous sense of community, nevertheless, his 'practical meliorism', as he called it, is evident, particularly at the very end of the novel. For the majority of people Farfrae's more efficient, scientific business methods mean cheaper, more plentiful bread, and even his impersonal, profit-directed methods of management are welcomed by his workmen because they no longer have the overwhelming personality of Henchard bearing down on them.

Murray's similarly ambivalent attitude to the past emerges in his first published poem, 'The Antiquary'. Murray's antiquary is no gentleman collector with a detached, aesthetic appreciation of the fine craftsmanship of the past. His enthusiasm and commitment go much deeper and are unrelated to aesthetic considerations so that, as the amusing description of his crowded cottage makes clear, much of what he has is junk rather than antiques and is strewn about at random rather than arranged and ordered. Clearly the things are an essential part of his daily life, like his old-fashioned clothes, and are not for display:

The horn-en' fu' o' craggins, quaichs, an' caups,
Mulls, whorls, 'an cruisies left bare room to stir;
Wi' routh o' swords an' dirks a' nicks an' slaps,
An' peer-men, used langsyne for haudin' fir.

The picture of the man and his environment emphasises that his attachment to the past is stronger and more intimate than that of the connoisseur: the antiquary lives not just with the physical remains of the past but also, to a large extent inhabits the *psychological* world of a previous age. His knowledge of spells and of various methods of foretelling the future are not just pieces of scholarly information but actually believed in, and the significance of the old silver sixpence he has kept 'Rowed in a cloutie, to preserve the glint' is described without any hint of scepticism. Whatever the poet himself believes, the antiquary clearly still believes in witches; his silver coin

. . . had shot a witch
Sae stark, she hadna left her like ahint
For killin' kye or giein' foul the itch.

As this suggests, the attitude to the past expressed in the poem is by no means a kailyard one. Like the silver sixpence, many of the details we are given about the antiquary and his possessions serve, like Hardy's stake or pool, to remind us of the superstition, cruelty and violence of the past. It is a grotesque, even grisly world, that the antiquary inhabits, despite the affection with which he is described, and even the old skills which he has preserved are of a grim kind:

He kent auld spells, could trail the rape an' spae,
He'd wallets fu' o' queer oonchancie leems,
Could dress a mart, prob hoven nowt, an' flay;
Fell spavined horse, an' deftly use the fleems.

The poem suggests that the idea of Murray as a poet of externals who, in Nan Shepherd's phrase, engages in 'no psychological probing', is only partly accurate. The antiquary's appearance and possessions tell us a good deal about the kind of man he is and the psychological world he inhabits.

It was a world which was only finally disappearing when Charles Murray was growing up; Hardy's older rustics (Tess's mother, for instance) inhabit it, and the latter's faith in the dream book is shared by the older women customers of Murray's packman who has in his pack 'A dream beuk 'at the weeda wife had hankered after lang.' But 'The Packman' is essentially a poem about the modernisation of the country area in which the packman himself operates – a process in which he himself plays a crucial part. His first step up the social ladder comes when he buys a pony and cart, then he takes 'a roadside shoppie', begins to employ others and to lend money. Finally he becomes principal local merchant and bank agent with three sons who have been to college and entered professions and a daughter married to a 'strappin' Deeside laird.' His career serves as a summary of the significant economic and social changes in a Scottish rural community in the later nineteenth century, and far from disapproving of this agent of change, Murray treats his rise with genial humour, approving of the energy and shrewdness which bring him success – hardly a surprising reaction in the light of his own family's similar, if less spectacular, rise in status. But also evident in the poem is Murray's sense that the traditional leaders of rural society, the gentry, are feckless and improvident, and now have to ally themselves with their social inferiors to save themselves from financial disaster. Though the packman's daughter is plain, the laird 'didna swither lang' about proposing,

> For he had to get her tocher or his timmer had to gang.

And in 'Jeames', we get the other side of the picture in the damage done to farming by the aristocratic addiction to field sports. Jeames has

> . . . banned the Laird upon the road –
> His bawds an' birds that connached sae the craft.

This sense that the gentry are idle, impractical and extravagant, largely doomed to economic extinction at the hands of hard-headed practical men, factors and feuars with an eye to the main chance, reappears in one of Murray's finest poems 'A Green Yule' (the title refers to the proverbial Scots phrase 'a green yule maks a full kirk-yaird'). It is a dramatic monologue, spoken by an old gravedigger who is just finishing a grave for the local laird. It begins with the old man's ironic comment on the attempt to maintain distinctions of rank beyond the grave, an attempt which has given him extra work:

> I'm weary, weary houkin' in the cauld, weet, clorty clay,
> But this will be the deepest in the yaird;
> It's nae a four fit dibble for a common man the day –
> Ilk bane I'm layin' by is o' a laird.

Events are being eyed from the church tower by a 'draggled hoodie craw' which seems the embodiment of the predatory spirit which animates the black-clad mourners who will, the old man predicts, take advantage of the ignorance and inexperience of the laird's widow to get possession of the estate:

> There's sorrow in the mansion, an' the lady that takes on
> Is young to hae sae muckle on her han',
> Wi' the haugh lands to excamb where the marches cross the Don,
> An' factors aye hame-drauchted when they can.
> Come spring, we'll a' be readin', when the kirk is latten oot,
> "Displenish" tackit up upon the yett;
> For hame-fairm, carts an' cattle will be roupit up, I doot,
> The policies a' pailin'd aff an' set.

As the son of a land-steward, Murray presumably knew what he was talking about, and his view of the gentry suggests that he shared, to some extent at least, the radicalism which William Alexander expressed in *Johnny Gibb*.

But one of the things which makes 'A Green Yule' such a good poem is the way in which it moves without strain from the social and topical to a timeless and universal level of significance, displaying just that union of the homely and exalted which C.M. Grieve saw as one of the peculiar strengths of the Scottish literary tradition. As the poem goes on, the gravedigger himself becomes an almost emblematic figure, related to the traditional image of Time the harvester with his scythe and even to Death himself, the grim reaper:

> The Hairst o' the Almighty I hae gathered late an' ear',
> An coont the sheaves I've stookit, by the thrave.

But he remains also a very human and tragic figure, resembling these legendary figures like Tithonus, who were burdened with eternal life without eternal youth. He is weary of life, his own family, even his children, are dead already so that he has nothing left to live for, yet death still has not claimed him. The man who lays others to rest cannot find rest himself. It is a powerful, almost medieval conception, strongly reminiscent of the episodes in Chaucer's *Pardoner's Tale* in which the three rioters in search of Death meet an old man who is able to tell them where he is to be found, although he himself has never met Death despite his desire to do so and is condemned to wander the earth seeking, but never finding, rest:

Thus walke I, lyk a restelees caityf,
And on the ground, which is my modres gate,
I knokke with my staf, bothe early and late,
And seye, "leve moder, leet me in!"

The short four-line stanzas which conclude *A Green Yule* suggest the tolling of the dead-bell and express its meaning, 'The tale of weird it tries sae hard to say.' The 'tale' with its catalogue of people of all kinds hurrying towards the grave inevitably suggests another powerful medieval motif, that of the Dance of Death:

Bring them alang, the young, the strang,
The weary and the auld;
Feed as they will on haugh or hill,
This is the only fauld.

Dibble them doon, the laird, the loon,
King an' the cadgin' caird,
The lady fine beside the queyn,
A' in the same kirkyaird.

Mighty o' name, unknown to fame
Slippit aneth the sod;
Greatest an' least alike face east,
Waitin' the trump o' God.

There are few things in modern Scots poetry nearer to the spirit of the great late-medieval makars than this; it is the poem which comes closer than any of his own perhaps to realising and vindicating C.M. Grieve's own slogan for the renewal of Scottish poetry: 'Not Burns – Dunbar!'

Suggestions for further reading:

There is no satisfactory critical treatment of the complex linguistic and cultural issues raised by the modern vernacular revival. Any reader who wishes to explore the nature and importance of the North-east contribution to the movement will find it more profitable to approach the poetry directly than via the standard literary histories. Because of prevailing critical attitudes, little of the work of the North-east vernacular pioneers is currently in print; even standard anthologies like the *Oxford Book of Scottish Verse* print only a very few of the most familiar pieces by Murray, Violet Jacob and Marion Angus and fail to reflect either their historical importance or the range and interest of their poetry. James Alison's *Poetry of Northeast Scotland* (Heinemann, 1976) offers a more generous selection of these poets and others and the poems included are less familiar, but the attempt to cover every historical period inevitably limits the space for individual poets.

Charles Murray is the only North-east poet whose work is currently available in its entirety in a reliable edition. His *Collected Poems* were published by Aberdeen University Press in 1979. Most of Mary Symon's Scots verse appears in *Deveron Days* (Aberdeen, 1938); while the bulk of Violet Jacob's vernacular poetry is included in the *Scottish Poems of Violet Jacob* (Edinburgh, 1944). Helen Cruickshank's *Collected Poems* (Edinburgh, 1971) was followed by *More Collected Poems* (Edinburgh, 1978).

The poems of Marion Angus and Alexander Gray have not been collected, but Maurice Lindsay has edited selections from both poets –

> *Selected Poems of Marion Angus*, with an introduction by Helen Cruickshank (Edinburgh, 1950)
> *Selected Poems of Alexander Gray* (Glasgow, 1948).

Both merit further exploration and interested readers are referred to the individual volumes of verse which they produced.

Notes:

1. *Hamewith: the Complete Poems of Charles Murray*, ed. Nan Shepherd (Aberdeen, 1979), ix.
2. *Press and Journal*, 12 November 1926, 8.
3. Donald J. Withrington, 'Scots in Education: a historical retrospect', *The Scots Language in Education*, Association for Scottish Literary Studies Occasional Papers no. 3 (Aberdeen, 1974), 13.
4. Alexander Mackie, Introduction and appreciation, in William Alexander, *Johnny Gibb o' Gushetneuk* (Edinburgh, 1908), xxi.
5. William Alexander, Preface to *Johnny Gibb* (Aberdeen, 1871).
6. *Chambers's Journal*, sixth series, IX, No. 248, 10 February 1906, 176.
7. C.M. Grieve, 'Charles Murray', *Contemporary Scottish Studies* (Edinburgh, 1976), 7.
8. Withrington, 'Scots in Education', 12.
9. J.M. Bulloch, Introduction to John Mitchell, *Bydand* (Aberdeen, 1918), vi.
10. Lewis Grassic Gibbon, 'Literary Lights', in Lewis Grassic Gibbon and Hugh MacDiarmid, *Scottish Scene* (London, 1934), 205.
11. Grassic Gibbon, letter to Cuthbert Graham quoted in *Aberdeen Bonaccord*, 15 February 1935.

12. Douglas Young, 'Scottish Poetry in the later Nineteenth Century', *Scottish Poetry: a Critical Survey*, ed. James Kinsley (London, 1955), 248.
13. David Buchan, *The Ballad and the Folk* (London, 1972), 4.
14. Bulloch, Introduction to Mitchell, *Bydand*, vi.
15. Robert Bain, 'Scottish Poetry of Today', *Burns Chronicle*, second series, I, 1926, 49.
16. *Northern Numbers*, ed C.M. Grieve, 3 vols. (Edinburgh, 1920 and 1921; Montrose, 1922).
17. Andrew Lang, Introduction to Charles Murray, *Hamewith* (London, 1909), xiii.
18. Grieve, *Contemporary Scottish Studies*, 7.
19. Grieve, *Contemporary Scottish Studies*, 13.
20. H.J.C. Grierson, Preface to *Edinburgh Essays in Scottish Literature* (Edinburgh, 1933), v-vi.
21. John Buchan, 'The Scots Tongue', *Scottish Review*, 5 December 1907, 259.
22. The first issue of *The Scots Observer* is dated 24 November 1888; Carrington (note 23) gives the date as 1889.
23. Charles Carrington, *Rudyard Kipling: his Life and Work* (London, 1955).
24. Maurice Lindsay, *History of Scottish Literature* (London, 1977), 375.
25. W.B. Yeats, *Autobiographies* (London, 1955), 343.
26. Thomas Hardy, Preface to *Select Poems of William Barnes* (London, 1908), xi-xii.
27. Richard Aldington, Preface to *Some Imagist Poets* (London, 1915), vi.
28. *Hamewith*, ed. Nan Shephard, ix.
29. C.S. Lewis, 'Kipling's World', *They Asked for a Paper* (London, 1962), 75.
30. Jack Webster, *A Grain of Truth* (Edinburgh, 1981), 33.
31. George Kitchin, 'The Modern Makars', *Scottish Poetry*, ed. Kingsley, 256.
32. Kingsley Amis, Introduction to the *Faber Popular Reciter* (London, 1978), 16.
33. George Orwell, 'Rudyard Kipling', *Collected Essays, Journalism and Letters* (London, 1970), II, 227-8.
34. Lindsay, *History of Scottish Literature*, 308.

ACTION AND NARRATIVE STANCE in 'A SCOTS QUAIR'

Isobel Murray

It has become part of received wisdom that the trilogy of novels forming *A Scots Quair* falls off, is disappointing, although critics have differed in their preference for *Cloud Howe* or *Grey Granite.*[1] *Sunset Song* is accepted always as the first and greatest of the three.

I want to suggest that the books differ by the author's clear intention. First, the vivid young Chris Guthrie of *Sunset Song* is the centre of consciousness in that novel, while in the later books she has matured. By the end of *Grey Granite* she is able to consider sexual questions from a new position, 'without hope or temptation, without love or hate, at last, at long last' (GG, Zircon, 468). This is very different from the Chris Guthrie whom Marget Strachan instructed in *Sunset Song*:

> It was over in a moment, quick and shameful, fine for all that, tingling and strange and shameful by turns. Long after she parted with Marget that evening she turned and stared down at Peesie's Knapp and blushed again; and suddenly she was seeing them all at Blawearie as though they were strangers naked out of the sea, she felt ill every time she looked at father and mother. (SS, Ploughing, 47)

So Gibbon has his character grow and develop from excitable adolescent to calm and detached older woman.

The narrative stance and method develop also. In *Sunset Song* Chris's involvement with the community is total, and the Song part of the book is dependent on Chris's consciousness, while Prelude and Epilude reflect a community voice more knowing, more ironic, more critical. In *Cloud Howe* Chris is the minister's wife, but no real part of Segget, and her consciousness is frequently replaced, usually by a Segget voice that delights in gossip and scandal, and low comedy like the tale of Jim the Sourock and the dead and bloody pig Dite Peat put in his wife's place in bed. In *Grey Granite* there are several more voices: Ewan had one section of *Cloud Howe*, reflecting life at the manse through a child's eyes, but here on more than a dozen occasions we read his adult reaction to experience. Also used as vehicles for the story are Ellen, Meg and Alick Watson, a chorus of the unco guid and an anonymous young worker identified as 'you' or sometimes Bob, who reflects on his reactions to industrial strife. (Bob is killed in the explosion at the Works.) (GG, Zircon, 468).

The way the main action is conveyed in each of the three books is necessarily different again. In *Sunset Song* action and narrative are practically inseparable, because Chris's consciousness dominates and treats outside events and inner thoughts alike. Some outside events certainly stand out, like the fire at Peesie's Knapp, the funeral of John Guthrie and the wedding of Chris and Ewan, and these are typically occasions when the community performs as a community, natural disasters or celebrations, and Chris's view of these events is strong, clear and often passionate.

In *Cloud Howe* most of the action is given through the Segget voice: the Segget voice relates town happenings, while Chris is preoccupied with Robert, Ewan and the manse. In *Grey Granite* Chris is even more a spectator of the action: her daily routine at Ma Cleghorn's is vividly handled, but the unemployment marches, the workers' hop, the murder at the Works gate, the explosion – all these are rendered by voices other than Chris's: the most she does is initiate an outing with Ewan and Ellen.

Effective criticism of *A Scots Quair* has tended to centre on the symbolic or mythical level on which Chris becomes 'Chris Caledonia' or 'Scotland herself'. This has perhaps tended to obscure the realism and immediacy with which she is presented in *Sunset Song*. Young Chris Guthrie is a very physical and a very emotional girl who reacts to experience with all her senses and her imagination. A clear example of this is found when she first realises she is pregnant: a storm of violent emotions in Chris, including hatred for Ewan, eventually produces a fight with him in very physical terms: her complex of responses to pregnancy is finely rendered. On a simpler level there is her sick and strange reaction to the tink who offers to relieve her of her virginity in the 'harvest madness' sequence in Drilling, or her confused memory of being kissed by a stranger on the road home after the fire at Peesie's Knapp:

> it was in her memory like being chased and bitten by a beast, but worse and with something else in it, as though half she'd liked the beast and the biting and the smell of that sleeve around her neck and that soft, unshaven face against her own. (SS, Drilling, 78)

The unique and unrepeatable emotional impact of *Sunset Song* is wholly involved with the character of Chris Guthrie and of the community, and the transient near identity of the two lasts just as long as the Song of the book. The Prelude shows us the whole community of Kinraddie in great detail, in the past and in the present. A map is provided, and the Kinraddie voice describes the place croft by croft, with all the inhabitants. For all their gossip and malice they form a small, cohesive group in a very real sense. It is important that they be established clearly before the more subjective, younger view of Chris takes over the narrative stance. Kinraddie is already well advanced in the historical process of dying: Gibbon uses Chris's youth, vitality and energy to transform it, at least in her imagination, and her Song is a celebration of life however late in the day. Chris comes to adolescence and maturity and begins a family, and it is her Kinraddie that we see. Even the degradation and death of Ewan Tavendale is finally transformed to a story of love and recognition by Chris: Harvest comes to a kind of 'happy ending' when Chris is reunited with the shade of her husband at the Standing Stone.

All this is to some extent oversimplified: in fact other voices, such as a Kinraddie one or Gibbon's own, do occasionally and unobtrusively take over from Chris, much as Dickens can supplant the sad older Pip in parts of *Great Expectations*, to exploit comic effects. Further, the reader is much more aware of the outbreak of the Great War than Chris is, for example, and anticipates some of its consequences. When Chae Strachan brings news of the war neither Chris nor Ewan can pay much attention: Ewan is absorbed in his crops, Chris in her pregnancy. But they have to become aware at least of the local effects of war: Chae Strachan volunteers, and both his absence and his tour of Kinraddie when he comes home on leave have some effect on Chris, and Chae and Long Rob both raise general questions about the war which Chris repeatedly ignores.

The local effects at least of the war are registered. Chae curses the felling of timber, ruining the land, and Long Rob's long ordeal of conscience and the minister's thinly veiled attack on him culminate in the nearest the book has to a battle, when the roused populace attack Rob and are attacked in turn by Rob with his gun:

> Folk ran to their doors, they thought the Germans had landed and were looting the Mearns; Chris, who had run across the Blawearie cornyard, shaded her eyes and looked over the country and at last she saw them, the running figures, like beetles in the distance, they fanned out and ran from the Mill as focus. And behind ran another that stopped now and then, and a puff of smoke went up at each stopping, and there came the bang of the gun. Mist was coming down and it blinded the battlefield, and through it the attacking army ran

> in an awful rout, Chris saw them vanish into its coming and Long Rob, still shooting, go scudding in chase.
>
> (SS, Harvest, 151)

The war then is to be much more terrible and to come much closer to Chris than she dreams possible, and Gibbon handles the awareness that he shares with the reader unobtrusively and well. The 'civilised world' shrinks down from Kinraddie to Blawearie, and again the reader has the advantage of Chris:

> So they were douce and safe and blithe in Blawearie though Kinraddie was unco with Chae Strachan gone.
>
> (SS, Harvest, 149)

But we know conscription is to come, and Ewan is at risk as well as the principled Rob, so that Chris's attempt to resist the outside world is specially pathetic:

> And to Chris it seemed then, Chae gone, Rob gone, that their best friends were out of Kinraddie now, friends close and fine, but they had themselves, Ewan and her and young Ewan. (SS, Harvest, 160)

She even plans a new pregnancy.

At the end of the novel, of course, Chris and young Ewan are all that is left, and they leave Blawearie. When Chris appears in the Epilude she is seen only from outside. The last throes of Kinraddie as a community are watched by a resilient heroine promised in marriage to the new minister.

The beginning of *Cloud Howe* is superficially similar to the beginning of *Sunset Song*: we are given an anecdotal account of Segget's past in a town voice, but no attempt is made to introduce the present characters, as is done in *Sunset Song*. The historical account is taken up with wars and killings, and in some degree the tone of disillusionment often found in the novel is prepared for by the scenes here, the boiling alive of the Sheriff of Mearns, the tortures of the Killing Times, James Burnes eaten alive by rats.

The structure of the novel again seems to follow that of *Sunset Song*: it is divided into four parts and each begins with Chris climbing the old castle of Kaimes and beginning a resume of what has happened to her since her last visit. But now a Segget voice boldly (and unrealistically) takes over the narration when required. In *Sunset Song* a double space between paragraphs characteristically intimated only a shift in time, space or mood for Chris, in *Cloud Howe* it can indicate that Chris's voice is replaced, usually by the anonymous Segget voice but exceptionally by Else Queen or Ewan.

The success of the novel depends on the dual narratives of Chris and the Segget voice, and Gibbon alternates them often because of his subject matter. Chris is no longer in every sense central. Of course she remains the chief character, but she is seen mostly in her involvement with Robert: she has very little to do with Segget. The actual difficulty of the minister's wife relating to any class or individuals in the town, her inevitable isolation, is mirrored by the narrative method. Chris is shown in her relations with Robert and her concern for him, but even here she has not shared his war experience, nor can she share his religious belief: her isolation is increased by his preoccupations, and completed by his visions which she so much distrusts.

In *Cloud Howe* as in *Sunset Song* we see things in general in the process of getting worse: here most of all we see the disintegration of the happy marriage of Chris and Robert and the collapse of the real family atmosphere found early on, when Robert plays with Ewan or when the whole household unites for the flitting. In the section of the novel called Cirrus a happy picture is established, and a hopeful atmosphere.

The social activities of the novel tend to be described by the Segget voice, and we read in Cumulus, for example, of the Segget Show and of the Armistice Day service. The hammer throwing at the Show is described in detail, and we find Robert Colquohoun himself competing, 'being pushed inside the ring by his wife' (CH, Cumulus, 245). The Segget voice is unobtrusive but effective: we gather that Robert will not really try to win against Jock Cronin, until one of the spinners cries: *'Jesus is getting a bit weak in the guts.'* This goads Robert to a particularly fine winning throw, and the Segget voice notes: 'he didn't say a word, just went off with his wife'.

Then we focus on Chris and Robert in close up:

> Chris said, *What's wrong?* Then he saw his hanky as he took it away from his lips; it was red. He said *Oh, nothing. Gassed lungs, I suppose. Serves me right for trying to show off.*
> (CH, Cumulus, 246)

The account of the Armistice Day service is given by the Segget voice, with a description of the respectable congregation and their backbiting:

> maybe in a minute there would have been a fine bit fight on the go, right there by the angel in Segget Square, folk round about looking shocked as could be and edging nearer for a better look, when they saw the minister coming from East Wynd, and the choir coming with him; and folk cried, *Wheest!* (CH, Cumulus, 265)

The voice describes the minister's tone and the message of his sermon, with a typical sideways glance at Chris, 'a common bit quean the minister had wifed' (CH, Cumulus, 266). The important bodies of the town come to attention at eleven o'clock.

> And faith! The quiet would have been fell solemn, but for a great car that came swishing up, from the south, and turned, and went up East Wynd.

We later learn that this is young Mowat's car.

On a previous occasion the town voice rejoiced in a comic description of the spinners interrupting a religious service: MacDougall Brown was preaching:

> Well, they were getting on fine and bloody, and having fairly a splash in the gore, when MacDougall noticed there was something wrong, the words all to hell, he couldn't make it out. (CH, Cumulus, 234)

It was the spinners, marching on singing 'WHITER than – the whitewash on the wall!' So we are prepared to be amused at the interruption of the Armistice Day service, until we are forced to notice that it is the spinners who are the war veterans, not Robert's congregation: the spinners are wearing the medals and singing their own political song. They drown Robert's hymn, and Jock Cronin invites all, starting with Robert, to join the Labour Party. Robert and Chris remain cool and calm, and go quietly home, but shortly after this Chris takes over the narrative and we see Robert taking it all very seriously: *'those spinner chaps – a perfect devil if they're right, Christine'* (CH, Cumulus, 269).

In this novel Chris is chiefly concerned with Robert, his belief and her lack of it, his black times and her retreat into herself. It is the Segget voice that describes most of the action and the grim comedy. The Segget voice early tells how being caught stealing Dalziel's hay rouses old Smithie to beat his ungrateful and tyrannical daughter: the reader is delighted to revisit this scene later when Smithie is given a bottle of 'Benny Dick Tine' and under its influence manages to oust daughter, son-in-law and all, and offer a home to Else and Alec Hogg. But the Segget voice has a wide range; it is not confined to comedy. There is for example the story of Jim the roan.

The story of Jim the roan puts an end to Else's subjugation by Meiklebogs. The Segget voice becomes almost a straight narrative, as it relates 'the real fine newsy tale of the happenings down at the Meiklebogs' (CH, Stratus, 287), and goes on to the shocking accident when the horse is impaled on the shaft of the cart. The town voice is not shocked by the horse's plight, or by Meiklebogs' determination to let the horse die a 'natural' death so that he can collect the insurance money: it is shocked by Ake Ogilvie's intemperate language, by Jess

Moultrie's distress, and by Robert Colquohoun's rage:

> And folk said that the Reverend Colquohoun swore awful – *The bloody swine, the BLOODY swine!* – a strange-like thing to say of a horse. But Ake Ogilvie said it wasn't the horse but the folk of Segget the minister meant. And that was just daft, if Ake spoke true – that Mr. Colquohoun could mean it of folk, real coarse of him to speak that way of decent people that had done him no harm. (CH, Stratus, 291)

But when Robert orders Ake to kill the horse, the cumulative effect is far from comic. For Else this is an awakening. She has put up with the enormities of Meiklebogs and his refusal to acknowledge the paternity of her baby, but the death of Jim the roan makes her 'as a body new waked out of the horror of an ill-dreamt dream' and she leaves the farm on the spot.

Robert Colquohoun attempts the same kind of desperate, doomed humanitarian intervention in the last horror story of the book, the story of how the Kindnesses were evicted and took refuge in a pig-ree, where in the night rats ate the baby's thumb. Robert races to give the family a refuge, to bring a doctor – but it is all useless, and too late, and the baby dies.

The intervention of the Segget voice throughout *Cloud Howe* makes possible a kind of patterning and contrasting that was difficult or impossible to achieve in *Sunset Song*. Chae Strachan's hardly presented relationship with his daughter Marget perhaps indicates a more natural and healthy one than John Guthrie's with Chris. But in *Cloud Howe* we find variations on some themes. Chris Colquohoun is frequently gibed at by the Segget voice, which calls her 'the common bit quean the minister had wifed', and the social inequality of her marriage to Robert is echoed in the romance of schoolteacher Jeannie Grant with railway porter Jock Cronin. This apparently develops into a lasting marriage, although Jock is criticised for having sold out the working class when he becomes a professional union man. The relationship of Dod Cronin to Cis Brown is another unequal match, and the two have to get married quickly, to the general rage, for people had been 'proud of Cis' (CH, Nimbus, 323) and the sexual purity they associated with her. Else's eventual marriage to the son of Hairy Hogg the Provost is another instance.

Gibbon's attitude to such unequal matches is hard to ascertain, in particular his attitude to Chris and Robert. There is a hint in *Sunset Song* that the perfection of the union of Chris and Ewan is fractionally marred by his lack of book learning or of imagination about the past:

> Ewan said they must fair have been fusionless folk, the bowmen, to live in places like that; and Chris laughed and looked at him, queer and sorry, and glimpsed the remoteness that her books had made. (SS, Seed-Time, 135)

The Segget voice frequently sneers that Chris is common and unworthy of Robert, but it seems an empty sneer, without authorial approval. In *Grey Granite* the question is still open: is Chris in some real sense of the wrong class for Ake Ogilvie, or is she spoiled for any other man by the fullness of her relation to Robert at its best?

> And now she stood by a stranger's side, she slept in his bed, he loved her, she him, nearer to his mind than ever she had been to that of the body that lay mouldering in France. (CH, Cirrus, 207)

Gibbon does not openly adjudicate, but we must feel Chris's book-learning is associated with her imagination and sensitivity, and that these make Ake an incomplete mate, whether or not on the grounds of class. By the end of *Cloud Howe* Chris is indeed a class refugee: she is no longer a crofter's daughter or a minister's wife; she has no recognised place in Segget or anywhere else.

If *Sunset Song* marked the end of peasant life in Kinraddie, *Cloud Howe* also marks endings. The industrial heart of Segget is destroyed. Young Mowat has been ruined and has swindled the bank out of five hundred pounds. The Mills are closed:

> And folk were saying they never would open, it wouldn't be worth it, with trade so bad; and nobody knew what the spinners would do that had waited for years for their jobs to come back. (CH, Nimbus, 340)

The death of Robert Colquhoun is a stark dramatic event, dramatising the last throes of an honest, idealistic mind that cannot find peace inside or outside the traditional Christian bounds. Robert built his last hopes on the General Strike and on Chris's baby, and both came to grief. It is the gravedigger John Muir who has the conviction after old Moultrie's funeral 'that something was finished and ended in Segget' (CH, Nimbus, 336). He seems to see the end of Christian faith:

> nothing enduring and with substance at all, kirk and minister, and stones all around graved with their promised hopes for the dead, the ways and beliefs of all olden time – no more than the whimsies a bairn would build from the changing patterns that painted the hills. (CH, Nimbus, 336-7)

The world of *Cloud Howe* is a grim one. Human nature is grimly exposed to the light. And the book seems to question human values and notions of human dignity in a constant stream of animal images. Segget's indifference to the appalling suffering of Jim the roan rouses Robert Colquhoun to a fury. Earlier the long saga of Jim the Sourock and the butchered pig in his bed is offered for our amusement: 'you couldn't but laugh when you heard the tale' (CH, Cumulus, 261). Here the Sourock's wife remembers the pig's fear of rats, and thinks of Dite Peat as a rat: the tale does no credit to the human race. In the end, rats prevail: James Burnes was eaten alive by rats in the Proem, and the Kindness baby is eaten alive by rats at the end of the book. Rough animal images abound; people are compared to horses (Ag Moultrie), to dogs (Ake Ogilvie), to a fighting cock (old Smithie), or a cow (his daughter), but the most loathsome image remains the rat, associated with Dite Peat and his brother Peter ('red-eyed like a rat'). 'The cry of human flesh eaten by beasts' is central to Robert Colquhoun's last sermon, and the picture of the hopeless Mrs. Kindness, 'with the shamed, strange eyes of a frightened beast' (CH, Nimbus, 344), remains with the reader as with Chris, 'and that memory that woke you, sick in the night, of the rats that fed on a baby's flesh'.

The third volume of the trilogy, *Grey Granite*, confronts new topics and new characters, and again Gibbon invents a singular, appropriate narrative method. But perhaps the greatest weakness of the book is in the character and role of Ewan. Like Chris, Ewan has no clear place, class or background: his fellow workers always call him a toff. But this is not enough to explain the two-dimensional effect of his presentation. He is meant to impress us as Chris's son, as Ellen's lover, as political leader and champion of the underdog, even as almost religious figure in his being beaten up and in the Judas-like betrayal of Alick Watson. The effect is of unreality, lack of authenticity.

Other novelists of the time, particularly in the United States, were trying to create revolutionary leaders in fiction and encountering snags. Perhaps the most effective such character is Fenian McCreary in John Dos Passos' *The 42nd Parallel* (1930). But the character of Mac succeeds by failing. In that book Mac comes to learn: 'A wobbly oughtn't to have any wife or children, not till after the revolution'. But he learns too late: he marries and has children, leaves them only to become a capitalist in a small way, abandoning his beliefs. So perhaps the would-be leader must remain single and childless?

> Ewan nodded and said that he saw that, there wasn't much time for the usual family business when you were a revolutionist. (GG, Zircon, 481)

In Steinbeck's *The Grapes of Wrath* the roles are divided out: the new leaders Jim Casey and Tom Joad are bachelors and almost doomed to death, to martyrdom, while the family is carried on by other characters, especially Ma Joad. Gibbon's martyr-leader fails to convince: his relations with fellow workers, with Big Jim Trease, with the police might work, but the relationship with Ellen is discordant.

Ewan is subject to extreme brutality at the hands of the police, is utterly degraded and humiliated. It is not entirely clear what particular sexual abuse he is subjected to, but only the devotion – and sexual normality – of Ellen can cleanse him. In as far as this relationship is convincing, Ewan's subsequent casting off of Ellen is unconvincing. Certainly Ellen is failing their political ideals, and aware of this, but Ewan is quite unreal: 'He stood up then, dark and slim, still a boy, and brushed her off carefully, and the snow from his knees' (GG, Zircon, 490). He is as always cool and collected and he calls her a prostitute:

> He stood looking at her coolly, not angered, called her a filthy name, consideringly, the name a keelie gives to a leering whore; and turned and walked down the hill from her sight.

The main difference in Gibbon's narrative technique, as he moves from *Cloud Howe* to *Grey Granite*, from Segget to Duncairn, is the widening of the narrative mode, reflecting far more of the characters' views. Chris is more of an outsider than ever; she is peripheral to the action of *Grey Granite*, no real part of Duncairn, working in Ma Cleghorn's boarding-house which itself houses refined and middle class characters, no part of a community, with the crucial exception of Ake Ogilvie. So the double space between sections is a far more important signal now. Among the narrators who may appear are Chris and Ewan of course, Ellen, the maid Meg Watson and her impetuous brother Alick, as well as Bob and anonymous workers. Further, there is a chorus of respectable voices reacting to events with hypocrisy and humbug: among these can be found the Reverend MacShilluck and his housekeeper-victim Pootsy, the self appointed Labour leader Baillie Brown, the Chief Constable, Ake's old companion the Provost, and so on.

The narrative technique here is inventive and unobtrusive. In fact, Gibbon's solution to the problems of this narrative is rather like the solution William Faulkner found to the narrative problems of *As I Lay Dying*. In each case there is a series of mixed individual voices, which Faulkner underlines by naming the speaker each time, while Gibbon leaves his reader to identify the different speakers. Faulkner's narrative emphasises the differences in the Bundren family, the different motives which urge the characters to cooperate in taking their mother's stinking coffin to Jefferson, while Gibbon uses almost the same technique to stress the random loneliness of city life, the lack of relationship between characters.

Chris can be absent now for long passages, and she has almost no connection with any of the action of the book. She has a vividly presented routine in the boarding-house, and works as hard as ever: she watches Ewan and cares for him, guesses much about relationships and does not interfere. The only action in the book that she initiates is the walk in the first section, when she is responsible for introducing Ewan and Ellen and furthering their acquaintance.

The action of *Grey Granite* is more obviously dramatic than those of *Sunset Song* and *Cloud Howe*: it involves violence, the march of the Broo men, their riot and Ewan's intervention to increase the violence. It involves strikes and beatings, treachery and betrayal, explosions and fire, and the final venture on a hunger march to London. There is still comedy of a sort, the comic adventures of Mr. Piddle and his work for the *Tory Pictman*, and Ake Ogilvie's tale of the Saturday outing of the Duncairn Council to High Scaur Hill, but the comedy always subserves a grim view of human behaviour.

Chris is a convincing character but peripheral to the action: Ewan fails to convince. But the action of *Grey Granite* is most strikingly conveyed by nameless characters. Gibbon invites the reader to share in the action, in the experience of the anonymous worker, discovering the tough facts of industrial life. The description of the marching Broo men marvellously catches a mixture of commitment and embarrassment:

> And all the march spat on its hands again and gripped the banners and fell in line, and looked sideways and saw the pavements half blocked, half Duncairn had heard of the march on the Town House – and och, blast it if there wasn't the wife again, thin-faced, greeting, the silly bitch, making you shake like this, the great sumph, by the side of those oozing creashes of bobbies, shining capes in the rain.
>
> (GG, Epidote, 394 - 5)

The build up to the murder of old Johnny Edwards holds real excitement:

> And then the fight cleared from its stance by the gates and went shoggling and wabbling over to the Docks, the dozen scabs held firm enough, the bobbies bashing to try and get them and rescue them. Old man though you were, you wouldn't have that, you pushed a foot in front of one of the bastards, down he went with a bang on the causeys, somebody stepped on his mouth and his teeth went crunch. And there, in the heave and pitch of the struggle, were sudden the

> waters of the Dock, dirt-mantled, greasy in oil from the fisher-fleet, the lights twinkling low above it, folk cried *In with them! Dook the scab swine!* (GG, Apatite, 439 - 40)

Arguably, the rendering of the experience of these anonymous workers is a unique fictional achievement.

Suggestions for further reading:

Two books have been devoted to Gibbon. The first, *Leslie Mitchell: Lewis Grassic Gibbon* by Ian S. Munro (1966) is a biography, and the second, *Beyond the Sunset: A Study of James Leslie Mitchell (Lewis Grassic Gibbon)* (1973), is a critical account of both the Scots and the English novels. There are interesting discussions in F.R. Hart, *The Scottish Novel: A Critical Survey* (1978) and articles in the *Scottish Literary Journal* by Ian Campbell (1 (2) 1974, 45-57) and Patricia J. Wilson (7 (2) 1980, 55-79) and in *Studies in Scottish Literature* (11 (1) 1964, 45-55) by David Macaree. Cairns Craig provides a stimulating reappraisal in 'The Body in the Kitbag: History and the Scottish Novel', *Cencrastus*, no. 1 (1979), 18-22.

Note:

1. For example, Douglas Young prefers *Grey Granite*, F.R. Hart prefers *Cloud Howe*. References by initials to the three novels of the *Quair* are to the one-volume edition of 1967, published by Hutchinson, in which the novels are paginated consecutively.

EDWIN MUIR AS A POLITICAL POET

Thomas Crawford

In Britain, as I write, over three million persons are unemployed. In Scotland, hearts are faint and spirits are low three years after the devolution referendum; the nation seems in limbo, with little will to seek Scottish solutions to Scottish problems. In Poland, social heroism and public virtue have once more been brutally assaulted; once more, an imposed communism has been shown to be morally and politically misshapen. And in every corner of the world, more insistently than at any time since the nineteen-fifties, people are haunted by fears of the violent destruction of all civilisation.

These issues have been with us in one form or another for more than half a century. And they were the concern, far more vividly and more profoundly than with any other writer featured in this book, of that most cosmopolitan of northerners, the Orkney-born Edwin Muir (1887-1959). It is a fact that seems quite extraordinary in view of Muir's reputation as a bookish symbolist and dreamer of mythical dreams, remote from the world of the senses: a writer whose sensitivity has been suspect as alien to the hopes and struggles of ordinary people. Yet a fairly large part of Muir's output can be described as, broadly speaking, political with social overtones. Muir often touches on the 'burning issues' already mentioned: unemployment, the plight of Scotland and other small nations, the anti-humanism of modern tyranny the threat to man's future and the continuance of life on earth. He wrote political poetry from the very beginning of his literary career. Thus some of his contributions to the periodical *The New Age* between 1913 and 1916 were 'versified propaganda on current politics, much what any clever young angry man might write.'[1] As late as the nineteen-thirties he could find release from the frustrations of those dismal years in experiments in modish political satire, like the two untitled, deliberately crude and almost Brechtian pieces about the contrast between the undernourished workless and the well-fed bourgeoisie and Church of Scotland ministers, which he published in 1935 in *Scottish Journey* (100, 152).

These two pieces on unemployment were not included in *Collected Poems*.[2] There was, however, a third poem in the travel book, the lines now entitled 'Scotland's Winter' (CP, 229), which rises far above the propaganda level. It was published again twenty-one years later in *One Foot in Eden* (1956) with the change only of one word from the 1935 text; and what marks it off from the two polemical pieces, apart from details of poetic technique, is the degree of aesthetic distancing involved. As Muir himself tells us, the poem had its origins in his 'impressions of Edinburgh, or rather of historical Scotland, my feeling of the contrast between its legendary past and its tawdry present' (*Scottish Journey*, 38). That contrast is made stronger and more significant by the trick of removing the present itself back some distance into the past. The winter season is symbolic of Edinburgh's and Scotland's political spirit because it is cold and frozen; it is rendered poetic by being personalised in a heroic, feudal way. The sun is 'helmed in his winter casket' like a warrior of the olden time 'and sweeps his arctic sword across the sky' (ll. 2-3). The 'tawdry present' is not, in the poem, embodied in 'the tastelessness and vulgarity' of the tearooms which are so mercilessly described in the Edinburgh chapter of *Scottish Journey* (20-22), or in the women who frequent them, whether bourgeois customers or proletarian waitresses, but in a slattern whom Muir has deliberately archaised. She was born, we feel, long after Percy and Douglas and Bruce (introduced into the poem as symbols of a vanished glory), yet she still belongs to the pre-industrial world:

> The miller's daughter walking by
> With frozen fingers soldered to her basket. (ll 7-8)

The dead heroes of Scotland, the bards and singers of feudal times

> Listening can hear no more
> Than a hard tapping on the sounding floor
> A little overhead
> Of common heels that do not know
> Whence they come or where they go
> And are content
> With their poor frozen life and shallow banishment. (ll. 22-8)

At first the miller's daughter seems an inappropriate symbol for what is keeping down the almost mythical heroes who stand for Scotland's spirit. That one word 'common' (l. 25) is surely a blemish: there is a trace of snobbery, of the arrogance of that Nietzscheanism which once dominated Muir's thinking.[3] Yet even so the girl cannot help her commonness. She is not herself responsible for what makes her jeer: she is ignorant, but has not herself chosen her ignorance, her 'frozen life' that is banishment from everything genuine and true in the *polis*, the nation and the tribe. Judged by purely technical canons – rhythm, versification, handling of assonance and alliteration, the manipulation of syntax and imagery, 'Scotland's Winter' is a triumph. Its dominant emotions are not anger and contempt, but sorrow and an aching heart for a land that is kingless and songless and whose people are spiritually dead. The fine last line ('With their poor frozen life and shallow banishment') shows that the poem has worked through to compassion for the miller's daughter and all she stands for. In the poem, distancing is achieved by the operation of what I can only call the cultural imagination – by the same order of insight shown in a remarkable prose passage that likens the psychological condition of the unemployed to the mood of the Cave of Despair in *The Faerie Queene (Scottish Journey*, 140-4). The ice in 'Scotland's Winter' is a heraldic beast that would not be out of place in Spenser; it has claws; the sun's helm and casket call up Arthurian associations; Percy, Bruce and Douglas are epic figures; the miller's daughter also fits into such a world. But the community about which the political statement is made remains particular; it is unmistakably Scotland; no *explicit* comparison is made with towns like Trieste or Stettin, as is done in the expository prose of the volume in which it first appeared (*Scottish Journey*, 27-8); the pity and sorrow in the author's voice are for his own country, fallen from a high estate. And the cultural imagination at work is at almost the opposite pole from the archetypes of dream which are generally thought to be Muir's special creative medium.

I use the word 'fallen' advisedly, for it touches a concept central to Muir's mental life, that of a cultural and historical Fall, present much more explicitly in 'Scotland 1941' (*The Narrow Place*, 1943; CP, 97). Here Scotland in the Middle Ages before the Reformation lives in an agrarian golden age, an age of folk balladry (conveyed by 'the green road winding up the ferny brae', l. 7, with its allusive reference to the ballad of 'Thomas Rymer', Child No. 37). It is the coming of Calvinism, to which Muir devoted an entire book, his prose biography *John Knox* (1929), that constituted the cultural Fall in Scotland:

> But Knox and Melville clapped their preaching palms
> And bundled all the harvesters away,
> Hoodicrow Peden in the blighted corn
> Hacked with his rusty beak the starving haulms.
> Out of that desolation we were born. (ll. 8-12)

If there is perhaps something of a sneer in the hoodicrow image for Alexander Peden, one of the covenanting martyrs of South West

Scotland in the seventeenth century, Muir nevertheless saw that those very qualities of heroic endurance, that 'courage beyond the point and obdurate pride' which 'made us a nation' in the days of Wallace and Bruce, were the very same ones that 'robbed us of a nation' (ll. 13-14) in the epoch of the Reformation and its seventeenth-century aftermath:

> Defiance absolute and myriad-eyed
> That could not pluck the palm plucked our damnation. (ll. 15-16)

To respond to the full emotional resonance of these lines one must be aware of a creative allusiveness in the poem reaching back to Books I and II of *Paradise Lost*, identifying Satan and his host of rebel angels with the revolutionary energy of Knox and the Covenant, and equating both with a Fall that has to be condemned and mourned at the same time as the positive bravery of devils and covenanters is admired. In 'Scotland 1941' Calvinism is indissolubly linked to the rise of capitalism, an idea that was commonplace in Labour and Communist party branches in the nineteen thirties and forties. The bravery of Montrose, Mackail, Argyle produced, says Muir's poem, 'this towering pulpit of the Golden Calf' (l. 34), which in its turn gave rise to cities like Glasgow 'burning in their pit' (l. 23) for profit, 'spiritual defeat wrapped warm in riches' (l. 31). Behind the concentrated poetic expression of these lines lie the horrors of Muir's years in Greenock and Glasgow, so memorably described in *An Autobiography* (90-150), and the poem ends with compassion for those Adams who wrought Scotland's historic Fall, the heroes of the Covenant themselves. But its backward-looking regret does not descend to the sentimental:

> Such wasted bravery idle as a song,
> Such hard-won ill might prove Time's verdict wrong,
> And melt to pity the annalist's iron tongue. (ll.39-41)

What saves the concluding lines is the witty conceit, the pun that blends together the ideas of melting emotions and white-hot metal, making the historian into an inexorably tolling bell and turning his organ of speech into a sonorous metal pendant.

The title poem of the 1943 volume, *The Narrow Place* (CP, 101), is the crystallisation of Muir's poetry of small nations and communities. Though the place is not named, one feels that Muir's experience of Orkney, Scotland and pre-war Czechoslovakia is profoundly and weightily present. The ground is 'parsimonious' (l. 22) and is 'so proud and niggardly and envious' (ll. 26-7) that it will allow

> Only one little wild half-leafless tree
> To straggle from the dust. (ll. 28-9)

If the landscape of 'The Narrow Place' is a dream landscape, the cultural imagination, fed by Muir's historical reading and by his experience of more than one *polis*, has been at work in the vision, side by side with forces from the unconscious mind and from religious myth. Just as in 'Scotland 1941' there was a positive – the ambivalent heroism of the Calvinist mártyrs – so in 'The Narrow Place' there is a positive, a more complex one. It has three aspects. First, under the stunted tree

we sometimes feel such ease
As if it were ten thousand trees
And for its foliage had
Robbed half the world of shade. (ll. 30-3)

Second, it is only when we sleep beneath the tree that we are truly able to see (ll. 38-42). And third, when we finally awaken we will behold

the club-headed water-serpents break
In emerald lightnings through the slime,
Making a mark on Time. (ll. 45-7)

Long before we have reached its threefold positive the poem has moved completely away from politics. The last image is one from the unconscious, fortified by memories of 'The Ancient Mariner', on to which has been grafted a metaphysical concept not completely integrated into the rest of the poem.

Another kind of poetry which Muir sometimes attempts is the poetry of imagined political experience, where the historical imagination is at work alongside the cultural, and where the poet identifies with individuals and groups in a political context. All the poems of this type feature 'man's inhumanity to man'. In 'Troy', for example (CP, 71), an old man has been left behind in the sewers after the sack of the city, his arms now meagre as a boy's with famine, scouring for scraps and fighting the rats in his delirium, taking them for Greeks. At last he is dragged to the surface by 'some chance robber' (l. 21):

They stretched him on a rock and wrenched his limbs,
Asking: 'Where is the treasure?' till he died. (ll. 28-9)

The poem speaks powerfully to an age where torture is the reward of the defeated and an instrument of policy. In 'A Trojan Slave', also from the 1937 volume (CP, 72), the speaker gives voice to the plight of many a nation whose ruling classes drag the whole community down with them because they refuse to recognise that the 'lower orders' are also part of the nation (ll. 26-9, 45-6). It is the paradigm of a folly that has been repeated again and again throughout history: yet it is more than a historical 'model', it is also a kind of analogue for the Fall. The slave is not, and therefore was not, completely innocent. There is a degree of meanness about his anger against his present Greek masters and against the dimly remembered ruling classes of Troy which is, for all its pettiness, the manifestation of an absolute evil.

Muir returns to the theme in 'The Castle', in the 1946 volume *The Voyage* (CP, 128). The citadel has been betrayed: 'The wizened warder let them through' (l. 20). As in 'A Trojan Slave', there is a twist provided by the character of the speaker:

> I will maintain until my death
> We could do nothing, being sold;
> Our only enemy was gold,
> And we had no arms to fight it with. (ll. 27-30)

The first of the lines just quoted (l. 27) is a signal that all is not what it seems on the surface: the speaker doth protest too much. And in his description of the town before it is taken (ll. 1-15), he unconsciously reveals another cause of the debacle: the garrison's crass and ignorant complacency, a 'flaw' whose role is similar to that of 'spite' in 'A Trojan Slave'. Once again, the reverberations of Adam's fall can be felt throughout a basically political poem. It is a point made much more explicitly in 'The Refugees' (CP, 95), from the 1943 volume *The Narrow Place*:

> A crack ran through our hearthstone long ago,
> And from the fissure we watched gently grow
> The tame domesticated danger,
> Yet lived in comfort in our haunted rooms . . .
> The good fields sickened
> By long infection. Oh this is the taste
> Of evil done long since and always, quickened
> No one knows how
> While the red fruit hung ripe upon the bough
> And fell at last and rotted where it fell. (ll. 1-4, 38-43)

It was not until after the second world war, during and after his period as British Council representative in Prague (1945-8), that Muir wrote his most original political poems. Even 'The Labyrinth' (CP, 163), a difficult poem about psychic unrest, seems in places to forecast the claustrophobic years ahead in central Europe. There are 'deceiving streets', 'rooms that open into each other', and Kafkaesque 'stairways and corridors and antechambers', which at one level are images of mental disturbance, at another connect with the spiritual blight of past fascism and stalinism to come, and at still another are linked to the more general plight of fallen man and fallen woman:

But the lie,
The maze, the wild-wood waste of falsehoods, roads
That run and run and never reach an end,
Embowered in error – I'd be prisoned there
But that my soul has birdwings to fly free. (ll. 66-70)

'The Usurpers' (CP, 187), also printed in the volume titled *The Labyrinth* (1949), ironically presents us with another kind of freedom, that of a materialist protagonist, who thinks he has conquered both superstition and the unconscious:

There is no answer. We do here what we will
And there is no answer. This our liberty
No one has known before, nor could have borne,
For it is rooted in this deepening silence
That is our work and has become our kingdom . . .
It was not hard to still the ancestral voices . . .
And the old garrulous ghosts died easily . . .
In this air
Our thoughts are deeds; we dare do all we think,
Since there's no one to check us, here or elsewhere.
We are free. (ll. 1-5, 7, 9, 11-12, 49)

It seems that Muir was consciously thinking of the Gestapo and SS (*An Autobiography*, 260-1), but the poem might equally have been written of stalinist 'apes of God'.

Another poem in *The Labyrinth* volume, 'The Interrogation' (CP, 182), conveys the reverberations of some sort of spiritual inquest, though at the purely literary level it is a finely imagined rendering of one of the stock confrontations of international revolutionary politics. But the major political poem from the Czech years is undoubtedly 'The Good Town' (CP, 183), which, as Muir himself put it in a broadcast on 3 Sept. 1952, 'is not really about Prague or any other place, but about something that was happening in Europe. Stories of what was occurring in other countries to whole families, whole communities, became absorbed into the poem, which I tried to make into a symbolical picture of a vast change' (quoted in Butter, 223). The 'I' of the poem, one of the old men of the place, asks why his good town has turned into a bad one. Was it because of external events, such as the two wars, or because good rulers were fortuitously followed by evil ones? The protagonist in 'The Castle', discussed above, would have answered 'yes' and postulated a wicked warder to let the bad men in. Not so this speaker. He asks point blank 'Could it have come from us?' (l. 77), and puts part of the blame on the tendency of ordinary humdrum citizens to ape the moral style of those in power.

Say there's a balance between good and evil
In things, and it's so mathematical,
So finely reckoned that a jot of either,
A bare preponderance will do all you need,
Make a town good, or make it what you see. (ll. 89-93)

Good ends perverted by bad means, the tragedy of the whole communist experience, of the God that failed – of any merely secular God, perhaps – is compressed into these lines:

We have seen
Good men made evil wrangling with the evil,
Straight minds grown crooked fighting crooked minds.
Our peace betrayed us; we betrayed our peace. (ll. 99-102)

Yet these same ordinary men can themselves be the vehicles of salvation, as in 'After 1984' (CP, 267) where they 'drove the murdering lies away' (l. 6) after the 'twisting chaos' within their apparently completely conditioned minds had 'turned on itself' (ll. 29-30).

The problem of how the ordinary man can preserve his humanity in a world of lies and Newspeak, where peace means war, love hate, and freedom tyranny, is posed more pessimistically in two pieces on which Muir seems to have been working just before his death, 'Ballad of Everyman' (CP, 290) and 'Nightmare of Peace' (CP, 291): they are clearly different versions of the same poem. Everyman goes as delegate to some peace conference, perhaps one of those that used to be staged by the World Peace Council. A 'battle-plated dove' (? Picasso's) swings from the roof 'in menacing love' ('Nightmare', ll. 8-9; 'Ballad', st. 2), but all is falsehood:

Two days he listened patiently,
  But on the third got up and swore:
"Nothing but slaves and masters here:
  Your dove's a liar and a whore.

"Disguised police on the high seats,
  In every corner pimps and spies."

('Ballad', st. 3, 4).

Everyman leaves in disgust. There is a search for him in a contraption as old and rickety as Icarus' chariot. From aloft a playing field is seen on which two sides are locked in combat. The players change into a beast that ravages the land; then the beast is entirely covered with staring eyes, which in 'Nightmare' are 'all dissolved in a common ring' (l. 43):

And the beast is gone, and nothing's there
  But murderers standing in a ring,

And at the centre Everyman.
  I never saw so poor a thing.

Curses upon the traitorous men
  Who brought our good friend Everyman down
And murder peace to bring their peace,
  And flatter and rob the ignorant clown.
('Ballad', st. 10-11).

In any selection of poems about the atomic threat, Edwin Muir's would occupy a place of great distinction. In 'The Day Before the Last Day' (CP, 300), the second last poem he ever wrote, he contemplates the worst of all possible outcomes, the total destruction of the human race and perhaps of life itself. He writes of the similarities and dissimilarities between men about to perish utterly after a nuclear exchange, and men awaiting the Last Judgment. At first, 'the dark ancestral dreams' (l. 25) tell them that what has happened *is* the Judgment, and they expect to see the dead arise, as in the traditional myth. 'And then a stir and rumour break their dream' (l. 34): it is not God's last day after all, but one they have brought about themselves, through their own technology and their own volition:

Mechanical parody of the Judgment Day
That does not judge but only deals damnation. (ll. 15-16).

They can get no 'sanctuary from grass and root' (l. 37); vegetable nature is expiring (l. 38); there is universal alienation; lovers are estranged; 'the generous do not try to help their neighbours' (l. 44); all 'think only of themselves and curse the faithless earth' (l. 49):

But all are silent, thinking:
'Choose! Choose again, you who have chosen this!
Too late! Too late!'
And then: 'Where and by whom shall we be remembered?'
(ll. 55-8)

Mankind's total self-destruction is also envisaged in 'The Last War' (CP, 282) when we will all

founder on common earth and choke in air,
Without one witness. (ll. 37-8)

The cause of the holocaust is ordinary, petty everyday evil – our inhumanity towards our fellows (the smile of the psychologically maimed, 'splintering a face', l. 45) and our malignity towards nature (the mistreatment even of a single tree, l. 44). If there is an atomic war it will be because we did not take the action necessary

To untwist the twisted smile and make it straight
Or render restitution to the tree. (ll. 74-5)

Such action is certainly personal and moral, but it is also political, involving the restructuring of the commonwealth. In the poem annihilation came because

> We who were wrapped so warm in foolish joys
> Did not have time to call on pity
> For all that is sick, and heal and remake our city. (ll. 76-8)

The personal and moral action open to us, craftsmanship and planting and reaping by which we know

> The simply good, great counterpoise
> To blind nonentity (ll. 70-71)

are not enough. It will not do merely to assert them in the face of evil. The only solution is an extra-mundane one, available even to those who die the atomic death, which Muir adumbrates in a vision of the entire human race passing before 'spirits of earth and heaven' around 'the well of life where we are made' (ll. 79-80). That all the persons in this procession are 'loaded with fear' as well as 'crowned with every hope' (l. 88) saves the ending from trite religiosity, though even so the vision has not been conveyed concretely or forcefully enough to make 'The Last War' a total success.

The second possible outcome of nuclear war – that there will be survivors – forms the background to 'After a Hypothetical War' (CP, 265) and 'The Horses' (CP, 246). In the first of these, anarchy prevails with no sort of social order; it is a world of mud and weeds, murder and obscene mutations, where harmful radiation from beyond the atmosphere can enter more easily than before:

> Even the dust-cart meteors on their rounds
> Stop here to void their refuse, leaving this
> Chaotic breed of misbegotten things,
> Embryos of what could never wish to be. (ll. 12-15)

'After a Hypothetical War' reaches a negative conclusion which, though its content is arguably more limited than the positive ending of 'The Last War', makes it artistically more satisfying. There is an element of distancing at the end which is just right, a detached pity for the human race that is the perfect comment on what has gone before:

> Poor tribe so meanly cheated,
> Their very cradle an image of the grave.
> What rule or governance can save them now? (ll. 24-26)

In 'The Horses', the emphasis is solidly on the positive. 'The seven days' war that put the world to sleep' (l. 2) – seven days of destruction corresponding to the seven days of creation (Butter, 259) – is in the past. A small community has survived, living by some coast. They would refuse to have anything to do with 'that bad old world that swallowed its children quick' (l. 19) if that were at all possible; even if there were oil for their tractors they presumably wouldn't use them. They have gone back to ploughing with oxen, 'far past our fathers' land' (l.30). And then, as suddenly as the outbreak of the seven days' war itself, 'the strange horses came' (l. 32), seeming as

strange to us
As fabulous steeds set on an ancient shield
Or illustrations in a book of knights (ll. 39-41),

because in the machine age even this farming community had grown out of touch with animals. But they are not heraldic beasts only, nor are they purely symbolic; they are real animals, 'creatures to be owned and used' (l. 47). The coming of the horses is utterly unexpected; it has the force of a miracle, and is an objective correlative for the power of miracle in the temporal, fallen world. The most miraculous of all, the 'half-a-dozen colts . . . new as if they had come from their own Eden', are paradoxically the most material, the most earthy; the choice of the monosyllabic verb 'dropped', with its four strongly articulated consonants, three of them vigorous plosives, perfectly conveys the physical reality of their birth – 'dropped in some wilderness of the broken world' (ll. 48-50). The parallel with the messy, material side of Christ's birth is not necessary for our aesthetic understanding of the poem. The horses offer freely to serve the survivors (l. 52). For once, the last line is perfect:

Our life is changed; their coming our beginning,

making a similar point in the context of atomic survival to one Muir had earlier made when writing of fascist and communist tyranny:

No: when evil comes
All things turn adverse, and we must begin
At the beginning, heave the groaning world
Back in its place again, and clamp it there.
Then all is hard and hazardous. ('The Good Town', ll. 95-9).

The difference is that in 'The Good Town' the beginning is to come solely from the survivors' own actions; in 'The Horses' there is help from outside.

A study of the political element in Muir's poetry forces us to reject or at least seriously to qualify the view that sees him as primarily an escapist poet, immersed in an arcane subjectivism. The poems we have examined deal with particular and general aspects of man's inhumanity to man, than which nothing could be muddier or bloodier. (A good example is the image of the rats skipping about in the sewers in

'Troy', ll. 7-8). More specifically, Muir comments on problems that are still among the most insistent facing western man – what unemployment does to the human spirit, the tyranny of right and left, the threat of nuclear war. The remoteness his critics sometimes complain of is the effect of concentrated poetic thought producing its objective correlatives through a type of imagistic generalisation (e.g. 'The Narrow Place', discussed above), and partly of that necessary aesthetic distancing without which political poetry is liable never to rise above the occasional and the ephemeral. Three types of imagination are at work in Muir's poetry – or perhaps it would be more accurate to say that his single imagination has three facets: the cultural, the historical and the archetypal. Myths, symbols and dreams which Jungians would see as coming from the collective unconscious are integrated by the historical and cultural imagination to make statements about the moral and political life of man. These statements from a northerner are addressed to all mankind; and their value, like that of all artistic statements, comes from their *beauty*: 'Beauty is truth, truth beauty', though not quite in the sense meant by Keats, or by his urn.

Suggestions for further reading:

In addition to *An Autobiography*, the following should be consulted as primary biographical sources: *Selected Letters of Edwin Muir*, edited by Peter Butter (London, 1974), and Willa Muir's account of her life with her husband, *Belonging* (London, 1968). *Scottish Journey* was reprinted again in Edinburgh in 1979 (Mainstream), with an introduction by Professor T.C. Smout. Besides *Edwin Muir: man and poet*, Peter Butter's earlier volume, in the Writers and Critics series (Edinburgh, 1962), is still in some ways better as a general introduction than Elgin W. Mellown's in the Twayne series (Boston, 1979). The best book-length critical studies are Christopher Wiseman, *Beyond the Labyrinth* (Victoria, British Columbia, 1978) and Roger Knight, *Edwin Muir: an introduction to his work* (London, 1980). There are signs of renewed interest in Edwin Muir as essayist and Andrew Noble, in a lengthy introduction to *Edwin Muir: uncollected Scottish criticism* (London, 1982) stresses the social orientation of these pieces. It is no accident that his best known prose collection is *Essays on Literature and Society* (London 1949 and 1965), or that his Charles Norton lectures at Harvard were given the socially relevant title of *The Estate of Poetry* (London, 1962). And it is surely significant that when J.M. Bullough reviewed *Scottish Journey* for both *The Daily Record* (22 Oct. 1935) and *The Sunday Times* (27 Oct. 1935) he saw in it a committed socialist message; and that in 1940, when pondering another biography, Muir should have considered tackling John Burns, the leader of the London dockers in the 1880s; R.B. Cunninghame Graham, socialist and nationalist; and James Connolly, whom he termed 'one of the greatest men of his time and one of the most interesting and moving' (To Herbert Read, 29 Feb. 1940, *Selected Letters*, 119).

Notes:

1. Peter Butter, *Edwin Muir: Man and Poet* (Edinburgh, 1966), 56.
2. *Collected Poems* (London, 1952); expanded 1960, 1963. Cited as CP, and all references are to the 1963 edition unless otherwise stated.
3. *An Autobiography* (London, 1964), 121 and *passim*.

THE NOVELS OF NEIL GUNN

G.J. Watson

Neil M. Gunn was born in 1891, in Dunbeath, Caithness, and died in 1973 in Inverness. The son of a Caithness fisherman, he entered the civil service as a young man, and worked as an excise inspector of distilleries in the Highlands and Islands. He resigned in 1937, and devoted himself thereafter to full-time writing. His novels have been highly praised by some of the most eminent critics of Scottish literature. Kurt Wittig, in *The Scottish Tradition in Literature* says that in Gunn's novels

> modern Scottish fiction reaches its highest peak . . . All his strength, his vision, his style comes from his people, from the Scottish tradition, from the Gaelic past, but he applies them to the crucial questions of our time. What he has to say is a concern of all men. Scottish literature here is national, yet knows no national limitations.[1]

And Francis Russell Hart, author of a comprehensive and definitive study of the Scottish novel, remarks: 'For me, Neil Gunn's twenty novels are the finest body of work as yet produced by a Scottish novelist'.[2] Yet, despite this generous and – as it seems to me – merited praise, Gunn's novels are not as well known as they should be even among Scottish readers, let alone those outside Scotland.

A possible reason for this is suggested by that still too prevalent critical dismissal of Gunn's work as 'provincial', despite Wittig's considered rejection of the charge. One would have thought that this hoary old *canard* might have been decently interred by now. Gunn's work is indeed firmly localised, but this is no drawback. His own defence of his choice of a 'small' fictional universe is mediated movingly through the words of Hector in *Young Art and Old Hector*:

> 'I like to be here. You see, I know every corner of this land, every little burn and stream, and even the boulders in the stream. And I know the moors and every lochan on them. And I know the hills, and the passes, and the ruins, and I

> know of things that happened here on our land long long ago, and men who are long dead I knew, and women. I knew them all . . . It's not the size of the knowing that matters, I think', said Old Hector, 'it's the kind of the knowing. If, when you know a thing, it warms your heart, then it's a friendly knowing and worth the having.' (ch. 17)

The warmth of Gunn's 'knowing', which avoids both sentimentality and elegiac nostalgia, is certainly one of the great pleasures to be found in his fictional world. But what is the relation between 'all these stories of poaching and fishing' (as I have heard a student dismissively characterise Gunn's work) and what Wittig calls 'the crucial questions of our time'? This essay will try to suggest that relation more fully later; here, it may be sufficient to draw attention to the dangers of making that kind of 'relevance', narrowly understood, our major criterion in assessing literary worth. Gunn himself, in his philosophic autobiography (or autobiographical 'philosophy'), *The Atom of Delight,* is clearly aware of the limitations of such a standpoint:

> When the poet is accused of escaping to his ivory tower he is being condemned for deserting the contemporary situation and taking refuge in illusion. But by whom? If the accuser is held so fast in the contemporary situation that all outside of it is illusion, then he himself is in his own ivory tower or his steel-and-concrete one. (ch. 44)

When we turn to consider the state of contemporary literature and criticism, another reason for the comparative academic neglect of Gunn becomes apparent. 'Advanced' literary thinking, whether that of the writer or of the critic, has tended in our time to be not only sophisticated but intensely self-conscious. From modernism to post-modernism to post-post-modernism, to the forbidding depths of deconstructionism, 'both the artists and the critics have taken as their subject the problematic status of their own authority to make statements about anything outside the systems of language and convention in which they must write.' (The quotation is from Gerald Graff's important recent book, *Literature Against Itself: Literary Ideas in Modern Society*, Chicago, 1979, 1.) Gunn is cheerfully and bracingly free from this hag-ridden introspective self-consciousness (books about writing books, the book as world, the world as book, post-structural paranoia, etc.) which has increasingly come to dominate our thinking about literature. By contrast, Gunn's work is confidently referential: it directs us unashamedly to that real world out there, to the smell of the cold sea, to the hiss of milk in the pail, to the taste of the hazelnut. All well and good; but this very quality of referentiality poses difficulties for the critic nurtured in the context of Joyce and Eliot, Borges and Beckett, and the oceans of criticism which are directed towards (or lap sluggishly around) such writing. As Gerald Graff puts it cogently:

> Unlike the words for talking about things like 'intertextuality' and 'reflexive structure', the words for describing what literature *says*, what it is 'about', are all marked with the stigmata of squareness and banality. There is no up-to-date jargon for talking about the referential values of literature. The jargon assists chiefly in other enterprises – questioning the possibility of literary truth, or translating that truth into psychology, epistemology, myth, or grammar. What gets lost in the translation as modern literature is assimilated, taught, and popularized, is its critical and explanatory power (13).

The paradox is to be encountered again and again in the teaching of modern literature: the more accessible the writer, the more difficult the critic may find it to discuss him. Gunn has, I think, suffered unduly for not being easily reducible to current critical fashions.

That much invoked, much maligned, and possibly illusory individual, the 'common reader', is – quite rightly – unlikely to find his enjoyment of Neil Gunn's novels dampened by such ink-horn considerations. The most immediately apparent quality of Gunn as a writer is his immense *readability*. His strengths as a novelist lie firstly in his descriptive powers – like Conrad and with like success, his task is 'by the power of the written word to make you hear, to make you feel – it is, before all, to make you *see*'.[3] Gunn's descriptions of storms at sea, of hairbreadth escapes, of perilous cliff-climbs, and of the tension and exhilaration of poaching, are all superbly realized and have the power to keep the reader almost literally on the edge of his seat. This is especially true of the two great chapters in *The Silver Darlings*, 'Out to Sea' and 'Storm and Precipice', concerning Roddie's first sailing to the fishing grounds of Stornoway, where we are plunged with the crew in 'countless herds of tumbling seas':

> For ever he had to be watchful, with stem or stern ready, and when they rose at a slant over a shoulder, Finn could see the backs of the seas, herds of slate-blue backs, racing over the endless wilderness, a sweep of wind round their mighty flanks, like brutes of ocean, hurrying to some far ultimate congregation. But always, from the lowest swinging trough, rising to out-top them, was the boat's stern, steadfast in its own wooden dream. (ch.15)

This whole sequence is as well-done as anything in Conrad, and also illustrates another similarity in its stress on the qualities of the small crew alone in the wilderness of heaving water – as J.B. Caird well says, Gunn is aware of the 'elemental qualities that make civilisation possible – courage, physical and moral, endurance, truth and sincerity, and, above all, loyalty. For Gunn, as for Conrad, betrayal is the ultimate crime.'[4] Similar passages occur in many of Gunn's novels, especially *Morning Tide, Highland River* and *The Green Isle of the Great Deep:* one thinks of Hugh's pride in his father's feat of seamanship in manoeuvring his boat into the dangerous harbour mouth as a storm rages, of Kenn's epic barehanded fight with the salmon, of Art on the run from the enemy – and there are many more. The pleasures of this kind of writing, which pitchforks us out of our 'sedentary trades' into elemental experiences where we may feel, like young Kenn in *Highland River*, 'all our ancestors come at us', should not be under-estimated or undervalued. At this basic level, Gunn's writing is deeply therapeutic, bringing vividly before us the life of action and instinct, attempting unpretentiously to redress (as Lawrence in a different way had attempted to redress) that imbalance between the head and the heart and instincts which Gunn feels is one of the sicknesses of our time.

Secondly, Gunn's novels embody some of the finest evocations of the experiences of boyhood that I know, taking their place in this respect quite without strain alongside the treatment of childhood in Wordsworth and Proust (two major influences whom Gunn acknowledges in *The Atom of Delight*), Dickens, Joyce and Lawrence. Gunn captures superbly the inner dramas of a boy's life, its intensities of resentments, its fears of demonstrativeness (as in Hugh's desperate hope that his sister will not shame him by crying, even though their brother is in mortal danger in the storm in *Morning Tide*), its exhilarations, its groping awareness of the cross-currents of family tensions, its wild bursts of suppressed anarchic laughter (as in the wonderful passage in *Highland River* where the brothers secretly compete with each other in the presence of the parents to see who gets off with speaking the shortest verse in the Bible: *Jesus wept*): above all, Gunn recreates through his depiction of boyhood that sense of the wonder of the world, which enables us in turn to participate in that vision of life where, to paraphrase Coleridge, our minds are awakened from the lethargy of custom and our eyes purged of the 'film of familiarity', which bedims the lustre and dries up 'the sparkle and the dew-drops'. The world of childhood is a private world, but one we all remember; and the lyricism of Gunn's evocation of it never becomes gushing or sentimental because it is so firmly anchored in sharp and precise detail. In *Highland River*, Kenn is thrashed twice in school on the morning after his great triumph in catching the salmon, once for a state of abstraction as he savours the memory (the master's attempt to elicit

Kenn's private reverie here is marvellously and sympathetically done), once for transposing the products of Birmingham and Leicester. One quotation here must suffice to try to convey something of the poetry, realism and tolerant comedy to be found in all Gunn's writing on childhood experience:

> But presently, when the master was taking another class, his spirit crept out again, its tender feelers searching the desk beside him, the room, and, lifting a little, the windows. Beyond the windows space rushed away to a blue sky with moving white clouds. His eyes on his book again, Kenn continued to feel this space, this wide freedom, down in the hollows of which wound the river. Listening acutely, he could hear the far cry of the brown water.
>
> The thrashing freed him from this school life and any obligation to the master; made him whole and secret and hostile. Outside this narrow prison with its captains and kings and their wives and small arms, was the free rushing world of light and earth and water, of which the master knew nothing but of which Kenn knew so much that he could stand up at that moment and tell him something that would astonish him! But he was careful not to smile to himself now. 'Leicester is famous for boots', he said, over and over. 'Birmingham for small arms'. But Birmingham was also famous for bicycles, hardware, rubber goods, edged tools, and other things including steam engines and buttons. And Leicester had hosiery, and machinery too. It was impossible to get a clear vision of Birmingham and Leicester. And unless Kenn saw a thing he could never with certainty remember it. This was all very trying. Particularly when his mind, like a curlew calling far in on the moor, told him the only thing worth remembering in the world, so important that it turned Birmingham, Leicester, and Henry VIII with his wives' heads to dust, was that the Well Pool was famous for its salmon. (ch. 2)

But although Gunn's boys are private, 'whole and secret', they are by no means solitaries or in any way highly specialised in the manner of Joyce's Stephen Dedalus. His third major gift as a novelist lies in his ability to evoke in an unforced and wholly authentic way the realities and the texture of community life. There is the child, then there is the family, especially the father and mother, and this unit is in turn contained within the small but intensely realized living organism of the Highland community with its traditional values and life-style. Father, mother and community all have their larger symbolic, even archetypal, significances in the novels, but again, Gunn's strength is that these significances do not seem imposed at the expense of the living realities of individual person or place. His art is firmly anchored in the everyday, and as Francis Hart puts it, is aware of 'the pitfalls of its own symbolic imagination'.[5] Thus Kenn in *Highland River* reflecting on his father's tendency to assume archetypal status in Kenn's own mind

> is sensitive to false symbolism here, but he knows the man, he sees his face, his eyes, his weathered stone-stillness. All that has happened is that in the acuteness of his vision the inessentials have faded out. The figure may be ageless, but it is a living figure to whom in time past his erratic emotions were directed: who once, in a bitter cold, took Kenn's hands and warmed them in his hair. (ch.4)

The same authenticating detail convinces us of the reality of Gunn's mothers whose stoical enduringness, like the fathers' reticent courage and manliness, might otherwise seem overdrawn – one thinks of Tom's mother in *The Serpent*, 'a waddling creature with an anxious face', whose strength and values are economically and movingly caught in the homely phrases of her letters to Tom, 'Take care of yerself now and see you and be eating all you can'.

The family and the community are inseparable, interpenetrate each other in Gunn's fiction, supported by and supporting a traditional way of life lovingly described with that warmth of which we have seen Old Hector speak above. We are made familiar with the arts and rituals of fishing, crofting, waulking, with the old music and songs, with the festivity of ceilidhs and the bitterness of emigration, with the joys of story-telling and the excitement of ploys connected with poaching: and with a folk-community itself sustained by its own awareness of these traditions. It is no small part of Gunn's achievement to have rendered so convincingly the experiences of a traditional community, experiences which, as George Bruce puts it, may be 'peripheral to urban society' but 'are not peripheral to life'.[6]

The convincingness is all, of course. Gunn knows this way of life from the inside, and it shows. There is no condescension to his material – one thinks of the slightly patronising tone of George Eliot, for example, in the 'rustic' scenes of *Adam Bede*, and of her elephantine attempts at humour. Nor is there the selectivity, the sense of closed doors, that one finds in a writer like Synge. Synge's work is always – it is one of its most genuinely compelling dramatic features – the work of an outsider: his Anglo-Irish inheritance cuts him off from the peasant communities that he so admired and idealised. I have explored more fully elsewhere[7] the effects of this tension (between the desire to belong and the knowledge of separateness) on Synge's art; it is enough here to note that Synge's portrait of traditional Irish communities is distorted – magnificent, but distorted. Such problems simply do not arise with Gunn: his knowledge of what he writes about is not only detailed, but intimate, his dialogue catches perfectly but unobtrusively the reticences of Highland speech and the influence on it of the older tongue, and he also manages to capture what may be called the rhythm of a whole way of life. The total effect is compellingly authentic.

Gunn does not see his traditional community through a roseate haze, of course. Novels like *The Grey Coast, The Lost Glen* and *Butcher's Broom* measure the full impact of the disasters of Highland history not just in terms of economic deprivation and 'things violently destroyed' (in Wordsworth's phrase) but also in more elusive but pervasive psychological terms – the sense of weariness, of the absence of hope, and of lacerating self-contempt which is a marked component in the psyche of 'colonized' peoples. But, while recognising all this, and giving it its due weight, Gunn remains an optimistic writer. He partakes of that enduringness which is such a marked feature of his characters. As he says in *The Atom of Delight*:

> You cannot rub out the whole way of life of a people by manipulating the powers in a charter, not unless you rub out the people themselves. And even if you add a new rent and protect the salmon, the old blood has its memories. (ch.15)

In the novels, Gunn's attitude is refreshingly free of the elegiac nostalgia and hostility to change which marks the work of his distinguished Irish counterparts, Yeats and Synge. In contrast, Gunn stresses in a novel like *The Silver Darlings* the resilience of people even in the midst of the most brutal kind of change. A good part of the pleasure to be derived from that fine novel consists in Gunn's ability to communicate to us something of the exhilarating excitement of the new herring fisheries, of the energies released in that 'busy, fabulous time among the common people of that weathered northern land.' And in *The Serpent*, one of the first details we are shown in the landscape of broom and juniper, whin and wild briar, is a red petrol pump. Tom, the protagonist, has himself introduced 'technology' and machinery into the community which has absorbed it without strain. As an older man, the 'philosopher', he reflects:

> Changes often appeared to be violent, and indeed were so frequently enough, but it was remarkable how, little by little, change was accepted in the lifetime of a man so fully, so fatally, that bitterness itself was forgotten. Children of the dispossessed, grown into men and women, reap, and sing as they reap, on the lands taken from their fathers . . . he saw figures singling their turnips in between the green cornfields on the narrow cultivated lands behind the houses. With their

> slightly bent heads they moved so slowly that it was easy to get the illusion of an inner meaning or design that never changed. (ch. 1)

And later in the novel, when the shepherd remarks '"It will never come back, the old life"', Tom replies (obviously with Gunn's endorsement) '"Yes, it will come back, but not in the old way . . . life will come back . . . with the old warmth"'.

The 'inner meaning or design that never changed', underlies, for Gunn, the surface accidents of history. It is, indeed, hostile to history. Gunn remarks in *Off in A Boat*: 'The Scots are pretty good at history which, perhaps, is why most of them mistrust it. For it is full of facts, most of them ugly'.[8] And in *The Serpent*, Tom reflects to his shepherd friend:

> History has so far been a remembering of the dirty business rather than an understanding of the arts and the way of life of the peaceful generation. I remember Alec Wilson getting a hiding in school one day because he couldn't remember all the high-up intrigues behind the bloody Massacre of Glencoe. The history of the Highlands to us as boys was a sort of enlarged massacre of Glencoe, and we had to remember the bloody bits or get walloped. (ch.14)

The opposition between the 'way of life of peaceful ("prehistorical") generations' and the 'bloody bits' of history is fundamental in Gunn's vision, and leads to a dismissal of history and a corresponding celebration of the historyless community, of the archaic, and of the folk. In *Highland River*, Kenn is introduced by Edinburgh friends to the illuminated Castle on its rock, which suggests the dramatic panorama of Scottish history; but for Kenn the history suggested by the Castle is irrelevant, something which merely flicks the surface of his mind:

> For on this night too . . . substance was given to his belief in the folk, of whom he was one. This belief has accompanied him with an elusive assurance of power. It explains to him why in history he always found the greatest difficulty in remembering the genealogical trees of kings or the dates of dynastic wars. In a profound sense they were of no interest to him. (ch. 17)

This belief in the supreme value of the experience of the folk in turn is related to Gunn's vision, shared with Grassic Gibbon, of the Golden Age. Future and past are linked here, and history obliterated, in the timeless vision, and in this respect Gunn's imagination has clear affinities with those of Edwin Muir and Mackay Brown, while he is more optimistic than Grassic Gibbon – earlier in the novel Kenn muses:

> It's a far cry to the golden age, to the blue smoke of the heath fire and the scent of the primrose! Our river took a wrong turning somewhere! But we haven't forgotten the source. (ch. 11)

For any Highlander, the Clearances are of course one of the really 'bloody bits' of history, and the effects are everywhere tangible. In one sense we can say Gunn is the most impressive historian of the Clearances, in *Butcher's Broom* and *The Silver Darlings* dealing with the subject head-on and in considerable detail. The former novel leads up to, the latter follows upon the event, but in both what we experience is the crashing intrusion of history on the timeless community. What is of critical interest and significance here is that sense of intrusiveness, where history is felt to be simultaneously powerful yet – in a fundamental way – irrelevant. These two novels have a narrative dynamism rarely encountered in Gunn's other fiction (this is especially true of *The Silver Darlings*, and may help to explain why that work is Gunn's most popular book), and this narrative dynamism comes from the drive of history; and yet even here, we can perceive that Gunn seeks to look beyond history. His characterization, for example, moves consistently from the particulars of time and place towards the archetypal and legendary, as in the famous sentence from *Butcher's Broom*:

> In the centre of this gloom was the fire, and sitting round it, their knees drawn together, their heads stooped, were the old woman, like fate, the young woman, like love, and the small boy with the swallow of life in his hand. (ch. 2)

(We may recall here Gunn's remark to Francis Hart that 'there is very little of the Clearances in *Butcher's Broom*. The tragedy is the destruction of a way of life, and the book is more about what is destroyed'.)[9] And in *The Silver Darlings*, something analogous occurs in the association of Catrine with the land and the past, and of Roddie with the sea; and beyond that, as Alexander Scott says, 'the characters appear as archetypes because they see one another as such'.[10] Finn at the end of the novel retreats to the ancient House of Peace, imagines himself as 'a white-haired old man, head of a tribe', and is encompassed by the 'immemorial calm' of the knoll. The two novels, then, use history and yet seek to deny its ultimate significance.

There is nothing wrong with this, of course. But Gunn's vision raises major problems of the novelist's art. Francis Hart in the preface to his monumental *The Scottish Novel* speculates on 'the haunting possibility that Scottish culture has features inimical to the novel.'[11] And certainly in the case of Gunn we can see that the distrust of history runs alongside, or produces, inevitably, a distrust in narrative. Cairns Craig, in a stimulating and thoughtful article,[12] identifies an underlying pattern in many twentieth century Scottish novels

> which oppose a static community, by-passed by the mainstream of history, to a world beyond whose essential meanings are defined by history. The opposition is not only of thematic interest, it is the key to central problems of narrative techniques within the tradition of the Scottish novel.

This is so because it may be argued that 'all history is founded upon the processes of narrative', as W.B. Gallie insists in his *Philosophy and the Historical Understanding* (London, 1964); to distrust history, to ignore it, or to feel that one has no access to it, clearly poses problems for the novelist's narrative strategies and impulses. As Craig puts it, speaking of the two major examples of 'intrusive history' in the Scottish novel, the Clearances and the First World War:

> What Scottish novelists have had to do again and again in recent times is to link their novel to some moment of historical dynamism which intrudes upon the historyless Scottish community: Scotland can only be known in these moments when narrative possibilities are forced upon a society that has lost all sense of its own narrative.

The argument about whether Scottish culture is, or feels itself to be, divorced from history, without a 'sense of its own narrative', cannot be gone into here; but certainly in Gunn's two great 'historical' novels, the sense of disjunction between the storyless community and the narrative of history is strong. In *Vanity Fair*, Thackeray writes of Amelia:

> So imprisoned and tortured was this gentle little heart, when in the month of March, Anno Domini 1815, Napoleon landed at Cannes, and Louis XVIII fled, and all Europe was in alarm, and the funds fell, and old John Sedley was ruined. (ch. 18)

Here the domestic and the historic are coupled effortlessly in a manner characteristic of the art of the whole massive novel. Compare Gunn's sense of the baffling distance between the domestic and the historic in this passage from *Butcher's Broom:*

> Here where they made their own clothing, their own shoes, built their houses, produced their food and drove a few cattle to market to get coin to pay rent, surely the forces that had so shut them in could do without them and forget them. It could hardly be within God's irony that a world which had forgotten their very tongue should be concentrating all its

> forces of destruction upon them. What could the pride and power of emperors have to do with this little pocket of self-sufficing earth lost in the hills, this retreat, this end of an age, this death of a culture which a millenium before had been no more offensive to the nations of the West than to set Christianity and learning amongst them? (ch. 1)

Insofar as in *Butcher's Broom* and *The Silver Darlings* Gunn has to take account of the destructive but dynamic intrusions of history we have novels with strong narrative patterns. But ultimately, as has been shown, Gunn opposes to history 'the inner meaning or design that never changed' and that is associated with the archaic, the folk and the idea of the golden age. There is certainly a lack of narrative momentum in most of Gunn's other novels, and in many of them (one thinks of *The Lost Glen, Wild Geese Overhead, The Drinking Well, The Key of the Chest, The Shadow, The Silver Bough* and *Bloodhunt*) the plots are either somewhat melodramatically contrived or are asked to carry a disproportionate amount of discursive political or philosophical analysis. But, on the other hand, we may query-especially since the impact of great modernist novels such as *Ulysses* – whether the novelist need commit himself wholly to a pattern based on 'the narrative of history'.

Gunn sees time in two main ways. On the one hand, there is the concern with what Hart calls 'primordial place and atavistic time', [13] which has been discussed above. On the other hand, there is his abiding preoccupation with 'the moment of delight' which informs much of his best writing, giving his work its impressionistic, poetic, and epiphanic organisation, explaining the importance of childhood in it, and forming the basis of his critique of the modern world. The moment of delight in Gunn may be related to the powerful epiphanies embodied throughout Wordsworth's *Prelude*, of which the poet says:

> There are in our existence spots of time,
> That with distinct pre-eminence retain
> A renovating virtue, whence . . .
> our minds
> Are nourished and invisibly repaired;
> A virtue, by which pleasure is enhanced,
> That penetrates, enables us to mount,
> When high, more high, and lifts us up when fallen.
> (1850, XII, ll. 208-218).

In these moments, as Wordsworth superbly puts it, 'the hiding-places of man's power open'. Indeed Gunn is an extremely Wordsworthian novelist – he too can say

> Fair seed-time had my soul, and I grew up
> Fostered alike by beauty and by fear.

For him too, 'life's morning radiance hath not left the hills'; and for him, too, the child is father of the man. Wordsworth could be describing Gunn's boys in *Morning Tide, Highland River* and *Young Art and Old Hector* when he writes of his own companions that they were 'fierce, moody, patient, venturous, modest, shy'.

The moment of delight – in the beauty of nature, in the achievement of a daring deed, in the sheer physicality of being, or in the sudden perception of 'belonging', whether to family or to the land – is dotted all over Gunn's early fiction, even in 'dark' novels like *The Grey Coast* and *The Lost Glen*. But it becomes an explicit and central issue first in *Highland River*. Kenn's quest for the source of his river is also a quest for the source of delight. It is Gunn's supreme achievement to realize so vividly, in this novel and in many others, such moments. Nearly twenty years after *Highland River*, he devotes almost the whole of his last work, *The Atom of Delight*, to an explicit consideration of the value-system based on the moment of 'sheer unconditional delight'. Large philosophical considerations are indeed involved, but Gunn's strengths lie in his essentially literary commitment to what Henry James calls 'solidity of specification'. As he says in that last book:

> What is this delight in its own moment, beyond consideration of thought, morals, politics, religion? Is it possible to hunt it out, to see how it happens, to realize how and when it comes about? And in the process to avoid as far as possible abstract words, as a naked boy avoids obstacles in his way when hunting a salmon in a pool? (ch. 1)

From the moment of delight comes the liberation of what Gunn calls 'the second self', a deep core of the personality that lies outwith the superficial social self, and is unbroken and unbreakable. This second self is attuned to the realities of 'primitive' vision, is freed from the 'meddling intellect' which – as Wordsworth, again, puts it – murders to dissect, and is instinct with a sense of the organic wholeness and harmony of life; yet all this is not speculation but is rooted in the tangible and the natural, as a passage in the *Atom of Delight* that can stand for many in the novels shows:

> The young savage of the Strath, then, was off and away from precisely everything that confined the culturally conditioned young boy of Combray [in Proust's great novel]. He burst loose and raced so fast that in a real sense he raced beyond himself, he left himself behind. And the self he left behind was the self that knew grown-ups, restrictions, home lessons and other home tasks. It was as if he had two selves and found the second self after going through the speed barrier. (ch. 12)

The second self has access, then, to the moment of delight which, as Douglas Gifford well says, 'blesses the human condition', [14] but also to a fundamental freedom. I have already praised Gunn's depiction of boyhood for its authenticity, but boyhood is more important to Gunn as a symbol of a life-enhancing state of freedom than as a catalyst for memory. As he says in *The Atom of Delight*:

> This sheer tenacity of the inner core of himself, the second self as I have called it, is remarkably strong in a boy, if not indeed imperishable. (ch. 12)

Opposed to this spontaneity and 'private' freedom, to be found especially but not exclusively in boyhood, is what, for Gunn, is true evil: the analytic, self-destructive, scientific intellect that has cut itself free from all emotion. As Nan writes to her lover, the coldly cerebral Ranald in *The Shadow*:

> I'm afriad . . . of those who think and *think only* . . . We need efficiency, we need certainty, we need thought more than anything . . . . If only we could also keep our eyes real eyes . . . . Don't you see the awful thing that has happened to us, the awful curse on us? Don't you see that I can hardly write two sentences without going all self-conscious and wanting to explain? . . . . We have murdered spontaneity . . . . The faces of analysts, everywhere; with bits of matter on slides, saying: That's all it is. And we wonder about war and horror! About murderers! (Part one, 19, 28)

The opposition between the moment of delight and all that it implies and the deathly analytic intelligence is explicit in this novel (indeed perhaps too explicit for the novel's entire success); but it is a theme which underlies all of Gunn's later fiction, and is articulated with superb success in *The Green Isle of the Great Deep*. This has been discussed extremely well elsewhere[15]; I have only space left here to say that Gunn shows here and throughout his work the relevance of his values to our totalitarian and murderous age, and delivers himself of the charge of escapism. 'Wisdom, knowledge, magic, love, these are the elements that exist within man but that have been so repressed . . almost entirely usurped by man's will-to-power and his unloosing of his rational and administrative faculties'.[16] It is a major theme in twentieth century art. What is refreshing in Gunn's treatment of it is his refusal to give himself over to the pessimism of writers like, say, Orwell, whose *Nineteen Eighty Four* is as bleak as Gunn's *Green Isle* is fundamentally optimistic. Nor does Gunn align himself with a writer like D.H. Lawrence in urging submission to the 'dark gods', the forces of 'blood' and the flesh. The optimism and the sanity of his vision in both these respects is intimately connected with his rootedness in the sustaining cultural context of the small Highland communities he knows best. From the strength of that cultural inheritance, however damaged it has been by the ravages of history, Gunn can survey the modern world. Wisdom, knowledge, magic and love – the talismanic words of *The Green Isle* – these are the values that Gunn's works offer his readers, in abundance.

Suggestions for further reading:

The most useful critical material on Gunn can be found in *Essays on Neil M. Gunn*, ed. David Morrison (Thurso, 1971), *Neil Gunn: The Man and the Writer*, ed. Alexander Scott and Douglas Gifford and the chapter on Gunn in Francis Russell Hart, *The Scottish Novel: A Critical Survey* (London, 1978). A major critical biography by Francis Russell Hart and J.B. Pick, *Neil Gunn: A Highland Life*, was published by John Murray (London) in late 1981, after the completion of this essay.

Notes:

1 Kurt Wittig, *The Scottish Tradition in Literature* (Edinburgh and London, 1958), 333, 339.
2 'Beyond History and Tragedy: Neil M. Gunn's Early Fiction', in *Essays on Neil M. Gunn*, ed. David Morrison, (Thurso, 1971), 52. Gunn's novels are: *The Grey Coast* (London, 1926); *Morning Tide* (Edinburgh, 1931); *The Lost Glen* (Edinburgh, 1932); *Sun Circle* (Edinburgh, 1933); *Butcher's Broom* (Edinburgh, 1934); *Highland River* (Edinburgh, 1937); *Wild Geese Overhead* (London, 1939); *Second Sight* (London, 1940); *The Silver Darlings* (London, 1941); *Young Art and Old Hector* (London, 1942); *The Serpent* (London, 1943); *The Green Isle of the Great Deep* (London, 1944); *The Key of the Chest* (London, 1945); *The Drinking Well* (London, 1946); *The Shadow* (London, 1948); *The Silver Bough* (London, 1948); *The Lost Chart* (London, 1949); *The Well at the World's End* (London, 1951); *Bloodhunt* (London, 1952); *The Other Landscape* (London, 1954). Also important is the autobiographical *The Atom of Delight* (London, 1956). Some of the novels are available in modern paperback editions published by the Souvenir Press, London.
3 Preface to *The Nigger of the 'Narcissus'* (Harmondsworth, 1963), 13.
4 'Neil M. Gunn, Novelist of the North', in *Essays on Neil M. Gunn*, 50-51.
5 'Beyond History and Tragedy', 57.

6 'Handling the Unbearable: *The Serpent* and *The Drinking Well*' in *Neil M. Gunn: the Man and the Writer*, ed. Alexander Scott and Douglas Gifford (Edinburgh, 1973), 217.
7 *Irish Identity and the Literary Revival: Synge, Yeats, Joyce, O'Casey* (London, 1979).
8 (London, 1938), 179.
9 Francis R. Hart, 'Neil M. Gunn: A Brief Memoir', in Scott and Gifford's critical anthology, 37.
10 'Folk Epic: *The Silver Darlings*', in Scott and Gifford's critical anthology, 37.
11 Francis Russell Hart, *The Scottish Novel: A Critical Survey* (London, 1978), viii. See also 326: 'the Highlands and Islands did not – could not – develop anything comparable to the socio-economic urban world that had served elsewhere as a pre-condition to the rise of the novel . . . The classic novelist's preoccupation with self and society was not a crux of moral identity. Rather, the crux was self and land, or self and archaic community, or self and suppressive theocracy.'
12 'The Body in the Kit Bag: History and the Scottish Novel', in *Cencrastus* 1 (1979), 18-22.
13 *The Scottish Novel*, 349.
14 'The Source of Joy: *Highland River*', in Scott and Gifford's anthology, 118.
15 See, for example, Hart in *The Scottish Novel*, 360-362; and Andrew Noble, 'Fable of Freedom: *The Green Isle of the Great Deep*' in Scott and Gifford's anthology, 175-216.
16 Noble, *art. cit.*, 196.

ERIC LINKLATER AS COMIC NOVELIST

Andrew Rutherford

When one of my colleagues, a contributor to this collection, admitted to me that he had never read any works by Eric Linklater, I politely refrained from comment but suggested that he might try *Juan in America* or *Private Angelo*. This advice stemmed from my own conviction that Linklater is at his best a comic novelist – a categorisation which may partly explain his current neglect. One of his early school reports read, 'On the whole he is doing fairly well, but is handicapped by a sense of humour'[1]; and this bias towards solemnity is not confined to pedagogues. The literary critic like the cultural nationalist retains a predilection for high seriousness, even for the portentous; whereas Linklater was in Auden's terms a follower of Hermes rather than Apollo.

The sons of Hermes love to play,
And only do their best when they
Are told they oughtn't;
Apollo's children never shrink
From boring jobs but have to think
Their work important.[2]

This alignment dates even from his days at Aberdeen Grammar School, which he attended from 1913 to 1916: 'Dirty-fingered,' he recalls, 'we sat at our desks – rough with deep-cut initials – and gave glum attention to *Samson Agonistes* and *The Cause of the Present Discontents*; but [the statue of] Byron, through the window, undid the schoolroom teaching that literature must be a solemn thing.'[3]

The central question about Linklater the novelist is whether his art mediates a comic vision which by a familiar paradox compels serious (though not solemn) attention, or whether it simply provides light entertainment. I would argue that at its best – but only at its best – it does the former.

He deliberately chose authorship as a career, but he also deliberately chose to stand outside the main literary movements of his day (which may be another reason for his falling out of academic favour). After war service in 1917-18 and a protracted period of study at the University of Aberdeen, first, unsuccessfully, in Medicine, then more auspiciously in Arts, he had spent two years in Bombay as an assistant-editor of *The Times of India*, and a further year in Aberdeen as Assistant to the Professor of English, his old mentor Adolphus Jack. Then came two years in the U.S.A. as a Commonwealth Fellow (1928-30). Based initially at Cornell, Linklater was ostensibly engaged in research on Elizabethan-Jacobean comedy, the kind of study, as he observes, that might have recommended him for employment in a provincial or Canadian university. 'But,' he goes on, 'I had already turned my back on a journalistic career in India, and now I dismissed all thought of a scholarly future. I determined to be a novelist . . . .'[4]

His first, rather awkward attempt at a novel, *White Maa's Saga*, had just been accepted for publication, and he had embarked on his second, the light-hearted but more accomplished *Poet's Pub*. Linklater wrote it, he tells us, 'with a total though not grave commitment'[5]; and the phrase can be applied more generally to his works, since throughout his career he took his writing very seriously in some ways, much less so in others. 'I am, of course, a serious writer,' he maintained in 1970: 'that is to say, I have always shown a proper respect for the language in which I write, a respect which is no longer general, nor even much applauded.'[6] Yet for all his careful craftsmanship he saw himself primarily as an entertainer, a provider of what he once called 'civilised amusement'. There is surely an element of wry self-portraiture in his presentation of Kyle, the once-popular novelist in *Roll of Honour* (1961):

> There's not much appetite [says Kyle] for what I used to write. I was never much given to causes, you see; unless you can accept tradition as a cause. In Western Europe there was a tradition, very painfully established, that the growth of civilisation encouraged the growth, enclosed in it, of civilised amusement; and another tradition that the proper use of language was a prime factor in the entertainment of civilised people. I never set myself up as a prophet or a preacher . . . but I've been loyal to two things: the English language and a liberal view of our need for entertainment.[7]

Linklater's own fiction is traditional in a further, that is to say a formal sense. He shows throughout a sense of style and a scrupulosity of craftsmanship (marred only by occasional early lapses into fine writing) which are themselves a source of pleasure to the reader, but he has little or no interest in technical innovation. In his first volume of autobiography he makes fun of the very conventional verses which he and his fellow-students had written at Aberdeen in the early 1920s:

> In the south, about this time, a new sort of poetry was stirring, a serious and disintegrated kind that reflected, but failed to synthesise, the spirit of the time: the broken thread, the frosty perception of wasted soil, the grim colloquialism, the bright skin of a scar new-healed but aching. The fashion, however, did not reach Aberdeen. We were remote from the contagion of intellect, and remained unserious, old-fashioned, and conventional.[8]

This assertion of provincial ignorance was, however, more a rhetorical flourish than a statement of fact. A later volume of autobiography makes it clear that he and some of his contemporaries were introduced to 'the brand-new verses of T.S. Eliot' by 'a young lecturer, Claud Coleer Abbott, a scholar and a good minor poet, who was aware of strange happenings in the south, and rebel movements in literature.'[9] These, however, made little impact on Linklater, whose impulses to rebellion were of a different nature. In *Poet's Pub*, which was published in 1929 (and which was later to be chosen by Allen Lane as one of the first ten titles to appear in Penguins), the poet-hero is resolutely old-fashioned in technique, and there are recurrent jokes at the expense of highbrow authors and reviewers. Even more outspoken are the comments on modern poetry in *Magnus Merriman* (1934), which has a dismissive reference to Eliot, an amusing parody of Hugh MacDiarmid, and an unflattering description of the movement as a whole: 'The poets of the post-war world were fairly united in their belief that poetry, to be poetical, must be unrhythmical, unrhymed and unintelligible: and by these standards their output was of a high order.'[10] Linklater's novels assume an intelligent, educated, highly literate but middle-brow reading public, and he shares with it a suspicion of the highbrow, an hostility to modernism in literature. This is partly due to the obscurity resulting from the modernist preoccupation with formal experiment. He was always mindful himself of a dictum of Adolphus Jack's: ' "A writer," he said, "should remember his manners, and for a writer the best of good manners is clarity. Clarity is also the debt he owes to his readers." '[11] It was in this spirit that Linklater praised Stendhal in a newspaper interview in 1951:

> He has the courtesy to make his story and his purpose as clear to his reader as labour and talent can achieve; but clarity and courtesy are not typically our present mode. He has, too, the traditional belief in the necessity of a managed

> story, and in the value of characters whom the reader can accept as credible and whose activities will hold the reader's interest; but this is not a faith that gets much respect from the intellectual writers of today.[12]

Linklater had, however, more fundamental reservations about writers of the *avant-garde* – objections which he tried to formulate when, flying to Australasia in 1951 to lecture on modern literature, he wondered what on earth he was to say:

> 'It has been a time of experiment,' I shall tell my audiences [he decided]. 'Not of absolute achievement – except in Ireland, where Joyce wrote a comic nonesuch – but of delicate trial and scrupulous exploration. A time of doubtful but conscientious authors with no great stomach for life (and who shall blame them?) but very sensitive fingers and sad, percipient gaze.' – Then I remembered a girl in Sweden, in the spring, a great golden, laughing girl who described a literary party to which she had been taken: 'And there were all the little poets looking at me with frightened eyes!' And that, unfortunately, broke my train of thought. . . .[13]

'Doubtful but conscientious' – 'no great stomach for life' – 'little poets' – 'with frightened eyes': such phrases (and the contrast with the great golden, laughing girl in Sweden, in the spring) modify the concessions of 'delicate trial and scrupulous exploration', 'sensitive fingers and sad, percipient gaze', converting them to items in an overall indictment, which points to an inadequacy in these writers' responses to life, a poverty of perception on their part, a lack of vitality, of zest, of the capacity for joy.

The indictment, whether justified or not, signposts us to qualities in Linklater himself which contributed to the notable success of his third novel, *Juan in America.* All three of his volumes of autobiography are to a significant extent travel books, packed with vivid descriptions and amusing anecdotes. They bear witness to his sense of fun, his eagerness for new experiences, his lively, inexhaustible interest in people and places. ('What a multitude of men you know & like,' Evelyn Waugh wrote, with a touch of envy, after reading *A Year of Space* in 1953.[14]) As a schoolboy he had been avid for 'the great adventure', enlisting in 1914 in a Territorial Battalion of the Gordon Highlanders. When war broke out he was rejected for service because of his eyesight, but in 1917 he contrived to get himself accepted by the Army and posted to France, where he served with the Black Watch until wounded in the course of the German Spring Offensive. As a young soldier he savoured the unique intensities of war experience. 'My few weeks as a sniper,' he recalled years afterward, 'gave to my life an excitement, an intensity, which I have never known since. I have, on the whole, had a happy life, and I have known much pleasure. But in my nineteenth year I lived at a high pitch of purpose, a continuous physical and mental alertness, that has never again suffused my brain and body – and which, in later years, my body and brain could not have sustained.'[15] As a student, his life was one of Bohemian zest, and his activities were multitudinous: he was President of the Debating Society, C.S.M. of the infantry contingent of the O.T.C., editor of the magazine *Alma Mater*, member of the University boxing team, and author of a musical comedy, *Rosemount Nights*, published in 1924. After leaving University he rebelled against the routine drudgery of the professions. By temperament he was more akin to Tennyson's Ulysses ('I cannot rest from travel: I will drink/ Life to the lees') than to the dull but dutiful Telemachus. The appeal of Medicine, he admitted subsequently, was the means it could provide for travel round the world. 'That was my real desire: to see the variety of Asia and America, and the seas around them. I never regarded the practice of medicine as an end, but only as the means of a vagrant livelihood. . . .'[16] Descended from seafarers and farmers on both his father's and his mother's side, he shied away from the life-style of the bourgeoisie. Indeed in several of his early novels we find him toying imaginatively with alternatives – the life of a perpetual student, a poet-publican, a Bohemian author, an Orkney farmer, or in a former age a Viking. But the perfect vehicle for his restlessness, his anarchic aspirations, his delight in life's variety, was provided by the picaresque novel, a traditional form which he revitalises in *Juan in America*. This transposition into modern, trans-Atlantic terms of Byron's comic epic gives us as hero a lineal descendent of Byron's Don Juan – an outsider, sometimes a detached observer, sometimes a passionate participant in the life around him, but a hero footloose, without ties or responsibilities, a modern *picaro* going from adventure to adventure and from one amorous involvement to another. It is based partly on Linklater's experiences and observations while travelling in the U.S.A., and partly on imagination issuing in sheer fantasy. Significantly, however, the fantasy matched that of thousands of potential readers: the creative writer, Stevenson once said, 'shows us the realisation and the apotheosis of the day-dreams of common men. His stories may be nourished with the realities of life, but their true mark is to satisfy the nameless longings of the reader, and to obey the ideal laws of the day-dream.'[17] This *Juan in America* unquestionably does; but it also engages very directly with 'the realities of life' in its affectionate, amused, at times almost anthropological scrutiny of the American way of life – from university football and campus loves to gangsters in Chicago and bootleggers in Detroit, negroes in the deep South, the bizarre phenomena of Hollywood, and burial customs in California (on which, as Linklater observes, he anticipated Waugh's *The Loved One*). The novel is a *tour de force* of comedy, combining the potentially conflicting elements of the anarchic, the satiric and the celebratory.

Juan in America was published in 1931, *Private Angelo* in 1946. Between these comic masterpieces came the rise of Fascism and the Second World War – events which tested the validity and limits of the comic mode as such. After his marriage in 1933 Linklater and his wife lived for a time in Italy; and in Florence he met some early victims of Nazi oppression. 'I . . . was moved,' he tells us, 'by indignation at what I heard from them to write an article, published in an English periodical of the time called *Life and Letters*, in which I spoke with a due and proper anger of the brutality already typical of German politics and German prisons.'[18] This immediately involved him in conflict with his German publishers, and in Italy too he was attacked with some animosity once he had disclosed his dislike of 'Fascism and its grosser practices.'[19] Yet he could still write a completely carefree novel like *Ripeness is All* (1935) – a light-hearted, *risqué* entertainment, unpolitical except for an ironic glance at the Communist and Fascist enthusiasms of public schoolboys, and this 'diagrammatic' poem attributed to one of the characters:[20]

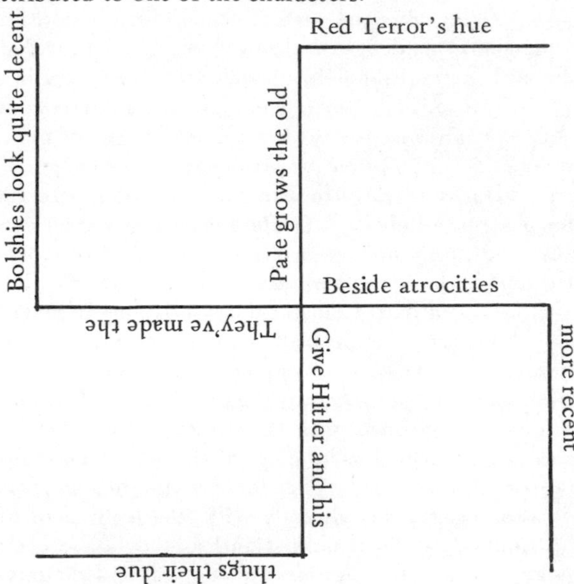

(On the basis of this send-up of experimentalism, Linklater later claimed – tongue in cheek – to have invented concrete poetry.)

Juan in China, however, the sequel to *Juan in America*, raises new problems. Linklater had visited China to get essential background for his story, leaving his wife and family in Orkney, where they had now made their home. On his way to the East he had seen one of Mussolini's troopships *en route* for Abyssinia; and in China itself he had seen something of the consequences of Japanese aggression. Yet he conceived of his new novel as 'a high comedy . . . set in the misery of war'[21] – a juxtaposition which caused some offence at the time, the book appearing as it did in 1937, the year when Japan renewed her attack on China. In retrospect too it seems oddly insensitive. The comedy of Juan's amours is itself less exuberant, less exhilarating, than his former exploits in America; and though the picture of Chinese inefficiency is ludicrous enough, the war can be seen as funny only by adopting a superior and patronising attitude to the participants. How absurd, it is implied, of Chinese patriots like Kuo Kuo to take the whole affair so seriously. There is certainly an element of truth in Bergson's assertion that comedy involves a momentary anaesthesia of the heart; and black comedy, so much in vogue in recent years, is based on the deliberate withholding of compassion from objects which would normally evoke it. Allowance must be made in some cases for deliberate shock tactics and for the implied presence of normative assumptions which remain unstated; but the magnitude of some disasters, the horror of some kinds of suffering, make detached amusement seem an inappropriate response – indeed a diminution of our essential humanity. Linklater's comic conventions cannot, in effect, contain the experiences which he treats in *Juan in China*.

On his return to Britain European political crises, unlike those of the Far East, affected him very deeply. Disturbed by the implications of the Spanish Civil War, disturbed too by the bungling of Western statesmen, he foresaw the outbreak of another major war. And in the cause of sanity, which by a fashionable aberration he identified with pacifism, he wrote *The Impregnable Women* (1938) to discredit the whole idea of war. An adaptation of Aristophanes' *Lysistrata*, it advocates the making of love instead of war, with the women withholding their favours till the men stop fighting. The idea is rich in comic potential, but the execution, as Linklater himself acknowledges, leaves much to be desired. He describes his imaginary war realistically, in terms of his own memories of 1917-18, bringing out both the heroism and the horror; but the women's counter-war is cast in terms of farce and of the mock-heroic, which are at odds with and diminished by the prevailing mode of realism. 'My novel was a failure,' he reflected later, 'because my cure for evil was less convincing than the evil I had evoked'[22]; but a more fundamental problem was that there was evil abroad much greater than the evil that he saw in war itself, and it was an evil that could be met only by war. The betrayal of Czechoslovakia at Munich filled him with moral revulsion, expressed obliquely through his novel *Judas* (1939): and like millions of others at that time he found himself having to reconsider his position.

Significantly, he described his moral dilemma in terms of the claims of alternative literary modes. His earliest allegiance had been to Romance, with its absolute polarities of good and evil and the necessary conflict these give rise to; but this had yielded place to comedy:

> I shall not claim [he wrote in 1941] that the comic view of life is either whole or ultimately satisfying, but it has no less validity than the tragic or romantic view, or what is known as realism. And in the years between the two German wars, the matter of comedy lay upon the world as thickly as forest leaves after a storm. But now [in the later 1930s], against my habit and hostile to inclination, my younger and less comfortable perception was beginning to return.
>
> There was good in the world, though worldly goodness was much blemished; there was evil in the world, though evil could whimper excuses for its birth; and when evil menaced the very existence of good, a man must put away the richness of comedy, the luxury of doubt, and stand with the angels. If victory were won, he could wear his conscience among the battle-ribbons on his coat; and if good were to be defeated, let him go down with virtue . . . .
>
> Now such an opinion, in the view of the comic years, would have been romantic and therefore ridiculous. In the comic years it was permissible – it was almost obligatory – to sympathise with the dragon and denigrate St. George. Dragons, one said, were wily and amusing creatures, while George in very truth was a Cappadocian war profiteer. But now the romantic view wore strangely a utilitarian look. Through stress and battle we must pursue a vision of justice, liberty, and peace, and in the realisation of that vision we should find our safety. We must do battle for the right and save our skins.[23]

In the Second World War his service was, perforce, less active than in the First. From 1939 to 1941 he commanded the Orkney Fortress Company, Royal Engineers. Posted thereafter to the Directorate of Public Relations in the War Office, he wrote pamphlets on several aspects of the Army at War, and also, in his personal capacity, a number of conversation-pieces on war aims. He served in Italy in 1944-45; and in 1951 he was to publish, for the War Office, an interim but fully authorised account of *The Campaign in Italy*, pending the production of the Official History. In that same year, holding the temporary rank of Lieutenant-Colonel, he visited the British forces in Korea on behalf of the War Office, the Air Ministry and the Admiralty; and it was while *en route* from Korea to Australia that he reflected so unfavourably on the writers of the *avant-garde*.

His critique, however, went beyond the points already cited. 'The more intellectual English writers,' he complains, '. . . have learnt a scrupulous, professional exactitude of thought and statement, they have acquired refinement and sensibility, but in their revulsion from all that is hearty and commonplace they have adopted . . . an anti-heroical view of life, when life in our century has demanded and been given, to retrieve its blunders, a dominating character of heroism.'[24] He expounds at length his view that in our century, through the two World Wars and beyond, civilisation has been preserved, the arts have flourished, normal life has been allowed to continue, because of a barrier sustained by the heroism – albeit sometimes reluctant – of soldiers, sailors and airmen. And he sees it as a serious limitation in contemporary writers that they fail to acknowledge this fact and pay tribute where it is due.

Linklater's own tribute is paid, firstly, through his wartime pamphlets and through military history in which he attempts simply to record the facts, as he does in *The Campaign in Italy* and *Our Men in Korea*, hoping that the facts will speak eloquently for themselves. Secondly, through the more confessional mode of autobiography, in *The Man on my Back, A Year of Space*, and above all *Fanfare for a Tin Hat* – the headgear in question being the steel helmet which he was wearing when he was shot in 1918 in the course of a fighting retreat, and which he preserved, with its jagged bullet-hole, for the remainder of his life. Thirdly, one might expect, through his art as a novelist; but as he explains in *A Year of Space*, he knew that the truth of battle could be told only by those who had fought; and he had chosen not to write extensively about the earlier war which he knew at first hand. The mood of the 1920s and 30s had led him, he admits in *Fanfare for a Tin Hat*, to make light of what had been for him 'a major emotional experience',[25] though one gets repeated glimpses of its importance to him in the early fiction. The Second World War, on the other hand, did provide him, through his first-hand observation of events in Italy, with the raw material for *Private Angelo*.

His reverting to the comic mode was partly no doubt a matter of basic temperament and professional habit. Something must also be attributed to the euphoria of victory: even when he began the novel in Rome in August 1944, it was clear that though hard fighting lay ahead, the tide of war had turned irreversibly in the Allies' favour. But comedy was also a means he deliberately chose to preserve emotional control in dealing with the tragic impact of war on the richness and beauty of Italian civilisation. 'War, in Italy,' he wrote afterwards, 'was a drunken, destructive and impertinent clown; to deal justly and truthfully with it one had to keep one's temper cool, one's judgement clear, and write a comedy.'[26] Yet this did not imply an absence of compassion where compassion was due:

> The pleasant little towns along the Appian Way had suffered, quite suddenly, such a change in their appearance as could only have been effected – without the help of science – by long eras of disaster . . . Of all the triumphs that had marched the Appian Way none had so spaciously shown the enormity of human power as this great spectacle of destruction; and the pity was that the refugees could not appreciate it as it deserved. The refugees were unimpressed by the march and majesty of science. They were thinking only about their homes. Tired as they were, and stumbling under their burdens, they hurried on towards their abandoned villages with hope in their straining muscles, hope in their bright eyes. And when they came to their villages, they sat down and wept.[27]

Private Angelo is not, however, in any simple sense an anti-war book. It derives both from Linklater's love of Italy and from his 'deep affection – born of admiration, nurtured by wide friendship – for the Eighth Army'[28]; and these disparate origins make for a conceptual conflict, a profoundly comic interplay of values. At the outset the eponymous hero, very unheroic in his flight from battle, seems a British wartime stereotype of Italian cowardice. Yet he is treated with tolerant amusement by the author, who comes to see him as epitomising Italy's good sense and good temper; and he becomes the spokesman for an alternative view of the Allies' crusade in Europe:

> 'All these people,' said Angelo, 'have been liberated and now they have nowhere to live. And before the war is over you will have to liberate northern Italy and France, and Greece and Yugoslavia, and Holland and Belgium, and Denmark and Poland and Czechoslovakia.'
>
> 'It may take us rather a long time,' said Simon.
>
> 'And when you have finished no one in Europe will have anywhere to live.'

'You musn't exaggerate. It won't be as bad as that.'
'*Speriamo*,' said Angelo.[29]

Nevertheless, the German presence in Italy is real and unquestionably evil. Fest, tortured in concentration camps and now pursuing an obsessive, solitary campaign of retaliation, reminds us of the bestiality of Nazism; and the oafish destructiveness, the wanton cruelty and the arrogance of other Germans, like the Count's gaolers or the temporary garrison of Pontefiori, confirm that this is a just and necessary war. We delight in Italian rascality and cynicism; we delight too in the sexual comedy (so much more humane than in *Catch-22*); but we applaud the carefree gallantry of Simon and his friends, with their nostalgia for the Desert (' "It's ideal country for a war .... You can't do any damage there, except to yourself and the enemy" '[30]), and the more stoical courage of the Army as a whole. If an ironic tone helped Linklater to avoid stridency in dealing with the waste and suffering inevitable even in a just war, it was also a safeguard against sentimentality or overstatement in praising soldiers and their virtues. We glimpse this danger in his panegyrics in *A Year of Space* ('In an age when much has failed and much been broken, only the soldiers have not been insufficient'[31]); but in *Private Angelo* his admiration is agreeably spiced with irony. 'To join and remain in Force 69 it was necessary that an officer should be naturally brave, uncommonly resourceful and know a great number of people by their Christian names.'[32] And his respect for the courage and innate decency of British troops does not preclude a clear-sighted acknowledgement of their peccadilloes, as in the description of a returning battle-patrol:

> The farthest houses had collapsed into grey mounds of rubble, and in a space between them, as if in a small ravine, stood two soldiers of savage and repellent aspect. Their faces were blackened, they wore stocking-caps . . . , their battle-dress was dark and filthy, over their shoulders were slung tommy-guns, and one had a long knife in his belt, the other a bludgeon. Each carried, dangling to the ground, a dead goose and a turkey.[33]

It is another gloss on the significance of 'liberation'.

The comic and heroic coexist in *Private Angelo*. Falstaff and Hal both have their say. The claims of love and war, of appetite and honour, of anarchy and duty are fully acknowledged, and Linklater sees some value in them all. The novel opens with the charge that Angelo lacks the *dono di coraggio*; and though in the interim he has to undergo a transformation, proving himself in battle, in the end he is acclaimed for courage of a very different sort, as he and his companions labour to restore their shattered countryside. The inhabitants of Pontefiori demonstrate a genius for survival and renewal, for love and acceptance; and with the end of the war the heroic modulates to pastoral. Indeed the synthesis established by the novel recalls one of Polonius's complex categories – 'tragical – comical – historical – pastoral'; yet the whole range of experience presented, grim or delightful, absurd or pathetic, is assimilated in the rich human comedy.

Suggestions for further reading:

Linklater on himself:

The Man on My Back. An Autobiography (London, 1941)
A Year of Space: A Chapter in Autobiography (London, 1953)
Fanfare for a Tin Hat: A Third Essay in Autobiography (London, 1970)

Entry in *Who's Who 1975.*

See also the present author's entry on Eric Linklater in the forthcoming 'Supplement 1971-1980' to the *Dictionary of National Biography*.

Notes:

1. *The Man on my Back* (London, 1941), 9.
2. See 'Under Which Lyre', in W.H. Auden, *Collected Shorter Poems 1927-1957* (London, 1966), 221-6.
3. *The Man on my Back*, 10-11.
4. *Fanfare for a Tin Hat* (London, 1970), 104.
5. *Ibid.*, 104.
6. *Ibid.*, 133.
7. *Roll of Honour* (London, 1961), 151-2. Cf. *The Man on my Back*, 199.
8. *The Man on my Back*, 70-1.
9. *Fanfare for a Tin Hat*, 86.
10. *Magnus Merriman* (London, 1934), 72.
11. *The Man on my Back*, 179.
12. *A Year of Space,* Reprint Society Edn. (London, 1954), 9-10.
13. *Ibid.*, 175-6.
14. *The Letters of Evelyn Waugh*, ed. Mark Amory (London, 1980), 390
15. *Fanfare for a Tin Hat*, 67.
16. *The Man on my Back*, 61-62.
17. Robert Louis Stevenson, 'A Gossip on Romance', *Memories and Portraits*, Tusitala Edn. (London, 1924), 123.

18. *Fanfare for a Tin Hat*, 147.
19. *Ibid.*, 149.
20. *Ripeness is All* (London, 1935), 375.
21. *The Man on my Back*, 295.
22. *Fanfare for a Tin Hat,* 159.
23. *The Man on my Back*, 333-4.
24. *A Year of Space,* 173.
25. *Fanfare for a Tin Hat,* 10-11.
26. *Ibid.*, 316.
27. *Private Angelo* (London, 1946), 146-7.
28. *Fanfare for a Tin Hat,* 300.
29. *Private Angelo*, 147.
30. *Ibid.*, 84.
31. *A Year of Space*, 175.
32. *Private Angelo*, 82.
33. *Ibid.*, 85.

FIONN MAC COLLA. UNITY THROUGH TRILINGUALISM

J. Derrick McClure

The autobiographical writings of Fionn Mac Colla (pseud: Tom MacDonald), the essay 'Mein Bumpf' and the short monograph *Too Long in This Condition*, give the outline of his life. He was born in Montrose, of a Plymouth Brethren family, in 1906; and – judging by the generous tributes which he pays to his family and his first teachers – spent a happy and stimulating childhood and youth there. He studied at Aberdeen College of Education, passing the final examinations with high distinction; and then took up a headmastership in the Gairloch, where he defied official educational policy by encouraging the use of Gaelic among his pupils. His next post was a lectureship with the Church of Scotland College at Safed, Palestine, which he held for three years. His return to Montrose in 1929 was prompted by the founding of the Scottish National Party, of which he was from then on an active member. *The Albannach*, published in 1932, immediately established his reputation as a writer. Despite this, his personal life in the thirties was one of daunting hardship; and though a teaching post in the Hebrides, which he held from 1940 to 1960, gave him financial security, the necessity of earning his living in an anti-Gaelic educational system was hateful to him. He retired from teaching in 1967, and lived in Edinburgh until his death eight years later. A body of work including at least two novels remains unpublished.

'A house divided against itself cannot stand.'

If there is a motto-text for Fionn Mac Colla's entire work, it is this. Throughout his writings, he emphasises his belief in Unity – the Unity of God, of mankind, of the nation, of the individual – and in the disastrous results that follow when this unity is breached. In a rhetorical passage put into the mouth of the priest Ninian Kennedy (*Clenched Fist*, 136),[1] he upholds the uniting and reconciling effect of sincere intellectual endeavour, and goes on to contrast this with the divisiveness of thought systems, such as Protestantism and Communism, which limit the truth to the beliefs and perceptions of their adherents. Among the protagonists of his novels, Rev. Ewen MacRury in *The*

Ministers and (ultimately Murdo Anderson in *The Albannach* are men of complete wholeness in all their faculties, set against antagonists whose spiritual meanness is reflected in grotesque and sickly physiques; Maighistir Sachairi in *And the Cock Crew*, torn by doubt and confusion, is reduced to an agonised helplessness. And one of the most tragic instances of a house divided against itself is Scotland.

The label 'nationalist' for Mac Colla is, as he says, a 'horrid, inadequate word' ('Mein Bumpf', 11). His awareness of the need for Scottish autonomy is profound, and few men have argued it with greater force and lucidity; but as with other major writers of the Scottish Renaissance, his political stance is on a far higher moral and intellectual level than the 'Scotland's Oil' nationalism of much contemporary discussion. In Scotland, a people who could have contributed a vast amount to the overall enrichment of human knowledge and culture have been paralysed by a distorted view of the world and of their own past. Scottish history, Scottish literature, Scottish music, Scottish art and architecture, and Scottish traditions and customs, receive so little attention in the educational system that most Scots are scarcely aware that a distinctive national culture has ever existed; or, to the extent that they are so aware, they perceive it in a grossly caricatured form (music-hall tartanry) fit only for ridicule. The Scots and Gaelic languages have been systematically denigrated to such an extent that even their surviving speakers characteristically regard them as inferior speech forms. (The present writer, a product of the Scottish educational system, had to acquire his systematic knowledge of Scots and the entirety of his knowledge of Gaelic long after his schooldays; though his grandparents were Scots-speaking, and his home county (Ayrshire) largely Gaelic-speaking until more recently than is often supposed. Even today he could have written this article more easily and convincingly in French than in either of the indigenous languages of his own country.) The music and song of the Gàidhealtachd (except in a somewhat trivialised form), its oral literature, and its poetry – which since the seventeenth century has included the work of several writers of incontestable genius – simply form no part of the basic knowledge of nearly all Scots. The dominance of the language and culture of England, and the minor place assigned to those of Scotland, in the process by which the mental habits of Scots are formed is a fact of Scottish life so fundamental as to be no longer even noticed, much less challenged, by most people in Scotland. These facts, once realised (that they are facts is beyond question), could not fail to disturb anyone concerned for Magnanimity and Truth – the two goals, as Mac Colla claims, of his life's pilgrimage (*Too Long in This Condition*, 1). And if a man feels sorrow at the deathblow of a culture as historically and geographically remote as that of Byzantium (54-5), it is hardly surprising that his discussion of such a state of affairs in his own country should take a powerfully impassioned tone.

The aim of Mac Colla's work is to expose, explain, and make what contribution one man can hope to make towards amending the present condition of Scotland. According to his interpretation of history, the Reformation breached the unity of the Faith and initiated fratricidal strife among Christians. In Scotland, the eventual triumph of the Calvinist party imposed a life-denying religion of despair on the nation. Not only this, but, because the success of the Reformation was due to the active assistance of the temporal and spiritual authorities in England, its result was to lay Scotland open to the influence of a power which had, for centuries past, been devoting massive efforts, both military and political, towards her subjugation. To ensure the continuance of their hold over the minds of the Scottish people, the Reformers imposed a rigidly sectarian discipline in education, in which the pre-Reformation past was deprecated or ignored and the close dependence on England elevated to a guiding principle in the national life. The combination of a religion which denied the value of all artistic and intellectual activity with the submission to a hostile and xenophobic power has had the ultimate result of virtually destroying Scotland. 'Only the inert is mute. Only total death has no statement to make.' (*Too Long . . .*, 46). This observation of George Steiner, the literary and linguistic scholar whom Mac Colla cites with admiration, is applied by him to Scotland: the state of the entire nation is symbolised by Maighistir Sachairi, who at a climactic moment breaks down in his pulpit in inarticulate sobs (*And the Cock Crew*, 147-8).

No summary on this scale could begin to suggest the full force of Mac Colla's thesis, supported as it is by profound psychological insight and – to some extent – historical facts. To some extent only, it must be admitted; for at least in his principal exposition, the extended essay *At the Sign of the Clenched Fist*, he is clearly guilty of selectivity and over-simplification in his account of the historical data. A particularly bad instance is that in his anxiety to counter the traditional notion that the pre-Reformation Church was vicious and corrupt he virtually dismisses it as the result of Reformation propaganda – though it is quite certain that the old Catholic Church, in Scotland as elsewhere, had become scandalously lax. Yet he has undeniably provided a novel, disturbing and stimulating exploration of the confused and stultified condition of present-day Scotland; and his views are worthy of detailed consideration.

We are here concerned with only one aspect of Mac Colla's attempt to restore Scotland's vitality by healing her internal divisions: his beliefs and practices in the matter of language. An immediately striking feature of his novels is his free use of Lowland Scots, Gaelic, and various types of Gaelic-accented English as well as standard English: his literary language is a personally-achieved synthesis of the three tongues of Scotland. This in itself entitles him to a unique position among Scottish writers: fluency in all three languages is rare enough, and the uniting of them all in a single literary idiolect is virtually unknown. Mac Colla, however, succeeds in this through his native familiarity with Scots and his thorough grounding in Gaelic; and the result is a style of kaleidoscopic variety.

The fight in the cafe and its aftermath in *The Albannach*, for example, provide occasion for some excellent snatches of patter in broad Glasgow demotic. In contrast to the sketchy type-figures of the keelies, Maister Byars in *And the Cock Crew* is a fully developed character portrait; and it is not only the powerful conception of this arrogant and brutal man, but the unerring authenticity of his Scots dialogue, that impresses him ineradicably on the reader's imagination.

Ane Tryall of Heretiks is notable not only for superb rhetoric and for the remarkable success with which Mac Colla presents a scholarly theological disputation in dramatic form, but for another striking linguistic effect: the appropriate register of sixteenth-century Scots is evoked by the use of archaic forms ('I will now declare to thee with authority, by virtue of mine office as ane bishop and pastor . . .' (86)), legal phrasing ('Ye are here compeared afore me . . . to be examinit anent certain heresies said to have been utterit and disseminated by you' (77)), and Biblical language ('Yea, of a surety, do unto me what ye will that am led as a lamb to the slaughter . . .' (87)). The last feature is strictly an anachronism, for the vernacular translations of the Bible that existed in the Reformation period can hardly have influenced popular speech in Scotland as profoundly as the language of the Authorised Version was to do in later centuries; but the licence is eminently justified by its results.

English spoken as a learned language by native Gaels is often represented; and it is noteworthy that the most heavily-accented dialogue is reserved for unsympathetic characters. The sycophantic Highland students in *The Albannach* express their degenerate acquiescence in the destruction of their culture with a superabundance of voiceless sounds:

> The '45 and the efictions were the Providence of God. But for them the Highlanders would neffer haff entered into their heritage, the map would not pee cuffered with Highland names . . . (147)

The pathetic quisling Lachlan Cearbach (i.e. clumsy or untidy) in *And the Cock Crew* can barely express himself in English: 'I wass tell him what I wass see myself in Gleann Mór agus an Srath Meadhonach . . .' (153). For the physically repulsive and morally outrageous Ar-Jai MacAskill in *The Ministers* a truly extraordinary eye-dialect is devised:

> 'They are sèhing, *ipsa facte* ant py eemplicèhtion, thaht aht the Reformèhtion the Cassolics were right ant the P-protestants were ronk.' (174)

Symbolically, their language marks these people as 'rejects': they have betrayed or abandoned their Gaelic origins, but have been unable to naturalise themselves in the rival culture. By contrast, Maighistir Sachairi in *And the Cock Crew* shows a splendid command of the learned language. Though he lacks the native Scots idiom of the Factor, his fluency and rhetorical skill make him fully the latter's match:

> 'Maister Byars! The Providence of God has seen fit to put this people in your power: and how have ye used your power! Sparing neither the grey head nor the bairn at the knee, ye have made all to rise out of their beds afore daybreak this bitter day and make their different ways with doubts and sore misgivings. Ye have feared them to death the space of three mortal hours and never took peety on their agony. And ye bear it in your heart to make them paupers and houseless wanderers and giving their hearth-stanes to four-footed beasts.' (25-6)

Mac Colla's interest in language, however, goes far beyond its potential as a source of literary effects. The historical development of the contemporary linguistic situation in Scotland, with English in a position of unchallenged dominance, Scots relegated to the status of a group of low-prestige dialects, and Gaelic in danger of total extinction, receives extensive discussion. Frequently he refers to the facts, firstly, that Gaelic was formerly spoken over the greater part of Scotland, and, secondly, that its recession has been the direct result of a deliberate policy of cultural genocide applied by first the Scottish and then the British governments with the Church and the schools as willing agents. This, it must be emphasised, is plain historical truth; and equally incontestable is that awareness of this national shame is suppressed by the educational system: as Mac Colla puts it:

> A lady teacher [in Montrose in the early decades of this century] would have as readily pronounced the word 'hoor' or 'shite' in front of her class as have mentioned that a language called Gaelic was once the predominant language there-

about. (*Too long* . . . , 81)

Mac Colla writes with the impassioned anger proper to a man who has understood the full implications of this neglected aspect of Scottish history: who has appreciated the sufferings inflicted on generations of Gaelic-speakers; has become acquainted, if only through its relics, with the artistic richness of the destroyed civilisation; and has realised the extent of the deception that has been practised on the present-day Scottish population in the concealment of these facts. In his non-fictional writing, he pulls no punches: one example will suffice:

> To kill a culture is to knock the Creator out of his universe. It amounts to the laying of sacrilegious hands on one incarnation of the Cause of being, to a defacing of the Infinite – And when the culture is of so unique an idiosyncrasy and enchantment as Gaelic culture, the offence is an act of unparalleled barbarism. Yet this in essence is what I [as a teacher] was expected to do, and I had superiors over me to see that I did it. The Enemy of Man, the Great Negator, the Father of Nay-say, ought officially to have another title – Director-in-Chief of Scottish Education. ('Mein Bumpf', 27-8).

Specific references to thc splendours of Gaelic literature appear in *The Albannach*: a fine lyrical passage (72) describes the effect of the poem *Birlinn Chlann Raghnaill* ('Clanranald's Galley'); and 'O Ree, what we have lost!' exclaims Murdo on being introduced by his Irish friend to old Gaelic poetry (97). For the honest, likeable, but superficial Rev. Macpherson Bain in *The Ministers*, a completely new light on his naive impression of the Jacobite risings and their consequences is cast by the much better-informed Ewen MacRury; to such an extent that when the latter points the conclusion 'It's as clear a case of . . . what's the word they're using nowadays? . . . genocide as anything in history. The murder of a whole race, a people.', Bain is forced to admit 'We-el . . . That's putting it pretty extremely, I would think . . . but . . . substantially . . . ye-es, I suppose . . .' (58). In an agonising speech during the long debate in *And the Cock Crew*, Fearchar the Bard is made to prophesy:

> 'The day she [England] looks for – and it is coming near, and this thing will hasten it – is the day there will be Albannaich no longer who speak our language or remember the ways of the forefathers and the things that belong to their nation: for that day she will have our country, we can never rise again. At the end of so long a time Alba will not be. The world will be, and nations; but *our* nation will not be.' (126-7)

The language conflict which both reflects and perpetuates the state of division existing in the Scottish soul has not only entailed the loss to common knowledge of a fine literature. Nor is its worst result the national tradition of inarticulacy which it has established: Mac Colla writes scathingly about the crass efforts of teachers who, 'tak[ing] it for granted it is simply *natural* to speak English,' (*Too Long . . .*, 44), have ridiculed and punished children for using their native language (be it Gaelic or Scots) in the classroom, thus hindering the intellectual and personal development of millions of Scots by making them unwilling or unable to express themselves verbally at all. Even the possibility – a serious one – that this has contributed to the crime and other social disorders endemic in Scotland, particularly in the cities, is not the most fundamentally disastrous effect of the forcible imposition of English. Still more important is the fact that the loss of a language is a catastrophe of a magnitude far greater than is commonly realised: a total loss to the entire human community.

The belief that 'each language gives its speakers access to a view of a special aspect of the Reality that surrounds and is in us, and which no human being would know otherwise in this life on earth' (*Too Long . . .*, 56) is of course not original with nor unique to Mac Colla, though he expounds it more eloquently than some. It has an established name, the Sapir-Whorf Hypothesis; and can be less poetically expressed by stating that since no two languages coincide exactly in vocabulary or grammatical structures, every language conditions the thoughts of its speakers in a way to a greater or a lesser extent different from that imposed by any other language. Everday experience with foreign languages confirms this in the most obvious and commonplace sense; and on a deeper level – that exploited in poetry and the art of poetic translation – the connotations of a word-sequence build up into a structure of meaning at once so powerful and so indefinitely complex that the task of transferring this, even approximately, to another language becomes manifestly impossible. It is to be expected that the greater the distance between two languages and their associated cultures (for a language is inseparable from the total culture – the literature, history, customs, traditions, beliefs – of its speakers), the more obvious and inescapable will be the difficulty of transferring concepts from one to the other: B.L. Whorf, who developed the theory in its most explicit form, cites modes of expression in American Indian languages which seem to presuppose a wholly different perception of events from that implied by English.[2] And it is not necessary to have had experience of Hopi or Shawnee to understand Mac Colla's insistence that his earliest recollection was of an event in the gairden at the back of the hoose: 'It is questionable whether any experience of significance could in those days have occurred to me in a garden, still less in a gahdn.' (*Too Long* . . . , 6, 17).

From this view of language, it follows that nothing could be more naive and shallow than the commonly-expressed view that the loss of a language is of no moment since its former speakers can adopt a language of wide currency like English or Spanish. No nation or individual has extended the capacity of the human mind for thought, learning and imaginative creation to its limits. A language in its entirety – which is not simply the contents of a compendious dictionary but the inconceivably (and yet increasingly) vast and complex mass of the associations acquired through centuries or millenia by each word – represents on this view *merely* the accumulated efforts of one group of speakers to discover order, regularity and intelligibility in the behaviour of the Cosmos and of human beings. Even a moderate knowledge of the language and culture of another people provides the learner with access to some insight into those mysteries which his own language does not afford. The disappearance of a language represents an irretrievable diminution of the actual and potential range of human thought and human knowledge. And it is the threat of this in Scotland that Mac Colla is attempting to counter.

The divisions which have so devitalised Scotland are not due solely to the existence of three languages; and there is no contradiction in Mac Colla's attempting to restore national unity by reversing the movement towards a uniformity of English monolingualism. The struggle of Gaelic against Scots, and the far more desperate struggle of both these against English, were never necessary; and could yet, at least in principle, end in reconciliation. Polyglot nations and individuals are not exceptional in the world but are, on the contrary, the established norm in many areas; and the existence of two or more languages within a state is no necessary barrier to an awareness of national unity. Belgium, Luxembourg and Switzerland are obvious examples from close at hand; and medieval Scotland, though linguistically and ethnically diverse, was one of the first countries in Europe to develop a national identity. It is an ascertained fact that normal individuals can, if exposed from childhood to two or even three languages, acquire complete fluency in them all with not the slightest detriment – again, rather the reverse – to their intellectual and personal development. What *is* harmful, and for many centuries endemic in Scotland, is any attempt at forcing a speaker to acquire a foreign language at the expense of – not as a complement to – his own: as can be all too readily observed, this generally results in confusion for the individual and grave social malaise for his community.

Of Scotland's three extant languages, Gaelic is in two simple and precise senses the 'oldest': it has been indigenous to Scotland for the longest time, and as the direct descendant of Old Irish it represents by far the oldest literary tradition (after Greek and Latin) in Europe. Of the two recessive tongues, Gaelic has suffered more severe and blatant discrimination, and over a longer time, than Scots: active efforts at suppressing Gaelic in its homeland began in the sixteenth century, whereas the social and educational dominance of English (considered as something distinct from and antipathetic to Scots) did not become a serious factor in the life of the Lowlands till the eighteenth. The most important step in restoring Scotland to linguistic health, therefore, must be a restoration of the Gaelic language and culture to a position of importance in Scottish life; a development which would not merely be an act of natural justice but would provide a powerful focus for Scottish national identity. (It is interesting to note that George Buchanan, the only Gaelic-speaker among the sixteenth-century Reformers and the only one whom Mac Colla exempts, however grudgingly, from his comprehensive dismissal of those men's intellectual powers (*Clenched Fist*, 131), in his historical writings contradicted much contemporary political thought by insisting on the Gaelic origins of the Scottish nation.)[3] The certainty that very few of his potential readers will have any Gaelic, however, at once imposes on Mac Colla a difficulty not so much practical as logical: how is he to demonstrate the value of the Gaelic language to readers who lack the slightest knowledge of it? To instil a historical awareness of what has been done to Gaelic and its speakers is one part of his purpose; and this he does, by the wealth of historical facts and arguments which he incorporates into his writing. But a more urgent aim is to acquaint his readers with the language itself.

His most sustained attempt at this is *The Albannach*; and his method is the use of a hybrid language: an English modified by the presence of Gaelic idioms, grammatical constructions, and actual words. The theoretical implications of this procedure are more extensive than is at first obvious. Since each language represents a unique perspective on the world, the act of forcing one language to assume in part the forms proper to another involves the superimposition of two perceptions of reality. Through his inescapable awareness of the difference between the Gaelic-accented language of the novel and normal literary English, the English-reader attains a sort of double vision: he is conscious simultaneously of his native and – so far as English, however modified, can present this – the exotic world-view. The impression of transference to a new, Gaelic, mode of perception which the reader receives is, of course, largely an illusion: the language of the book may be closer to Gaelic than is most English writing, but it is English and not Gaelic nonetheless. Yet the illusion is in itself a remarkable linguistic achievement; and it is skilfully maintained.

The Gaelic patina on the language is achieved in several ways.[4] Most obvious is the incorporation of actual Gaelic words, in both the dialogue and the narrative sections of the book. The title itself embodies both an invitation and a challenge to the reader. Few people in Scotland will know the meaning of *Albannach* (simply 'Scotsman') – and, incidentally, non-Gaelic-speakers are absolutely certain to mispronounce it: it does not sound like almanac but like, approximately, 'Allah-punnoch', with a dactylic rhythm and equal pitch-prominence on the first two syllables – but most will at least recognise it as a Gaelic word. Those who pick up a book with this title may therefore be presumed to have some interest and curiosity, and perhaps goodwill, towards Highland life. The presence of Gaelic words in the novel confirms the reader's naturalisation in the Gaelic milieu, by the tacit assumption that he is able to understand them, or willing to make the required effort. From another point of view, they represent a kind of forcible instruction in the Gaelic language, since the reader is faced with the choice of either ascertaining, deducing or guessing their meanings, or losing part of the story.

When a Gaelic word appears in the narrative, Mac Colla occasionally supplies a gloss: 'It [the 'path' of life on which Murdo's parents are bound] was cumhang, strait and narrow' (10); 'The òran buana, the reaping song' (274); 'The murmuring noise they [rivulets] made, the toraman' (285). In some such cases the English translation does not cover the full implications of the Gaelic word: *cumhang* has connotations – very appropriate in the context – of narrowness of *mind*, and *toraman* suggests, besides a murmur, the sound of a musical instrument, often specifically the drone of pipes. Much more frequently, the words are left unexplained: 'as if he had met a bochdan [hobgoblin] itself' (48); 'as if the feilleadh [kilt] itself was flapping at the back of his knees'; 'jumping from ploc [tussock] to ploc' (280). However, in most such cases the context enables the reader to make a reasonable guess; and thus his initiation into Gaelic becomes a stimulating rather than an exhausting experience.

In the dialogue, Gaelic phrases other than simple interjections and conversational tags (such as *thig a stigh* 'come in' (65), *oidhche mhath leibh uile* 'good night, everybody' (74)) are often followed by a translation. In such instances, the form of the text is somewhat peculiar: despite the punctuation, it is not to be presumed that the speakers actually said 'Tha oidhche bhreagha ann, there's a beautiful night in it' (56), or 'Eudail mo chridhe, cho breagha 's a bha e, Jewel of my heart, so beautiful it was' (69). However, the effect of this on the reader has

Iain Ruaidh? [i.e. Murdo (son) of Red John] Yes, still, but with the emphasis no longer on Iain Ruaidh!' (205) might be lost on a reader unacquainted with the custom. Mac Colla is, in fact, frankly and even pointedly inviting the reader to explore the Gaelic language; and thus attempting to breach the barrier of ignorance and hostility that has divided the two parts of the Scottish nation for centuries.

A stylistic feature frequently employed in the novel, and one which has been adopted by many since Mac Colla, as he ruefully points out in 'Mein Bumpf' (14), is the use of Gaelic syntactic patterns: 'It's a poor crop we'll be having the year if there won't be more rain in it' (91). More interesting and less obvious is the use of English words in idiomatic senses peculiar to their nearest Gaelic equivalents. An English-speaker will certainly be impressed by the vivid and unusual phrase 'the black mouth of winter' (2); but will probably take it to be an imaginative metaphor devised by the author. In fact is is a transference of an accepted sense of the word *beul* (mouth), which appears in many idioms of weather and time with the meaning of 'oncome' or 'imminence' (e.g. *beul an latha* 'mouth of the day' is dawn). Again, the expressive phrase 'the blazing red shame' (51) follows a regular use of the colour-word *dearg* to indicate an extreme degree of some violent or painful emotion. 'Bright yellow music' (77) is not, or not only, an arresting synaesthesia: *buidhe*, as well as meaning 'yellow' or 'golden', has implications of gratitude and joy. 'Greatland' (210), much more evocative than the standard *mainland*, is a borrowing of the regular Gaelic *tìr mór*. 'Open weather' (279) reflects a use of *fosgailte*, which means 'freed' or 'unbound' as well as 'open (like a door or a box)': the sky becomes *fosgailte* when clouds disperse. By imparting to the English words the polysemy of their Gaelic counterparts, Mac Colla presents startling new perceptions to his non-Gaelic readers; and, more generally, demonstrates the peculiar facility of the Gaelic language for metaphorical and poetic expressions.

> If there is any magic in anything I have written, any express lucidity, anything shining with an especial light, anything above all that is at once durable and sweet, they are derived from *that special sighting of Reality which can not be attained save through the window of the Gàidhlig.*
>
> *(Too Long . . .*, 56).

The language of *The Albannach* is a fine illustration of the meaning, and the truth, of this claim.

If there is a paradox in Mac Colla's achievement, it is that a Scots-speaking Lowlander, representative of what is for Gaelic an enemy culture little different from that of England, should have done more than any other recent Scottish writer to harmonise the two sides of a subtle appropriateness to Mac Colla's intention. A translation in a footnote or a parenthesis outwith the speech-marks would emphasise the reader's place as an outsider: one incapable of participation in the Gaelic culture of the novel. By putting into the speakers' mouths both their actual words and something which conveys their meaning (while retaining a Gaelic flavour by virtue of the non-English syntax), the author presents the reader with the illusion of having literally understood the Gaelic; and thus enhances his sense of identification with the Gaelic setting. On one occasion a similar trick is played by a quoted exchange: Annie's first words on her return to Murdo's house (276) are 'An d'ith thu fhathast, a Mhurchaidh?', and Murdo's response is given as 'I did not eat,' – though Murdo's whole character and his frame of mind at that moment make it inconceivable that he would actually have answered her in English. The form in which his reply is written lets the reader know what Annie's question was; but it has a further significance. Annie has until now affected English, even though she speaks it imperfectly; and this, her first use of Gaelic in the novel, clearly suggests her reconciliation not only with Murdo but with her Gaelic identity. The reconciliation is extended to the reader by allowing him to understand Murdo's acceptance.

The use of place-names and personal names in their Gaelic forms serves to emphasise the Highland setting of the novel. More than this, it presents considerable interest to readers who are prepared to follow the hint given in Duncan's speech:

> 'Say Achadh nam beith to a Gaelic man and he will be seeing in his mind a level place and the birch trees growing here and there, and they white and slender. Say Achadh nan siantan and he will be seeing a little plain between great mountains and the rain driving down on it. But will a man of you tell me what Achbay or Achnasheen will mean in the Beurla [English], or what kind of a place is in Lowestoft or Dover?' (70-71)

Drum Uaine (Green Ridge), Allt Dubh (Black Burn), Eilean Sona (Blessed Island), Baile na Creige (Village of the Rock) and the other Gaelic names have meanings instantly accessible to a reader whom the novel may tempt to pick up a Gaelic dictionary. Personal names demonstrate the custom – still prevalent in the Gàidhealtachd – of using patronymics or nicknames rather than official surnames: Mina Bhàn is Fair-haired Mina, Kenny Mhurchaidh Bhig is Kenny (son) of Wee Murdo, Calum Mac Dhonnchaidh Odhair is Calum son of Mousey-haired (or perhaps Sallow-skinned, or possibly even Unwashed) Duncan, Calum Bàn Mac Ruaraidh 'Ic Ailean Mhóir is Fair-haired Calum son of Rory son of Big Allan. The significance of 'Murchaidh

Scottish civilisation. This he has done by applying his remarkable gifts as a writer to his extensive knowledge of the two cultures, their histories and their languages. One of his intentions in writing *The Albannach*, he says, was to administer 'a sharp awakening slap in the matter of language' ('Mein Bumpf', 14). If it and his other works were more widely known, that slap could yet awaken Scotland to the reality of her present condition.

Suggestions for further reading:

The only published work of Mac Colla not cited in the article is *Scottish Noel* (Edinburgh, 1958). This and *Ane Tryall of Heretiks* are actually sections of a long novel of the Reformation, not yet published in its entirety.

Readers whom Mac Colla's advocacy entices to explore the history and culture of the Gaidhealtachd will find an excellent aid in Derick Thomson, *An Introduction to Gaelic Poetry* (London, 1974). The only popular history of Gaelic is Kenneth Mackinnon, *The Lion's Tongue* (Inverness, 1974); but it is sketchy and in places wholly inadequate. Readers prepared to venture into the subject in greater depth could not do better than to begin with Nancy Dorian, *Language Death* (Philadelphia, 1981).

The quotations from George Steiner in *Too Long in This Condition* are from his essay 'The Language Animal' in *Extraterritorial* (Harmondsworth, 1975). Steiner will make fascinating, though demanding, reading for anyone interested in Mac Colla's views on language: the discussion of *The Albannach* in the present essay draws on his examination of other 'interlingual' works in Chapter 5 of *After Babel.*

A translation of the Classical Gaelic poem quoted in *The Albannach* (216-7) can be found in *The Penguin Book of Irish Verse* (72-3). Hugh MacDiarmid's translation of *Birlinn Chlann Raghnaill* is included in the various editions of his collected poems.

Notes:

1. The editions of Fionn Mac Colla's works used are the following: *The Albannach* (Edinburgh, 1971); a reproduction of the original 1932 edition. *And the Cock Crew* (Glasgow, 1962); originally published 1945. *The Ministers* (London, 1979). *At the Sign of the Clenched Fist* (Edinburgh, 1967). *Too Long in this Condition* (Thurso, 1975). 'Mein Bumpf' in *Essays on Fionn Mac Colla*, ed. David Morrison, (Thurso, 1973). *Ane Tryall of Heretiks* is incor-

porated in *At the Sign of the Clenched Fist*, and quotations from it are from this source.

2. *Language, Thought and Reality* (Cambridge, Mass., 1956).
3. See A.H. Williamson, *Scottish National Consciousness in the Reign of James VI* (Edinburgh, 1979), chs. 5, 6.
4. I am grateful to Donald MacAulay for consultation on this section of the essay.

TRADITION AND PATTERN IN THE SHORT STORIES OF GEORGE MACKAY BROWN

J. Graeme Roberts

George Mackay Brown is an Orkneyman. Born in 1921 in Stromness, he has lived there all his life except for periods of study, first in 1951-52 at Newbattle Abbey, where his fellow Orkneyman Edwin Muir was Warden, and then at Edinburgh University. In 1960 he graduated with an honours degree in English before going on to do postgraduate work on Gerard Manley Hopkins. Besides his collections of short stories, he has published a play, two novels, and several volumes of poetry, as well as a book of essays about Orkney.

His short stories, like his other work, are rooted almost exclusively in the history, folklore and communal life of the Orcadian archipelago, where, as he says in his Introduction to *Witch and Other Stories* (1977), 'the art of story-telling had been practised for many generations' (vi). He himself is very conscious of being 'part of a tradition' that comprises Norse sagas, oral tales and Scottish ballads:

> I am not an isolated storyteller writing in the late twentieth century; I draw from a treasury of narrative written and unwritten out of the islands' past. (*Witch*, x)

The effect of this native narrative tradition on his approach to the art of the short story is the subject of this essay.

The saga tradition is most obvious, naturally enough, in tales like 'The Story of Jorkel Hayforks' (*A Calendar of Love*, 1967), 'Tartan' (*A Time to Keep*, 1969) and 'The Fires of Christmas' (*Hawkfall*, 1974), stories whose characters, incidents and general ethos are drawn from the world of the *Orkneyinga Saga*, which records the lives and deeds of the Norse Earls of Orkney and their followers. The Vikings' laconic acceptance of fate, for example, is reproduced not only in 'The Fires of Christmas,' which re-tells the story of Earl Rognvald's ominous slip of the tongue shortly before he is killed by his uncle Earl Thorfinn, but also in the comment made by the fictional Jorkel when one of his companions falls to his death while sheep-stealing on Fair Isle: 'Flan's descent is much quicker than his going up' (149); or when another companion dies of seasickness on the crossing to

Orkney: 'Mund will not be needing dinner any more' (150). Similarly, stories such as 'Sealskin' (*Hawkfall*) and 'The Book of Black Arts' (*The Sun's Net*, 1976) draw their material from folktales and ballads.

Native tradition, however, is probably more important as an influence on Brown's narrative style than as a source of material for his stories. What it offered him, at least in his earlier stories, was a model of narrative economy, particularly of presentation.

> I admire the 'pure' art of the sagamen, everything extraneous, such as the detailed descriptions of people and places and comments by the author on what is happening, is ruthlessly excluded. Perhaps Hemingway of modern authors comes closest to that tough bare austere style. (*Witch*, x)

'The ballad-maker,' he writes in an essay on 'The Last Ballad', printed in *The Listener* (20 June 1968), 'is not interested in the details, only in the central situation, the skeleton of the story' (p.800). The effect of paring down the narrative to its essentials is to throw such detail as remains into sharper relief, so that it acquires an added significance. Thus in traditional tales told round the winter fire, Brown writes,

> all unnecessary details are left out, such as the colour of a character's eyes or the acreage of his fields, and out of the starkness the hero looms larger than life, and every word he utters is simple and portentous. (*Witch*, viii)

A good example of how Brown's own 'tough bare austere style' can be at once 'simple and portentous' is provided by the opening section of 'A Time to Keep':

> We came down through the fields, Ingi and I.
>
> The wedding was still going on in her father's house in Osmundwall, ten miles over the hill.
>
> There were lacings of snow across the valley and the upper hills were white.
>
> We saw our house in front of us, a clean new house of sea-washed stones. There was no earth-weathering on the walls yet. I had built the house myself between harvest and Christmas. Fires had been lit to burn the dampness out of it, but there was no fire yet for food and companionship. Beside the dwelling-house were byre and barn and stable that the mason had built the winter before. The thatch on the four roofs was new springy heather, covered with wire-netting and weighted with stones.
>
> Ingi went alone into the house. I went into the byre to see that the two cows were all right. There was a sheep here and a sheep there on the field above, seven sheep in all on the hill. One sheep wandered across a line of snow, gray against white.

> A new plough leaned against the wall of the barn. The blacksmith must have delivered it that afternoon. I took it inside, a gray powerful curve.
>
> This was our croft, Ingi's and mine. I turned back towards the house. Blue smoke was rising from the roof now. The first true fire had been lit. (*A Time to Keep*, 38)

Most of the sentences in this extract are simple, and on the whole the language is monosyllabic and rather plain. As a result, the exceptions are inevitably foregrounded, thus drawing attention to their possible symbolic significance. There is, for example, a contrast signalled syntactically between the 'fires . . . lit to burn the dampness out' and the 'fire . . . for food and companionship.' There is also a contrast between the 'clean new house of sea-washed stones', thatched with 'new springy heather', built by the narrator's own hands for Ingi and himself and the 'byre and barn and stable that the mason had built'. The symbolic fire on the hearth tended by the woman turns out to be one of the most potent recurring images in the story that follows:

> Always the smoke was rising out of the roof, sometimes gray smoke, sometimes blue, sometimes black. But the flame beat in the hearth, the house was alive. (39)

The fire dies when Ingi neglects it in order to join the other women at the Good Friday service, and at the end, when she dies in childbirth, her friend Anna comes to look after the child and to tend the fire in her stead: 'The fire wasn't out after all. There was a deep glow in the heart of the peats' (62). Other important details highlighted by the language are the 'sea-washed stones' of the croft and the 'gray powerful curve' of the 'new plough'. These are emblems of that 'interweaving of sea and land, tilth and salt' which Brown finds 'peculiarly quickening to the imagination of a storyteller' (*Witch*, vii).

Another story which illustrates the emotional effectiveness of Brown's terse, almost impersonal style is 'Witch' (*A Calendar of Love*), the tragic tale of an innocent young farm servant who is tried and executed on a blatantly trumped-up charge of witchcraft. After Marian has been found guilty and condemned to death, she is taken back to her cell.

> And at once came to her William Bourtree, Simon Leslie, John Glaitness and John Beaton, with shears, razors, and pincers, who cut off her hair and afterwards shaved her skull clean, denuding her even of her eyebrows. Then one by one with the pincers John Glaitness drew out her finger-nails and toe-nails; and this operation caused her much pain. (119-20)

The following day she is taken to be strangled and burned at Gallowsha.

> Because her toes were blue and swollen after the extraction of the cuticles, she could not walk but with much difficulty. Therefore they bound her arms and carried her out on to the street. There was much laughter and shouting at sight of her naked head. Every alehouse in town had been open since midnight, the earl having decreed a public holiday. All night people had come into the town from the parishes and islands. There was much drunkenness and dancing along the road to Gallowsha. (121)

The cruelty, injustice, ignorance and superstition of Marian's tormentors, together with her courage and patience in the face of appalling suffering, is all the more strikingly conveyed by reason of the matter-of-factness and impersonality of the narrative style, which purports to be a clerk's record of the proceedings against her. Our normal sense of decency, justice, and humanity is outraged not just by what is done to Marian, but by the flat, emotionless, objective way in which it is reported by the narrator.

The narrative economy which is such a feature of stories like 'Witch' and 'A Time to Keep' is much less in evidence in Brown's later collections, which sometimes suffer from excessive ornamentation and verbal prolixity. In 'Hawkfall', for example, no less than five stories from different periods of Orkney's past are held together by little more than the presence in them of members of a single family, whose distinguishing feature is 'a curiously flattened nose' (*Hawkfall*, 14). Another five stories are loosely joined together in 'Cinquefoil', and presented in a curious mixture of narrative modes – sermon, diary, essay, letter and newspaper report, as well as more conventional first and third person narration. 'Sealskin', for all that it reveals about Brown's view of art, is an unsuccessful attempt to graft a 'portrait of the artist' on to a traditional 'selkie' tale.

The narrative economy that Brown admires in Norse sagas and oral tales is, of course, a widely recognised feature of folk literature. 'Modern literature,' according to the Danish folklorist Axel Olrik, in his 'Epic Laws of Folk Narrative',

> loves to entangle the various threads of the plot amongst each other. In contrast, folk narrative holds the individual strand fast . . . Everything superfluous is suppressed and only the essential stands out salient and striking.[1]

A similar comment is made by David Buchan in *The Ballad and the Folk* (1972): 'the reductive impulse compels the oral maker to jettison ruthlessly all extraneous matter in order to concentrate on the story's essence'. (54) Such economy and concentration is also, however, the most important characteristic of the classic short story as the genre was defined by such influential nineteenth century critics as Edgar Allan Poe and Brander Matthews. According to Matthews, for example, the short story should deal with 'a single character, a single event, a single emotion, or the series of emotions called forth by a single situation'; 'compression,' he wrote, 'a vigorous compression, is essential'.[2] It is for this reason that narrative economy, whether of subject matter or style, is probably a less significant example of the effect of tradition on Brown's approach to the short story than another characteristic of his earlier work, his use of very marked verbal and structural patterns, something that seems to derive from orally composed and transmitted narratives like the ballad.

Patterning, according to David Buchan in *A Scottish Ballad Book* (1973), is how 'the oral maker controls his material' and expands his 'bare narrative essence'.(2) This patterning is of two kinds, verbal and structural. Verbal patterning usually consists of formulas, stock modes of expression; structural patterning has to do with how the narrative is built up: the way one part relates to another and to the story as a whole. Although the parts of an oral narrative, he points out, tend to be organized paratactically, such a narrative often exhibits more complex structural patterns, which manifest themselves 'in all kinds of balances and parallelisms, contrasts and antitheses, chiastic and framing devices, and in various kinds of triadic groupings' (*The Ballad and the Folk*, 53). Such patterns were memorably defined many years ago by Axel Olrik as the Law of Opening and Closing, the Law of Three, the Law of Repetition and the Law of Contrast.

Brown's most common use of the framing device (Olrik's Law of Opening and Closing) is to unify his narratives. This is seen at its simplest in 'Five Green Waves' (*A Calendar of Love*), where the story of a schoolboy's initiation into the mysteries of ale, the sea, women and death is framed by two sentences. The first – 'Time was lines and circles and squares' (41) – alludes to the formal, regulated world of education and the various learned professions to which it gives entry, a world from which the narrator has been temporarily excluded at the start of the story for failing to prepare a geometry lesson. The final sentence – 'Time was skulls and butterflies and guitars' (60) – refers to the extra-mural world of death, freedom, beauty and love which the boy discovers on his way home and which makes him choose to become a sailor rather than the minister, doctor or lawyer his merchant father proposes. At a verbal level, of course, the Laws of Contrast, Repetition and Three reinforce the structural pattern here. The arrangement of the boatman's 'singing' speech in verse form at the beginning and end of 'The Seller of Silk Shirts' (*A Calendar of*

Love) provides a similar narrative frame.

Framing devices are to be found in other stories. In 'The Storyteller' (*A Time to Keep*) it is merely a mechanism for linking three separate stories that at first sight have little connection with each other, even though the third story incorporates the telling of the other two on a previous occasion. In 'The Three Islands' (*A Calendar of Love*) the device is more effectively used. Here three vignettes from Orkney's Viking past are embedded in a rather flat narrative about a fishing trip to the islands of Eynhallow, Gairsay and Egilsay. The effect, however, is to contrast the banality and ignorance of the present with the heroism and piety of the days of Sweyn Asleifson and St. Magnus. Similarly, in 'A Treading of Grapes' (*A Time to Keep*), three sermons on the same text delivered at different times over the centuries in three churches built on the selfsame spot are brought together in such a way as to point up the obvious moral and spiritual impoverishment of contemporary religious life. The framing device not only introduces the sermons and thus sets up the invidious comparisons, but at the end reminds the reader of the continuity and common destiny of all human life:

> The wind from the sea soughed under the eaves of the Kirk, and among tombstones with texts and names newly chiselled on them, and those with withered half-obliterated lettering, and those that have lost their meanings and secrets to very ancient rain. (75-76)

These stories also illustrate Brown's fondness for 'triadic groupings'.

The operation of the Law of Three is, indeed, frequently to be seen. In 'Tam' (*A Calendar of Love*), for instance, the hero's cousin has 'three bright-eyed, apple-cheeked daughters' (101), with each of whom Tam sleeps in turn the night before he puts to sea: Tam disappears, but 'three bonny bairns, born within a week of each other, played on the steps of the close where Jock the shoemaker lived' (103). In 'A Carrier of Stones' (*A Time to Keep*) Rolf is offered 'three ships trading in Ireland' (149) if he will agree to marry one of the laird's three daughters, to each of whom he is introduced in turn. In 'The Story of Jorkel Hayforks' three offers are made to Finn the poet before he consents to stay and marry the daughter of his host. Three utterances are made by Mund before he dies of seasickness; and three different explanations are offered by Sweyn, Valt and Jorkel for the disappearance of Thord: one at vespers ('He will have gone after the women of Papa Westray'), one at compline ('No doubt he is stealing eggs and cheese'), and one at matins ('Thord has repented').

In some cases Brown exploits the Law of Three for special narrative effects. In 'A Carrier of Stones', for example, Rolf's rejection of the third daughter, the youngest and most beautiful, comes as a surprise to the reader, disappointing as it does his conventional expectations, and prepares the way for Rolf's eventual application to become a monk. In 'Tartan' (*A Time to Keep*) a three times repeated remark is used for ironic effect. When Kol wets his feet crossing a burn, he says 'No doubt somebody will pay for this' (135). When he bumps against the door of the weaver's cottage, he says again 'Doubtless somebody will pay for this' (137). Finally, when he is stretched out in the lee of Duncan's house to sleep off his drunkenness, he says 'A great many people will suffer' (138). However, when his companions return they find Kol 'where they had left him, at the wall, but he was dead. Someone had cut his throat with a cornhook' (139).

Repetition, of which the Law of Three is but a special case, is the most common type of structural patterning in Brown's stories. In 'The Seller of Silk Shirts' there is the Sikh boy's round of his customers; in 'The Wheel' (*A Calendar of Love*) Robert Jansen's 'ritual' enquiries after his dead friend Walls; in 'The Ferryman' (*A Calendar of Love*) a series of different passengers; in 'Stone Poems' (*A Calendar of Love*) a collection of seven runes; in 'The Story of Jorkel Hayforks' a diminishing band of seven Vikings; in 'The Whaler's Return' (*A Time to Keep*) a succession of stops for refreshment. Brown has been accused by Robin Fulton of misusing this fictional device and of employing it 'quite mechanically.'[3] However, it could be argued that by mimicking the paratactic organization of oral narrative, it does contribute to the traditional flavour of his stories. More important, it is a device that lends itself to the creation of effective climaxes, yet another feature of the classic nineteenth century short story. In 'The Troubling of the Waters' (*A Calendar of Love*), for example, it enables Brown to score yet another point in his unrelenting battle against the effects of Progress. Having described in rich poetic detail seven varieties of home-made whisky formerly distilled on the island of Quoylay, he concludes:

> Nowadays there is a licensed grocer at the cross-roads, a Mr. MacFarlane from Dalkeith, where the island people buy their whisky in sealed bottles at two pounds one shilling and sixpence a bottle. (85-86)

Repetition, together with contrast, provides the basic structural and symbolic patterns in 'Celia' (*A Time to Keep*), the story of a girl with a drink problem caused by her excessive sensibility and idealism. In order to satisfy her craving she entertains men at night in the little dark seaward room of the house she shares with her stepfather, the shoemaker. To this room come a succession of visitors: on Monday, Per Bjorling, skipper of a Norwegian whaler, with a bottle of vodka;

on Tuesday, Mr. Spence the jeweller, with a half bottle of whisky; on Wednesday, William Snoddy the builder's clerk, with a flask of gin (here the pattern is broken, when he is refused admittance by the shoemaker and is met by Celia in the shadows outside); on Thursday, Ronald Leask the crofter, her fiance, who sends the shoemaker off to buy a bottle of brandy. On Friday the pattern is again varied, for the visitor is the minister, to whom Celia pours out her confession, and the drink is a bottle of wine Celia has provided for herself. Saturday night sees Bjorling, Spence, Snoddy and Leask all drinking in the same bar, where Leask picks a fight with the Norwegian over Celia. Later that evening, however, as her stepfather lies ill, Celia is visited by Snoddy and Spence but refuses to admit them or accept the drink they bring.

This obvious structural pattern based on repetition and contrast is reinforced by an equally obvious set of symbolic contrasts between light and darkness. As Bjorling approaches the house, the shoemaker's room has 'a lamp burning in the window but the other room next the sea was dark' (1). The visitor having been announced, 'the seaward room remained dark; or rather, the window flushed a little as if a poker had suddenly woken flames from the coal' (1). Celia, it emerges, needs darkness and the glow of alcohol before she can confront the world. There is the same contrast in Section 3 between Celia's 'dark seaward window' and the 'lamplight' of the room where Mr. Spence plays two perfunctory games of draughts with the shoemaker before entering her 'dark room', where he finds Celia 'bending over the black range, stabbing the coal with a poker:'

> At once the ribs were thronged with red and yellow flames, and the shadow of the girl leapt over him before she herself turned slowly to the voice in the doorway. (4)

Similarly, as Snoddy argues on the doorstep with the shoemaker, 'the lamp was burning in the work-room but the room next the sea was in darkness' (6). When Celia accosts him outside, 'her face in the darkness' is 'an oval oblique shadow', and together they move 'into a segment of deeper darkness' (8). Exactly the same contrast between light and darkness is to be found during Leask's visit in Section 6: 'The lamp was lit in the old man's window but Celia's room, as usual, was dark' (9). When the two men enter, they see her 'outline against the banked-up glow of the fire' (10). Celia refuses to light her lamp: 'I like it best this way, in the darkness' (10). While the shoemaker goes for brandy, Leask and Celia sit 'in the growing darkness':

> The only light in the room was the dull glow from the range. Ronald could see the dark outline of the girl beside the fire. (12)

Then the brandy arrives and the scene is transformed.

> She picked up the poker and drove it into the black coal on top of the range. The room flared wildly with lights and shadows. The three dark figures were suddenly sitting in a warm rosy flickering world. (12)

Later when the shoemaker tries to light the lamp, Celia quarrels with her fiance and sends him away.

> The flames were dying down in the range. Celia and Ronald and the shoemaker moved about in the room, three unquiet shadows . . .
>
> The last flame died. In the seething darkness the girl and the old man heard the bang of the outer door closing. (14)

It is in 'half darkness' (15) that Celia makes her confession to the minister, who urges her to 'have faith':

> The girl's window was full of stars. The sky was so bright that the outlines of bed and chair and cupboard could be dimly seen, and the shapes of an empty bottle and a glass on the table. (22)

In the final section, the shoemaker's room is feebly lit as he lies fighting for breath. This time it is Celia who comforts him and sends the night visitors away. The shoemaker looks forward to her marriage to Leask and 'an end to this darkness' (35). Finally, as she leaves his room the dawn is breaking outside: 'The sun had not yet risen, but light was assembling in broken colours over the Orphir hills'. As she looks across the harbour towards her fiance's farm, 'the sun rose clear of the Orphir hills and folded the girl in the light of a new day' (37).

What we find in 'Celia', then, is that the structural and symbolic patterns are exactly matched: in each pattern there is a set of repetitions of incident or image, and in each the culmination, the climax is marked off by contrast.

'It is in contrast,' declares Brown, 'that a storyteller finds his greatest delight' (*Witch*, vii). It is no surprise, therefore, to discover that it is this device that provides the basic structural pattern in 'A Calendar of Love'.

The narrative pattern is obvious from the very start. 'January' begins:

> The fisherman Peter lived in a tarred hut above the rocks with his boat, his creels, his Bible.
>
> Jean Scarth lived with her father (men called him Snipe) in the pub at the end of the village . . .
>
> Thorfinn Vik the crofter lived in a new wooden house at the edge of the moor. (9)

Peter is a fisherman living by the shore; Thorfinn Vik a crofter living beside the moor: thus each is associated with one of the 'primitive elements of land and sea out of which,' according to Brown, 'men have, with danger and endurance, to drag their livelihood' (*Witch*, vii). Peter is religious, a total abstainer, an attender of Gospel meetings; Thorfinn a compulsive womaniser and drinker, an habitue of dance-halls and public houses. Together, as their names suggest, they embody the contrasting traditions and mores of Orcadian life, the Christian and the pagan. 'February' begins:

> After the gale in the second week of February there was much sea for days. Peter sat over his stove with the evangelical magazines. The ten lost tribes of Israel were not lost at all! They were here, in the islands of Britain, and Peter was one of them, Peter was an Israelite! He read on and on.
>
> * * *
>
> The van cost Thorfinn fifty pounds second-hand. Now he could go to dances in the farthest parishes and see new women. He had not passed the driving test, he had neither licence nor insurance, but he took the risk, driving at night, with no L-plates. (10-11)

Between Peter and Thorfinn, literally in the extract from 'January' and metaphorically in their rivalry for her love, stands Jean, who before the cycle of the year is complete, bears one of them a son, conceived either in Thorfinn's van as the March thaw 'unwove the stubborn snow' (13), or in Peter's 'hard religious arms' (14) the night Jean's father dies.

The story is built out of the contrasting actions and speeches of the three characters in passages of tightly patterned dialogue and narrative. The section entitled 'June', for example, consists of a montage of patterned speech: 'Thorfinn said to Jean . . . Jean said to Peter . . . Peter said to Thorfinn . . . Thorfinn said to Peter . . . Peter said to Jean . . . Jean said to Thorfinn' (17-18). 'July' focusses on the contrasting activities of Thorfinn, Peter and Jean 'on the last day of the Carnival Week in Stromness' (18), abruptly cutting no less than six times from Thorfinn to Peter to Jean. 'August' advances the story by means of three contrasting advertisements from the *Orcadian*:

> THE TEN LOST TRIBES OF ISRAEL – *where are they*? They inhabit the British Isles *today*! We are THE CHOSEN PEOPLE in a world *hastening to its end*! Those who would like to know more about this *undoubted fact* are invited to a public meeting in Ingsevay Community Centre on (D.V.) 15 August, at 8 p.m.

> Experienced full-time *barman* wanted for Ingsevay Inn. Wages £8 10s. per week. Apply Miss Jean Scarth, The Inn, Ingsevay.
> FOR SALE – A green Morris van, 1945, in first class running order. Can be seen. Apply Box No. 3124. (24)

In 'September' Thorfinn and his fellow crofters take part in 'the great shining ceremony' of harvesting the corn – 'stooping, rising, burdening and disburdening themselves as in some ritual of birth and death' (25). Peter, on the other hand, gathers limpets by himself on the shore and discovers the corpse of a drowned woman. In 'October' both men in turn visit Jean's inn, ask to see her and are refused by the hired barman. Here the pattern of repetition and contrast is put to comic effect:

> 'Jean's not seeing anybody,' said James Firth.
> 'Tell her *I'm* here,' said Peter.
> 'It wouldn't matter a damn if I told her the Archbishop of Canterbury or the Dalai Lama was here, she wouldn't see them,' said James Firth . . .
>
> James Firth said, 'She isn't seeing anybody.'
> 'Tell her it's me,' said Thorfinn.
> 'It wouldn't matter,' said James Firth, 'if you was Robbie Burns, Casanova and Don Juan all in one.' (28-29)

'November' describes how each character in turn reacts to 'the first snowflake of winter'. To Peter, disappointed in his expectation of the end of the world, it is a sign from the heavens, a reminder of the eternally cyclic pattern of life. To Thorfinn, preparing to do battle with the police, it is a 'kiss of peace'. To Jean, however, indifferent to the child in her womb, it brings spiritual and emotional release:

> suddenly everything was in its place. The tinkers would move for ever through the hills. Men would plough their fields. Men would bait their lines . . . And forever the world would be full of youth and beauty, birth and death, labour and suffering. (33)

This epiphany, of course, lies at the very heart of Brown's vision of life: 'Birth, love, labour, death,' he writes in *An Orkney Tapestry* (1969), 'this was the rhythm of the crofter-fisherman's life, generation after generation' (36).

The paratactic structure of oral narratives like the ballad, according to David Buchan, does not result in looseness 'because binding rhythms unify the poems and produce highly patterned artefacts' (*The Ballad and the Folk*, 53). We have seen how Brown uses the same 'binding rhythms' of repetition and contrast to shape and unify his stories, and have witnessed the 'highly patterned artefacts' that result.

However, in Brown's case the complex patterning is not merely a device for controlling and unifying the narrative; it is also something he clearly admires and values for its own sake. For to Brown pattern is the essence of all art. 'Poetry, art, music,' he writes in his novel *Magnus* (1973), 'gather into themselves a huge scattered diversity of experience and reduce them to patterns' (140). One reason why 'I rarely write a story about the 1970s' he tells us, is that 'passing events are difficult to grasp, form, pattern' (*Witch*, x).

Nevertheless, Brown does not ultimately subscribe to the doctrine of art for art's sake. 'Art must be of *use*', says Storm Kolson, the old blind Orkney fiddler in his play *A Spell for Green Corn* (1970, 83), a sentiment echoed in 'Sealskin' by Magnus Olafson, who discovers the 'task of the artist' is 'to keep in repair the sacred web of creation' (*Hawkfall*, 139). For Brown, 'a really great story' has more to offer than 'superb craftsmanship': it must satisfy 'some basic hunger in our nature' (*Witch*, viii-ix).

It is by virtue of what Brown, in *An Orkney Tapestry*, calls its 'ceremonial quality' (130) – its ritualistic element, its structural patterns, recurring images, and rhythms, that art fulfills its social function. 'Ceremony,' writes the young novelist in 'The Tarn and the Rosary', 'makes everything bearable and beautiful for us. Transfigured by ceremony, the truths we could not otherwise endure come to us' (*Hawkfall*, 198). Elsewhere, Brown describes how Grimm's Fairy Tales and certain Old Testament stories first taught him 'without realising it, how narrative is shaped and given rhythm': 'later', he adds, 'these seminal stories became still more precious as I grew to understand that they were, as well, fables of the human condition.'[4] In his essay on 'The Last Ballad' he suggests that it is the 'ritual quality' of the ballad-maker's words that hints at the 'fuller significance' of his story. So, in his own case, the 'ritual quality' created by Brown's structural and symbolic patterns leads the reader to recognise the 'fuller significance' of his best short stories, transforming them indeed into 'fables of the human condition'.

Suggestions for further reading:

Besides the collections of short stories referred to in the text, there are Brown's two novels, *Greenvoe* (1972) and *Magnus* (1973), both reprinted in paperback, and *Selected Poems* (1977), which contains poetry from three earlier collections. The only critical study of Brown's work is by Alan Bold (1978).

Notes:

1. *The Study of Folklore*, ed. Alan Dundes (Englewood Cliffs, 1965), 137-38
2. See J. Graeme Roberts, 'The Short Story as a Literary Form', *Chapman* 17 (1976), 2.
3. *New Edinburgh Review*, No. 4 (1969), 7.
4. 'Writer's Shop', *Chapman* 16 (1976), 22.

THE ENGLISH POETRY OF IAIN CRICHTON SMITH

J.H. Alexander

Iain Crichton Smith was born in 1928 in Lewis and grew up there. At the end of the war he came to Aberdeen to read English, and after graduating he embarked on a distinguished career as an English teacher, mainly at Oban High School. He has published eleven major collections of poetry in English, containing nearly 500 poems, and in addition he has produced, also in English, numerous uncollected poems, five novels, and five collections of short stories. As a native Gaelic speaker, he has written extensively in verse and prose in that language, and he has translated several of its poetic classics into English. Radio and television works and a not inconsiderable amount of literary criticism, mainly in the form of reviews, add to a corpus which was already of daunting proportions, when in 1977 Smith retired from teaching to devote himself exclusively to writing. The present essay offers a brief introductory account, in chronological order, of his major collections of English verse, which suggest that he is a very remarkable and individual poet, though a decidedly uneven one.

Smith's first volume, *The Long River*, appeared in 1955. It had only nineteen poems, but they were enough to indicate that he was a writer of exceptional promise. The title is drawn from the longest poem in the collection, a somewhat incoherent 'Meditation Addressed to Hugh MacDiarmid', in which Smith praises 'That masterful persistence of the spirit / that wears like a long river through the stone' (21). The fact that this poem is addressed to MacDiarmid is important, as is its celebration of sustained creative effort, for *The Long River* is a deeply earnest set of poems, beginning with a wider tribute to 'The Dedicated Spirits' whose 'perpendiculars of light / flash sheerly through the polar night / with missionary fire' (9), and including a roll call of the 'elemental ones', 'Catullus Shelley Burns / Sappho Blake and Clare' (14). Like the young Keats, Smith is consciously using his first collection to dedicate his poetic powers, and in the process both his elevated and austere conception of poetry and the extent of those powers become evident.

In *The Long River* poetry is an arduous quest for beauty, which 'has to be earned / in terror lightning and calm' by 'a blind man hunting a key / on a night of terror and storm' (14-15) and which when found offers 'more grief than gaiety' (17). Smith's early poetry is on a cosmic scale, seeking, even at the risk of great pain and emotional ferocity, to cast off all insensivity and boredom and to invest the whole gamut of human experience with the 'subtle radiance' of a high, passionate romantic lyricism (12-13, 24).

The devotion to beauty that has terror comes near to being matched by Smith's poetic ability in this first volume. What will immediately impress each reader, along with his technical versatility and fluency, is his extraordinary image-making faculty. On almost every page there is at least one unforgettable image, from the opening lines of the first poem, where 'The dedicated spirits grow / in winters of pervasive snow / their crocus armour' (9), through Prometheus' question 'Has too much suffering dulled / the liquid eye that ran / like a fine hound over the earth, / scent and colour one?' (12), to the grotesque picture of modern ennui: 'Time sagged in the middle / like a sack void of grain / as if turning in a bed' (24). It is true that this fondness for highly original images can lead to obscurity and a clotted density which impair the argument, but this is not an unusual failing in a young poet and, along with the fluency, it is here a sign of an exceptionally richly stocked and active imagination. Not all of Smith's imagery is strikingly original, and one finds in his work repeated and varied use of a number of common images derived from the natural environment of the west coast. In the impressive 'Poem of Lewis' (16) he distinguishes between the 'fine graces / of poetry', to which Lewis folk are in general immune, and the natural splendours of the landscape where

The sea heaves
in visionless anger over the cramped graves
and the early daffodil, purer than a soul,
is gathered into the terrible mouth of the gale.

It is this landscape -- pure, bare, harsh, haunted -- which characterises much of Smith's poetry with the hardness of stone, the impersonal cruelty of the gulls, the fitful glory of light and the terrible splendour of lightning, a cold environment surrounding an ardent humanity, and everywhere the infinitely variable sea.

The title of the second collection, which was included by Edwin Muir in *New Poets 1959, The White Noon,* is taken from its most important and accomplished piece, 'In Luss Churchyard'. This poem embodies forcefully that visionary and aesthetic ecstasy which is a prominent feature of Smith's early work. In the churchyard the speaker experiences an intense awareness of natural energy 'where living and dead turn on the one hinge / of a noon intensely white, intensely clear'. Smith's poetry is exceptionally full of colours and hues: green, blue, red, yellow, orange, black, and above all white. They are not in general used systematically, but whiteness habitually suggests extreme purity, spirituality, and atemporality, and it is often linked, as here, with the force of light which 'strikes the stone bible like a gong', 'the noon's implacable sea / of hammered light'. This is a meditation of unforgettable intensity and goes a long way towards justifying Smith's emphasis on the supreme importance of the aesthetic in art. In a cooler poem, which shows the influence of Wallace Stevens' mandarin speculations, he calls the 'Beautiful Shadow' of the aesthetic attitude 'beyond the anguish of the ethical / my best follower and my truest friend' (31), and in five sonnets under the title 'Grace Notes' which end the collection, he opposes to theological grace a number of secular graces, among them the intuitive vision of the poet which goes beyond the pretty to the truly beautiful:

> The grace I ask is otherwise. It's not
> what will, like moonlight, make all rubbish seem
> the mellow music that rewards your thought –
> rather the blind man's grace who, in a dream
> of tapping whiteness, makes his way round what
> would dump the seeing in a raging stream. (38)

In spite of a few fine ambitious poems, *The White Noon* is a rather miscellaneous collection with a high proportion of pieces which must be reckoned failures on the whole – forced, obscure, or inconsequential. Obscurity is also a problem in the third collection, *Thistles and Roses* (1961), where a handful of poems defy all efforts at comprehension and knotty passages are legion. The major development in this volume is a pronounced movement away from the high aesthetic ecstasies and the tendency to write poems about poetry which were evident in the first two collections. The title *Thistles and Roses* does not refer to a specific poem but suggests a general conflict between severity and softness. There are no thistles as such, but there are repeated references to roses. The sonnet 'Luss Village' begins with one of Smith's most daring and successful collocations:

> Such walls, like honey, and the old are happy
> in morphean air like gold-fish in a bowl.
> Ripe roses trail their margins down a sleepy
> mediaeval treatise on the slumbering soul. (10)

The sleepy geriatric mildness here is innocent of any hint of thistles, but in the striking poem 'Kierkegaard' the cold northern environment and the philosopher's father pictured as Abraham cutting his son 'to the head and heart' are opposed to the influence of Regine who 'sank her roses into his cold desert' and 'drove his body deeper into art'. The resulting art fused tragedy and comedy

> Till the new category, the individual,
> rose like a thorn from the one rose he knew.
> The crucifixion of the actual,
> by necessary acceptance brought him through
> to where his father standing calm and new
> cutting his head and life made one from two. (35)

(The repetition of 'rose' in the second line can hardly be a pun, so it must be ascribed to that carelessness which not infrequently accompanies Smith's fluency.) Here the rose helps to give birth to an individual tough enough to accept the crucifixion and the paternal knife. No such fusion, however, took place at the Scottish Reformation in 'John Knox', with its opposition between 'false French roses' and Knox's ruthless scythe (18). One result of this is that nowadays 'A Young Highland Girl Studying Poetry', coming from an affectionate but unsoulful stock at whose mouth 'The foreign rose abated', experiences poetry as 'an angled plough' which 'drives its lines into her forehead' (41). Lacking Kierkegaard's healing fusion in her upbringing, the young girl finds poetry a puzzling and harrowing experience. The basic opposition in the collection would thus seem to be between the harshness or bareness of Scotland's Reformed sensibility, impervious to Kierkegaard, and the very diverse softnesses of 'foreign' refinement and the Eventide Home.

A similar conflict appears in this collection's concern with the status of art. Smith finds that the artist is not readily accepted or taken seriously by his society. 'About that Mile' introduces a theologically and morally earnest interlocutor who talks of the 'shining moral knife', the construction of fences (a recurring symbol for the protection of the ego), and crucifixion, and opposes them to an interlude of relaxation in his own past; he asks 'why two people living in a mile / of perfume and vast leisure failed their task', and when the speaker presses him on this subject he makes his low estimate of poetry clear:

> 'About that mile,' I said, 'about that mile
> you talked of there.' 'Well,' he pursued, 'what then?'
> 'Do you not,' I questioned with a half-smile,
> 'dream of it sometimes, wish it back again?'
> But he with an equal smile said then to me:
> 'I turn to poetry for such foolery.' (20)

The subject is taken up again in two sonnets under the title 'Studies in

Power'. The speaker, attending a meeting and listening to the debate, doubts the value of his own 'dwarfish verse' in the face of the violent 'in / black Roman leather' (Roman severity is a frequent image in Smith's work) and the beautiful 'in her deadly silks', But then, in an image which recurs several times in the verse and prose fiction to represent perfection, he has a vision of the integrity and comprehensiveness of art which resolves his doubt for the moment:

> Till suddenly there I saw a vase in bloom
> gathering light about it clearly clearly
> in adult daylight not by a moon obscurely,
> and its harder language filled the small room
> with its bare constant self, its paradigm
> of straining forces harmonised sincerely. (47-8)

In *Thistle and Roses* Smith's visions lose something of their former afflatus, becoming rather harder and barer, and they have more directly to do with harsh reality and common humanity. The celebrated opening poem, 'Old Woman', is tightly observed, over-explicit in the middle, but ending with a sea image at once aesthetically perfect and in close keeping with the subject:

> And nothing moved within the knotted head
> but only a few poor veins as one might see
> vague wishless seaweed floating on a tide
> of all the salty waters where had died
> too many waves to mark two more or three. (9)

The humanity which can form part of the aesthetic attitude is evident also in the communal vision of friends in the pure 'By Ferry to the Island', in another art in the following poem 'A Blind Negro Singer', and in love in 'Three Sonnets': all of these poems are full of light and whiteness. In answer to the persistent doubts about the value of art, and in particular the suggestion that it shields one from the searing flames which the puritan confronts directly, Smith can only insist that art is truly graceful, comprehensive rather than single, fertile rather than barren (11-12), and that the fragile orange sunshade which 'shield[s] us from the fire' justifies itself by its poise and its beauty (17).

In the same year which saw the appearance of *Thistles and Roses*, 1961, Smith published in *New Saltire* an ambitious and important poem in fourteen sections called 'Deer on the High Hills – A Meditation'. (It was included in the *Selected Poems* nine years later, where two less important subsequent sequences also appeared, along with a number of shorter poems selected from earlier collections and elsewhere.) The concern of this sequence (which is by no means always easy to follow) is with the fragility of beauty, and the impersonality of the natural world and the extent to which it can play a part in imaginative work. For part of the sequence the deer are made to function as a natural correlative to the force and grace of art, arrogantly aloof, often ignored but dangerous in times of crisis, poised between the mundane and the visionary, between earth and sky. The poet is asked to know the mundane world thoroughly and to use the hard, bare, intractable landscape as the stuff of poetry rather than raiding the myth-kitty, to use Larkin's phrase, so that he may achieve a deer-like grace:

> You must build from the rain and stones
> till you can make
> a stylish deer on the high hills,
> and let its leaps be unpredictable! (*Selected Poems*, 31)

The deer is both amoral and completely at home with its own fragility, untroubled by the 'languaged metaphor' of evil (33) or 'The rampant egos of the flat plains' ever clinging to their identities, whether stones or humans (37). Thoroughly sensuous, graceful, and alert, the deer surveys the world at its feet 'vigilant always like a tiptoe mind / on peaks of sorrow, brave and scrutinous' (39). Yet the poem ends with an acknowledgement of the 'otherness' of the natural world, of the falsity inherent in using it metaphorically. The deer itself may be 'a world away, a language distant' (40), but man in his loneliness must continue to establish imaginative contact with landscape and its inhabitants, while recognising their integrity, and follow the deer's example in his art:

> So being lonely I would speak with any
> stone or tree or river. Bear my journey,
> you endless water, dance with a human joy.
>
> This distance deadly! God or goddess throw me
> a rope to landscape, let that hill, so bare,
> blossom with grapes, the wine of Italy.
>
> The deer step out in isolated air.
> Forgive the distance, let the transient journey
> on delicate ice not tragical appear
>
> for stars are starry and the rain is rainy,
> the stone is stony, and the sun is sunny,
> the deer step out in isolated air. (41)

This sequence is a bold imaginative effort, playing abstract words deftly against concrete and handling the three-line stanzas with an exalted and passionate delicacy befitting its subject. 'it is both words and music together, it is what one wants poetry to be.'[1]

Smith's concern with the nature of grace and his argument with his society are continued in the fourth collection, *The Law and the Grace* (1965). Here there is a limpid title poem, in which the poet answers the call to conform to a church and a society where grace has been legalised with a proud defence of his own angels, which

are free and perfect. They have no design
on anyone else, but only on my pride

my insufficiency, imperfect works.
They often leave me but they sometimes come
to judge me to the core, till I am dumb.
Is this not law enough, you patriarchs?

In 'Hume', as fine a short poem as any he has written, Smith examines the additional challenge to this inner law and grace of art which is offered by rationalism, and he employs for the purpose an extraordinary and completely successful set of images, unobscure, witty, haunting, making the point of the poem by example:

More than this I do not love you,
Hume of the reasonable mind.
There was an otter crossing the sound,
a salmon in his cold teeth.

This mist came down. Between two capes
there was no road. There was a French
salon, an adoring wench.
He picked the salmon with his teeth.

Delicate Hume who swims through all
the daring firths of broken Scotland,
there were no roads across the land.
The causes, like old fences, yawned

gravely over wit and port.
Diplomacies are what displace
the inner law, the inner grace,
the Corrievreckan of bad art.

(Corrievreckan is a whirlpool between Jura and Scarba.)

Smith's low regard for eighteenth-century rationality results from his awareness that beneath rational argument and calm behaviour there is a more profound life of will and passion. Having established his own poetic identity in his earlier poems, he is now moving towards a critique of that bourgeois society of which he is a member, and several poems are devoted to exposing the passion or the anxieties which lie below its apparently calm surface. One of the poet's functions is to tap the dionysiac and loosen the rigid as Burns does for the Covenanters in 'The Cemetery near Burns' Cottage', to be a lone rider, one of 'the careless ones' who are on hand to rescue the plodding settlers 'with their wagons all weighed down / by women's hysteria, furniture, design' (55): the last word there is nicely ambiguous.

In each of the four collections discussed so far, the force of the whole has been somewhat lessened not only by the presence of inferior work but also by the lack of that overall cohesion between the poems which one finds supremely in Yeats. It is true that the same themes and images often recur, but one is still very much aware that most of the poems are occasional pieces. Smith's fifth collection, *From Bourgeois Land*, is a bold attempt to produce a fully coherent set of poems in criticism of bourgeois values. An epigraph for the volume may be found in the thirteenth poem where, in answer to an interlocutor's suggestion that it is inevitable that young rebellion should mature into acceptance, the speaker says:

> Ah, it is difficult. I know it well.
> But surely it is possible to remain
> a spy within the country and to gain
> a hard-won honesty from hollow hell.

As a spy in bourgeois land Smith has come in for some criticism. It has been argued both that his critique is superficial, that (in the words of his own criticism of some of Sorley Maclean's political poetry) it is 'too one-sided to be true at a poet's level of perception',[2] and also that the subject has led him to produce poetry of less density and resonance than formerly. There is some truth in both these accusations. The collection contains several distressingly slick poems, making easy points easily, and the richness of the earlier style is less in evidence, but *From Bourgeois Land* is nevertheless a substantial achievement.

The fundamental point of the volume is made in the first poem: lack of imagination can lead to unquestioning obedience and, in the extreme case, to the tidy administration of genocide. In the exploration of those barely hidden forces in bourgeois Scotland which, in different circumstances, might result in the extreme case Smith covers a remarkably wide variety of topics with a new lucidity and displays his mastery of a formidable arsenal of poetic tones. In appropriately neat stanzas he introduces, for example: grotesque comedy, as the bourgeois 'weeps all day for the minutest error / and snores from tidy pillows like a frog' (23); poignancy, with an old photograph of a girl, in a Free Church Manse, which is 'almost rusted in this world of grace' (11); and in one four-line poem (No. 25) a massively Blakean epigram which sees eternity in a grain of sand:

I take it from you – small token of esteem –
this ponderous watch that holds a soundless scream

and give you back – a gift that haunts your sky –
the howling faces of eternity.

It has been objected that Smith offers as an alternative to bourgeois conformity only a slightly self-conscious bohemianism, but he is a poet and his true alternative is the poems themselves; if his audience should fail him (47) then there is love, and in the last two delightful poems there are children.

The new unity of subject matter evident in *From Bourgeois Land* is maintained in *Love Poems and Elegies* (1972). The love poems are mostly very brief and may strike the reader as somewhat inconsequential, but sometimes they can encapsulate in half a dozen lines or less a world of tenderness, anxiousness, fierceness, and terror:

I think we are both sick.
When our heads touch they seem to scorch each other.
Our lips are drinking each other's ruin,

quietly just quietly breathing in unison.
Your eyes are wedged open, staring at me
just like a badger's frightened in the dark. (51)

The elegies (which come first) were written when Smith's mother died and adopt the broken style of a notebook of deprivation pioneered by Robert Lowell in *Life Studies*. Again, there is a risk that such poems will mean more to the poet than to the reader, but several factors help to make the set of elegies an impressively austere achievement. The great variety of invention in these poems on death is remarkable, yet they are united not only by their subject but by the relentless variations on funeral black, reaching their climax in a bunch of grapes which is seen as a clutch of black stars (29) and a black jar for which one feels that, like Turner, Smith wants a blacker colour than black (31). Further, the choice of words and images often moves just beyond the ordinary without breaking the self-imposed decorum:

There is no site for the unshifting dead (12)

In that brown picture you all look very old
for twenty-year-old girls and you're all gazing
to a sun that's off the edge and is made of salt. (13)

Most importantly, many of Smith's favourite images recur with poignant force in the elegies, so that they may be seen as a retrospective survey of his poetic world in the perspective of death: here are the roses, the fences, the daffodils, moon and stars, the stone, deer, the light and lightning, the vase, grace, and the ticking watch. In the year preceding the publication of these poems Smith said: 'everything I have ever done is really eventually coming to this question. What is death? What is a dead person, and in the end what is the value of writing when one is confronted by a dead person?'[3] The attitudes adopted in the face of death are those Smith has developed over the years – a stark honesty, the cultivation of the 'truly human', and acceptance that

> Being who we are we must adore the common
> copies of perfection, for the grace
> of perfect things and angels is too cold. (32)

The retrospective element in the elegies is also evident in *Hamlet in Autumn*, published in the same year. Hamlet had already played a prominent role in *From Bourgeois Land* as the sensitive prisoner of a grotesquely corrupt society which he experienced as a hall of mirrors, distorted reflections in a spoon (18, 25). The new volume offers an autumnal picture of this society in decline, beginning with meditations on the fierce revealing light of tragedy from classical times to the present (8-11) and ending with 'Finis not Tragedy' (59) and a Stoppard-like punning evaporation glancing once more at the mirror:

> It was just that I was not looked at.
> It was just
> an injustice of the glass. (61)

Hamlet himself is seen as being half in love with death: he 'chewed it, fed on it, watched for it in mirrors' (17), as the Chekovian Russians exclaim in their ennui 'Help us, let something happen, even death' (18). This is a picture of a weary, bored society, distrusting the intellect, aware of the fact 'That the slaves / sustained our libraries', surviving the decay of Empire, under the threat of nuclear annihilation (34, 36, 49, 43). Idiots bounce balls (7, 22); Napoleon's 'subtle genius' is defeated by 'the dense ignorance of life itself' (32); Francis Bacon's figures scream (7, 27); Chaplin 'pulls / thick cultures down' and 'trudges on / to thriving emptiness' (30).

The weariness which is the volume's subject matter (and which effectively draws the varied poems together) is unfortunately reflected in the rather tired language and flaccid structure of some of its contents. The most successful poem, 'For Keats', is a dense and tightly imagined piece. Keats was a major influence on Smith's early poetry, and now that autumn is a theme he appears openly with allusions to the three great odes, fused with the death of Tom (during whose last illness Keats had felt his identity threatened) and his own visit to Scotland in search of that nobility and objectivity which he eventually achieved in his last ode 'To Autumn'. This poem gains, as do many others in the collection, from reminiscences of Smith's earlier meditations — the perfect vase opposed to the imperfect bird, the 'helmet' frequently used for the human spirit, and the recognition of the otherness of nature:

> Fighting the scree, to arrive at Autumn,
> innocent impersonal accepted
> where the trees do not weep like gods
> but are at last themselves.
>
> Bristly autumn, posthumous and still,
> the crowning fine frost on the hill
> the perfect picture blue and open-eyed
> with the lakes as fixed as your brother's eyes,
> autumn that will return
>
> and will return and will return, however
> the different delicate vase revolves
> in the brown mortal foliage, in the woods
> of egos white as flowers.

This marvellous little poem is complemented by an equally noble elegy 'For John Maclean, Headmaster, and Classical and Gaelic Scholar'. The technique of this formal poem is not flawless, but it contains some of Smith's most successful ruminations, as he pays tribute to Sorley Maclean's brother, a fine representative of two dying cultures who knew 'that what protects us from the animals / is language healthy as a healthy pulse': the last three sections are particularly full of retrospective allusions and form a memorable natural hymn, drawing on autumn's splendours as the crown of the year.

In 1974 Akros Publications brought out a thin pamphlet of 24 pages, *Orpheus and Other Poems*, which is among the least known of Smith's collections but which contains his most impressive single poem. Most of the pieces in it are short and not of great importance ('In the Dark' is a notable exception) but the title poem 'Orpheus' is superb. This gravely joyful set of sonnets consists mainly of a dialogue between Orpheus and Pluto in which several of Smith's central concerns are examined lucidly and imaginatively in the most elevated tone. Pluto explains to Orpheus what he has already subconsciously willed, that his love for Eurydice had to come to an end so that now in writing about her his poetry may be 'more clear / barer and purer'. Pluto's own music, played on Orpheus' lyre, is such 'as the zodiac / if made of solid heavy massive chains might make / which yet were banked with elegies and fire', speaking 'in joy / with its own elegance, intense and sparse'. Orpheus experiences a desire to stay in the underworld, so as to avoid the egotism of life on earth, but he is persuaded to return to the upper world and incorporate in his poetry the rich textures of ordinary life. It appears that Smith is thinking of the development in his own verse from *The Long River* to *Love Poems and Elegies* as he writes:

And so his lyre had a graver heavier tone
as if containing all the possible grains
that can be found in marble or in stone.
What he had lost was the sweet and random strains
which leaped obliquely from the vast unknown
concordances and mirrors but the gains,
though seeming sparser, were more dearly won

as less in mobile warfare than in trench
one sees the faces closer as they loom
in their thorny helmets whether German, French,
or some quite other nation; and they seem
so like his own – the cheeks, the teeth, the chins –
that he must love them not as in a dream
but on this smoky field of green and orange. (14)

The grave abstraction and flexible pentameters of the penultimate stanza, and in the final stanza the daring image and sudden colour after the monochrome of the rest of the poem, indicate the assurance and range of this piece, which puts one in mind of Wordsworth's 'Laodamia' and some of Landor's most typical work.

The influence of 'Orpheus' is clearly felt in the first part of *The Notebooks of Robinson Crusoe and Other Poems* (1975). This part contains a group of fine formal poems with the gravity of their predecessor, several of them dealing with the aesthetic potentialities of common city life, and a number of delicate and sensitive treatments of love which maintain the new lucidity. The short second and third parts of the volume have less to offer, but there is one uniquely wry 'Chinese Poem' full of a rare mandarin wit. This anticipates the 41 short sections of the extraordinary 'Notebooks' themselves which make up the final part. One of the aphorisms in the thirtieth section may stand as epigraph: 'The world of one man is different from the world of many men.' Smith's awareness of the double movement in his own poetic personality comes to the surface in the 'Notebooks'. Crusoe is repelled by society, seeing it as 'a Hall of Mirrors in which my face like all faces swells like a jester's in a world without sense' (87); becoming in his imagination

> my own god worshipping my own images, I would not wish to enter, unshaven and hairy, the monotonous climate of the mediocre, but would prefer my extreme pain to their temperate ordinariness. (82)

In his proud isolation he is at once obsessed by and fearful of his own personality, trying unsuccessfully to keep away from the large mirror in which his wolfish face appears at shaving time (67-8, 85). In these circumstances he finds that language disintegrates under scrutiny into pointless wordplay and childish babblings (which at times approach concrete poetry). In spite of all his reservations Crusoe is driven back into an acceptance of society, since for better or worse 'Language is other people' (87). His prayer is:

> O Lord, let me know my mortality: let me cast myself on the common waters. Let me be resurrected by the cheap tarnished glorious tinfoil light. (82)

That this social world may be in its way also unreal, a 'new dream', a cinematic fiction, is an unavoidable danger.

The 'Notebooks' are written with a scrupulous economy of means, brisk precision, and an attractive wit. They fluctuate easily between verse and prose, avoiding almost entirely both the tendency to wordiness which mars a good deal of Smith's poetry and the conscious lack of stylistic distinction with which the often depressing characters of his fiction tend to express themselves.

Smith's most recent collection of poems, *In the Middle* (1977), continues the ironic tone of the 'Notebooks', and the concern with common life evident in earlier volumes becomes a pity for that human suffering which is distressingly similar in every country (15). Irony and pity meet in sad amusement at the grotesque comedy of existence. The title may be taken in a number of senses, but the most direct reference is to a poem of the same title (44-5) which suggests in a somewhat confusing way the busy confusion of life experienced by a middle-aged poet in the midst of a society which is itself betwixt and between. The main sense in the collection is of the continuity of life's processes:

> The new children are taught their alphabet,
> and the new mothers enjoy their miracles.
> What is in the water but more water?
> If you close your eyes, you hear the endless footsteps. (10)

Even in sleep 'We go back to bed, / joining the endless river' (27). The sense of flux is increased by Smith's familiar conviction that western culture is in decline, the culture of a fading élite (13), where

Lycidas is drowned in a pile of supermarket goods (21) and scholars take part in a grotesque charade (47-50, 60).

The verse is spare, highly controlled, largely unrhymed. At times the danger of inconsequentiality is not avoided (18-19, 23-5), and an occasional note of cheapness and easiness is disconcerting (12, 17), but at its best this collection is no less impressive than the dedicatory poems with which Smith's career began. There is less obvious technical virtuosity, and the absence of rhyme from the work of such a fine rhymer is an impoverishment, but the early obscurity has largely been purged and there is a classical inevitability about much of this work which is the fruit of long discipline and which justifies the noble assertion in 'We Poets':

Whatever one sees
the other sees.
It is strange how we start from different premises
and see the same landscapes.

Poets of my heart, poets
of a different country. Our language
may be uniquely different.
Nevertheless our words sound
back from the same sounding board
with the same plangency of autumn
the same prints in the frost.

Suggestions for further reading:

Most of the poems discussed in this essay have been included in *Iain Crichton Smith Selected Poems 1955-1980*, selected by Robin Fulton (Loanhead: Macdonald Publishers, 1981). This generous selection from the whole range of Smith's poetry, incorporating a number of important poems hitherto unpublished, will satisfy most readers' needs, though the early collections and *From Bourgeois Land* are under-represented. *Lines Review*, 29 (June 1969) contains a select bibliography by the poet himself. More recent articles and reviews by Smith, together with reviews of his work and a handful of critical essays, have been listed each year since 1969 in the *Annual Bibliography of Scottish Literature*, a supplement to *The Bibliotheck*. Smith's own critical work is usually of considerable interest, and he has in general been well served by his reviewers and critics, but the following may be particularly recommended:

Smith, 'On Modern Scottish Literature', *SSTA Magazine*, 23 (1968), 40-1.

'Poet in Bourgeois Land' (interview with Lorn Macintyre), *Scottish International*, September 1971, 22-7.

Untitled article by Smith on his work in *Chapman*, 4:4 (Summer, 1976), 12-18.

Robin Fulton, 'The Poetry of Iain Crichton Smith', *Lines Review*, 42-3 (September 1972 - February 1973), 92-116; reprinted as Chapter II in his *Contemporary Scottish Poetry* (Loanhead, 1974).

Edwin Morgan, 'Poets of the Sixties - I: Iain Crichton Smith', *Lines Review*, 21 (Summer 1965), 9-17; reprinted as 'The Raging and the Grace: Some Notes on the Poetry of Iain Crichton Smith' in his *Essays* (Cheadle Hulme, 1974), 222-31.

Notes:

1. From Smith's review of Sorley Maclean's *Selected Poems*, *Glasgow Herald*, 21 April 1977, 8.
2. 'Modern Scottish Gaelic Poetry', *Scottish Gaelic Studies*, 7 (1953), 201. For the adverse criticisms see: *Times Literary Supplement*, 14 August 1969, 898; Alan Brownjohn in *New Statesman*, 79 (2 January 1979), 18-19; and John McQueen in *Lines Review*, 29 (June 1969), 46-8.
3. *Scottish International*, September 1971, 27.

Index

(Works discussed in this volume are indexed under the name of the author)

TREASURE ISLANDS 2

AN ADULT GUIDE TO CHILDREN'S WRITERS AND ILLUSTRATORS

Michael Rosen and Jill Burridge

PICTURE CREDITS

BBC Books would like to thank the following for providing photographs and for permission to reproduce copyright material. While every effort has been made to trace and acknowledge all copyright holders, we would like to apologise should there have been any errors or omissions.

Page 15, illustration taken from *Peepo!* by Janet and Allan Ahlberg, 1981. Published by Kestrel Books 1981 and in Picture Puffins 1983. Reproduced by permission of Penguin Books Ltd.; p. 34, © Quentin Blake. Publishers Jonathan Cape; p. 41 © 1983 Anthony Browne. Permission granted by the publishers Walker Books Ltd.; p. 58, © Quentin Blake, 1988. Publishers Jonathan Cape; p. 80, *Alfie Gets in First*, Shirley Hughes. Harper Collins Publishers Limited; p. 91, © Jonathan Allen, 1989. Publisher J. M. Dent; p. 96, © Jill Murphy, 1986. Permission granted by the publishers Walker Books Ltd.; p. 112, © Maurice Sendak, 1963. Publishers: The Bodley Head; p. 129, © Barbara Firth. Permission granted by the publishers Walker Books Ltd.; p. 134, *Max's Dragon Shirt*, Rosemary Wells. Harper Collins Publishers Limited.

AUTHORS' NOTE

Please note that all the book prices listed are accurate up to the time of going to press but may change subsequently

This book is published to accompany the R4 series entitled *Treasure Islands*

Published by BBC Books,
a division of BBC Enterprises Limited,
Woodlands, 80 Wood Lane
London W12 OTT

First published 1993

ISBN 0 563 36773 3

Front cover illustration from *Willy the Wimp* © Anthony Browne, 1984.
Permission granted by the publishers Walker Books Limited.

Set in Century Light by Selwood Systems, Midsomer Norton
Printed in Great Britain by Clays Ltd, St Ives Plc
Cover printed by Clays Ltd, St Ives Plc

CONTENTS

THE MAIN ANNUAL CHILDREN'S BOOK PRIZES

THE SMARTIES BOOK PRIZE:
Sponsored by Smarties and administered by Book Trust, there are three categories of age groups 0–5, 6–8, 9–11, with a winner in each category and an overall winner for the Grand Prix.

THE CARNEGIE MEDAL:
Presented by the Library Association for an outstanding book for children.

THE KATE GREENAWAY MEDAL:
Presented by the Library Association to an artist who has produced the most distinguished work in the illustration of children's books.

THE KURT MASCHLER *Emil* AWARD:
For a book of excellence where text and pictures work in harmony to enhance and balance each other.

THE *GUARDIAN* CHILDREN'S FICTION AWARD:
For an outstanding work of fiction for children by a British or Commonwealth author.

THE CHILDREN'S BOOK AWARD:
Organized by the Federation of Children's Book Groups, the children select their best book of the year.

THE WHITBREAD LITERARY AWARD CHILDREN'S NOVEL:
Sponsored by Whitbread and administered by the Booksellers Association, this award is for a book for children of seven and up written by a British or Irish author.

THE MOTHER GOOSE AWARD:
For the best newcomer to British children's book illustration.

THE *SIGNAL* POETRY AWARD:
Sponsored by the journal *Signal: Approaches to Children's Books* the prize honours excellence in children's poetry.

THE ELEANOR FARJEON AWARD:
Presented annually by The Children's Book Circle and sponsored by Books For Children in recognition of outstanding service to children's literature.

INTRODUCTION

Children's literature is a strange phenomenon. It is something that virtually all of us come across; it involves millions of people as its audience and millions of pounds changing hands and yet very few adults take it seriously. This is even more remarkable in the light of the nationally-voiced concern about the level of children's reading standards. There may be many reasons for this mis-match between a public and visible business enterprise, and a lack of public and visible concern, but one reason must be something to do with the way we think about children.

There is much clamour over the recently-introduced standard achievement tests, an idea which seems to regard children as if they were raw chassis waiting at one end of a production line – all that is needed to make them readers, is to put the chassis through a few processes, then chunks of knowledge will become attached and eventually a finished, fully-reading product will emerge. The one problem with this approach is that it overlooks the fact that children are human beings. Human beings find it difficult to learn anything if their human-ness isn't taken into account. As far as reading is concerned this means finding books that interest children and listening to what they say about them. It is not enough, to put print in front of children and expect them to warm to the idea of reading, simply because it's there. Nor is it a great incentive to most children to suggest that a certain kind of book is worth reading simply because it'll do them good.

The idea behind this book is, then, to help anyone interested in children's literature – parents, librarians, teachers, booksellers and, of course, children – to explore what is available. It is only through exploring, browsing and following your nose that reading really becomes enjoyable. A two-year-old scrabbling around in the book box in the children's library, is no different in kind from a university professor reading the long list of books at the back of a scholarly work. If we want our children to be readers, we have to show them that the world of books is there for their benefit too. Reading has to be rewarding whether it's a baby in the bath playing with a plastic book, or a fifteen-year-old discovering Alice Walker, a twelve-year-old reading a pop-music magazine, or an eight-year-old reading a joke book. This means finding every possible way to bring alternatives and choices of books and print in front of children: comics, magazines, TV tie-ins, hobby manuals, sport histories, travel guides, catalogues, concert programmes and, of course, books. But what kind of books? It is nothing less than tragic that so many adults seem pitifully unaware of the huge range of children's books available today. When I was a child, there were really only two kinds of book: the picture book and the story book. The picture book was about the size of A4 and the story book was about A5. And that was it.

Nowadays you can have books that are in the shape of the object it's about: if it's about a sandwich then the book can actually be a paper-and-card sandwich. It can be a pop-up, it can have revealing flaps and holes. Books can tell stories in pictures and no words, partly in pictures and partly in words. They can look like comics or colour supplements, advertizements or letters. As for subjects, there is virtually no limit from the totally trivial to the deeply serious, the rude to the safe, the disgusting to the very proper. Almost any theme or subject that has cropped up in the public eye over the last twenty years has been approached by children's books: nuclear war, shopping malls, single-parent families, table football, neo-Nazis, cutting fingernails, truancy, and paper aeroplanes. It is a cornucopia and any adult interested in helping their children to read cannot claim to be serious unless they help their children see the range.

How does this book contribute? It is a set of profiles of some of the best-known, most widely read, and most critically acclaimed children's writers today. The profiles are all the result of face-to-face encounters with the presenters of the BBC Radio 4 programme 'Treasure Islands', so what you read here is a combination of background information, selected passages from the books, booklists and most importantly, the writers' own words describing how and why they write. It is a window onto a process. Just as we stand fascinated at the Craft Fair watching the blacksmith or the cabinet-maker, we can read this book and see the commitment, pleasure and skill of writers for children. From there I make the jump of thinking that anyone who comes to see this will inevitably be drawn into appreciating the vitality, exuberance and genius of today's children's books. This, in turn will lead you into an enthusiastic sharing of books with the children you know and care for. This may be wildly optimistic but then working with children and books can make you like that.

Some observers may notice that this tone is a far cry from the various pessimistic noises we hear in the press: children can't read, don't read, no one writes books as good as the ones we had, children's books today aren't serious enough, aren't funny enough, aren't scary enough and so on. What always baffles me about these moans is how ignorant they are. Almost *any* objection that can be made about 'children's books' can be answered by simply taking the objector by the hand into a good children's library or bookshop. There, I guarantee, they will find some books that come up to the standards they think are lacking. If what our objector wants is the classics, there they'll be. If they think one or other section of society has never been represented, they'll find something there. If they think everything has gone too cosy, they'll be able to find something that'll give you nightmares for weeks . . . and so on. Maybe there isn't enough of what this objector likes, but it won't be completely absent.

So what's being said here is: there's no excuse. If you care about children's reading – no! what am I saying? – if you care about *reading*, then this book should interest you. No matter how it looks, there is no separation between adult and child reading. The one doesn't happen without the other. If you think this matters, then listen to what some of our best writers are trying to do with books. This brings me back to what helping children read really means: *finding books that interest children and listening to what they say about them.*

Michael Rosen

JOHN AGARD

'I enjoy the contact with children. The work takes on a living dimension when you perform it with children.'

One of the most distinctive voices writing poetry for children at the moment is John Agard. His collection *I Din Do Nuttin* is a firm favourite with many children, and he spends an enormous amount of his time visiting schools, libraries and festivals. The children who are lucky enough to see him, very soon discover that he's someone who makes poetry dance.

John was born in what used to be called British Guiana, but is now Guyana. He came to England in 1977 and published his first book for children in 1979, *Letters for Lettie and Other Stories*. He writes poetry mostly, but he's also written texts for picture books, usually with a lyrical, rhythmic pattern to them, too.

He enjoys the contact with children that he's found on the hundreds, if not thousands of visits he's made over the years. 'It's a great joy, a great delight. The work takes on a living dimension when you can actually perform it with children.' Of course, it's very difficult, as a visiting writer, to evaluate what the children get from the experience, but he remembers that after one visit to a nursery school how flattered and excited he was by what the teacher told him. One of the children had said that instead of hearing the usual bedtime *story* that night, she would ask her mum to read her a bedtime poem. Small wonder, when he produces infectious pieces like this from *No Hickory, No Dickory, No Dock*:

So-So Joe
de so-so man
wore a so-so suit
with a so-so shoe.
So-So Joe
de so-so man
lived in a so-so house
with a so-so view.
And when you asked
So-So Joe

de so-so man
How do you do?
So-So Joe
de so-so man
would say to you:
Just so-so
Nothing new.

When John performs his poetry to children, he sometimes improvizes with them, using a chorus, inventing lines as he goes along. He sees this as similar to the way a musician might improvize depending on the vibes he gets from the audience. 'So you might have a chorus on the page. It's only written once or twice, but in actual fact, when you perform with the children, if the energy level begins to rise, and they are all involved, you wouldn't necessarily confine the repetition to, say, twice, as it is on the page. So the words on the page could become a kind of score. And from that musical score, you just take off . . .'

This is what inspired his poem 'How do you do?' He got the idea because at one school in the North of England, the Headteacher said to him, 'Oh, Mr Agard, just go in the staff-room, make yourself at home, get a cup of tea, I'll be with you shortly. Up here in the North of England, we don't say, "how do you do", quite as much as the folks in the South. I ask you a question, "How do you do?" What's your answer? Another question – "How do you do?"' This conversation set John thinking and he came up with a poem called 'The howdooyoodoo':

Haven't you heard
of the how-doo-yoo-doo
how-doo-yoo-doo?

I'm surprised
you haven't heard
of the how-doo-yoo-doo
how-doo-yoo-doo

Spend a day or two
in a place called England
and I'm sure you'll meet
the how-doo-yoo-doo
how-doo-yoo-doo

But for those of you
without a clue
the how-doo-yoo-doo
is a creeping kind of plant
that takes you by the hand
and says how-doo-yoo-doo
how-doo-yoo-doo

And if by chance
you should say
I'm feeling down today
I got a tumour in my brain
and my old grandmother
keeps haemorrhaging
drops of rain
that doctors can't restrain

Then the how-doo-yoo-doo
gets embarrassed
almost a fright
retreats into itself
and begins to wither

So upon meeting
the how-doo-yoo-doo
the most peculiar plant
don't be alarmed
be polite
just take it by the hand
and say how-doo-yoo-doo
how-doo-yoo-doo
how-doo-yoo-doo
how-doo-yoo-doooooooooooooooooo

At a school with this poem he gets the children joining in, shaking hands, saying, 'How do you do?' 'But even though I'd conceived that as a poem I'd do with adult audiences because of the whole satirical element of people being surface polite without giving their heart, children really respond to it very positively.'

Teachers often put it to him that there's a problem for them that if they don't speak in the same way as John does, then they don't know how to read his poetry out loud. He replies by asking them to picture him, in the Caribbean as a boy, within a British educational system. His teachers, he says, didn't have a Chaucerian accent. 'I don't think I have a Chaucerian accent myself, but when I see the words on the page, I've got to give it some kind of spirit.' He can read Chaucer's opening lines of *The Canterbury Tales*:

'*Whan that Aprill with his shoures soote*
The droghte of March hath perced to the roote ...'

so teachers should be able to read his poetry too. He says to them, 'Respond to it naturally with your own regional accent.' He feels that if they try to imitate a Caribbean accent, it can become a caricature.

But he doesn't only write in his native Guyanese dialect or language, he often writes in standard English or even switches between the two, as in this poem from *Laughter is an Egg*:

Round and round in supermarket circles
ain't much fun,
but weekend shopping must be done.

Every Friday, same old story
staring at things like cabbage and broccoli
when all you want is crisp and lolly.

Hear Dad: That's a nice piece of braising steak.
Hear Mum: This shopping always gives me a headache.
Hear Dad: Don't know why you never make a list.
Hear Mum: Must pick some cherries for the cake.

What about crisp and lolly?
And bet they'd say no
if you ask to have a go
at pushing the trolley.
But what can you do when you're only two?

Only sit trapped in little trolley basket,
round and round in supermarket,
and wait for your turn to get to the queue.

When will they reach crisp and lolly
underneath cabbage and broccoli
and that big big box of soap powder?
O how you wish they'd hurry.

Suddenly Mum and Dad are in a flurry.
Hear Dad: Look what you've done, silly.
Hear Mum: You've broken one of the eggs, Billy.

Round and round in supermarket circles
ain't much fun
but you like it when an egg is smiling.

'As a writer, it's very exciting having that heritage of standard English as well as Creole.' John explains that you can explore the resonances. He gives the example of the line: *Hear Dad: That's a nice piece of braising steak*. To say, 'Hear Dad' like that, is very West Indian. To say 'Listen to Dad' isn't the same. For him, it loses the poetry.

John began writing his poetry in Guyana; at Secondary school, one of his favourite subjects was English. He had a priest who used to teach his class, a Scottish priest by the name of Father Maxwell. He made words very exciting. At the time they didn't have television, so they used to listen to the radio. John used to hear this 'very strange man called John Arlott'. 'When I listened to cricket, I might suddenly pretend that I am the commentator, and make up fictitious commentaries – "Here comes Freddy Truman from Yorkshire coming up to bowl to Garfield Sobers. He cracks it. Magnificent boundary. Four runs . . ." '

Looking back at those times, John feels that what really excited him wasn't the commentary itself. It was the language: 'A gentle breeze blowing across the carpet . . .' Those little imitations of cricket commentaries was a budding love for the magic of words.

John Agard often works with other Caribbean poets like James Berry and Grace Nichols. Before these, and a few others, were visiting schools, black children were unlikely to have seen a black writer. As John puts it: 'I've been in schools where children have this idea that a Caribbean poet is like a strange invention. Cricketers fine. Reggae singers, fine. Limbo dancers, fine. But we have been conditioned, for many years, when we think of a poet, we think of male and white.' This image was reflected in a number of anthologies and that's why John Agard has produced the book *Life Don't Frighten Me At All*, an anthology of poetry for teenagers. He wanted teenagers to realize that a poet can be tall, short, man, woman, black, white and not necessarily just in the arts. With John Agard around, there'll be more and more children coming to realize just that.

John Agard

FAVOURITE TITLES

Calypso Alphabet	**PB** Lion £3.99
Dig Away Two-Hole Tim	**PB** Picture Knight £3.99
No Hickory, No Dickory, No Dock	**PB** Puffin £3.50
I Din Do Nuttin and Other Poems	**PB** Red Fox £2.99
Lend Me Your Wings (with Adrienne Kennaway)	**PB** Picture Knight £2.50
Laughter is an Egg	**PB** Puffin £2.99
Go Noah Go!	**PB** Picture Knight £3.50
The Emperor's Dan-Dan	**HB** Hodder & Stoughton £7.99

JANET AND ALLAN AHLBERG

'The way a piece of work gets made is often like a piece of knitting without a pattern.'

Janet and Allan Ahlberg have become one of the most successful duos there has ever been in children's books. *Each Peach Pear Plum, Peepo!, The Jolly Postman,* winner of the Kurt Maschler *Emil* Award in 1986, *Burglar Bill* have all delighted millions of children and adults. Their first books together were the *Brick Street Boys* series, a knockabout set of stories based on a group of inner-city children, and since then they have scored almost every year with a line of modern classics. Allan's words catch the rhythms of ordinary speech, catch-phrases from everyday life and joyful borrowings from popular rhymes and stories. Janet's illustrations have a naive quality to them, the figures stand out clearly from their backgrounds, but with little contouring. This makes them highly approachable and clear.

Of course, when two people work together, we often become curious as to how they go about the business of co-operating. Allan puts it like this: 'Usually what happens is one of us gets an idea that we like the sound of, talks to the other about it. And we bat it around then, like table-tennis. Eventually the time comes to start a book. We move in on it and continue to knock the words and pictures back and forth over quite a long period.'

Janet's version is that Allan usually gets the very first idea for something – often when he's out running. 'He comes back in, dripping, and rushes for a little scrap of paper and a pencil. I start to speak to him and he says, "Just a minute," usually because he wants to write down what he's thought of.'

They do have separate spaces to work in, Janet works above the garage in what used to be a hayloft but is now full of newspapers and old books, while Allan has a shed down the garden. It's smaller and simpler, he says, and he needs to be completely on his own and silent when he's working. But then they had a baby. This was to change their books. First to come was *The Baby's Catalogue*, the style of which picks up on that fascination children have with mail-order catalogues. This is both used and parodied as the book is almost a catalogue *of* babies rather than one *for* babies. *The Jolly Postman* was stimulated by their daughter too, and anyone who has read (or should one say 'played with'?) the book can testify to children's pleasure at taking the letters out of the pouches and reading the parodies.

Peepo! is both a game and a powerful evocation of a moment in English social history. Allan picks up the story: 'With *Peepo!*, the initial idea for that book was the hole. I thought it would be very nice to sell holes. I used to be a gravedigger. That's probably where I got the idea. Anyway, we played around with lots of forms of book that would justify or require the hole. It was only when we thought of the game Peepo, and peeping through the hole to see what was happening on the next page, that the book fell into place. We had a lot of narratives, some of which were quite surreal, and then suddenly I found myself writing about myself. In fact,

He sees his father sleeping
  In the big brass bed
And his mother too
  With a hairnet on her head. *Peepo!*

the baby in the book is me growing up in a working-class terrace in the Black Country in the Forties.'

In fact, several of the Ahlbergs' books have a sense of the past both in the text and the pictures. Janet is self-confessedly fascinated with objects from the past. 'I like the pram in *Peepo!*. It's a wonderful, huge sort of black thing and it isn't like modern prams.' But there's a developmental reasoning here too: 'We do the detail because children are very interested in tiny things and can actually see a lot. Their eyesight is incredibly good. On the other hand it's also easy to over-stuff a picture with too much. So I think I have to be careful about not overdoing it.'

Bye Bye Baby tells the story of a baby who goes out to look for a mother. It's an idea, like other books the Ahlbergs have done, that takes a conventional situation and twists it round, or plays with it. This began with an image, the symbol for StartRite shoes where there are two little children walking hand-in-hand. We see a back view of a little girl and boy. 'There's a certain kind of poignancy and power in that image which we've always liked. But the way a piece of work gets made is often like a piece of knitting without a pattern. I mean this book just started: There was once a baby who had no Mummy. Having got that sentence, the next follows the line of knitting and gets tagged on. You don't know where the story's going. The words lead you.'

Allan also writes poetry without Janet's artwork, as with the hugely successful, *Please Mrs Butler*. Rather surprisingly for someone so popular, he is strangely diffident about this: 'I find myself in a curious position in relation to verse, which is that I want to write it; enjoy writing it, but know almost nothing about it. I feel quite uncomfortable sometimes.'

With *Please Mrs Butler* and *Woof!*, a short novel for young children, there's quite a critical edge of schools and teachers:

During Assembly, Mr Blocker talked about how Jesus loved the little children and suffered them to come unto Him. He talked about some boys who had been having a spitting competition in the back playground. He warned what would happen if they did it again.

He admits that his attitude to schools is ambivalent. He is 'deeply fascinated' by primary schools. He worked in one as a teacher but, he says, he's unhappy and uncomfortable with the whole notion of schooling, 'because schools are, in many ways, pretty awful places. No one starting from scratch would propose to take thirty children and put them in a room with one adult and expect anything particularly good to happen. They excite me and amuse me and I want to write about them. But I think, God, they could be so much better than they are.'

Perhaps it is just as well Allan Ahlberg is 'fascinated' by schools, no matter what reservations he has, because the result has been some of the funniest and most inventive writing for children today.

Janet and Allan Ahlberg

FAVOURITE TITLES

PICTURE BOOKS

The Jolly Postman	Heinemann	£8.99
The Jolly Christmas Postman	Heinemann	£9.99
The Baby's Catalogue	**PB** Puffin	£3.50
Bye Bye Baby	**PB** Mammoth	£3.50
Funnybones	**PB** Mammoth	£3.50
Burglar Bill	**PB** Mammoth	£3.50

VERSE

Each Peach Pear Plum	**PB** Puffin	£3.99
Peepo!	**PB** Puffin	£3.99
Please, Mrs Butler	**PB** Puffin	£2.99

FOR OLDER CHILDREN

Woof!	**PB** Puffin	£2.99

JOAN AIKEN

'Adult books tend to be for entertainment. A lot of adults, if they read fiction, want to rest themselves and be entertained, whereas children, when they read, are really reading to learn about life unconsciously, or they should be, because reading is a tremendously important part of their experience.'

If a child has not read one of Joan Aiken's novels, then he or she will surely have come across her short stories which crop up in anthologies and many new-reader series. She is one of the best-known, and most widely read children's authors today, creating amusing stories about extra-intelligent animals for younger children, haunting ghostly tales, as well as magical and fantastical short stories for children aged between seven and eleven, and imaginary historical novels for older children. She won the *Guardian* Children's Fiction Award in 1969 for *The Wolves of Willoughby Chase*.

Chilling ghost stories slipped into Joan Aiken's repertoire as an author from an early age. She was the child of two different writers, her father Conrad Aiken and also her stepfather, Martin Armstrong. Both were keen to encourage her to write, both enjoyed the technique of creating the short story and they each produced, at one time or another, a classic ghost story.

'Naturally our house was stuffed with anthologies of ghost stories and when I was a child, I read them all with my hair standing on end and somehow got into the habit of it, and I've never stopped writing them since. They are a lot of fun to write because it's rather an easy pattern. Children say to me, "How do you write a ghost story?" and I say, "Well, what you do is, you think of a horrific situation and then just lead up to it." It couldn't be easier really.'

Judge for yourself how simple but how scary these stories can be, with a collection such as *A Goose on Your Grave*.

It was Martin Armstrong, Joan Aiken's stepfather, who led her into writing for children. As an adult novelist, he had just one foray into the children's book world with a series for BBC Children's Hour called 'Said the Cat to the Dog' which was so successful that Joan decided to have a try herself. She, too, wrote a story for Children's Hour. It was accepted and at the age of sixteen, she launched her literary career, initially writing for children, then later for adults as well.

Two of her most popular characters for young children must be Arabel and her monstrous raven, Mortimer. Mortimer has a penchant for diamonds, slot machines and the inside of fridges, but his vocabulary is limited to one word, 'Nevermore'.

'He came absolutely out of the blue. "Jackanory" asked me if I would like to do a story for them and I had this idea of two characters, one perfectly good, intelligent, sensible and rational and the other absolutely, unutterably awful, just doing whatever he wanted. So then I thought one of them would be a girl, the other would be some kind of bird, then I thought, he'll be a raven. Then I had terrible time trying to think of his name, because I knew it had got to have three syllables. Then the name

Mortimer slotted in and I thought about how he was going to appear in the first place inside a refrigerator absolutely stuffed with food, and it just sort of built up from there. Arabel is the ego, the perfectly sensible good side and Mortimer is the id, unrepressed passion, and they kind of balance each other.'

'There's a great awful bird *in the fridge!' sobbed Mrs Jones, 'And it's eaten all the cheese and a blackcurrant tart and five pints of milk and a bowl of dripping and a pound of sausages. All that's left is the lettuce.' . . .*

Arabel opened the fridge door, which had swung shut. There sat the bird, among the empty milk bottles, but he was a lot bigger than they were. There was a certain amount of wreckage around him – torn foil, and cheese wrappings, and milk splashes, and bits of pastry, and crumbs of dripping, and rejected lettuce leaves. It was like Rumbury Waste after a picnic Sunday.

Arabel looked at the raven, and he looked back at her.

'His name's Mortimer,' she said. . . . And she put both arms round the raven, not an easy thing to do, all jammed in among the milk bottles as he was, and lifted him out.

Mortimer creates anarchy wherever he goes, with a level of absurd madness which young readers find greatly appealing.

'I keep a little notebook always and in it I write down anything that strikes me as I go along. Like, for instance, coming up in the train today, there's a house which has a moose head on the outside. This, in fact, I have made use of in a story because it seems so extraordinary. My notebook is now stuffed with things like this and it's no trouble at all just to whizz through it and combine three or four different ingredients and make them into something.'

For older children, Joan Aiken has invented an imaginary historical world with a series of events and people who have never existed. So, you have Richard IV, a Roman America where they speak Latin, and a channel tunnel already in action, two hundred years before its time. This invented historical framework first appeared with *The Wolves of Willoughby Chase* and has been carried forward with titles such as *Black Hearts in Battersea* and more recently, *Dido and Pa* and *Is*. The novels are full of wild improbabilities, with a language to match.

'Everybody out,' Mrs Bloodvessel bawled in a voice so loud that it made Dido jump. 'Come on, out of it, you slobby little tadgers, you.'

To Dido's amazement, out of the narrow door there began to appear what seemed like a never-ending stream of children, most of them barefoot, dressed in tatters, undersized, shock-headed and bleary-eyed.

The room they had entered was a dark, dank basement, not large. Dido was astonished that so many children could have emerged from it. She was puzzled also by the forest of ropes that dangled from bacon hooks in the ceiling, with knotted loops at their lower ends, as if this were a kind of hangman's warehouse. Then she guessed what their use must be as she saw Mrs Bloodvessel march over to a corner where a sleeping boy dangled motionless with his head, arms and shoulders through the loop of the rope and his feet dragging on the flagstones. Mrs Bloodvessel extracted a long steel pin from her nightcap and handed it to Mr Twite, who jabbed it into the boy's arm. He woke with a yell, tugged his head and shoulders free from the loop and made off, with terrified haste, as Mrs Bloodvessel bawled after him, 'Six o'clock striking. Can't you hear Marychurch church bells across the water? Get out, you lazy young lollop, or you'll have to pay for another night.'

'I started it doing *Black Hearts in Battersea* and I got hold of this wonderful book called *The Elizabethan Underworld*, which gave reams and reams of the most marvellous thieves' cant, and it just seemed to be a terrible waste that these words weren't brought back into circulation.'

A sharp, cockney heroine called Dido Twite, the foggy underworld of London, and the harsh realities of life during the Industrial Revolution bring flavours of Dickens to mind in these novels.

'Dickens was a terrific influence on me, because from about the age of seven on, my mother used to read Dickens aloud, especially *Oliver Twist*. In fact, I pinched one whole character from Dickens which somebody spotted recently. I'm not going to tell you which it is.'

Any ideas?

Joan Aiken

FAVOURITE TITLES

Arabel's Raven & other books about *Mortimer*	**PB** BBC £2.25
A Necklace Of Raindrops	**PB** Puffin £3.99
A Last Slice of the Rainbow	**PB** Puffin £3.50
The Kingdom Under the Sea	**PB** Puffin £4.50
A Goose on Your Grave	Gollancz £6.95
A Fit of Shivers	Gollancz £8.95
The Wolves of Willoughby Chase	**PB** Red Fox £2.99
Black Hearts in Battersea	**PB** Red Fox £3.50
Dido and Pa	**PB** Red Fox £3.50
Is	**PB** Red Fox £2.99

NINA BAWDEN

'I think a great many children are guilty and jealous and they're ashamed of these feelings, which is why it's quite sensible and interesting to write about them.'

Nina Bawden is both a truly serious and truly popular children's writer. She is prepared to look at children in her books as people who think deeply about emotions and people's motives. Among her best known novels are *Carrie's War*, *The Peppermint Pig*, which won the *Guardian* Children's Fiction Award in 1976, and *Keeping Henry.*

She was brought up in East London, went to university, has been for a time a Justice of the Peace and has always been active in the world of books, having written over twenty adult novels. It has been pointed out that she is one of the few children's writers who admits to making a conscious adjustment to writing for children. Jill Paton Walsh says that 'perhaps because she also writes for adults she is singularly free from the temptation to write for adults in the guise of children's books'.

Nina Bawden says that her family was 'rich in secrets; people always kept things from each other'. She remembers her childhood very clearly, best from about nine upwards, and this is the age she draws from most when she's writing. She thinks this is partly because the Second World War happened when she was twelve, and this made a kind of watershed, so that she knew what happened 'before' and 'during'. She lived with her mother and her brothers while her father was at sea. 'We lived a very closed-in life, I think, and so all the outside bits and going out and seeing things were very important.' She was evacuated with her school, which then seemed very strange and exciting, while all the time her father was away on North Sea patrol. He was only seen occasionally. She feels that this period of the evacuation was the most important part of her childhood, living amongst strangers in the Welsh valleys. Anyone who has read *Carrie's War* which tells the story of a girl, Carrie, and her brother evacuated into a Welsh village, will recognize the outline of the story in Nina Bawden's life.

She says that at the time, she was 'very emotional and rather violent'. 'I was always being told not to tell lies and not to get so agitated and not feel things so much.' One of the distinctive features of Nina Bawden's writing for children is that the child characters are psychologists. That is to say, we hear their figuring out of people's motives and wishes. In *The Outside Child* one of the children says, '*So I don't get angry with him as I do with the aunts. It's the people you live with who make you angry.*' It's Nina Bawden's view that children often are this kind of person. Children, other than your own, she says, tell you about how they think and feel much more than adults do. This is because it's their only way of survival, keeping an eye on the adults and seeing what they're up to. 'Adults can do anything to you. They can remove you from your home, they can stop you doing something you want to do.'

This philosophy makes Nina Bawden give her child characters a sense of power. They develop real knowledge about the world in her books, and they are real people seeing why and how they operate in the world. She says, perhaps she makes them more knowledgeable and understanding than they would naturally be, but it's a way of showing the characters as people who can 'help themselves a bit better'.

He took the kettle from its hook above the fire and filled it at the sink. He hung it back in its place, then knelt to put screwed-up newspaper and kindling in the grate. When it flared up he put the coal on, small lump by small lump as Aunty Lou always did, and as Carrie watched him, doing Aunty Lou's job, all the anger went out of her.

He said, 'Soon get it going. Cup of tea, bit of breakfast. Bacon, I thought. Fried bread and tomatoes. Something hot to set you up for the journey.'

Carrie said in a small voice, 'Not for Nick. The grease might upset him. He gets sick on trains.'

'Porridge, then?' He looked round, rather helplessly.

'I can do that,' Carrie said. . . . 'Aunty Lou?'

'Gone. Off with her fancy man.' . . .

Carrie said, 'Are you – are you angry?'

He sucked his teeth thoughtfully. 'Ate a lot, your Aunty Lou did. Always at it, munch, munch, nibble, nibble, just like a rabbit. Now she's gone there'll be one less mouth to feed. One less mouth to eat up the profits. . . .'

This piece is, of course, from *Carrie's War* and in the book, Nina Bawden has one of her young characters, Albert, saying '*I wish I was a grown-up. It's a fearful handicap being a child. You have to stand there and watch. You can never make anything happen.*' Which is precisely how she felt when she was evacuated. 'I had no control over what happened there or anywhere.'

At the outset, when Nina Bawden is writing a novel, she spends a long time working on the first three or four pages, because it's difficult to know exactly how she's going to tell it – whether it's going to be a centrally focused third-person, a first-person narrator or through a narrative where you take the point of view of several characters in the story and move between them. 'Until I've written it in different ways I can't be sure which kind of angle I'm going to use. I started off *The Outside Child* from a third-person point of view and it didn't work because you needed the emotional excitement of the central character discovering something.'

Today, there was a new picture. It was of a girl and a smaller boy, both of them younger than I was. Their picture had not been there before – I was sure of that – and yet, somehow, I felt that I knew them. . .

I picked up the picture and said, 'Who are they?'

My father and Aunt Sophie turned in the same moment, and they both seemed to freeze, as if I had held a frame in a video. . . .

Aunt Sophie said, 'Oh Edward, how careless!'

He looked very bright-eyed, a bit sly and embarrassed. He said, 'Sorry. . . .'

'You'd better explain to her, Edward.'

She looked at him, waiting, but he didn't speak, only sighed.

'Oh all right.'

She turned to me and said in a funny, flat voice, 'Their names are Annabel and George. Annabel is your father's other daughter and George is his son. So they are your half-brother and sister.'

Nina Bawden is adept at bringing her readers up with a start. She can surprise them with a sudden revelation, or shock with a quick horrific scene. In *The Outside Child* you find yourself worrying with the narrator whether she really has done something terrible to a baby, and in the opening of *The Peppermint Pig* we have, what has now become quite a celebrated scene, the finger-chopping episode.

Old Granny Greengrass had her finger chopped off in the butcher's when she was buying half a leg of lamb. She had pointed to the place where she had wanted her joint to be cut but then she decided she needed a bigger piece and pointed again. Unfortunately, Mr Grummit the butcher was already bringing his sharp chopper down. He chopped straight through her finger and it flew like a snapped twig into a pile of sawdust in the corner of the shop.

It was hard to tell who was more surprised, Granny Greengrass or the butcher. But she didn't blame him. She said, 'I could never make up my mind and stick to it, Mr Grummit. That's always been my trouble.'

Here Nina Bawden quite candidly admits to writing the finger-chopping scene to shock and titillate. It was a family story. 'My Grandmother used to tell it to me and I wanted her to tell it over and over again, because the idea of someone having her finger chopped off at the butcher's was so wonderful. And she went on telling me the rest of the story which was how the lady always kept her hand hidden. When she died and was laid out on her bed, my Grandmother wanted to see it, so she crept upstairs and pulled back the covers and the fingers were hidden in a pair of gloves.

When she went back downstairs, her Aunt knew where she'd been and said, 'Emily, will you go upstairs to the front room and fetch me my scissors and my thimble.' She had to go back up into the room where this dead woman was lying with the sheet pulled back and her gloved hands lying there ...

But Nina Bawden has always done much more than 'shock and titillate' her readers. Of writers writing for children today she is one of the best for describing sensitive, touchy and sometimes unpleasant feelings. 'Children often feel guilty and jealous. Things that they may have done are things that frighten them greatly. I think I was a guilty, jealous child. I think a great many children are guilty and jealous and they're ashamed of these feelings, which is why it's quite sensible and interesting to write about them.' Because Nina Bawden engages with emotions like these, her books are intriguing, magnetic and powerful. Not many writers for children dare to cover such areas, and we have to be grateful that we have a children's author who has chosen this way of writing.

Nina Bawden

FAVOURITE TITLES

Carrie's War	**PB** Puffin	£2.50
The Peppermint Pig	**PB** Puffin	£2.99
Keeping Henry	**PB** Puffin	£2.50
The Outside Child	**PB** Puffin	£2.99
The Robbers	**PB** Puffin	£2.99
Squib	**PB** Puffin	£2.99
A Handful of Thieves	**PB** Puffin	£2.99
The Finding	**PB** Puffin	£2.99
The Witch's Daughter	**PB** Puffin	£2.99
Humbug	Gollancz	£9.99

JAMES BERRY

James Berry has helped provide children living in Britain with a new voice. He has brought into children's literature scenes, characters and language that had mostly been ignored or – worse – misrepresented. His book of poems, When I Dance *won the* Signal *Children's Poetry Award in 1989 and his book of short stories,* A Thief in the Village *won the Smarties Grand Prix Award in 1987.*

James was born and brought up in Jamaica and came to England in 1948. At first he worked in International Telegraphs – now British Telecom – but he is now a full-time writer. He has often been put in the position as a spokesperson for 'ethnic' writers, but it's a term that James doesn't like. He says, 'I dislike these labels like "negro" and "coloured" and "non-white". I dislike "ethnic" because it separates off people.' What James prefers is 'getting to know each other on both sides'. He puts the issue into perspective by looking at the matter autobiographically.

'When I was a small boy in Jamaica, it always seemed to me that a white man was never a man at all. He was a white man. This was so because he would never meet me and pick me up and tickle me and shove his hand in his pocket and give me a penny to buy sweets or give me fruit. He would sit on his horse and I always suspect and feel and know that he is critical towards me, almost as if something's wrong with me. Since I've come to England and worked with people here I've come to realize that a white man is also a man. Similarly, I hope that, in the other way round, the bogeyman, the black man also becomes a person, a human being. It's a two-way thing.'

James grew up in a coastal village in the parish of Portland, Jamaica. As a child he was part of the agricultural way of life, helping parents, doing a share of work, fetching and carrying and making sure that he was in time for school. He was a Sunday School boy at the local Church of England. In the books at school, he says that no black person was ever portrayed as good. He was always a rebel, lazy or stupid. 'I had no real characters to identify with.' The two kinds of literature he was stimulated by was the Bible and the orally told Anansi stories.

James has written his own collection of twenty of these stories. *Anancy Spiderman* comes from the Ashanti people of what is now Ghana. 'He came to Jamaica through my ancestors when they came from Africa. The stories have become very popular in the Caribbean because, in a psychological way, they offer a form to express the kind of relationship between the overlord and the slave.' The stories truly belong to James because he heard them orally told right from when he was young. 'As a child we told these stories to each other and each individual had their particular stories that they tell over and over. On dark stormy nights, we didn't have electricity, we sat around telling these stories.'

The Anansi stories tell the tales of a trickster figure, Anansi, who can be a man moving around amongst people, playing tricks on them, sometimes successfully, sometimes not, and then when he gets into hot water, he can turn himself back into a spider. He is for that reason seen as a great survivor, rather like black people themselves and their culture surviving capture, transportation and slavery.

His book *A Thief in the Village* is set in a village in Jamaica. It's a set of stories about different people in that village. Though the stories aren't linked in plot or character, they build up a picture of a whole way of life. They were stories, he says, that he wanted to tell about a way of life he was fascinated, worried and puzzled about in terms of human behaviour. 'How we were all isolated and felt shut away.'

... Granny-Flo sat breaking coconuts and pulling out the pieces. Her blunt, stumpy machete came down hard on a coconut gripped in her left hand. Cracking it, then opening it, she then let the coconut-water drain from the hollow inside into a bucket. With her strong slender knife, she skilfully prised the white coconut kernel from its shell....

Fanso stood almost behind the squeaking wooden mill. He turned and turned the handle like mad. Turning the mill's grater-roller, cutting each coconut piece into white shreds caught underneath in a trough, Fanso milled as if he would never stop.

Granny-Flo rested down her short machete. 'Whoo!' she said. 'It so boilin' hot. Sweat runnin' in mi mouth. Jesus, Jesus – we need rain! All we need is rain, rain, rain!' ...

Fanso said nothing, though he'd slowed down his milling to listen. He quickened his work again then stopped thoughtfully.

'Granny-Flo,' he said. . . . 'These days – I keep wonderin', mam – wonderin' – what – what my father looks like. How he look, mam. Is my father tall, short, fat, thin, black, brown or fairskin?'

Granny-Flo stopped. The question made her look paralysed. Silent, not moving, Granny-Flo stared ahead rigidly. . . .

In a sharp, flat voice Granny-Flo said, 'You' father?'

'Yes, mam. Mi father.'

'You' father not worth talkin' 'bout.'

The book represents a way of life that belongs mostly to a generation before children today, but James doesn't see that as any kind of problem. 'Where would English literature be without a Charles Dickens?' He sees the stories as filling in a gap and he hopes that will form a link to the background of children born here of Caribbean parents. But he wants the books to be something to share between white pupils and parents too, as part of 'getting to know each other on both sides'.

James spends a huge amount of his time visiting schools and libraries, putting on performances and running workshops. They are, he says, very interesting and very important to him. 'One of the things that you come to recognize as a result is that there's a new relationship that black and white people have had through there being a black population in England. There has been a whole different attitude. When I first came here, people could hardly talk to me ordinarily without shouting at me as if I was deaf, or getting a little bit red in the face, or behaving oddly. In other words, bristling like a strange animal meeting another.'

Now he sees a change has happened. He can go to some remote part of Britain, to a village school, say, where all the children are white and they've only seen black people on television, and he feels that they're very happy to work with him. 'We must realize that humans have this tremendous capacity to share the difference that others have. We have it in us.'

James's collection of poems, *When I Dance*, has been very well received. In it we hear the voices of the Caribbean, and British black people, young and old, male and female. Sometimes we hear the traditional sound of Jamaican proverbs and riddles and then we hear a girl in England complaining about the way her dad expects her to behave.

In this poem it's a boy talking about his sister:

Listn Big Brodda Dread, Na!

My sista is younga than me.
My sista outsmart five-foot three.
My sista is own car repairer
and yu nah catch me doin judo with her.

I sey I wohn get a complex.
I wohn get a complex
Then I see the muscles my sista flex.

My sista is tops at disco dance.
My sista is well into self-reliance.
My sista plays guitar and drums
and yu wahn see her knock back double rums.

I sey I wohn get a complex.
I wohn get a complex.
Then I see the muscles my sista flex.

My sista doesn mind smears of grease and dirt.
My sista'll reduce yu with sheer muscle hurt
My sista says no goin keep her phone-bound –
with own car mi sista is a wheel-hound.

I sey I wohn get a complex
I wohn get a complex.
Then I see the muscles my sista flex.

As with John Agard, a poem written out like this, using what has now become a fairly standardized form of Creole, has provoked some people into making remarks about 'condemning people to the ghetto'. James sees such criticism as an attempt to defend a one-culture society, as if standard English were the only language just because it is dominant. 'Our British way of life is made up of many cultures. We'd be much poorer if we were to kill off all other languages and all kinds of regional voices, just in order to hear one kind of picked-out, trained-up voice.'

He sees Caribbean people as inheriting two languages – standard English and the language that has a West African background. Traditionally, Caribbean writers use both languages. 'It comes out of our plantation situation and offers a language that has roots in where people grew up, have lived and had experience and history. Rather than set up proud directives, we need to understand and to share and appreciate other languages.'

There is no finer way of understanding what James is saying here than to read his stories and poems, and indeed children's literature in Britain is much richer for having found a place for James Berry's work.

James Berry

FAVOURITE TITLES

VERSE	
When I Dance	**PB** Puffin £3.50
FICTION	
A Thief in the Village	**PB** Puffin £2.99
Anancy Spiderman	**PB** Walker £2.50
Isn't My Name Magical?	**PB** BBC £2.50
The Future-telling Lady	Hamish £8.99

QUENTIN BLAKE

'Very often, the first thing that you think, is right. One of the problems in doing a book, is keeping your first idea into the final drawing.'

Quentin Blake is one of the most recognizable, most loved and most influential artists working in children's literature today. He has both illustrated other people's work, most famously Roald Dahl's stories and poems, collaborated on a regular basis with Michael Rosen and John Yeoman and produced masterpieces on his own with such characters as Mr Magnolia, Snuff, Patrick, Angelo and Mrs Armitage. If you look, you can find common elements with his characters; they are often slightly dishevelled, chaotic, cranky types, often loners tackling a fantasy or a problem in some slightly absurd way.

Quentin Blake started drawing for magazines when he was still at school. 'I invented jokes and did little drawings for them and submitted them – which seemed a wonderful thing to do if you were a schoolboy.' He didn't have a formal art training. He studied English at university and followed that with a year's teacher training. It was then that he knew that he wanted to be an artist and he was already doing drawings that were being published. But he was conscious he didn't know enough about it and so he went down to Chelsea Art School in London and said, 'Can I come and do Life Classes?' which they let him do. Not that there was any certificate at the end of it, he says.

Humour is very important in all of Quentin's work but, he says, it's something he finds quite hard to talk about. Sometimes when he's been discussing books and illustration, he realizes that he's talked for some time without having mentioned humour at all. He says it's something that's very hard to define. 'It's something about the way you are, the way you see things. What is important to me about humour, is that it came out of starting professional life as a cartoonist. I knew that was a way of doing funny drawings and getting paid for it. But I realized after some time that that wasn't exactly what I wanted to do. I didn't want to illustrate jokes. I think the funniest things to me in drawings are living through what is happening.'

What Quentin means here is that the humour in his work arises out of the situation. Sometimes he doesn't know exactly what it's going to be. Only by trying out things does something start to become funny. 'I mean, after a while, you know that if you make a pig's ears wave about, it's going to look amusing. But the best bits, I think, are the things that you stumble across, something that your hand draws because you're imagining the reactions of the people to what is happening in the picture, like the mice in *Mouse Trouble*.'

When Quentin Blake has worked with writers like Roald Dahl, Russell Hoban and John Yeoman, he has had the problem of illustrating a character created by someone else and deciding whether he should add his own dimension to that character. He does a lot of reading before he starts drawing. The manuscript is very, very important. But if he has an idea in his head, it isn't necessarily what comes out as he starts to draw it. The ideas develop in the process of drawing. Sometimes these emerge straight away, at other times it happens later. 'Though I think, by the time I've finished the book, I always knew what that person looked like. Yet when

I look back at the old drawings which are lying around in corners of the studio, I find that I didn't. They didn't look like that to begin with and something has happened while I was drawing them.'

One of Quentin Blake's most successful collaborations was with Russell Hoban on *How Tom Beat Captain Najork and his Hired Sportsmen*. He says it was an astonishing experience, reading Russell Hoban's manuscript for the first time. 'It was . . . what? . . . two and a half pages of typing. I knew as soon as I'd read it, that it was something that I wanted to illustrate. It was as though it had been written specially for me. What was so "taking" about it, was that it was exactly the sort of thing I liked, yet it wasn't anything I could have thought of. Which is really one of the wonderful things about working with authors.'

When Quentin Blake and Russell Hoban came to do a sequel to that book – *A Near Thing for Captain Najork* – Quentin said to Russell, 'Did you find it hard to write another one?' He was very touched when Russell Hoban said, 'No, because I knew what the people looked like.' Generally what happens is that initially, there is no collaboration. Because two names appear on the cover, sometimes people think that Quentin sits down together with Russell Hoban, or John Yeoman or Roald Dahl, and they say, 'What shall we do a book about next?' That never happens, he says and he thinks it's right like that: 'The author writes.'

But of course Quentin Blake also writes and draws his own books. The inevitable question is, which does he prefer doing?

'I like both and it's a constant pleasure to think that I can do both.' He doesn't have to opt for one or the other. He very much likes doing his own books because he feels then that he is in charge of the whole thing. 'That is a special satisfaction: you've designed the whole thing. But I think the question of working with an author is something that has got more interesting to me, partly because you never know what's going to happen next. It pulls you into drawing things that you perhaps wouldn't have thought of. One can make a sort of analogy with a film or a theatre production. I like being the producer and the director as well as the actor. So it's a sort of interpretative function.'

As soon as he's reading a manuscript, he's reading it in the way that anybody reads a story, but he's also thinking which bits of this would make a good drawing? Which drawings would bring out what's happening? Which drawings can he do that will add something to it and not take away from it? How can he divide up the text so that it goes across however many pages it is – 32, 64, 96 – so that it all falls into place nicely and helps to tell the story? 'All those things are turning round in my mind.'

The other thing, which is nice, he says, is when you get an author who has a sense that this is going to be a visual production as well as something you read. 'With *Mouse Trouble*, like others by John Yeoman, John knows that I'm going to do the pictures. So, in that book there's a reference to the cat who chases the mice, and the cat spends some time pretending to catch mice, or pretending to be thanked by the miller for catching mice – things he never succeeds in doing. That's the author feeding you something you can use.'

This interview took place while Quentin was working on *Quentin Blake's ABC*. He explained that to start off with he had drawn things very, very quickly, not for the sake of drawing them quickly, but to get down all his initial ideas. 'Very often, the first thing that you think is right. One of the problems in doing a book, is keeping your first idea into the final drawing.'

Quentin was in his studio so he talked through the drawings he was doing for 'V is for vet'.

'There's a little boy here. His pet is some kind of dinosaur with spikes along its back and the vet has got his stethoscope which he's feeling the dinosaur's chest with. I've drawn that as quickly as I could. I thought I'd try it with a crocodile, but it didn't seem to be as interesting on the page.

'Later on I'm doing drawings on watercolour paper. Here there are quite a few more people and a gorilla got into the background and I thought perhaps that was too much, so that when we came to the final drawing, I left out the gorilla and there's just that rather rough-looking character with a sick parrot at the back.

'I can't tell how many stages it goes through. It goes through a rough, probably a second rough and then, in theory, the next picture could be the finished picture. Sometimes it happens like that and other times, one just goes on until it seems to come right. The problem is keeping it to look as though you'd only drawn it once.'

So what about influences? Has Quentin Blake been influenced by other artists? In one sense he's been influenced by any artist who has been interested in narrative, anyone interested in using drawing to tell a story. And then again he's been influenced, he says, by anyone who's been interested in linear drawing, using line in a clear way. But if he had to 'fish out' three he would choose Honoré Daumier, the nineteenth-century

V is for Vet,
when your pet has a pain
Quentin Blake's ABC

artist whose main work comprised 4000 lithographed cartoons for the satirical newspapers of the time. He was Quentin's first hero, because, he says, Daumier was able to show that you could draw people, 'as it were acting on an almost empty stage'. He is very fond of George Cruikshank, especially the illustrations to Dickens: 'full of life and intensity and things going on, conveyed through line'. Caran D'Ache interests him too. He was a late nineteenth-century French cartoonist who knew how to tell a story in a sequence of pictures. In fact, he virtually invented the short comicstrip joke. 'They're very economical in line, but they're wonderful narratives, very economical and controlled. All those people, I'd steal anything from them.' There are plenty of people who would say the same of Quentin Blake.

Quentin Blake

FAVOURITE TITLES

PICTURE BOOKS

Mr Magnolia	**PB** Lion £2.99
Snuff	**PB** Lion £3.99
Patrick	**PB** Lion £2.99
Angelo	**PB** Lion £3.50
Quentin Blake's ABC	**PB** Lion £2.99
Quentin Blake's Nursery Rhyme Book	**PB** Lion £2.99
Cockatoos	Cape £7.99
All Join In	Red Fox £3.99
You Can't Catch Me!	**PB** Puffin £3.50
How Tom Beat Captain Najork and his Hired Sportsmen by Russell Hoban Illustrated by Quentin Blake	**PB** Red Fox £2.50

JUDY BLUME

'I write popular books. It's funny that if children like it, it can't be good for them. You write what you can write, then other people categorize you.'

She's the most widely read author of contemporary children's fiction, her books have sold tens of millions of copies and yet she's also been described as the most censored children's author in the United States. Judy Blume writes across the age range: *Tales of Fourth Grade Nothing* for seven-year-olds and upwards, then on to books like *Are You There,*

God? It's Me, Margaret, and for teenagers *Forever*. There are many more titles and they are still coming; *Fudgamania* was published in 1992.

Most young readers feel enthusiasm for her books, they're captured by the characters in the stories and feel they can closely identify with their experiences and the humour, particularly in the books involving young Fudge. 'Fudge was originally based on my son Larry when he was a toddler, but the first Fudge book was written twenty-something years ago, I think, and much of what Larry did as a toddler is in *Tales of a Fourth Grade Nothing* – eating under the table, Frisky the cat, all that sort of thing. But now Larry is twenty-eight years old and when I was writing *Fudgamania*, he told me a wonderful story about how, when he rides his bicycle around New York City, pedalling hard, you know how when you're breathing hard your mouth is open, well, he has on occasion, swallowed a fly. So then I wrote the chapter in *Fudgamania* called "The ISAF Club" – the I Swallowed a Fly Club, so I'm still getting inspiration from that guy who was the little Fudge and is now grown up.'

The idea of writing stories about 'issues' appals Judy Blume, but she often concentrates on a protagonist with a problem, and using that as the focal point of the book, weaves the story around the problem. Because she chooses problems that many children will experience in their day-to-day lives, they can quickly identify with the characters. *Blubber*, for example, is about a girl who is bullied, a situation as prevalent today as it ever was.

'When my husband and I checked in to our hotel, we turned on the television and there was some show about a young woman here who had killed herself because of bullying at school. This is a subject that fascinates me. *Blubber* is about a kid who's victimized in the classroom. I wrote it many years ago, when my own children were involved in the same kind of situations, and they're not really bullying her, or victimizing her because she's fat. It's very clear at the beginning of the book, that the fattest kid in Fifth grade, these are ten-year-olds, is Bruce, but no one is victimizing Bruce. Why are they picking on Linda in this way? That's what really fascinates me about it.'

We all looked over at Linda. She had her lunch spread out on her desk. Two pieces of celery, one slice of yellow cheese and a package of saltine crackers.

'Hey,' I said, 'Blubber's on a diet.'

'Is that right?' Wendy asked.

'Yes,' Linda said. 'I'm going to lose ten pounds and then you won't be able to call me that name any more.'

'What name?' Wendy said, and we all giggled.

'You know.'

'Say it.'

'No, I don't have to.'

Wendy got up and went over to Linda's desk. She made a fist at her. 'Say it.'

'Blubber,' Linda said, very low.

'Louder.'

'Blubber,' she said in her regular voice. . . .

'Now say, "My name will always be Blubber,"' Wendy told Linda.

'No, because it won't.'

'Say it,' Wendy told her and she didn't look like she was fooling around any more. . . .

'My name will always be Blubber,' Linda said. There were tears in her eyes . . .

'Why do kids do this? Why do some of them use their power in such an evil way? I have my own strong feelings about it and that is, if a classroom teacher sets the tone and the climate within the classroom, if it's one of nurturing and caring and that teacher can bring such things out into the open, it is not going to happen. But in *Blubber*, the teacher in that book is not aware at all, and it happens.'

You might think that some of Judy Blume's books would seem dated to children today, after all, *Are You There, God? It's Me, Margaret* was first published in 1970. But the wistful anticipation of Margaret as she dwells on the process of growing up; periods, breasts, and her first bra, all compounded by religious doubts, comes across with an easy good humour which makes the anxieties and emotions universal and timeless. Certainly, Judy Blume's readers write in their thousands to express their appreciation and to say how clearly they see their own feelings reflected in the stories.

Forever has been Judy Blume's most controversial book. It is the story of Katherine and Michael, both eighteen, who share the joys and disappointments of first love. Their first experience of a sexual relationship is described explicitly in a way that twelve- and thirteen-years-olds will understand and this has led to the book being banned from some libraries and schools.

'I wrote it in 1975, and when I wrote the book, I felt that sexual responsibility was extremely important. I believe that even more today. Kids have got to understand that they are responsible for their own actions and if they are going to become sexually active, whether it's at sixteen, seventeen, eighteen or in their twenties, it is their responsibility to make sure that they're not going to become pregnant, that they are protecting themselves and their partner against sexually transmitted diseases. All of these things are still very important.'

Judy Blume feels that *Forever* is a book for twelve-year-olds and over, and for parents who are concerned about the frank and open way she writes about sex, then the answer is to read the book too, and be prepared to discuss the issues it raises with your children.

'Forbidding a book makes it very exciting, very tempting. What is in this book that they don't want me to read? So, far better to sit down and talk to your kids and if your family values are different from Katherine's family values, tell them. Explain to them why Katherine's behaviour is not right for your family and why.'

Around the children's book world, some people have made the distinction between popular writing and serious literature and somehow serious is important and popular is not. Judy Blume is most certainly a popular writer for children, she has broken barriers and tossed taboos to one side to deal directly with the subject she has chosen to write about. She is popular because she can remember with sensitivity and with humour what it was like to be young.

'I think we want kids to read. If we want them to be lifelong readers, we have to make sure that they taste books that are wonderful fun. I have a new baby grandson, my first, and I'm already excited about the books that I'm going to be able to share with him. But I want him to love books and so I'm going to get him books that he'll giggle at and then books that touch something inside him and then let him explore and move in any direction, but let him read.'

Judy Blume

FAVOURITE TITLES

Tales of a Fourth Grade Nothing	**PB**	Pan	£2.99
Superfudge	**PB**	Pan	£2.99
Fudgamania	**PB**	Pan	£2.99
Freckle Juice	**PB**	Pan	£2.99
Are You There, God? It's Me, Margaret	**PB**	Pan	£2.99
Tiger Eyes	**PB**	Pan	£2.99
Otherwise Known as Sheila the Great	**PB**	Pan	£2.99
Then Again, Maybe I Won't	**PB**	Pan	£2.99
Blubber	**PB**	Pan	£2.99
Forever	**PB**	Pan	£3.99

ANTHONY BROWNE

'I think that picture books work at their best when the words change for the pictures and the pictures change for the words.'

Anthony Browne is one of the most innovative and intriguing artists working today in the field of children's literature. His first book, *Through The Magic Mirror* was published in 1976. *Bear Hunt* and *Bear Goes To Town* followed, but it was his book *Gorilla* which won both the Kate Greenaway and the Kurt Maschler *Emil* Award in 1983 and has since become a modern classic. Some of his other titles include *Willie the Wimp*, *Piggybook*, *The Night Shimmy* and *Zoo*. It is impossible to categorize his style, he uses fantastic imagery which is often symbolic, but the description that is most often applied to his work is 'surrealist'.

'I've got to admit that surrealism has been a big influence on my work and probably always has been since I first saw a Magritte painting at the age of ten or eleven. The way that surrealists tried to look at things anew, as if for the first time, is a sort of equivalent to the way that children see things for the first time. By putting disparate objects together as a surrealist often did, it gets to that freshness of a child's eye view. Now when I decided to use surrealism in children's books, I wasn't thinking this, it was just how it came, just how I happened to do children's books.'

The dream imagery of surrealism is especially relevant, Anthony Browne believes, to a child's imagination. As adults, we tend to lose our ability to interpret visually because we are taught to grow away from pictures and into words. The picture book is left behind as children grow up into novels. By adding different levels and dimensions to his picture books, Anthony Browne has ensured that these will not be left behind as children get older. They can be enjoyed by children of all ages. Youngsters pore over incongruous details; the image of a gorilla in the portrait of the Mona Lisa, a sausage impaled on the park railing, or the piggy rosette on the male chauvinist's lapel, images that surprise and amuse on every page. Apart from the story, there are other implications to be drawn from the text and the illustrations.

'I think there are different ways of looking at the same story. Picture books at their best, at least my picture books at their best, are those where there is one main story going on which can be read at one level. Older children, or more aware children perhaps, read deeper insights into the same story. I try to make sure that the hidden details or the jokes, actually comment on part of the story. For instance in *Gorilla*, Hannah was obsessed with gorillas, therefore I'd fill the background with images of gorillas; banisters which were in the shape of a gorilla's head or the Mona Lisa gorilla on the wall behind her as she's going to bed.'

The background may be filled with detail but there is, nevertheless, a quality of isolation in Anthony Browne's books. His characters are lonesome protagonists dealing with such feelings as jealousy or boredom, they are survivors learning to care and to be resourceful. His chimp hero *Willy the Wimp* is indeed weak, but he's a survivor and so too, the girl in *The Tunnel* who wins through at the end of the story with kindness. These characters echo some of Anthony Browne's own childhood experiences.

'It's a story about a boy and girl who discovered this tunnel. The boy walks down. The girl is afraid but she has to go down eventually to rescue her brother. I think that related to my own childhood. My brother and I used to play in this horrifically dangerous tunnel. Neither of us were brave

They danced on the lawn.
Hannah had never been so happy. *Gorilla*

enough to say we were too scared to go down the tunnel. I think in childhood, particularly for a boy, one spends a lot of time pretending that one's not frightened, trying to cope with the world. I think that *Willy the Wimp*, for instance, is about a boy trying to cope with an adult world.'

Anthony Browne did not set out to be involved with children's books. He did a degree in graphic design at the Leeds College of Art and then became a medical illustrator, a job that he feels gave him the best possible training. It required great accuracy and technical precision, combined with an understanding of anatomy, but more importantly, he had to tell the story of an operation in pictures. Because operations are messy procedures, photographs are not usually much use and medical illustrators have to clean everything up, but still paint a realistic sequence of pictures; telling the story, in a way.

Achieving the balance between picture and text is the dilemma facing every writer and illustrator of children's books. For Anthony Browne the balance is probably the hardest aspect to get right.

'It's not like writing a short story and then illustrating it. It never works for me like that and that's why I think it's difficult whenever I'm given a text by an author and then have to illustrate it. The balance doesn't seem to be right. I think that picture books work at their best when the words change for the pictures and the pictures change for the words. So, for me, it's like planning a film. I have the idea of the plot and I plan it as shots of a film, so that I've got to tell the story in twenty-six shots, or whatever. Those first ideas are, in a way, neither visual nor verbal and I'll make a story board (a sort of dummy book) with twenty-six little rectangles and scribbles in. The scribbles don't mean anything to anybody else, but I know that they're telling a certain part of the story. So it works like that and if things change as I paint the pictures, say I've changed my original ideas of the words, then as I change the words, the pictures will also change. It's very much a two-way thing.'

Despite the difficulties he has encountered working with other people's texts, Anthony Browne has illustrated such stories as *Hansel and Gretel* and *Alice's Adventures in Wonderland*, for which he won the Kurt Maschler *Emil* Award in 1988. Both these classic stories in theme and content lend themselves ideally to his style of illustration.

'*Hansel and Gretel* is a story I remember vividly from childhood. I started by drawing Hansel and Gretel, their father and mother, walking through the forest and at some stage I suppose I must have decided to put them in modern dress, probably Fifties dress, which is when I grew up. But I don't actually remember making a conscious decision to do that and I certainly didn't think that I'd make the story more relevant by bringing it up to date, that's just how it happened.'

The illustrations for Lewis Carroll's *Alice* concentrate on the dream quality of the story, with visual puns and puzzles conveying the strange and alluring tale. As with all his work, it provides hours of pleasure and entertainment, surprises and interpretations, appealing to all ages.

Anthony Browne

FAVOURITE TITLES

Through the Magic Mirror	**PB** Mammoth £3.50
Bear Hunt	**PB** Hippo £1.95
Bear Goes to Town	**PB** Beaver £3.99
Gorilla	**PB** Mammoth £3.50
Willy the Wimp	**PB** Mammoth £3.50
Piggybook	**PB** Mammoth £3.50
The Tunnel	**PB** Walker £3.99
Zoo	Julia MacRae £8.99
ILLUSTRATOR	
Hansel and Gretel Grimm	Julia MacRae £6.95
Alice's Adventures in Wonderland Lewis Carroll	Julia MacRae £12.95

BETSY BYARS

'My strength is in writing realistic fiction.'

Betsy Byars is one of the most popular writers for children today. She is a winner of the prestigious American award, the Newbery Medal, which she won in 1971 for *The Summer of the Swans*. There are well over thirty more books to her name. They are full of dialogue and humour, but underlying the lively chat, there is something serious going on: children and teenagers discovering what their feelings really mean.

This is no more apparent than in *The Summer of the Swans*. Charlie is a boy with learning difficulties, and hardly communicates with his sister, Sara, or any of his family. One day he disappears and in the panic to find him, we find out what Charlie means (or doesn't mean) to all the people who know him. The boy who was rumoured to have victimized him turns out to be the good guy, Charlie and Sara's father isn't there when they need him, while Sara's friend Mary has other things on her mind.

Mary and Sara were up in the field by the woods. They had been searching for Charlie for an hour without finding a trace of him.

Mary said, 'I don't care how I look. I am taking off this scarf. It must be a hundred degrees out here.'

'Charlie!' Sara called as she had been doing from time to time. Her voice had begun to sound strained, she had called so often. 'Charlie!'

'Sara, do you know where we are?' Mary asked after a moment.

'Of course. The lake's down there and the old shack's over there and you can see them as soon as we get up a little higher.'

'If *we get up a little higher,' Mary said in a tired voice.*

'You didn't have to come, you know.'

'I wanted to come, only I just want to make sure we don't get lost. I have to go to Bennie Hoffman's party tonight.'

Betsy Byars says that the more serious the theme, the more humour you need in the book. They have to be there, she says, for the readers' relief – and, as it happens, her relief too in the writing-process. Much of this humour comes out in the dialogue. 'I'm the greatest eavesdropper in the world,' she says. 'I love to listen to other people's conversation and sometimes I hear something really human and I think I'll use that in a book.'

These dialogues don't always push the plot on, nor for that matter do they necessarily develop character. Rather, they are spaces in which her characters explore their feelings. Betsy Byars says that this usually only comes to her when she's on her third or fourth re-write. Only then does she 'start knowing what that person is thinking and feeling'.

She is also excellent at building tension and concern for her child characters. In *The Midnight Fox* this surrounds a boy who is afraid that his 'Uncle' Fred is going to shoot a fox. What creates the tension is that the boy is away from his parents on an enforced stay with relatives and the only thing that has relieved the situation is a growing obsession with a wild black fox. Uncle Fred doesn't know this and enlists the boy's support in helping him track and kill the fox the boy loves so much.

The story started life from a moment when Betsy Byars was on holiday too. 'We have a cabin in West Virginia and we always saw beavers, deer and racoons. One day, I was in the woods and I saw a fox. It wasn't a black fox but it was a stunning moment. The fox just turned around and looked at me and that was really the basis of the book.'

The book takes a child through some difficult moments, especially when first, Uncle Fred breaks open the fox's den and carries off the cub and then when he puts the cub in a hutch as a decoy to attract the mother, so that he can shoot her.

It seemed to get dark quickly that night. Uncle Fred was already out on the back porch. He had brought out a chair and was sitting with his gun beside him, pointing to the floor. I never saw anyone sit any quieter. You wouldn't have noticed him at all he was so still.

I stood behind him inside the screen door. Through the screen I could see the tiny fox lift his black nose and cry again. Now, for the first time, there was an answer – the bark of his mother. . . .

. . . In a frenzy now that he had heard his mother, the baby fox moved about the cage, pulling at the wire and crying again and again.

Just then there was the sound of thunder from the west, a long rolling sound, and Aunt Millie came to the door beside me and said, 'Bless me, is that thunder?' She looked out at the sky. 'Was that thunder, Fred?'

'Could be,' he said without moving.

'Look!' Aunt Millie said, 'I swear I see black clouds. You see, Tom?'

'Yes'm.'

'And feel that breeze. Honestly, when you think you have reached absolutely the end of your endurance, then the breeze comes. I could not have drawn one more breath of hot air, and now we are going to have a storm.'

We stood in the doorway, feeling the breeze, forgetting for a moment the baby fox.

Then I saw Uncle Fred's gun rise ever so slightly in the direction of the fence behind the garage. I could not see any sign of the fox, but I knew that she must be there. Uncle Fred would not be wrong.

Betsy Byars says that she has loved animals all her life. 'As a child I had no interest in becoming a writer. I wanted to work in a zoo and take care of the animals whose mothers had rejected them. I was very fond of the animal that was in distress. And I think children can confide in their animals in a way that they can't confide in people.'

Another great love is flying which is the setting of *Coast to Coast*, a book that shows how a flying-trip across the United States changes a girl and her grandfather. Like a lot of Betsy Byars' books there are several storylines running concurrently. Grandfather is about to put himself into a retirement home but the girl is worrying about an old poem that she's found that had been written by her now dead grandmother. The poem seemed to be saying that there was a baby who died. Who was the baby?

'My favourite books to write are the ones where you have several plots that you can investigate. Sometimes if it gets complicated, I have to lay out the book so that I can see that I keep the plot going in the right way. I have a 24-chapter kitchen-table so I can get it all out there and look at it.'

Betsy Byars' protagonists are often isolated, having to face life and its problems alone. In *The Eighteenth Emergency*, Benjie (nicknamed Mouse) faces the problem of the school tough guy, Marv Hammerman. The other seventeen emergencies, are situations of terror that might face someone: emergency four is facing a crocodile; solution: prop a stick in its mouth to prevent it biting. Emergency eleven, if attacked by a werewolf, draw a six-pointed star and get inside it. But the eighteenth emergency is facing Marv Hammerman who is enraged that Benjie has made fun of him.

As soon as he saw Mouse, Ezzie got up and said, 'Hey, what happened? Where'd you go after school?'

Mouse said, 'Hammerman's after me.'

Ezzie's pink mouth formed a perfect O. He didn't say anything, but his breath came out in a long sympathetic wheeze. Finally he said, 'Marv Hammerman?' even though he knew there was only one Hammerman in the world, just as there had been only one Hitler.

'Yes.'

'Is after you*?'*

Mouse nodded, sunk in misery. He could see Marv Hammerman. He came up in Mouse's mind the way monsters do in horror movies, big and powerful, with the same cold, unreal eyes. It was the eyes Mouse really feared. One look from those eyes, he thought, just one look of a certain length – about three seconds – and you knew you were his next victim.

We soon find out why Hammerman is after Mouse ...

'Well, when I was passing this chart on my way out of history – and

I don't know why I did this – I really don't. When I was passing this chart, Ez, on my way to math ' He swallowed, almost choking on his spit. 'When I was passing this chart, Ez, I took my pencil and wrote Marv Hammerman's name on the bottom of the chart and then I drew an arrow to the picture of the Neanderthal man.'

Betsy Byars has drawn on her childhood and her own children for her books. In fact, her son, on reading the Bingo Brown books said, 'Mom, I'm Bingo,' and she said, 'Well, I think a lot of boys are.' Bingo is only eleven but is very concerned about his love life. 'I can remember when my son was maybe eight or nine and I would look out and I would see girls on the lawn and I'd say, "What are they doing on my lawn?" Well they're interested in Guy. So I realized these things start very early and with great emotion.'

It's because of these kinds of observations that Betsy Byars reaches right into children's lives and produces the funny-sad, riotous-serious books that she does.

Betsy Byars

FAVOURITE TITLES

The Eighteenth Emergency	**PB** Puffin £2.99
The Midnight Fox	**PB** Puffin £2.99
Goodbye, Chicken Little	**PB** Puffin £2.50
The TV Kid	**PB** Puffin £2.99
After the Goat Man	**PB** Puffin £2.50
The Summer of the Swans	**PB** Puffin £2.25
Bingo Brown and the Language of Love & other books about *Bingo Brown*	**PB** Puffin £2.99
The Not-Just-Anybody Family & other books about the *Blossom* family	**PB** Pan £2.50
Coast to Coast	Bodley Head £8.99
The Moon and Me	**PB** Bodley Head £8.99

HELEN CRESSWELL

'I don't feel there's that big a gulf between fantasy and poetry.'

Helen Cresswell is one of the most popular and prolific writers for children. She writes of a world that is of not quite today, not quite yesterday and with a flavour all of its own – funny and original.

She was brought up in Nottinghamshire, went to university where she read English and has in her time been a literary assistant, a fashion buyer and a teacher. Her first book for children *Sonya-by-the-shore* was published in 1960. Her most famous titles are the stories from *The Bagthorpe Saga*, and the *Lizzie Dripping* stories which were adapted for television as was her *Secret World of Polly Flint*.

With some of her stories it seems as if she has created some kind of new time-band all of her own. She is typically self-mocking in her explanation as to why: 'I think it's partly through sheer bone-idleness because I'm absolutely hopeless at research and historical detail. So, while I want them to be set in the past, I really don't want to pin myself down to any particular time.' She says that she used to wonder where she got her characters from, but then discovered Kilvert's Diary and 'recognized' them – the grown-ups, anyway.

Helen Cresswell has been quoted as saying, 'I do not particularly believe in what most people call reality. I really only believe in the truth of the imagination.' In interview she added to that: 'I'm actually saying something that I felt right from childhood itself. It's probably because I read so much as a child. It seemed to me that the things that were happening inside my own head were infinitely more real than the events outside. Whether most children feel this and then gradually adapt themselves, I don't know, but I've never adapted myself.'

At the beginning of *The Bongleweed*, Helen Cresswell has put a quotation from the Russian writer, Turgenev: '*Whatever a man prays for, he prays for a miracle. Every prayer reduces itself to this. Great God grant that twice two be not four*,' which she thinks means almost exactly the same thing: that we don't have to accept the world as totally predictable, 'That there is a sort of numinous other layer. In fact, we can actually create this ourselves, if we want to. It opens the whole universe out if you don't believe that two and two are four.'

One of Helen Cresswell's recurring characters is a William Morris craftsman-type. This may be because her father was like this. He was a great gardener and he grew chrysanthemums to the pitch of perfection. 'I can remember I used to go round with him helping him drop lighter-fluid oil down the canes to keep the earwigs from them. It was this total single-minded concentration on making something beautiful.

Like a lot of writers, Helen Cresswell refers to her writing as a 'craft'. Practising it very seriously as a craft as a child, she would set herself exercises. One day she would study a Keatsian ode, first breaking it down, then trying to write one. Then the same with the 'sprung rhythm' of the poet Gerard Manley Hopkins and the same with a Spenserian stanza. 'I really was dedicated to poetry,' she says. 'In a funny kind of way, I think that if you write fantasy you are drawing on a lot of the same processes. There's an awful lot of subconscious stuff. There's an awful lot of image. In a way, I don't feel there's that big a gulf between fantasy and poetry.'

There are passages in nearly all Helen Cresswell's books where she feels so strongly that they must be perfect that she makes endless drafts, and keeps drafting them out and altering just the odd words, as when writing poetry. 'I polish it and change the words exactly as if it were a poem.'

Her 'secret favourite' book is *The Bongleweed*.

Till now, she had thought of the Bongleweed as a rogue, a rascal, an outsize botanical scallywag. But now she saw that it was beautiful too.

The mere fact that these flowers were flowers at all was amazing enough under the circumstances. But that they should be so outsized, so unrepentantly and wickedly beautiful, was more than even Becky herself had bargained for. Their very colour was flagrant, russet and nasturtium and apricot, depending on whether they were in shadow or sun, half-furled or fully opened. In the centre of some she glimpsed dark brown stamens, inches long, antennae. The texture of the petals was such that the flowers seemed to float among the foliage rather than grow out of it, waft, more like moths than blossom. In a way, they hardly seemed to belong to the weed at all – hothouse flowers, pinned on to a sturdy, all-seasons perennial.

And more than ever now, the weed seemed what Becky had called, 'alive' (for want of a better word) because of the perpetual stream of its colours down the wind, and the glint of its great leaves . . .

Helen Cresswell also does a lot of writing in tandem with television serials – such as 'Moondial' or 'The Secret World of Polly Flint'. She feels that they've strengthened her books, because she didn't really know the meaning of the word 'plot' for a great many years. She says she would just start, ramble on and then finish, whereas if she knew she was doing something for television, she came to realize that there had to be at least five points in the story where something interesting is happening and there's going to be some kind of a cliffhanger. It forced her to make some kind of structure.

But writing for television started by accident. She was asked if she could write a one-off drama, to which she said yes, she could, even though she had no idea how to. This was the first 'Lizzie Dripping'. 'Because I didn't know how to write a script, I thought, what I'll do is: I'll write it as a story first and then I'll turn it into a script and they'll never know. It was only at the very end, I thought, well I can confess now. I said, "Actually I had to write them as stories first." And they said, "Oh, where are they? Come on, we'll publish them."'

Helen thinks television is very ephemeral so if she's going to put large amounts of energy into something, she wants to make something permanent which means making a book out of it. 'I don't want it just to flicker over someone's screen and go. So I put the book first. Always.'

The Bagthorpe books are, she says, totally exaggerated, but are pretty well based on her own family as a child and Daisy Parker is an amalgam of her two daughters. Mrs Bagthorpe, though, owes quite a lot to Helen Cresswell's mother who was a Christian Scientist. 'Mrs Bagthorpe thinks positively. Well, you can't get more of a positive thinker than a Christian Scientist, can you? And my mother believed this. She said, "If you believe in yourself, you can achieve anything." So we all had to go to elocution lessons and take the violin and the trumpet and achieve.

'But poor Jack – well, we're all poor Jack, aren't we? I mean, he's just like everybody else.'

'You could borrow some money off Zero,' suggested Jack helpfully. 'He'd lend you some, wouldn't you, old chap?'

Zero made a movement of his tail that could, in no way be described as enthusiastic. And Mr Bagthorpe pushed back his chair and stood up.

'That piece of uncalled-for sarcasm is all I needed,' he said. 'The day I am reduced to borrowing money from a dog and in particular

a numskull, pudding-footed, matted-up hound like . . .'

'Don't, Father,' pleaded Jack, 'I'm sorry. I didn't mean it like that. I didn't mean to be sarcastic.'

Jack did not even know how to be sarcastic. He often wished he did so that he could keep his end up with the rest of the family. Mr Bagthorpe flung out. He was muttering under his breath, but Jack could only hear the odd words like 'bankruptcy' and 'last ditch' and 'penury'.

'What a pity, Henry, you're so impulsive and so bad-tempered,' remarked Grandma, spooning up honey. 'You should have taken up the offer of a loan from a dog, interest free.'

Helen Cresswell thinks her American readership is different. 'For one thing, American librarians are terribly keen on English fantasy and they whoop with joy and give rave reviews on your latest fantasy. I don't think the American children read them all that much. And certainly, for every letter I receive from the States about a fantasy, I receive five about the Bagthorpes. I put this down to the fact that, number one, the Bagthorpes are anarchic, and everyone likes that. And number two, I honestly think that they think that this is how English families are, you know. It sort of fulfils their picture of an ideal, zany British family.'

Helen Cresswell

FAVOURITE TITLES

Title	Format	Publisher	Price
Lizzie Dripping and the Little Angel and other books about *Lizzie Dripping*	**PB**	BBC	£2.25
Meet Posy Bates & other books about *Posy Bates*	**PB**	Red Fox	£2.50
The Bongleweed	**PB**	Puffin	£2.99
The Bagthorpes Abroad, *Bagthorpes Unlimited* & other books about the *Bagthorpes*	**PB**	Puffin	£2.99
The Night-Watchmen	**PB**	Puffin	£2.50
Moondial	**PB**	Puffin	£3.50

The Secret World of Polly Flint	Faber £6.50
Dear Shrink	**PB** Puffin Plus £3.99
The Return of The Psammead	**PB** BBC £6.99

GILLIAN CROSS

'The only way that I can write stories is by imagining that I am one of the people in the story.'

Gillian Cross is a Carnegie Medal winner, an award she won in 1991 for *Wolf*. In 1992 she also won the Whitbread Award and the Smarties Award for *The Great Elephant Chase*. These came after more than ten years of success with such titles as *The Demon Headmaster* and *The Mintyglo Kid*. She was brought up in London, studied English at university and could technically call herself 'Dr Cross', as she has a D. Phil from Oxford. At one point in her life, she could have become an academic, but just as she was on the verge of taking it up, she made the leap of becoming a children's writer. It came about partly as a result of having children herself. In fact one of her children spurred her into writing the book that many children know her for, *The Demon Headmaster*.

What happened was that her daughter, having read *Save Our School*, was fascinated by the story that one of the characters had written. One bit of it goes like this:

Cracking his whip over the children's heads as they cowered in the corner, the wicked Headmaster smiled ferociously and twirled his moustache. 'You will never escape,' he shouted, 'I've put a bomb somewhere in the school . . .'

Gillian Cross's daughter, Elizabeth, said to her, 'That's much better than the sort of stories you write. Why don't you write a book like that?' And Gillian said, 'I will one day, when I'm not busy, when I'm not writing a great work, I'll write you your book.'

Elizabeth kept on at her about it. She kept saying, 'You haven't written that Headmaster book yet.' Till in the end Gillian Cross knew that she would have to do it. 'When I began to think about how you would actually write a book about a wicked Headmaster in a real school, in the sort of school that most people go to, I saw that it couldn't be done simply – because, if my children had terrible troubles with their Headmaster, or their Headteacher, they would come back and tell me and I would stomp in and beat the place up. But there was one way that a Headmaster in a day school could actually do terrible things: that was by hypnotizing all the pupils. The moment I thought of that I could see how the book was going to go. So, to shut Elizabeth up, I wrote it.'

But Gillian Cross's Carnegie Medal winner, *Wolf*, began life in a different way. What she first thought of was what happens at the very beginning of the book where Cassie, the girl, is lying in bed, in the flat, and she hears feet coming along the balcony. The padding feet she had in mind was the sort of atmosphere that one associates with wolves, 'That kind of Red Riding Hood, things-leaping-in-the-night atmosphere.

'When I was researching it, I went to London Zoo, and I was lucky enough actually to be taken into the enclosure where they keep the wolves. What happened – which I describe in the book and is the only thing I've ever described in my whole life exactly as it happened to me – was that we walked into the middle of the enclosure and the wolves made a circle round us. They moved as if they were working together. One of them sniffed our footsteps, where we'd been. It was very beautiful to see because wolves are very beautiful and it was a perfectly wolfish thing to do. But at the same time, it was the feeling that I would associate with being in a dangerous, urban place; being in a part of a city where I didn't feel very safe. And I knew, because I'd read about wolves, my feelings didn't actually have a great deal to do with real wolves. It was that twin pair of things, those two things coming together that really fascinated me all the time I was writing the book.'

He was standing by the window, with his back to her, looking out into the garden. His tracksuit hood was pulled up over his head and he was hunched slightly forward. . . .

'Lyall –'

He turned. For a split second her brain froze, putting everything into slow motion. Repeating the same image, over and over again. He turned – and instead of his face there was a senseless, nightmare shape. He turned – and the yellow teeth gnashed suddenly as his jaw snapped open. He turned – and the long grey muzzle flickered at her from every mirror in the room, at a hundred different angles, tinted blue, or pink, or yellow. He turned – Cassie screamed. Wolf!

The wolf where no wolf should be. Behind the door. Invading the house. Inside the skin of a familiar, trusted person . . .

Gillian Cross says that once you've grown up, it's very difficult to read Red Riding Hood, and actually get those same feelings out of it. We can only remember that we had those feelings about it when we were a small child. What she wanted partly to do was to make it happen again. This interweaving of different kinds of text and different kinds of statements about wolves, some factual and some mythological, makes the novel very 'modernist'. Gillian Cross explained that that was not what she was trying to do at the outset.

'What I always set out to do, what I really, really want to do is to set out and write a very simple story that starts at the beginning and goes through to the end with one narrative thread. And what keeps happening to me, and I keep fighting against, is that I see that, if I just have my single thread, I can't get in something that I want to get in. I can't get in some kind of feeling, or some kind of atmosphere, or some kind of juxtaposition of two viewpoints. So I always end up putting in something else. I'm always trying not to write a scissors-and-paste novel, but to write a thrilling tale. And I will succeed in the end.'

In *Chartbreak*, Gillian Cross tells the story of Janis, a tough, cynical girl in the pop world. She thinks it's the only book she's written where somebody in the story actually tells the story.

'I wasn't thinking terrifically feminist thoughts when I was writing it. It was just that I was thinking about *her*. I knew how she was. It was her character and her voice that was the starting point for the book. She's 'driven', because, in fact, everybody says that about her. Everybody says she's very tough. But I have never seen her like that. I was amazed when somebody first said that to me. I see her as extremely vulnerable. She's an extremely vulnerable person who actually runs away because she feels very unhappy and unwanted. And that comes out in aggression. It comes out in her determination to fight her corner. Because she's lucky enough not to be a pretty little thing, she can't use that particular weapon. So she uses the other one. I suppose in a way that's a feminist point.'

I wanted to grab hold of him.

... I just wanted to clutch him and hold him as close to me as I could ... There was no way, no way at all that I was going to give myself away like that, on stage, for the whole world to see. Oh, if I'd been small and pretty I might have done it and serve Christy right if he didn't like it. But as it was – I could just imagine the laughter ...

I breathed. I got the last notes out. And then Christy made to take another step towards me, closer than I could bear, daring me. My hands went out before I could stop them, gripping his shoulders ...

At the same moment, the song finished, and the lights cut out. For a second I was locked into violence, digging my fingers into Christy's shoulders and shaking him in total darkness. Then my eyes adjusted and I saw Dave and Rolo coming to pull me off.

'For God's sake, Finch ... Are you crazy?'

One could easily imagine that it would take an enormous amount of research to conjure up the pop world, with the language of the sound engineers, the pop musicians and the glitzy boys behind the scenes.

When Gillian Cross found that she was going to write *Chartbreak* she was appalled when she thought of the story. Nothing could be less like the kind of thing she knew anything about. When she was a child, her family used to listen to 'Juke Box Jury'. 'My parents used to turn the sound down when the songs were on, so that you could only hear the comments. But I had this character in my head. I had her voice. I knew I had to write the story down. So I just batted it from all directions.' She read all sorts of teenage magazines, especially things like *Smash Hits*, which give the words and they give the profiles of the bands.

It seems as if research is very important for Gillian Cross but she describes it as a 'trick' for herself. 'I think all writers have tricks that they operate on themselves, to get themselves writing. I think mine is to do with research and actually making myself able to see what's going on. The only way I can write stories is by imagining that I am one of the people in the story. They don't have to be telling the story, but I will see everything from the point of view of one particular person in a book or in a chapter. I think it's an identification-thing really. It's the sort of thing that led me to write for children, because I think that what children, even more than adults want out of fiction – is to be able to identify with characters.'

Gillian Cross

FAVOURITE TITLES

The Great Elephant Chase	Oxford £8.95
Wolf	**PB** Puffin £2.99
The Mintyglo Kid	**PB** Mammoth £2.99
Chartbreak	**PB** Puffin Plus £3.99
The Demon Headmaster	Oxford (Eagle) £5.50
Save Our School	**PB** Mammoth £2.99
The Dark Behind the Curtain	**PB** Hippo £1.50
A Map of Nowhere	Oxford £7.95
Roscoe's Leap	**PB** Puffin £3.50
On The Edge	**PB** Puffin £3.50

ROALD DAHL

'My crusade is to teach small children to love books so much that it becomes a habit and they realize that books are worth reading.'

If the best children's author was a title that children could award, then without doubt it would be Roald Dahl. From 1961, when he published *James and the Giant Peach* until his death in 1990, he produced a string of books that have sold all over the world in their millions. In 1983 he won The Children's Book Award and the Whitbread Award for *The BFG*. Adults have sometimes found his mixture of beastliness and greed a little hard to take, but very few children have found anything to object to. Quite apart from what he wrote about, Roald Dahl was immensely readable, using a style of writing that talks directly to the children, as if they were in the room with him.

There isn't space here to describe his remarkable life, and anyway he does it himself in *Boy* and *Going Solo*. One of the most affecting aspects of his childhood was that he went away to boarding school which meant that he was separated from his much-loved mother. At school he was profoundly upset by the relentless and purposeless beating he and his friends received at the hands of his schoolmasters. Without delving too deeply into psychology, this may explain the sharp division one finds in Roald Dahl's adult female characters, between the perfect and the totally revolting. Perhaps a little bit of unconscious blame was channelled into his writing. If anything, this tendency to write clearly defined characters, sometimes grotesque, like the 'Twits', sometimes perfect like Danny's father in *Danny, Champion of the World*, makes him terribly attractive to children. In fact, he always wrote for both adults and children – his first children's book *The Gremlins* was published in 1943 and his first book for adults, *Sometimes Never*, in 1948.

Matilda is the story of a child prodigy and she is one of his few girl central characters.

'Who taught you to read, Matilda?' Miss Honey asked.

'I just sort of taught myself, Miss Honey.'

'And have you read any books all by yourself? Any children's books, I mean?'

'I've read all the ones that are in the Public Library in the High Street, Miss Honey.'

'And did you like them?'

... 'I liked "The Lion, The Witch and the Wardrobe,"' Matilda said. 'I think Mr C.S. Lewis is a very good writer but he has one failing. There are no funny bits in his books ... There aren't many funny bits in Mr Tolkein either.'

... 'Do you think that all children's books ought to have funny bits in them?' Miss Honey asked.

'I do,' Matilda said. 'Children are not so serious as grown-ups and they love to laugh.'

Clearly, Dahl was writing his own philosophy into the character of Matilda there because as he put it himself, 'I think children love to be made to laugh, especially if you're giving them a very dicey, possibly cruel passage. Crude, if you like. It's got to finish in a laugh to relieve the tension.' Roald Dahl saw laughter as an essential ingredient. 'It's part of their lives,' he

Her own small bedroom now became her reading-room
and there she would sit and read most afternoons,
often with a mug of hot chocolate beside her.
Matilda Illustrated by Quentin Blake

said, 'they're miserable if they don't laugh.' He admitted quite freely that he laughed at his own jokes, the reason he gave being that he had a childish mind. At the same time, he said, 'You've got to be serious about making people laugh, as any comedian will tell you.'

With *The BFG*, he is the first and perhaps the last children's writer to have come up with a formula that would satisfy publishers that they could bring out a book in which a character breaks wind in front Queen Elizabeth II. Part of the trick was to invent words to cover the indecency – 'whizzpoppers'. Once again, Dahl explained this by considering how children think. 'Children are terribly rude compared with us snotty grown-ups. They're coarse and crude and rude. As for the business of writing about farting, I'm surprised I hadn't tried it before. No one else has tried it. I don't quite know what's funny about it, but it is funny.' This is precisely what is intriguing about Roald Dahl that he was sure he knew how children think – and if sales of books is anything to go by, then he got some of that right – but he was never quite sure *why* children think the way they do. *The BFG*, the Big Friendly Giant, was a huge bestseller the moment it came out. It tells the story of Sophie and her giant friend and their dealings with the not-so friendly giants. It isn't all knockabout stuff, there is some real fear and tenderness in the story too.

'We is now having a swiggle of this delicious frobscottle and you will see the happy result.'

The BFG shook the bottle vigorously. The pale green stuff fizzed and bubbled. He removed the cork and took a tremendous, gurgling swig.

'It's glummy!' he cried. 'I love it!'

For a few moments the Big Friendly Giant stood quite still, and a look of absolute ecstasy began to spread over his long wrinkly face. Then suddenly, the heavens opened and he let fly with a series of the loudest and rudest noises Sophie had ever heard in her life. . . .

'Whoopee!' he cried. . . . 'Now that *is whizzpopping for you.'*

While liberally slapping on the fun, Roald Dahl has tackled some quite serious themes. In *James and the Giant Peach*, right at the beginning, a group of children are abandoned, James's parents are wiped out. Dahl always felt very strongly about children who were in bad or desperate situations, but when he was wearing his writer's hat he saw that this could lead to a reader's gratification. 'It's a classic, unalterable fact that the more you can start a child off in a rotten situation, the more wonderful it is when he becomes a hero or finds the treasure.' This, for him, meant that it was essential that the child at the outset is withdrawn from a normal kind of relationship. His books, he says, are basically fantasies, so he started his characters off in a world that the child reader hasn't quite ever seen. 'If you start them off in their own cosy living-room and the mum and dad are sitting around, it's no good.'

And yet though he said that, Matilda in the book of the same name, starts off in a desperately realistic world, a very uncosy, domestic setting where she's got an enormous amount to fight against.

'Every single car that comes through my hands gets the treatment,' the father said. 'They'll all have the mileage cut to under ten thou before they're offered for sale. And to think I invented that all by myself,' he added proudly. 'It's made me a mint.'

Matilda, who had been listening closely, said, 'But Daddy, that's ... disgusting. You're cheating people who trust you ... It's dirty money ... I hate it.'

Two red spots appeared on the father's cheeks. 'Who the heck do you think you are?' he shouted. 'The Archbishop of Canterbury or something? ... You're just an ignorant little squirt who hasn't the foggiest idea of what you're talking about.'

'Quite right, Harry,' the mother said. And to Matilda she said, 'You've got a nerve talking to your father like that. Now keep your nasty mouth shut so we can all watch this programme in peace.'

Clearly, underlying this passage is a view about children's rights to speak and offer opinions on parents, justice and decency. As Dahl put it, 'I have very strong and almost profound views on how a child has to fight its way though life. All their lives, they're being disciplined. When you're born, when you're one or two or three, you are an uncivilized creature. From that age, right up to twelve or thirteen, if you're going to become a civilized member of the community, you're going to have to be disciplined. "Stop eating with your fingers." "No spitting on the floor and swearing." And who does the disciplining? Two people. It's the parents and the teachers. Therefore, subconsciously in the child's mind, although the child loves her mother and father, they are the enemy. There's a very fine line, I think, between loving your parents deeply and resenting them.'

Largely as a result of *The Witches* Roald Dahl has been accused of being sexist, and certainly it's hard to read the opening pages of the book without thinking this is certainly a possibility. This accusation always annoyed Dahl. 'I'm the opposite. I'm madly *for* women and therefore it comes as a bit of a surprise to be called either anti-women or sexist. I can't stand these women who go around calling people sexist unless everyone is dead equal. Some people aren't as good as women and *vice versa*. And there it is. I don't think everyone's equal. If I look back on some of the fifteen, sixteen books I've written, I've got at men sometimes too. In fact I jolly well have with Mr Twit. So if I suddenly decide to have a go at women, I don't see why I should be accused of being sexist?'

'Children smell!' she screamed. 'They stink out the vurld! Vee do not vont these children around here . . . So here are my orders! My orders are that every single child in this country shall be rrrubbed out, sqvashed, sqvirted, sqvitted and frittered before I come here again in vun year's time. Do I make myself clear?'

This is from *The Witches* which, rather unusually for a Dahl book, doesn't all end up with a satisfying resolution. Instead, the child who has been transformed into a mouse, stays a mouse. This would seem to fly in the face of the Dahl formula. He insists that to have done the usual would have been a cliché. 'Everyone expects a child who was turned into a mouse by witches to be turned back into a human for a happy ending. Actually, I think it is a happy ending, as I've tried to point out in the book: what's wrong with being a mouse compared to a little boy? They don't have the worries of little boys. They don't have to pass GCSEs.'

When it was put to him that the readers, though, are boys not mice, he said, 'But they've got to throw themselves forward and imagine what it's like to be a mouse. If you can avoid mousetraps and various other things you don't have a bad life. Think of the worries we have all our lives. I mean, mice don't have them.' This is classic Dahl, where he delights in saying the perverse and one can't be totally sure that he's serious.

One strong feature appears in his books: an anti-bullying, anti-blood-sports line. He was against cruelty in general. 'The longer you live', he said, referring to himself, 'the more you subscribe to a kind of religion which is anti-cruelty. The number one attribute, I think, of all humans should be the simple word, "kind". If you can achieve that, and try to be kind to people, you don't go far wrong.'

Every one of Charlie's grandparents was over ninety. They were as shrivelled as prunes and as bony as skeletons, and throughout the day, until Charlie made his appearance, they lay huddled in their one bed, two at either end, with nightcaps on to keep their heads warm, dozing the time away with nothing to do. But as soon as they heard the door opening and heard Charlie's voice saying, 'Good-evening, Grandpa Joe and Grandma Josephine, and Grandpa George and Grandma Georgina,' then all four of them would suddenly sit up and their old wrinkled faces would light up with smiles of pleasure and the talking would begin.

And thus, for perhaps half an hour every night, this room would become a happy place and the whole family would forget that it was hungry and poor.

Roald Dahl always saw his writing of children's books in the context of children's reading development. 'My crusade is to teach small children to love books so much that it becomes a habit and they realize that books are worth reading. Books, if you are going to be anything in life, are vital.

'But it isn't only for your profession. If you are a fit reader, there are times in people's lives, when they're lonely or ill, when, if you're able to read books, enjoy them and love them, you've got the whole world of literature at your feet. You can go and find another book and get lost in it.' Or, as he put it in *The Giraffe, and The Pelly and Me*:

We have tears in our eyes
As we wave our goodbyes,
We so loved being with you, we three.
So do please now and then
Come and see us again,
The giraffe and the Pelly and me.

All you do is to look
At a page in this book
Because that's where we always will be.
No book ever ends
When it's full of your friends
The giraffe and the Pelly and me.'

It's quite likely that Roald Dahl will always be there, as a page in a children's book, as one of the most popular writers for children there has ever been.

Roald Dahl

FAVOURITE TITLES

The Giraffe, and The Pelly and Me	**PB** Puffin	£3.99
Matilda	**PB** Puffin	£3.99
The BFG	**PB** Puffin	£3.99
James and the Giant Peach	**PB** Puffin	£3.50
George's Marvellous Medicine	**PB** Puffin	£2.99
The Witches	**PB** Puffin	£3.99
Fantastic Mr Fox	**PB** Puffin	£2.99
Charlie and the Chocolate Factory	**PB** Puffin	£3.50
The Twits	**PB** Puffin	£2.99
Esio Trot	**PB** Puffin	£2.99

BERLIE DOHERTY

'I think writing for teenagers is a very important, a very exciting area to write in. When I was a teenager, you left children's books behind and you plunged straight into the classics or adult books. Of course, many teenagers do today, but I think it's a shame if they can't continue to travel with themselves through their reading and I think that's what books for teenagers offer. There's still an awful lot to be explored when you are a teenager. You are becoming an adult, but there's still very much a child in you and there's a lot of turmoil.

Berlie Doherty writes for all ages, but perhaps mostly for older children, often about situations and issues that affect them in everyday life. She has won the Carnegie Medal twice, first of all with *Granny was a Buffer Girl* in 1987 and then again in 1992 for *Dear Nobody.*

Dear Nobody tells the story of a teenage pregnancy and the way it affects not just the girl, Helen, but also her boyfriend, Chris, their parents and grandparents. 'Essentially I wanted to write something about a teenager that actually affected not just that person, but their family and I felt that a pregnancy would do exactly this. When I first knew that I wanted to write a novel about teenage love, I went down to the local comprehensive school that my three children had all been to, and I talked to fourth-, fifth-, and sixth-formers there, about love. Then, when I decided that Helen and Chris would go the whole way and she would become pregnant, I then broached the subject of pregnancy with them. It's incredible really, that the students and the people that they introduced me to, would talk so openly about what being a teenage parent meant emotionally.

'It was difficult to get the boys to talk until I got rid of the girls, and then the boys would talk and talk. They felt that they weren't really allowed to talk about love.

'Although, of course, it's Helen's dilemma, the important thing for me was to make it also Chris's dilemma, to make it a story that affects boys as much as girls, because such a situation should affect a boy, just as much as a girl.'

Two voices tell the story throughout. Chris is the narrator, but Helen's voice is heard through a series of letters that she writes to her unborn baby during the pregnancy. This technique allowed Berlie Doherty to express Chris's feelings and emotions directly, but also to let Helen write about her anguish and bewilderment in the letters addressed to 'Dear Nobody', the child she does not yet know.

Dear Nobody,

When she came home from Auntie Pat's my mother, your grandmother, walked past me as if she didn't know me. I was sitting in the kitchen waiting for her to come and when I heard the car, I went to open the door. She walked past me and went upstairs, and on her way up she said, without looking at me, 'You've let me down, Helen.'

Dad came in behind her with his car keys dangling in his fingers.

'What did she say?' I asked him.

'She's very upset, Helen.'

'Of course she's upset,' I told him, 'But will she let me stay here?'

'Good God, she's not going to kick you out into the streets.'

'But will she let me live here, with a baby?'

'You're not really going to keep it, love?' His voice was pleading. 'You're throwing your life away.'

'I think writing about love is a very, very difficult thing to do, but I think it is an important thing to do because love is a very important part of teenagers' lives. It is an important part of everybody's lives, but sexual love is an important part of teenagers' lives. Falling in love is an important experience, but I don't think we should romanticize what love is all about. I think lots of books are written about romantic teenage love. I always try to look at love in a much more serious way.'

Berlie Doherty approaches a subject like love, by looking into the characters themselves. There is plot and action there too, but the story seems to be driven by the characters and the way they develop. *Granny was a Buffer Girl* for instance, is a novel constructed around a family group. Each chapter is, in a way, a contained short story, with one or two people moving events forward. So, a girl about to leave home for the first time, to go to university, listens to the stories of her parents and grandparents when they were her age, and as each story captures a particular moment, so the format lets you see inside that life from a particular perspective.

'None of us are just ourselves. We are our parents, we are our grandparents and great-grandparents. We stretch back for generations and generations and I think particularly with teenagers, they're so self-important. I mean, that's good, that's the way they should be, but I don't think we should forget that there are traces and elements, going back hundreds and hundreds of years and that we are very much affected by our parents and grandparents.'

One of the stories comes, in fact, from Berlie Doherty's own family: Catholic Bridey and Protestant Jack fall in love, but they are afraid to tell their parents because of the religious divide that separates them. So they marry in secret, and go back to their individual homes, to carry on as normal until they're found out.

Much more up to the minute is *Tough Luck*, a school story featuring Twagger, the classic school refuser and Naseem, who has recently arrived from Pakistan and has to find her way in a strange country and a strange school. They are both outsiders and underdogs, the sort of lonely protagonists that often appear in Berlie Doherty's novels.

'I think all writers are interested in outsiders and underdogs, perhaps because writers see themselves as being outsiders, looking in on things. I think in the same way that I don't like to see old people dismissed, I don't like to think that we forget that they were young once and have had very full lives, that's how I feel about outsiders. They're easily dismissed because we can't make friends with them because it's difficult to make friends with them because we're shy or afraid of them, or whatever. Through the novel, we can explore the outsider and come to know them a little better.'

As writer in residence for a term at a school in Doncaster, some years ago, Berlie Doherty had a class of fourteen-year-olds for an hour each Wednesday morning. By the end of the term, *Tough Luck* was well on the way. 'They were so nice. As soon as I met them, I liked them and I thought, I don't want to spend these eleven visits doing eleven different writing exercises, I'd really like to do something sustained with them. So I was literally thinking on my feet, when I said, "Would you like to write a book with me?" and they all thought that was a good idea and I told them that they could choose what it was going to be about. We had a secret ballot and more than half the class said that they wanted it to be a book about themselves.'

Direct contact with her audience is obviously invaluable for Berlie Doherty. She has rarely ventured into the world of fantasy, but *Spellhorn* is a notable exception and with this novel, she once again called on the help of children as she developed the plot. BBC Schools asked her to write a radio play about a unicorn, and in creating for this medium, she decided to involve blind children.

'We have a school for the blind, for the visually handicapped in Sheffield. So, I went along there and met four children and very soon after meeting them, I made two important decisions. One was that as well as writing the play, I'd write a novel, so that I could read it to them chapter by chapter, as it was developing. Also I decided that the novel would be about a blind child. I don't think I would have had the courage to write about a blind child, if I hadn't met these children and seen a little bit into their worlds. I think really it's their huge enthusiasm for a start, but also their very vivid imaginations that again gave me courage to take huge steps into my own darkness, the darkness of the imagination.'

The blind child in *Spellhorn* travels to another land, a wilderness which is a young world, peopled by primitive tribes. It is a stage of innocence where the magic of the unicorn is carefully guarded and the child, with powers of her own, can be in control. Inevitably, she has to choose between this life, and life in the real world. The story gives a powerful insight into the world as it is for children who are visually handicapped and the magic of the adventure will certainly appeal to ten-year-olds and over.

Berlie Doherty

FAVOURITE TITLES

Snowy	**PB** Lion £3.99
Tilly Mint and the Dodo	**PB** Lion £2.25
How Green You Are	**PB** Mammoth £2.99
The Making of Finger Finnigan	Pied Piper £6.50
Paddiwak and Cosy	**PB** Mammoth £2.50
Spellhorn	**PB** Lion £2.99
Children of Winter	**PB** Armada £2.99
Granny was a Buffer Girl	**PB** Armada £2.75
White Peak Farm	Methuen £6.95
Dear Nobody	**PB** Lion Tracks £3.50

ANNE FINE

'One of the loveliest things about being a writer is that when you feel there's social injustice, you can get out the pen.'

Anne Fine defies the stereotype that women can't write humour. Her novels are hilarious depictions of family and school life. That said, though, she is not strictly speaking a comic writer, as her humour is very much rooted in real life experiences. In other words, in reading her books, we're never far from serious themes about how and why people need each other in relationships, and how and why people keep getting it wrong.

She was brought up in Northampton, and went on to university and teaching. Her first book, *The Summer-House Loon*, came out in 1978 and she's written over twenty since. She's always been drawn to humour. She believes that all writers write for a reader hidden inside themselves and in her case that reader has always been someone who likes reading funny books, so when she started to write, the humour 'just sort of trickled in there automatically'.

But the humour is serious. 'The darker the subject when you make a joke out of it, the funnier the joke seems.' One reason why the subjects of her books might appear to be 'dark', she says, is because of the way she works. It usually takes her a whole year to write a book, so because she is, as she sees it, a slow worker, she has to have a topic that will interest her for a whole year's-worth of writing.

The topic that recurs in her books is the tension that crops up in families. In her childhood reading she was given rather conventional books to read and picked up the idea that in fiction 'Mother' was a hand coming out from nowhere with a plate of sandwiches at the end. Then everybody had the sandwiches and the hand disappeared and that was 'Mother'. 'That isn't how life is. More and more, children stay in the home. They're not so safe out on the streets as they used to be. They don't lead the lives that, twenty years ago, children lived. They would go out cycling and they would be called in when it was dark. Now they're very much stuck in the home, often quite complicated homes. I think family relationships probably interest children more than they did when I was young.'

In *Goggle-Eyes* Anne Fine tackles the issue of a girl's view of her divorced mother's new man, the potential stepfather. This she feels mirrors the kind of family set-ups in our society. Her children go to school where they have had to walk under a poster that says: Since the time you passed this poster yesterday, 436 children got divorced. 'I think some people perhaps try and pretend that it isn't true. But it's a fact.'

'Kitty, could I come in your room for a moment?'

. . . 'What for?'

He swung the hammer and the wrench.

'I'm searching for an airlock in the pipes. I think it's probably in there with you.'

... 'I suppose so.'

I pulled the door back as far as it would go.

... 'Can you open the door?'

'I have,' I told him, 'This is as far as it opens.'

'What's wrong with it?' (Oh, you could see it in his eyes: Goody! Another little job to help me suck up to my lovely Rosalind.)

'Nothing is wrong with it. It's just that there's one or two books lying behind it on the floor.'

'One or two books? ... You must have the whole National Scottish Collection behind there to jam it that much.'

I said nothing. I think he knew perfectly well what I meant by my silence ...

He slotted himself in sideways and peered through the gloom.

... 'Why haven't you opened your curtains?'

I stepped back, tripping on wires from my computer and my hair crimpers tangled all over the floor.

'I haven't had time yet.'

... He flung the curtains open. Light flooded the room.

There was a stunned silence ... then,

'Dear Gods! ... Designer compost.'

In spite of the antagonism here expressed by the girl towards the step-father figure, the book ends on a reassuring note. This is deliberate: 'I certainly think there is no place in a children's book for despair. I would hate any child to put down a book of mine and think, "Well, I feel a lot worse for reading that!"' So Anne Fine says that she would always want to end a children's book with some element of hope for the future – not necessarily with everybody ending up happily ever after – but just a sense of where they're going to go from now.

With *Round Behind the Ice-House* we have a book that's written from a boy's point of view. She describes it as an introspective piece of work and thinks that when authors are writing about someone of the opposite sex, somehow they can kid themselves that they're more protected, more hidden. This way they can go just a little deeper into their own psyches.

She sees this book as immensely personal, with regard to the growth of self-esteem. Tom, the narrator, has a sister, Cass, and she is way ahead of him in her social and verbal development. Tom feels this particularly strongly because they're twins, and he's working out how he can grow a bit more. 'He's a late bloomer,' Anne Fine says, 'In some ways, I was a late bloomer myself and the book is important to me.'

These more realistic novels are complemented by some books of Anne's that are more exaggerated. In *A Pack of Liars* all the 'penpal' letters sent to a class of children prove to be written by one resourceful burglar. In *Crummy Mummy and Me*, 'Mummy' is a raving punk, Crusher Maggot is the live-in boyfriend and also a punk. Anne admits this is a kind of weakness. 'I love farce. I've always loved pantomimes. I've always liked that sort of edge of things, almost tipping over.' *Madame Doubtfire* is a comedy about what happens after a divorce when the children are fine in Mum's house, fine in Dad's house but they'd do a lot better if there was more ease of access between the two. Dad ends up dressing as a cleaning lady, calling himself Madame Doubtfire, and getting a job in Mum's house because he feels this is the easiest way of seeing his children. 'At some level this is obviously entirely farcical, but I have tried to write it so that it just could happen.'

Again, in *Bill's New Frock*, there's an impossible situation of a boy changing into a girl, and going to school and facing all the petty condescensions and discriminations that girls experience. Under the humour, one senses someone who is writing partly out of anger. 'I'm very interested in socio-political issues. Everything that happens in your life has a sort of political resonance and I do think children can take on board quite subtle issues.' She points out that a girl will come home from primary school saying, 'It's not fair. They always ask the boys to ... (whatever)', 'It's not fair, they always ask the girls to ... (whatever).' She says that she used to haunt her children's school, along with other parents and say, 'Don't you think it's a bit sexist?' But she was fobbed off with the same old responses, 'I don't think anybody else is bothered about this, Mrs Fine. Nobody else has complained.' One of the things Anne enjoys about being a writer is that when you feel there's social injustice, you can get out the pen.

'On with your work, down there on table five,' warned Mrs Collins promptly.

She meant him. He knew it. So Bill picked up his pen and opened his books ... He wrote more than he usually did. He wrote it more neatly than usual too. If you looked back through the last few pages of his work, you'd see he'd done a really good job, for him.

But you wouldn't have thought so, the way Mrs Collins went on when she saw it.

'Look at this,' she scolded, stabbing her finger down on the page. 'This isn't very neat, is it? Look at this dirty smudge. And the edge of your book looks as if it's been chewed!*'*

She turned to Philip to inspect his book next. It was far messier than Bill's. It was more smudgy and more chewed-looking. The writing was untidy and irregular . . .

'Not bad at all, Philip,' she said. 'Keep up the good work.'

Bill could scarcely believe his ears. He was outraged. As soon as she'd moved off, he reached out for Philip's book, laid it beside his own on the table and compared the two.

'It isn't fair,' he complained bitterly. 'Your page is much *worse than my page. She didn't say anything nice to* me.*'*

Philip just shrugged and said, 'Well, girls are neater.'

Anne says that she wrote the book for a purpose. 'I wanted to make all the children who read it look at their day in the primary school with clear eyes, able to label what they see.' In other words, she wanted every child to look at the world freshly, having been shown it in a different light by the book. It's probably what most writers hope they're doing with their books. It's just that Anne Fine is more explicit about it than most.

Anne Fine

FAVOURITE TITLES

Bill's New Frock	**PB** Mammoth	£2.99
Anneli the Art Hater	**PB** Mammoth	£2.99
The Granny Project	**PB** Mammoth	£2.99
Crummy Mummy and Me	**PB** Puffin	£2.50
Madame Doubtfire	**PB** Puffin Plus	£3.50
Goggle-Eyes	**PB** Puffin	£2.99
Round Behind The Ice-House	**PB** Puffin	£2.50
A Pack of Liars	**PB** Puffin	£2.50
The Summer-House Loon	**PB** Mammoth	£2.99
The Stone Menagerie	**PB** Mammoth	£2.99

RUMER GODDEN

'To hold children, a story must have two things: it must have conflict, and it must have a crisis. A book has a pattern; it starts slowly, then rises to a small crisis and a slightly larger one, then comes up to the real crisis, which is where you hold the attention. A true storyteller is always dramatic.'

Rumer Godden has been writing for children for more than forty years. With over sixty books to her credit, she appeals to a wide age-range, from four-year-olds to early teens. Her first book, *The Dolls House* was published in 1949 and is still popular with six- and seven-year-olds today, then in 1973 she won the Whitbread Award for her novel *The Diddakoi*, about an orphaned gypsy girl, who is determined not to conform to accepted social patterns.

More recently, she has turned to Eastern themes for her books and *Great Grandfather's House* is set in Japan.

'The book seemed to ask for Japan, because in Japan the old ways, the old values are disappearing very quickly and are overlaid by modernity. Children grow up without any knowledge of their heritage at all. People will tell you that a couple like Great Grandfather and Grandmother don't exist any more, but they do. To make this point the little girl in the story is sent to stay, much against her will – she's very spoilt, very blasé, very "city", very sophisticated and extremely selfish – with her Great Grandfather, who is an artist, in the country. There, she discovers what is really childhood's right: not second-hand television and too many toys, but the real meaning of play, the real meaning of life and nature and creation. That sounds a very serious theme, but it worked very well in the book.'

The story may be set in Japan, but it is relevant to children all over the Western world. Rumer Godden believes there is a danger that children today, obsessed with computers, television, electronic toys and other gadgetry, are losing their ability to be creative in their play.

'Left to themselves, the spirit is still there, the trouble is that they don't get time, they're so organized and in a way they're being robbed of their childhood. I would hate to have a book with a moral, but it is I suppose, in a way, a kind of "missionary" book. It's for the child to discover what it means to create, to make their own toys. It's not that I'm condemning toys, but they have too many and what I do dislike, is the perpetual organization which leaves a child no time to be himself or herself.'

Rumer Godden began writing for adults and it was almost by accident that she decided to experiment with stories for a younger audience. She had always been fascinated by the miniature and wanted to see if a strong plot would work in the compass of 'a dolls house'. Once hooked, she discovered that other aspects about writing for children attracted her.

'There's a far greater discipline in writing for children than there is in writing a novel. In a novel you can do anything. In a book for children, there are rules and the smaller the child, the more stringent the rules. For instance, you cannot have flashbacks, which a novelist loves. The story has got to go from a beginning to an end and if your character has a background, that's got to be conveyed in the present, you can't go popping back.

'I remember one book I wrote called *The Story of Holly and Ivy*, where the little girl is an orphan and I had to convey her whole orphan past. Well, I couldn't go back and do it, so I did it in Ivy's present feelings, that in this little girl Ivy, there was a hole which seemed empty and it ached and ached and she so wished that she could have a father and a mother and particularly a grandmother. Now in those few sentences, you've got what would have been in a novel, a whole series of flashbacks.

'Then they won't take a lot of description, they get very bored with it. Also the words matter tremendously, it's not that you want simple words, but a children's book is made up of fewer words than a novel, therefore they've got to be chosen very, very carefully.'

Her own childhood was spent in India and Rumer Godden did not have formal schooling until she was twelve. She and her sisters were taught at home by their mother.

'I remember that as a little girl, I had a tree which grew in our garden in India, and it was a cork tree that flowered beautifully, great white flowers in the spring, and it had a hole in it where I used to keep my poems and my stories, because I've always written, since I was five.'

At the age of twelve, Rumer Godden was sent to boarding school in England. She experienced at first-hand how it felt to be the stranger, the unwanted newcomer, and in her novels, it is often the outsiders, her kindred spirits, who come across most forcefully. Kizzy, in *The Diddakoi* is half-Gypsy and an orphan, who is fostered by the local squire, but rejected and disliked by the local children at school.

'Yesterday we sewed up her coatsleeves, so she couldn't get it on. . . . Today Prue and Mary Jo asked to go to the loo and nipped out to fasten a string across the lane, low down where she couldn't see it. Cor! she came down full tilt . . .' and, when Kizzy was down, they pounced. . . .

'Don't go too near, she smells.'

'Doesn't now, Barmy Admiral's bought her new clothes.'

'That's why she's so uppity and high and mighty.'

'Mighty-tighty.'

'Dandy-spandy diddakoi.'

'Where's yer cloes pegs, diddakoi?' . . .

'Let me go home,' said Kizzy through tight lips.

'Go on, we're not stopping you,' but Kizzy had not felt one of them skilfully looping a skipping-rope round her ankles and making a slip knot; as she turned they pulled it tight and Kizzy went smack on to the lane path. . . .

'Go on, then. Go home. Run, tinker, run.' They pulled her up by the arms. 'We'll make you run.'

Kizzy is a survivor, who wins through by persistently being herself and not giving in, but perhaps in a way the story is too well resolved, too rounded to reflect the reality of everyday life.

Characters with the same determination, but with very different goals in mind, appear in her ballet stories including *Listen to the Nightingale*. Here, Rumer Godden reflects the demands put upon children who have a special talent and the sacrifices they have to make in order to commit themselves wholeheartedly to dance. She herself taught ballet in a school in Calcutta in the 1930s, experiencing the dedication and disappointments of these children.

'Parents always want a gifted child, but they don't realize what it means and I wrote the book to show what extremely hard work a child musician or child ballet dancer has to go through, doing their training and their schoolwork and also they have to make tremendous sacrifices in their home and social life.'

These stories are not daydreams of what might be, but a representation of the aches and pains, the fatigue and frustration, as well as the exhilaration and success, which eight- to eleven-year-old dancers will share, understand and enjoy. And this commitment to a profession, a chosen career, be it ballet, music or writing, is something with which Rumer Godden can sympathize.

'If you've got an overwhelming talent, or gift, you don't choose it, it's chosen you and you can't get away from that. I'm a storyteller, storytellers are born, not made, it's something that you have to do. It's as if you have been taken over. You are really the instrument of some greater force and people say to me, "Isn't it time you stopped writing?" because I'm very old now, but what they don't understand is that you don't give up writing until writing gives you up.'

Rumer Godden

FAVOURITE TITLES

A Kindle of Kittens	MacMillan £3.50
Tottie: The Story of a Dolls House	**PB** Puffin £2.99
The Story of Holly and Ivy	**PB** Puffin £2.99
Candy Floss and Impunity Jane	**PB** Pan £2.99
Mr McFadden's Halloween	**PB** Pan £2.99
Fu-Dog	**PB** Walker £5.99
Great Grandfather's House	Julia MacRae £8.99
The Diddakoi	**PB** Pan £2.99
Thursday's Children	Pan MacMillan £8.95
Listen to the Nightingale	Pan MacMillan £9.99

RUSSELL HOBAN

'An idea will come to me as a concentrated short burst, comparable to poems as opposed to prose. Then it seems right for a children's book. Sometimes, it's because the matter of which I'm writing is too deep or too metaphysical for adults.'

Russell Hoban, author of sixty books for children, is an American who has lived in this country for more than twenty years, writing mainly picture book and short story texts for young children, as well as adult novels.

As he works with an idea to mould it into a story he is not aware to start with, which audience he is writing for. 'I don't know until I've got something down on paper and I can see where it's going. At the moment, I'm fifty-three pages into something which, if I'm lucky, will be a novel, and it began with the buying of an Inuit artefact, a carved sperm-whale tooth. This got me thinking and made me wonder about various things having to do with the carving and finally, it settled into an attempt at a novel. But it's getting into things of the deepest sort which, at the same time, are more interesting and more willingly read by children than by grown-ups.'

His picture book texts for young children share one strong characteristic, they are a deliberate play on words with an anarchic sense of humour which appeals to adults, as much as younger readers. *How Tom Beat Captain Najork and his Hired Sportsmen* (illustrated by Quentin Blake) follows the fortunes of a small boy called Tom, who is given to fooling around, in a small-boy sort of way. He has to contend with his Aunt Fidget Wonkham-Strong who wears an iron hat and takes no nonsense from anyone. She calls upon the services of Captain Najork and his Hired Sportsmen to lick Tom into line, but of course, Tom's foolery is just what is required to beat the Captain at his games of Womble, Muck and Sneedball and he wins through triumphant, as any young child should when mucking about and fooling around for pleasure.

The Hired Sportsmen brought out the ramp, the slide, the barrel, the bobble, the sneeding tongs, the bar and the grapples. Tom saw at once that Sneedball was like several kinds of fooling around that he was particularly good at. Partly it was like dropping things off bridges into rivers and fishing them out, and partly it was like fooling around with barrels in alleys.

'I had better tell you,' said the Captain to Tom, 'that I have played in the Sneedball Finals five years running.'

'They couldn't have been very final if you had to keep doing it for five years,' said Tom.

The Twenty-Elephant Restaurant is another piece of sheer, unexpurgated fun.

'That has a very distinct and specific origin. When we moved into the house where we now live in Fulham, the first thing I did was to build an asymmetrical desk into a bay window for my writing. The second thing I did was to build a couch into the wall for my napping after lunch. The couch was very powerfully built with a number of square, four-by-four legs that were glued to both the couch and the floor. I said to my wife, after I finished making the couch, "That couch is really strong, elephants could dance on that couch," and she said, "How many?"'

Russell Hoban's best-known books feature Frances the badger, who with her father and mother, baby sister and best friend Thelma, confronts many of the problems that will be familiar to most children between the ages of four and seven: sibling rivalry, fear of the dark, the sexism of little boys. They are dusted liberally with Russell Hoban's quirky humour, but they are comforting stories, reassuring for the very young.

'On my birthday, I had a large number of flat brown envelopes from elementary schools in various parts of America, all with a letter from the teachers and then enclosures from the children and one of the letters said, "We like these books because they all have a little lesson in them."'

The sentences are carefully structured with repeated phrases, and simplified vocabulary, so that children who are learning to read can feel confident about completing the story for themselves. *The Mouse and his Child* is a longer book for children over the age of ten. At its most basic, it is a quest story about the triumph of good over evil. A pair of clockwork mice, father and son, are rescued from a dustbin, by a passing tramp. Their search for a safe-haven, a renovated dolls house, and their desire to become self-winding and independent, leads them to fall prey to the infamous Manny Rat, a cruel and vicious predator. The mood of the book alternates between scary and poignant, sparked with sardonic humour and touches of maverick invention.

'What came first was the actual clockwork toy which was one of a collection of toys that some friends of ours kept under their Christmas tree. After about three years of looking at it, I found I wanted to write something about it, so I began what I thought would be something longer than a picture book. As I wrote, I found that I was having a go at trying to write a novel and I had to learn how to do it as I went along. At first, it was completely linear, like knots on a string, and I had to learn how to put things over and under and weave them in and out. It was quite difficult for me. We lived in a big house, with quite a long living-room. I think the living-room was twenty-four feet long and I used to lay the pages on the floor for the whole length of the room and walk up and down, trying to get the whole story so far, in my mind, so that I could continue.'

A large rat crept out of the shadows of the girders into the light of the overhead lamps, and stood up suddenly on his hind legs before the mouse and his child. He wore a greasy scrap of silk paisley tied with a dirty string in the manner of a dressing gown, and he smelled of darkness, of stale and mouldy things, and garbage. He was there all at once, and with a look of tenure, as if he'd been waiting always just beyond their field of vision, and once let in would never go away. . . .

The story is just the tip of the iceberg, it is a sort of social satire, an allegory for our times. The mice learn that no one is ever completely self-winding, *'That's what friends are for,'* and Manny Rat, apparently reformed, lingers menacingly at the end of the book. *The Mouse and his Child* is widely recognized as a modern classic.

'For better or for worse. I internalized the English standard of writing, as the standard that I wanted to work to. Ever since childhood, I've admired English writers and I've always wanted to get that sort of wordage down on paper. When I was writing *The Mouse and his Child* I was trying to make as English a children's book as I possibly could.'

Russell Hoban

FAVOURITE TITLES

A Bargain for Frances	**PB** Mammoth £3.50
Best Friends for Frances	**PB** Faber £2.95
Bread and Jam for Frances	**PB** Puffin £2.99
Jim Hedgehog and the Lonesome Tower	**PB** Puffin £2.50
Dinner at Alberta's	**PB** Red Fox £2.99
How Tom Beat Captain Najork and his Hired Sportmen	**PB** Piper £2.50
Dancing Tigers	Cape £5.95
The Twenty-Elephant Restaurant	Cape £6.99
The Marzipan Pig	**PB** Puffin £2.50
The Mouse and his Child	**PB** Puffin £3.50

SHIRLEY HUGHES

'A picture book text isn't just words with pictures added. It's unthinkable without the pictures. Like a film, you're putting it together from the word go.'

Shirley Hughes is an artist-storyteller melding narrative and pictures in a way that very young children can interpret and appreciate. Her first picture book, *Lucy and Tom's Day* was published in 1960. Since then, she has illustrated over two hundred children's books, creating such favourites as the 'Alfie' stories, *Dogger* (which won the Kate Greenaway Medal in 1977) and the families of Trotter Street. Her work is known all over the world and in 1984 she was presented with the Eleanor Farjeon Award for distinguished services to children's literature.

Shirley began writing and illustrating at a time when great changes

Alfie ran on ahead because he wanted to get home first.
Alfie Gets in First

were in the air for children's book publishing. During the Sixties, advances in printing and production techniques meant that large-format picture books, as we know them today, began to roll off the presses in a blaze of colour. It was this renaissance and the challenge it presented that fired Shirley Hughes with enthusiasm.

'I was a line artist at that time and I found colour quite difficult to come to. I don't regret it because the actual underlying drawing of any colour work is important, but I didn't really pluck up courage to get into picture books until I had young children of my own.'

With three children of her own to watch and observe, Shirley Hughes has created picture books which develop from real situations with which small children can identify. The stories are set in a city background with a wealth of domestic detail and everyday events which will be part-and-parcel of most children's daily life: going shopping, going to school and going for a walk in the park. But there is always a touch of humour or an incident to be discovered in the pictures and it is the illustrations that carry the story, encouraging children to create their own interpretation of characters and events from the pictures they see.

From childhood, before she completed her formal training at the Ruskin School of Art in Oxford, Shirley Hughes was a practised observer of life.

'I was always drawing or sketching, usually using just a pencil and a sketch book. I enjoy looking at real people, having an eye for movement and the way people group themselves, particularly children when they're absorbed in conversation or a game, having an eye for a face or a telling gesture, that's terribly important, because it's observation of real people that gives fluency to your imaginary people.

'I've got a slightly myopic, rather close vision of life, so I get very charged and interested in the detail and I think it does tell you a lot about the story. Even very young children can absorb a great deal of detail, they can examine pictures and re-visit them, enter the picture and linger there. It's something they can only do with a book.'

The idea for a picture book can evolve quite slowly.

'It starts like every other idea in one's head; like an iceberg, it floats about mostly under the surface. Then something triggers the idea urgently into view and because I am an illustrator, I reach for a pencil almost immediately to get the people, the characters down.

'For instance, when I first drew Alfie, who is a four- or five-year-old hero of mine, he was rushing up the street ahead of his mother, who was trundling behind with the shopping and the baby in the buggy. I knew that Alfie was absolutely pink in the face, determined to get into the action as soon as I got him down on paper. So just as authors say that when they start to write a character into a situation, the character has a life of their own, so that happens for me when I draw them.'

Occasionally, an idea for a story has come from a real piece of the past. 'Dogger' is an old soft toy which Shirley Hughes discovered languishing at the back of a cupboard one day.

'Almost every family has one child who has a toy without which they can't go to sleep and there comes that awful moment when its lost at bedtime. Because Dogger reminded me of a very powerful, emotional situation which of course happened in our family, I thought I'd write a story about him and it just seemed to come. It just fell on the page.'

Here, as so often in her books, the real story lies beyond the narrative. Shirley Hughes conveys feelings through pictures and it is this close affiliation with children and their emotions that makes her such an accessible writer and illustrator for five-year-olds and under.

As the story unfolds in each book, a new surprise awaits the child with every turn of the page. Shirley Hughes plans the design of her books to give a variety of small pictures and close-ups, contrasted with double-page illustrations which are expansive scenes packed with action. The design is an integral part of encouraging children to 'read' pictures, as well as text.

'You are moving the eye, you are moving in close, breaking up the page and the text with the pictures. Before I do the dummy, or the rough draft of the book, I write the story and I distil the words into the actual storyline and then put them in place on the page, so that you know on each page what the print is going to look like and what sort of pattern the writing and the pictures make together. So you will allow yourself a big double-page spread where you have Alfie at a party or something big is happening and you want to show the whole thing in pictures with just two lines of text. Then on another page, you may have rather more text and you break it up so that your eyes move across and around.'

With her series of *Chips and Jessie* books, Shirley Hughes has used a different design technique to appeal to a slightly older audience; children who are just starting to read on their own. Using a comicstrip approach, the characters talk to one another via speech balloons, with some justified text alongside. Once again the page is divided in an innovative way.

'You've got Chips having a terrific up and down row with his mother about whether or not he can bring the hamster home from school. So you've got him shouting across the page. I wanted to lapse in and out of the strip cartoon and have some justified text as well and that creates a different page altogether. I think the actual page of a book is rivetingly interesting and has an enormous number of different connotations and different ways of expressing a story.'

In another development of the comicstrip, Shirley Hughes has created a story without words; she calls this type of book 'a Mount Everest' for illustrators! *Up and Up* is a kind of mime where the whole story is conveyed through facial expressions and movement. A book without words can appeal to all ages, offering any child, whatever their reading ability, the opportunity to interpret the story themselves.

You may feel that Shirley Hughes's approach sometimes presents a world that is altogether too cosy for children today. Her stories are all carefully resolved without much menace or danger and present an image of family life that is comforting and reassuring. But this is a criticism that she rejects.

'I think the whole marvellous fabric of children's literature has to contain two poles. Children need the excitement and the controlled sense of violence that you get in fairytales, to be pleasurably frightened. They also need the other pull towards the walls of security at home. Every child needs to run off in their imagination, to be an adventurer, a wayfarer, to take risks. They also need to feel they have a little place of their own kitted out as they want it. So in children's fiction, we need to supply or present this whole spectrum for them. I just happen to be in the reassurance spectrum. But having said that, I think the borderline which we all walk, the tightrope between sentimentality and sentiment, is a challenge for children's authors, because sentiment is wonderful, sentimentality is awful and you have to rouse emotion in a way that is not bland.'

Shirley Hughes

FAVOURITE TITLES

Lucy and Tom's Day	**PB** Puffin £3.50
Dogger	**PB** Red Fox £3.99
Up and Up	**PB** Red Fox £3.50
Alfie Gets in First	**PB** Lion £2.50
Chips and Jessie	**PB** Lion £2.50
Angel Mae	**PB** Walker £3.99
Out and About	**PB** Walker £3.99
Wheels	**PB** Walker £3.99
The Big Alfie and Annie Rose Storybook	**PB** Red Fox £4.99
Here Comes Charlie Moon	**PB** Red Fox £2.50

DICK KING-SMITH

'I sit down and think, I'm going to write another animal book. What sort of animal shall I write about? Then I choose one. Then I have fun putting words into its mouth. I love writing dialogue.'

Dick King-Smith is one of the best humorous writers working for children now. His books are hilarious upside-down affairs, where babies are talking geniuses, pigs can round up sheep, swim, and, yes, fly. *The Sheep-Pig* won the *Guardian* Children's Fiction Award in 1984.

He was born in Gloucestershire, served in the Grenadier Guards during the Second World War. He's been a farmer and a teacher and presented television programmes. His first book was *The Fox Busters* in 1978 and since then he seems to produce as many as eight books a year.

He grew up reading a lot of animal stories, where animals spoke – *Winnie the Pooh, The Wind in the Willows* and so on. He quite happily concedes that all this means is that really a person is translated into an animal, but it all happened by mistake. Pigs seem to be a particular favourite with him. This, he thinks, may almost be as some kind of compensation for the fact that he hasn't got the room to keep pigs any more. He had liked them on his farm because, contrary to what most people think, pigs are extremely clean. 'Unfortunately we give them a bad press, but given half a chance, leaving aside its loving to roll about in mud, it is, in its personal habits, extremely clean. But what really endears me to pigs is the fact that they are so bright. Pigs are clever.'

The sheep-pig idea, where a pig becomes a sheep-herder, came from keeping dogs. He's always kept lots of dogs but he'd never owned a real sheepdog because he didn't keep sheep on his farm. The germ of the idea of the sheep-pig was a little incident at his local village fête in Gloucestershire. There, at the fête, was the mandatory little pig, in the corner and people were required to guess its weight. 'I began to fantasize about somebody buying it, taking it home, having it adopted by a Collie and from there things led on . . .

. . . Babe expected, and at that moment got, the command 'Come by, Pig,' to send him left and so behind the sheep and thus turn them towards the corner.

The pig cleared his throat. 'If I might ask a great favour of you,' he said hurriedly to the sheep, 'could you all please be kind enough to walk down to that gate where the farmer is standing and to go through it? Take your time, please. There's absolutely no rush.' ...

No one broke ranks or tried to slip away, no one pushed or shoved, there was no noise or fuss. From the oldest to the youngest, they went in like lambs.

Then at last a gentle murmur broke out as everyone in different ways quietly expressed their pleasure.

'Babe!' said Fly to the pig. 'That was quite beautifully done, dear.'

'Thank you so much!' said Babe to the sheep ...

In spite of all this chatting between animals, Dick King-Smith doesn't shy away from the realities of farming in his books. The pigs are destined to become bacon, which could possibly set up problems for children. Dick feels that children should accept it – 'if that doesn't sound too preachy'. The subject often crops up in schools. He finds himself saying to children, 'If you don't like meat, that's fine, be a vegetarian. It's your option. If you don't like reading animal stories where death arrives as well as birth, well I'm afraid you're the wrong reader for me because I can't see any point in covering these things up, hushing them up. It's something that happens to all of us.' In the same way, although he doesn't make a great hoo-ha about natural functions in the animal stories, if they have to do them, 'they jolly well do 'em'.

Writing came to Dick fairly late – he calls it a 'late flowering' because he had spent many years doing other things. He'd always loved messing about with words, and he'd always written a lot of verse, some of it romantic stuff, 'the way that young men did in those days', but quite a lot of lampooning doggerel, comic verse. But for most of his life, he'd never thought about writing a novel, much less one for children, until he had a 'rather wacky idea' which turned out to be the first book, *The Fox Busters*. He wanted to have a situation where the weak overcame the strong. The weak were the chickens and the strong were the foxes. 'I couldn't think of any way in which this could be done except by direct and violent attack. So I dreamed up the idea that, A) these chickens had the power of flight, and, B) by chance they learned to lay eggs in flight, and, C) after a great deal of clever work by their mother, they hard-boiled these eggs inside them by sitting in hot greenhouses and that kind of thing. So they were eventually carrying lethal missiles.

Jefferies was already airborn, hovering forty feet above the roof of the Dutch barn. And as the vixen began to climb, Jefferies swooped vertically down upon her so that it seemed to the watchers that the two must meet head on. At the last instant the pullet levelled off, and they could see her beak open in the triumph-shout:

'Egg gone!'

Simultaneously, her missile struck the climbing vixen full on that long nose that was, for the flock, the symbol of all they hated most about their enemies. The beast lost her footing and cartwheeled away to the ground, to rise, stagger and fall again beneath the blood-stained beaks and talons of the mob.

His experiences as a farmer feed into the books. It was also a help being a soldier, as in a book like *Saddlebottom* where a pig becomes a soldier. He's also kept pets all his life and they appear – or aspects of them – in a book like *Yob* about a dog who gets knocked down and hears everything backwards. He has ten grandchildren who draw stories out of him too. One of their favourites is *Harry's Mad* about a boy who inherits a parrot in his Great Uncle's will.

'What sort of games d'you like playing, Mad?' Harry asked.

'You mean football and stuff? Guess I ain't built for that, Harry.'

'No, no, I mean games that you and I can play together, you know, like cards.'

'Now, cards,' said Madison, 'are real tricky. Trouble is my foot ain't designed for holding a playing card any more than a pencil. . . . No, what I like are board games, you know? Where I can use my beak to pick up the pieces? . . .'

'Draughts?'

'Draughts? Never heard tell of that.'

Harry fetched a box of draughtsmen and a board from the cupboard where he kept all his toys.

'These.'

'Oh, checkers. That's what we call it. Yeah, sure, we played checkers'.

As with Madison, nicknamed Mad, there's a lot of fun with names in the books: *Daggie Dogfoot* is a piglet, his mother is called Mrs Barleylove and in the other sties there's Mrs Swedechopper, Mrs Maizemunch and Mrs Gobblespud. The combination of fantasy, madness and harsh reality was not very fashionable when Dick started writing. At the outset, he would occasionally be told, 'You can't do that sort of thing.' Ironically, his second book was turned down by the publishers for being too mild so he ended up re-writing the whole thing making it incredibly bloodthirsty. Once again he was told, 'we can't possibly publish this'. So, he sees himself as an old dog who's learnt new tricks and now, without a doubt his books are amongst the most-loved by children today.

Dick King-Smith

FAVOURITE TITLES

Title	Format	Publisher	Price
Sophie Hits Six	**PB**	Walker	£2.99
Paddy's Pot of Gold	**PB**	Puffin	£2.50
Martin's Mice	**PB**	Puffin	£2.99
The Fox Busters	**PB**	Puffin	£2.99
The Sheep-Pig	**PB**	Puffin	£2.50
Saddlebottom	**PB**	Puffin	£2.50
Harry's Mad	**PB**	Puffin	£2.99
Daggie Dogfoot	**PB**	Puffin	£2.99
Magnus Powermouse	**PB**	Puffin	£2.99
Super Terrific Pigs	**PB**	Gollancz	£2.99

JOAN LINGARD

'I am very interested in the whole transitional period of adolescence. I think it's an absolutely fascinating and extraordinarily difficult time, from the point of view of those going through it and the parents. I've been through it with three daughters and it's a time of major change

and upheaval. It's like coming to the crossroads of life, deciding which way you're going to go and what you're going to do. Also deciding, are you going to carry on with the ideas and ideals of your parents, or are you going to forge new ones of your own? Are you going to reject some of their prejudices?'

These are the themes and ideas that come across with compassion and humour, in Joan Lingard's books for teenagers. She enjoys a well-established reputation as an adult novelist, but in 1970 she changed tack and began writing for young people. It was a decision brought about by the start of the troubles in Northern Ireland in the late 1960s.

'It was one of those instances when I had a book in my head. It was as if it was waiting to be born, kind of whole. It was really my strong desire to write something for young people which would be against prejudice and wouldn't be for one side or the other, but would be for both sides, seeing the good and the bad in both. Once I had written *The Twelfth Day of July*, I wanted to go on and write the second book and so forth.'

There are five books in the series about Catholic Kevin and Protestant Sadie who live in the heart of Belfast in similar back-to-back terrace houses but in religiously segregated streets. The novels depict the bitterness and hatred dividing the city in a setting that was familiar to Joan Lingard. She was brought up in Belfast, having moved there from Edinburgh at the age of two, and as an adolescent, she was well aware of the hardened prejudices dividing the communities.

There is no doubting that Joan Lingard is a political writer, because she believes that political events touch all our lives, but her aims as a writer are threefold; firstly, to entertain. If her books do not fulfill that criteria she feels that they have failed from the start. The reader needs to be involved from the first page to want to continue and to be absorbed in her world. Secondly, Joan Lingard wants to stimulate the imagination, and thirdly, to stretch the mind.

In several novels, Joan Lingard has explored the idea of displacement. From the personal perspective of families displaced through re-marriage in *The Gooseberry* and *Strangers in the House*, to the more dramatic displacement of families through war. *Tug of War* is the story of a Latvian family fleeing the advancing Russian army in 1944. Again in this book there are echoes of Joan Lingard's own family history.

'Inevitably, as a writer you lower the bucket down into the well of your experience and it doesn't come up in any kind of chronological order, but you bring things up at different times. My husband is Latvian. He and his family had to flee in the wake of the advancing Russian army. They waited until the very last minute, then they left to catch the train to the Baltic coast and they missed it. So they had to set off on a trek, the young ones walking, the older ones riding in carts, travelling by night because the German and Russian bombers were attacking during the day. It took them six weeks to make this journey and then they went through the Baltic Sea and arrived in Poland, which was occupied by the Germans. Everything was in chaos and they became DPs – Displaced People – refugees in Europe for four years.

'I didn't write the book directly about my husband's family. I'm a fiction writer, so I create characters. I created twins who were fourteen when they had to leave Latvia and they are separated. This is my plot, the separation of the twins through war and as a writer you have to put yourself in those experiences. I really felt as if I had lived through those refugee camps in Europe by the time I had finished the book.'

The sequel to *Tug of War*, called *Between Two Worlds*, follows the family in the post-war period when they move to Canada to start a new life, strangers in an alien land. The emotions, the hardships, the prejudices are all there in this novel, which explores a theme only too relevant today.

'Come in, if you're coming in. And close that damn door.'

Hugo did as he was told and pulled the door to behind him. There was little room for him and, immediately, he wished that he had stayed outside. He was being looked over.

'DP?'

Hugo nodded.

'Where you from?'

'Latvia.'

'What?'

Hugo repeated the name of his country. His country! He could scarcely imagine it any more. The name did not seem to ring a bell with the men.

'Which side were you on during the War?'

'No side.'

'Come on. Everyone was on a side. I fought in Europe, nearly got it from a Jerry shell, so I should know!'

Hugo was sweating. The cross-examination from this burly man with the bullish shoulders and huge hands were bringing on a headache.... How could he begin to explain the complicated history of the Baltic states, battered by everybody, torn apart by bigger powers? How could he explain in his halting English?

Not all Joan Lingard's books concern conflict and danger. She also writes with humour about families and individuals. The novels about Maggie, a Glasgow girl, who wants to go to university and extend the boundaries of her life, have been a popular TV series. *Rags and Riches* and *Glad Rags* are stories based around a second-hand clothes shop in Edinburgh, where an eccentric family tease their way through life, marshalled by Granny, Manageress of the local supermarket. It is light-hearted fun and reflects the pleasure that Joan Lingard finds in writing for a teenage audience.

'I think it's immensely rewarding. Much more rewarding than writing for adults. I'm not talking about financially, I'm just talking about the response you get. When you write for adults, people will say in a diffident way, "I enjoyed your book". But the warmth that comes back from children when they write and tell you, "I thought that book was absolutely fantastic", or the way their eyes light up, that makes it all worthwhile.'

Joan Lingard

FAVOURITE TITLES

The Twelfth Day of July	**PB** Puffin Plus £2.99
Across the Barricades	**PB** Puffin Plus £3.50
Tug of War	**PB** Puffin Plus £3.50
Between Two Worlds	**PB** Puffin Plus £3.99
The Gooseberry	**PB** Beaver £2.99
Strangers in The House	**PB** Beaver £2.99
Maggie series	New Windmill £3.99
Rags and Riches	**PB** Puffin £2.99
Glad Rags	**PB** Puffin £2.99
The Guilty Party	**PB** Puffin Plus £3.50

MARGARET MAHY

'I think we all probably get a lot of very intensely coded information when we're children. Some people I know, seem to have very little memory of their childhood, but I think that I do have quite strong memories of my childhood and a sort of continuity of idea and image. Now whether I have that because I remember my childhood, or whether it's there anyway and I've just been led to notice it, I can't really say for sure. But I think I write for children because I am interested in decoding quite a lot of the information I received when I was small.'

Margaret Mahy delights and amazes children of all ages with her wild imagination. From her native New Zealand, she is known all over the world and in this country has been awarded the Carnegie Medal twice: in 1982 for *The Haunting* and again in 1984 for *The Changeover*, both books for older children. Her picture books are usually a blend of fantastic fun and romping action. *The Great White Man-Eating Shark*, for instance, tells the story of obnoxious little Norvin, who looks like a shark

Out of plastic he made himself the dorsal fin of a great white man-eating shark. *The Great White Man-Eating Shark* Illustrated by Jonathan Allen

and terrorizes the bathers, so that he can have the beach all to himself.

'Norvin is a vision of myself. I was in a swimming pool, a very small swimming pool, which I was sharing with two other people who were obviously enormously fond of one another, because they stood at one end of the swimming pool embracing passionately, while I swam up and down. As I swam towards them, I did have this feeling of intruding into private space which, after a while, began to get on my nerves and I began to try to work out ways in which I could frighten them out of the swimming pool. One of the things I thought about was getting dressed up as a shark. I didn't imagine actually, in real life that if I did this I would be particularly terrifying, but what I did do was to take a note about it and then later on use it as the basis for the story of *The Great White Man-Eating Shark*.

An element of the fantastic is usually an important ingredient in Margaret Mahy's stories. There's *The Man Whose Mother Was a Pirate*, *The Queen's Goat* or in *Jam: A True Story*, the family who had so much jam, they started to repair the house with it.

'I think fantasy gives you a certain amount of room to negotiate with the world. I certainly find that the world does have a sort of fantastic shimmer running through it. A variety of things happen to us in life and as well as the fact of the things that happen, you have also at your disposal, certain ingredients, which mean you have a variety of ways you can interpret what's happening. The interpretation depends, sometimes affects, the way you actually cope with it.

'As an example, there's an occasion when our car caught fire and we jumped out and ran down the road. The children were very frightened by this and I was scared too. I thought the car was going to blow up. I've seen that happen a lot on television and I always find it convincing. As we ran down the road, however, I thought I should try and make things a bit better for them. So I was saying to them, "Look on this as an adventure." I was saying it to myself as much as to them. I was saying, "This is an uncomfortable thing, but we're going to live through this and we'll come out and it will be a story to tell and it will become part of our imaginative structure of the world."'

Margaret Mahy began writing when she was a child. Looking back at her first story *Harry is Bad*, which she wrote when she was seven, it seems to her a highly moral tale about a little boy who hated work, but, trapped by a witch who sets him tasks, he grows to love it. There was a clear understanding, even then, about the way in which certain stories will work as a narrative.

As a child, she loved to read about pirates, she romanticized their swashbuckling lifestyle and ever since, lured by the taste of adventure and danger, such buccaneers have been firm favourites with Maragaret Mahy. In her story, *The Great Piratical Rumbustification*, written for six- or seven-year-olds, she introduces the idea that not all pirates are on the high seas; there are, in fact, bank managers and businessmen who are secretly pirates. They are not the heroes of her childhood, but rather inefficient characters, trying to act out their traditional roles.

'In *The Pirates Mixed-Up Voyage* the pirates set out to be pirates but they can't read, so they don't know which way to hold their treasure map. They go to school to learn to read and the teachers are even tougher than they are, so I think there's something working in there in which the adventurous, anarchic, romantic spirit is modified by all sorts of systems in the world, including the school system.'

For older children, in novels like *Dangerous Spaces* Margaret Mahy explores the paranormal. As a child she was fascinated by stories involving the psychic and the supernatural.

'I think it does have an imaginative effect. I think that for a variety of reasons, our nervous systems are very anxious that we shouldn't be too alarmed, even though we live in an alarming world. They try to filter a lot of the surprise out of our lives. We learn to take things for granted and some stories which have supernatural elements in them, by restoring astonishment and a certain amount of fear and mystery to life, actually enable us to take a true imaginative look at things.'

The photo in the frame showed the crack in the world. A jagged gash running across a snowy slope. It seemed almost life-size, certainly much larger than the picture on the card, and incredibly clear and deep. Beside it stood the boy, facing her, pointing to the crack with one hand and in the other holding out the same stereoscope that Anthea herself held at that very moment. And it seemed to Anthea that, coming out of the crack beside him, was a hand on a scratched wrist, groping upwards, just as if someone were trying to pull herself up out of the cleft. Anthea's own hand began to shake as it jerked the card along its tin grooves. . . . 'Look what I've found.'

Flora looked, but was not surprised. She had seen it before.

'Henry's stereoscope. ... Lionel's brother, dead Henry. That one there.' Flora pointed at one of the old photographs over the bookcase.

Sure enough, there he stood, holding the stereoscope, just as she had seen him a moment ago on the edge of the crack in the world. He smiled a little, triumphantly, she thought, like someone who has a space all his own, held safely between his own two hands. But it seemed to her that this was a space he was offering to share.

Dangerous Spaces is in some ways a ghost story, the psychic element is a means of healing for Anthea, who is trying to come to terms with the death of her parents. For her, it is also a way of accepting, being reconciled with the past and through that, looking for a new interpretation of the present. Margaret Mahy covers similar ground in *Underrunners*, the story of Tris, whose parents have split up. But, by contrast, this is a thriller, strongly linked to the isolated peninsula in New Zealand, where the story is set.

'Between writing *Dangerous Spaces* and *Underrunners*, that particular peninsula actually came up for sale and, although it's not much use for anything for a variety of reasons, including erosion, I bought it, so I've looked at it since then with a much greater intensity.

'I was walking over the land with somebody from the Ministry of Forestry and we were talking about planting native bush on it and he said, "Oh, you've got very big underrunners here." I've known that there were these little caves in the ground, they don't go back far, but they're big enough, in this case, for an adult to get into. So I suppose I've been aware of them and thinking about them unconsciously for a while and it seemed to me to provide a very good metaphor for life. It looks fun on the surface, but is, in a lot of cases, tunnelled underneath in mysterious ways, sometimes benign, sometimes not benign, but that there are all these tunnels that run under our lives.

'In many ways, people like the father of Tris, in *Underrunners*, relate to the pirates we were talking about earlier. He has a romantic vision (and I don't use the word romantic in any pejorative sense) but he does have a romantic vision about how life should be lived, but he can only live it inefficiently. He doesn't do it as efficiently as it needs to be done. So he has some areas of success, but also big areas of failure, which is also true of my personal romantic life. So that, I guess some of these things have got biographical elements, although the people aren't anything like me.'

Margaret Mahy

FAVOURITE TITLES

Title	Publisher
The Great White Man-Eating Shark	**PB** Puffin £3.50
The Man Whose Mother Was a Pirate	**PB** Puffin £3.50
Horrendous Hullabaloo	Hamish Hamilton £8.99
Downhill Crocodile Whizz & other stories	**PB** Puffin £2.99
Keeping House	**PB** Puffin £3.50
The Pirates Mixed-Up Voyage	Dent £7.95
The Great Piratical Rumbustification	**PB** Puffin £2.99
The Haunting	**PB** Mammoth £2.99
Dangerous Spaces	**PB** Puffin £2.99
Underrunners	Hamish Hamilton £8.99

JILL MURPHY

'People often think that you write for children you have, or children that you know. You don't. You write with a part of you that comes from not having really grown up.'

Author and illustrator Jill Murphy scored an instant hit when her book *The Worst Witch* was published in 1974. She followed that success with two more bestsellers about young Mildred Hubble whose talents as a trainee witch never quite meet the expectations of her Headmistress, Miss Cackle. She's matched her doubtful heroine with a story about *Geoffrey Strangeways*, a highly imaginative young lad whose aim in life is to become a knight. Then there are a string of picture books for younger children including *Peace At Last*, *All in One Piece* and *Five Minutes' Peace* which won the *Parents* Best Books for Babies Award in 1987.

'It's always the story that suggests itself first. I've been writing and drawing since I was very small and I thought everybody could draw, so I just took that for granted. I loved writing stories and it was all I ever really did.'

Five Minutes' Peace is the sort of story which has great appeal for children under five and will strike some familiar chords with many parents. The Large family happen to be elephants but the story came directly from everyday family life, courtesy of a friend who was expecting her fourth child.

'We were trying to have a quiet cup of tea before we went off to the shops. We were just chatting while my friend was sitting in the bath resting her teacup on her pregnant stomach. Really the little ones did the book. They all trooped up the stairs, marched in and the youngest ended

She poured herself a cup of tea and lay back with her eyes closed. It was heaven. *Five Minutes' Peace*

up dropping all the toys in the bath. I remember thinking that it would make a funny story because it laid itself before me, so I just wrote it down on bits of paper, then the pictures came later.'

Peace At Last, the story of Mr Bear's search for a quiet place to sleep during a particularly disturbed night, traces a sequence of events, noises and phrases which very young children quickly learn to repeat.

'It was a story I made up for a little boy when I was a nanny. He was a quiet little boy and I told him the story for fun on the way to playgroup. To my surprise, when I went to collect him later on, he'd actually tried to tell it to another child who in turn came and repeated it to me. So I wrote it down and later on, I used it with children during library sessions. They actually learn it by heart very quickly and that helps them with their reading because they see the blocks of words, so they actually think they're reading and it gets them interested.'

By contrast, *The Worst Witch* was actually an adaptation of Jill Murphy's own time at a Roman Catholic school. The nuns in their long black robes, the girls in dark, scruffy school uniform, hair backcombed with hats perched on top; it all seemed to fit with witches.

'I've no idea how I got the idea. It was like a light bulb appearing above your head just as they show in comics. I thought instead of velour hats, they could have pointed ones. Instead of bicycles, they could have broomsticks and you wouldn't even need to unlock the school gates, they could all just come over the wall. Then I always wanted to have animals at school. We only had stick insects and you can't get very excited about stick insects, so I thought supposing you all had a cat to train or an owl. After that I just basically added stereotypes, because at school, there are always some mean girls and some nice girls.'

'I think Miss Cackle gave you that cat on purpose,' Ethel sneered. 'You're both as bad as each other.' . . .

'Look, Ethel,' Mildred said, 'you'd better be quiet, because if you don't I shall . . .'

'Well?'

'I shall have to turn you into a frog and I don't want to do that.'

Ethel gave a shriek of laughter. 'That's really funny,' she crowed. 'You don't even know the beginners' spells, let alone ones like that.'

Mildred blushed and looked very miserable.

'Go on, then,' cried Ethel. 'Go on, then, if you're so clever. Turn me into a frog. I'm waiting.'

It just so happened that Mildred did have an idea of that spell. She'd been reading about it in the library. By now, everyone had crowded round, waiting to see what would happen, and Ethel was still jeering. It was unbearable.

Mildred muttered the spell under her breath and Ethel vanished. In her place stood a small pink and grey pig.

The Worst Witch was written by the time Jill Murphy was eighteen. It had appeared in her school rough-books with drawings added three years earlier, but when she sent it off to various publishers, they all rejected it. So, that seemed to be the end of her writing career and she went off to work in a children's home and later became a nanny.

'Then by an amazing fluke, a friend of mine went to a publisher's party and mentioned me and they actually said they'd like to see me. I went along and met them and they loved it and printed five thousand. I remember thinking, "Where will we find five thousand people who will buy this?", but it just took off all on its own. It was all such a treat.'

The Worst Witch books appeal to children who have mastered the basic skills of reading, but need confidence to go further. They are enticing and amusing, mixing basic ingredients like friendship and school with magic and invention so that readers are quickly drawn into the plot.

A change of gender and a change of scene comes with *Geoffrey Strangeways*. This young man has his sights set on being a knight, but he's not very competent and he allows his vivid imagination too much rein. His fantasies are akin to the daydreams that Jill Murphy remembers from her own childhood.

'At school, I was rather a hopeless case. I couldn't really do anything very well. I could write interesting stories but nobody seemed to take any notice of that. I actually remember standing in Assembly, imagining that robbers, dressed in striped jumpers, had rushed in and grabbed the Headmistress, dragging her off the rostrum. I would rush up there and save her, and then everyone would say, "How wonderful! We always knew this girl had it in her." I know that a lot of children at school are in that position, hoping they might do a bit better or be noticed a bit more.'

This affinity with children and their emotions comes through in Jill Murphy's writing. In her book *Worlds Apart* she has ventured into the realistic world where family relationships can founder and fail, leaving children confused and hurt. She is aware that in life a happy ending does not often ensue, but in children's fiction she feels it's important to give that reassurance.

'All my books have happy endings, that's how a book comes out of me, so I can only do it that way. I don't think that children need too much harsh realism, particularly when they're small.'

Jill Murphy

FAVOURITE TITLES

Peace At Last	**PB** MacMillan £3.50
On The Way Home	**PB** MacMillan £3.50
All in One Piece	**PB** Walker £3.99
Five Minutes' Peace	**PB** Walker £3.99
A Piece of Cake	**PB** Walker £3.99
The Worst Witch	**PB** Puffin £2.99
The Worst Witch Strikes Again	**PB** Puffin £2.99
A Bad Spell for The Worst Witch	**PB** Puffin £2.99
Geoffrey Strangeways	**PB** Walker £2.99
Worlds Apart	**PB** Walker £2.99

JILL PATON WALSH

'I do, without apology, offer children literary books, because I think the pleasures of literature are what books have to offer, that other forms of entertainment cannot give. I don't see the point of writing a very lightweight, frivolous book, like a television soap, for a child because it's never going to be as easy as watching the soap, or as prettily coloured or as fast-moving. You're always going

to be asking for more effort from the reader, than you would be from the viewer on the sofa, and I think you need to be absolutely sure you have sufficiently rewarded the extra effort when you get it.'

Widely regarded as one of the best writers for children today, Jill Paton Walsh has won a host of prizes on both sides of the Atlantic, including the Whitbread Award in 1974 for *The Emperor's Winding Sheet* and the Smarties Grand Prix Award in 1986 for *Gaffer Samson's Luck*. The settings of her novels vary; sometimes historical, sometimes contemporary, but the story is always accessible with a strong plot.

She began her career teaching English in a girls' grammar school in north London and then when family life assumed more importance, Jill Paton Walsh turned to writing for children. Now that her own children have grown up and left home, she has begun to explore more adult material and her recent book, *Grace*, reflects this change. It gives a new perspective to the famous story of Grace Darling, the lighthouse keeper's daughter, who saved nine people from the wreck of the *Forfarshire*, in 1838. Jill Paton Walsh tells the story of the shipwreck, the rescue and the aftermath through the voice of Grace Darling.

'There is just one side of the story that's well known. There's another story that isn't well known at all and that's how the lifeboat went out from Seahouses, the same morning, at terrible risk, and rowed thirteen sea miles in the teeth of the gale and arrived twenty minutes after the last seaman was safely inside the lighthouse. That is to say, too late to have any official share in the bounty that would undoubtedly be paid on every soul saved living from the shipwreck. There was a terrible stink about it. Half of England worshipped Grace for the rest of her life, as though she were a sort of early Beatle or something, wanting bits of her clothes, bits of her hair; and all the local people hated her, because they thought she hadn't done anything brave enough to deserve the recompense she had received, compared to the scant recognition and much smaller recompense that the lifeboat crew had received for going into greater danger.'

You might think that there is little for a teenager today to relate to in this story, but it is all about adolescent dreams of fame and fortune, and the reality of that dream is the same today as it was for Grace Darling. It meant isolation from local friends, a loneliness that wealth cannot compensate for and a change of lifestyle which was dramatic and unwelcome. Jill Paton Walsh invites her readers to look forward out of childhood to see adult dilemmas. For Grace Darling, her brave action brought personal stress which certainly contributed to her early death. There are many people today who share her dilemma.

Having said that, *Grace* is a demanding read for twelve- to fourteen-year-olds. The language and the structure of the sentences and the style of the book reflect the nineteenth-century voice of this story. The book would not have been convincing told in the modern idiom, but some readers may be put off by this approach.

Fireweed, a story about the London blitz, and *The Dolphin Crossing*, concerning Dunkirk, have much more in the way of pace and plot, perhaps because they're told from personal experience. Jill Paton Walsh grew up during the Second World War, and it all comes alive in these books. You can imagine her a quiet observer of every passing personality and incident.

'I spent a lot of my childhood trying to read *Jane Eyre* down an air-raid shelter and the people round me were reacting in very different ways. They were of all social rank and all kinds and I suppose the writer in me started, as a little child, wide-eyed, watching the milkman hitting the bank manager to stop him yelling in a raid. Then seeing the two of them courteously bidding each other "Good morning" on the street the following day and beginning to think about people under stress and in danger and finding them very mysterious when I was a child and, let's face it, still finding it infinitely mysterious and infinitely interesting, how people react in crisis.'

A crisis of a very different kind, comes with *A Parcel of Patterns*, the story of Eyam, the Derbyshire village which, when the plague struck in 1665, accepted voluntary isolation to stop the spread of the disease. At the heart of the book there is a powerful love story and the dilemma of the lovers – should the girl from the plague-ridden village continue to meet the shepherd from a neighbouring village?

'The past is always what we see from the rock we stand on now. So that, as the present rock changes, the panoramas of history that we are considering change. There's no interest in an historical subject for a novelist if it does not connect with a contemporary situation. Now choices about individuals pursuing individual happiness, as against pursuing communal happiness, arise in trivial ways all over childhood. Are you going to put your own personal chances in life ahead of everything else? Are you going to be loyal to your friends?

'I also feel fairly sure that children read forward. They read about situations they haven't yet encountered. That's part of their preparation, part of their thinking about life. So I don't much mind if the book is about the sort of dilemma that usually hits people in adult life. I'm sure that the thirteen- and fourteen-year-olds of my acquaintance are already thinking about what young adult life is going to be like.'

By contrast, *Gaffer Samson's Luck* is a quieter, more contained story, which will appeal to nine- to twelve-year-olds. James goes to live in a Fenland village where he is an outsider caught between two factions, the children who live in the village, and the children from the estate. Trying to come to terms with his new surroundings, James makes friends with Gaffer Samson, who lives next door. The old man lends him his bike and this new found freedom gives James the chance to explore this strange and alien landscape, but it also leaves him open to the menace of the village boys.

A vast sky overhead, a vast land all around. . . . It made James dizzy. The landmarks danced in space as he rode . . . and from the corner of his eye he caught movement far over on his right. Miles and miles away, riding on another road parallel to his own, he saw a group of cyclists going east with him.

Even without seeing the pale blue speck of Terry's anorak, he would have known they were the village, chasing him. He put his head down and pedalled furiously. The bike went at an amazing speed, but all the time, along the other road, the other bikes kept up with him. No nearer and no further, but full in view. . . .

Black panic overtook him. Wherever he rode they would be able to see him. For miles and miles there was no cover, no tree or wood, only flat and naked earth. . . .

In the bleak Fenland country, James is forced to pit his wits and courage against the village boys. There are more threads to the plot though, for Gaffer Samson is terminally ill and in order to die, the old man believes that he needs to have back a lost talisman, his 'luck', a little Stone Age arrowhead which James must find. So, through this strand the story is woven around a life turning full circle. Gaffer Samson wants to die and he accepts that it is time for him to go if only James can find the means to release him.

'In most families' lives, some grandparents will die before the end of childhood and I'm wanting children to see that in a not too frightening or resisting way. I think we think of childhood as being protected from metaphysical concerns about the meaning of life; good, evil, suffering and so on. In fact, it isn't. It's impossible to protect children from death, from pain, from accident, from loss, from change, from personal stress. They have it and it is unfair of us not to reach out to them with some kind of human solidarity and try and show them that in these situations and feelings and wonderings and resentment against God, or whoever might be responsible for the loss of your pet, or worse, they were not alone. You have to show them that this is a general human thing that they're going through, not a curious, isolating, personal aberration. I think real fiction for children ought to address them as full human beings and it ought to because they are full human beings. They're at the same risk as any of us on the face of this uncertain world.'

Jill Paton Walsh

FAVOURITE TITLES

Gaffer Samson's Luck	**PB** Puffin £2.50
The Butty Boy	**PB** Puffin £2.99
The Dolphin Crossing	**PB** Puffin £2.99
Fireweed	**PB** Puffin £2.99
Torch	**PB** Puffin £2.99
The Chance Child	**PB** Puffin £3.50
Babylon	**PB** Beaver £3.99
Matthew and the Sea Singer	**PB** Simon & Schuster £3.50
A Parcel of Patterns	**PB** Puffin £2.99
Grace	Viking Kestrel £8.99

PHILIPPA PEARCE

'I think the main thing is a story, isn't it?'

Philippa Pearce is one of the truly great children's writers of the modern era. Her book, *Tom's Midnight Garden* is generally regarded as a modern classic on a par with anything produced in the so-called Golden Age of children's literature before the First World War.

She comes from Cambridgeshire, went to university in Cambridge itself during the last War. She has worked as a scriptwriter and producer at the BBC, as an editor for Oxford University Press and again at André Deutsch Children's Books. She won the Carnegie Medal in 1959 for *Tom's Midnight Garden* and the Whitbread Award in 1978 for *The Battle of Bubble and Squeak*.

She can remember quite clearly how *Tom's Midnight Garden* came about because it had a local, personal reason to it. It is actually about the garden and the house where she was brought up. Her father had been born there. It was the millhouse and he was the miller and his father had been the miller before him. 'It was a terrible wrench, a real attack on my feelings, when I heard that my parents, who were then elderly, were going to move and leave it. That was one of the main causes of that story: thinking about my childhood in the garden and my father's childhood in the same garden.' Philippa remembers walking round the garden, at the time when her parents were selling the house, trying to see her grandfather. She had never known him because he had died just after she was born, so she was trying to see him as a sort of ghost. But she never did. 'I think as a family we're not very ghostly.' At that time, she made a note with pen and paper of all the things in the garden, the plants that grew and the trees and the layout. 'I didn't think I might write a book, as I did; but I never, never needed to refer to that list. It was all in my mind forever.'

There is a time, between night and day, when landscapes sleep. Only the earliest riser sees that hour; or the all-night traveller, letting up the blind of his railway-carriage window, will look out on a rushing landscape of stillness in which trees and bushes stand immobile and breathless in sleep – wrapped in sleep, as the traveller himself wrapped his body in his great-coat or his rug the night before.

This grey, still hour before morning was the time in which Tom walked into his garden. He had come down the stairs and along the hall to the garden door at midnight; but when he opened that door and stepped out into the garden, the time was much later. All night – moonlit or swathed in darkness – the garden had stayed awake; now, after that night-long vigil, it had dozed off.

Tom is bored and lonely staying with a childless aunt and uncle in a flat which is part of the house. He discovers the garden at night where he plays with Hatty, who is – here Time slips – a Victorian child. If that was all there was to the book, it would never have become the classic it is. The point is, Hatty grows up and in so doing reveals to Tom the painful truth about coming to terms with change and growing up. It has been seen as a reply to *Peter Pan*. This makes the book enjoyable and moving for adults too. In fact, this movement between adult and child audiences has happened to another of Philippa Pearce's stories, *What the Neighbours Did*.

It would be wrong to give the impression that Philippa Pearce's stories are cerebral – she considers story terribly important. She learnt the craft of getting over a good strong storyline when writing twenty-minute scripts for radio. 'You had to get it right, quickly, if you only had twenty minutes. It always seems to me to be a gorgeous luxury now to write a short story which could take, you know, even three quarters of an hour to read aloud.'

She also has the ability of finding a sense of fear, an arresting moment. There's a point in *The Way to Sattin Shore* where the child looks in the mirror and sees her father.

She peered deeply into the mirror. Behind Kate Tranter's face lay the dimness of Kate Tranter's bedroom, all reversed and strange, as though strange things might begin to happen there.

In that background dimness a slight movement attracted her attention. The just-open door wavered as in a draught – swung open a little wider – a very little wider. There was something else, too. Not Syrup, the cat, because Syrup would have appeared almost at ground level. This was much higher, at human eye level.

She looked, and her eyes met other eyes, through the shadowy gap of the door. Too dark to see the face properly; but she knew it was there, because the eyes looked at her. . . . The eyes of a stranger looked at her from over her shoulder, from the dim depths of the mirror. . . . She could not have imagined it.

Philippa thinks ghost stories are interesting because people are both easily afraid yet are willing to be made afraid. 'They want to know what they're afraid of and why. I've felt it myself. I think ghost stories can be very revealing to people. They're images of certain basic fears that we have.'

She's also a creator of other worlds as with the child's fantasy world in *A Dog So Small*. She says that if you lead a full adult life, you also have a full fantasy life. 'Your dream life is just a safety valve for what's going on.'

In a tube train, for instance, Ben could sit with his eyes shut for the whole journey and if anyone noticed, no one commented. . . . When other passengers got out at their various stations, he stayed on, going round and round the Inner Circle. . . . No one ever saw what he was seeing: a fawn-coloured dog of incredible minuteness.

If Ben were sitting he saw the dog on his knee. If he stood, he looked down with his eyes shut, and saw it at his feet. The dog was always with him, only dashing ahead or lingering behind in order to play tricks of agility and daring.

It has been spotted that Philippa has two recurring images in her books: water and dogs. The dogs, she feels, are a soft-spot from her childhood. 'We had a dog when I was a child and although I had a loving mother and father, two brothers and a sister, the dog meant to me almost as much as any of them.' Then when she became a parent, she acquired a dog and found that her daughter was as 'dotty' about dogs as she was. 'I think dogs are so lovely because when I go home in the evening, she'll be there and she'll be so delighted to see me. None of that "Why haven't you come before?" or "I haven't had a satisfactory supper." Just total unconditional love, which is very nice to have.'

As far as the water image is concerned, this goes back to her childhood in the millhouse. The river ran by the garden, and the family had a canoe, her brothers went fishing and it seemed natural to have water at hand. She observes here that in those days it also seemed natural that boys should do things like fishing while girls did 'different things'. This, perhaps, led her at the outset to make her main protagonists boys, though in her later books she says she would be as likely, or even more likely to put a girl in the central position. She says, 'If you think what it was like to write in the Fifties, certainly for somebody who was brought up between the Wars as I was, it was natural to think of the boy perhaps as the central character if there were going to be active things done. I had two elder brothers. They were awfully nice to me but they were the ones who really did things.' Meanwhile her elder sister was being 'terribly feminine' and didn't do the energetic things the brothers did. 'I think it was just cultural conditioning.'

As it happens Philippa feels that it's a pity sometimes to say that the central character is *either* a boy *or* a girl. This whole issue of gender in books is one of the changes Philippa has lived through. Another concerns language. 'My language is always as pure as the driven snow, simply because I've trained myself like that. It was in my childhood anyway.'

Nowadays, she feels out of date, technologically, and this becomes a problem if you're going to set a story in the present. 'I used to introduce television sets when I hadn't got a television. I now ought to be introducing all sorts of other things, and I don't even understand the language. But of course *humanity* doesn't change all that much.'

No matter what Philippa writes in the future, her position as a writer of some of the best children's stories ever, is secure.

Philippa Pearce

FAVOURITE TITLES

Who's Afraid? and Other Strange Stories	Puffin	£2.99
The Battle of Bubble and Squeak	**PB** Puffin	£2.99
Mrs Cockle's Cat	**PB** Puffin	£2.50
Lion at School & Other Stories	**PB** Puffin	£2.99
What the Neighbours Did & Other Stories	**PB** Puffin	£2.99
Minnow on the Say	**PB** Puffin	£3.50
Tom's Midnight Garden	**PB** Puffin	£2.50
The Way to Sattin Shore	**PB** Puffin	£3.50
A Dog So Small	**PB** Puffin	£2.99
The Shadow Cage and Other Stories of the Supernatural	**PB** Puffin	£2.99

ANN PILLING

'However authentic a novel seems to be, a children's novel is slightly fantasic.'

Ann Pilling, who also writes under the name of Ann Cheetham, has established herself as a writer whose fiction can terrify – with her ghost stories like *The Pit* – but who can mix humour with self-discovery and revelation with a novel like *Henry's Leg*. This won her the *Guardian* Children's Fiction Award in 1986 and was adapted into a very popular television series.

She came originally from Lancashire, studied English at university and worked for a while as a teacher and as an officer for the Federation of Children's Book Groups. When she first started writing it was in order to win a competition. This turned out later to be *The Year of the Worm*, published in 1984. One of the requirements of the competition was that the story should be funny and she remembers sitting with a pad and a pencil scratching her head, thinking, 'Can I be funny?' Slowly she realized she could be. But underneath, there was always the compulsion to write about the victim, the anti-hero. Her first anti-hero, Worm, was one such victim and Ann Pilling sees that as a pattern which has emerged in her writing. Her characters are learning how to survive – 'in a hard world, but a world that is full of humour'.

She has been accused of only writing for boys, but she points out that there are both sexes in her books. The reason she started off with a male hero was, she says, because she has two sons. They were her starting point. She remembers an elderly friend saying to her, rather whimsically, 'There's nothing like the world of the small boy.'

There's something unconventional about her heroes. Henry, in *Henry's Leg*, for example, is a kind of clumsy eleven-year-old, with big feet, and hoards of junk, rubbish and animals in his room.

Across the road, outside a dress shop, he saw three big dustbins all lined up neatly for the chewer, and out of the middle one something was sticking straight up. It was a human leg.

The long wet road, with its façades of dreary little shops, felt empty suddenly, and somehow threatening. The sidestreets had turned into shadowy canyons where monster cats lurked. The drizzle was becoming a downpour and Henry's hair was plastered to his head. But he didn't even notice. His brain was working overtime and he just stood there goggling ... The body had been hacked to pieces and stuffed into a dustbin outside Alice Modes Fashions.

It was an old-style dress shop, expensive but 'good' ... sandwiched between a betting shop and a run-down newsagent's, its two big windows full of pink corsets and middle-aged hats, and there was this leg, in one of its dustbins. Henry crossed the road to have a closer look.

It had obviously come off a fashion model but there was no sign of the rest of the body, no trunk or arms in the gutter, no odd hand lying on the pavement. Just the leg, with its red toenails, pointing straight up at the tin-coloured Darnley sky.

He walked on, very slowly, then stopped and looked back. He quite fancied that leg. He didn't know why, he just wanted it ...

This casual kleptomania lands him right into the middle of a thriller. The local gang are very interested in the leg too, and seem prepared to stop at nothing to get it back. But Ann Pilling is very interested in relationships, especially the ones between children and adults, unlike, say, the classic children's fiction that 'kill off' the adults in the opening pages – as with *The Lion, the Witch and the Wardrobe*. She hopes that her adults are seen from the point of view of the child. This comes partly from eavesdropping, from hearing the way young teens talk about their parents, from listening to their grievances. However, she's concerned that some children's writing at the moment emphasizes adult pre-occupations with children from the adult point of view. This is the wrong balance, she feels.

Yet, it has to be said, that Ann Pilling's characters are often beset with adult problems: financial difficulties, one-parent families and the like. She sees this as a 'survival pattern'. 'The hero or heroine has a problem, and nearly always it is a problem with domestic circumstances, but solve something.' This is because no matter how authentic a novel seems to be, children's fiction is always 'slightly fantastic'. 'We know really that it's unlikely Henry could solve his parents' problems by finding a leg in a dustbin, and yet you can write that in a children's novel. Not only can you do it, you can succeed in making it convincing. It doesn't become ridiculous, because underpinning the semi-fantastic, is real life.'

Another key element in Ann Pilling's writing is melodrama. In all her books there are moments of high tension, as, say, in *On the Lion's Side*, when the children get stuck down a disused mineshaft in Wales. Ann feels that there isn't enough adventure in many recent children's novels. She sees plenty of fantasy, and domestic drama but those old features of getting swept out to sea, clinging with your fingernails on to the edge of cliffs seem to have gone. So what she did with *On the Lion's Side* was to inject this. 'The first thing that happens to Robert, my hero, is that he goes out on the moors and this Welsh lad points a gun at him . . . and it goes downhill from there.' What Ann sees as important about adventure is that it takes you on an incredible journey.

A very different kind of adventure can be found in *Vote for Baz* which deals with elections and selection in education. The story was taken from real life. A school had an election at a time of a General Election and it was taken very seriously. As the time for voting drew near, it became evident to everybody around that the Anarchist Party was going to win, because it had captured the imagination of everybody. It caused great humour and disruption. They were seen as wicked. The Headmaster of the school realized that wasn't good news for him, so he changed the rules. He announced that the staff – and it was a big staff – would be allowed to vote. He calculated that this would sway the count in the direction of the Conservative Party, which was what he wanted. And it did!

People were definitely interested; he'd got them, he could tell. Undoing his jacket he stuck out his chest and pointed to the trumpet logo. 'Everyone supporting me is wearing one of these today . . . You see it's all very well old Julius going on about fine feathers and that, but that's not it, *is it? Does it really matter what people wear, I mean now,* does *it? So long as they are comfortable in their clothes and they don't go around embarrassing other people? What's wrong with a pair of sneakers for Heaven's sake?' and he stuck out one rather beaten-up trainer, for inspection. 'What's wrong with the odd ear-ring? What's wrong with* colour *in life, and choice and* individuality? *That's what Mr Lyme wants to encourage in this school, I know. He wants us to think for ourselves, don't you, sir?'*

That was daring. 'I certainly do, Bradshaw,' Slime said with an icy smile . . . He obviously didn't like what he was hearing.

'Of course this is a great school, but . . . if you vote for me, you'll make it even better. You see, I want fairer chances for people . . .'

With books like this, there's always a danger that the adult view appears too imposed on to a children's book. Ann admits that perhaps she did do this in respect of her views on 'haves' and 'have-nots'. 'I was very anxious, when I planned the book, to explain how the hero, Baz (Bradshaw), got into this old-fashioned school. The Comprehensive, where he was, and from which he was plucked, by winning the scholarship, is actually next door. So we always have a juxtaposition. He's gone to the old grammar school for the sake of his father, who is dead.' In other words, Ann Pilling is saying that the conflicts and tensions over class, are rooted in conflicting loyalties within Baz's family. As with all her books, the human dimension to the themes she's exploring, is always strongly felt.

Ann Pilling

FAVOURITE TITLES

Dustbin Charlie	**PB** Puffin £2.99
The Big Biscuit	**PB** Young Knight £2.50
The Jungle Sale	Blackie £2.95
Henry's Leg	**PB** Puffin £2.99
Vote for Baz	Viking Kestrel £8.99
The Year of the Worm	**PB** Puffin £2.99
Our Kid	**PB** Puffin £2.99
On the Lion's Side	**PB** Piper £2.99
The Big Pink	**PB** Puffin £2.50
Stan	**PB** Puffin £2.99

MAURICE SENDAK

'To me, drawing is composing.'

Maurice Sendak is one of the most distinguished illustrators this century. He's a New Yorker who worked first as a cartoonist and as a shop-window display artist. His very first illustration work was for a book called *Atomics for the Millions* in 1947, and the first book he wrote and illustrated was *Kenny's Window* in 1956. Kenny is, in part, the product of Sendak's interest in psychoanalysis. He's a boy who escapes into dreams and fantasies to discover some painful sides to his life. Perhaps Sendak's best known picture book is still *Where The Wild Things Are*, which came out in 1963 and is now a classic. It was, at first, the subject of much controversy. Some people thought it too frightening, too

That very night in Max's room a forest grew. *Where The Wild Things Are*

strong meat for children. This has always been a puzzle to Sendak, because to him it just felt like 'the next book I did'. He says, 'I didn't have any sense of doing anything unusual. So I was stunned when it came out mostly to hostile criticism. "It was frightening", "it was ugly", "no American child would behave in this particular way". Well of course American children "behaved in this particular way" '.

The point was, it was a key moment in the history of children's books. What Sendak portrayed in *Where The Wild Things Are* had never been done before. 'Unknowingly, and sort of clumsily, I had sort of bumped into historical facts: there had been angry children, but none with Max's temper.' Maurice Sendak feels that people were worried by the depiction of the child: that the child was angry and rude to his mother. Worse yet – the mother was rude back. Then on top of that, he went to this extremely rude place where horrendous creatures – as they were then thought – terrifying creatures, threatened him with: '*We'll eat you up, we love you so.*' It was considered too frightening for children.

Meanwhile, the book was becoming hugely popular. 'Children were just devouring the book. It became a children's crusade book. Now it's considered a fact.' Bruno Bettleheim, the child psychologist, was very much against the book when it came out. But when he wrote *The Uses of Enchantment* he suggested that we read such books to children so that they get rid of their fears, so that they can exorcise their fears. So Maurice Sendak feels that he's come full circle, accepted for doing the right thing.

A question that has always arisen about the book, is who actually are the Wild Things? The answer is disarming:

'Honestly? Honestly, they're relatives. They are uncles and aunts, people I hotly loathed when I was a child for no other reason other than that they came, poked us, pinched us, said absurd, patronizing things to us, took up all the room in the house, ate up all the food, were just no-gooders as far as I could see. And they were dangerous because they looked at you as though they could devour you. I didn't like them, simply.'

He feels that there is no way of knowing exactly what frightens children. 'When I was a child, it was Charlie Chaplin who frightened me. It would stun my father, who adored Charlie Chaplin. I couldn't go to a Charlie Chaplin movie because he walked – in what I thought then – was the way a dead person would walk. The Invisible Man was the most frightening creature in the world because he could be anywhere in the house. You could never see him. So I had a year of insomnia, thanks to the Invisible

Man ... but children are frightened of the simplest things. In fact, we don't know what triggers it because it's already there in the child waiting to be triggered.'

Looking at Maurice Sendak's work, it is clear that there are many styles at work which would suggest that he's allowed himself to be influenced by several different artists. He says that most of what he's learned came from looking at other people's work. The people he looked at most were the English illustrators. He gives the example of George Cruikshank. 'I was cross-hatching back in the Fifties and everybody thought that was such a novel, new way of illustrating.' He also mentions Randolph Caldecott, Walter Crane, Beatrix Potter, Arthur Hughes, Samuel Palmer and William Blake. 'I ripped off swathes of English artists, and some German and some French. But it was all looking and taking. I really do believe in taking.'

With Beatrix Potter it wasn't the graphic style, it was literary style. It was her sense of candour and straightforwardness that he says he liked so much. 'I love her drawing, but her drawing and water-colouring was nothing I could use personally. But it was what she stood for. It was the mini-Jane Austen that she is. The very straightforwardness of her, the severe honesty of those books. It was a wonder she got away with it because, 'Peter Rabbit', famous as he is, is a lethal story – just barely escaping death. The threats that lurk in her books, they are the real threats of life – like the Roly Poly Pudding, in *The Tale of Samuel Whisker*, where some rats roll a kitten up into a pie and get ready to eat him.'

But of course, Maurice Sendak's influences are not only European. His book, *In The Night Kitchen* is absolutely and directly American. It belongs right in the tradition of mainstream American popular art.

Sendak is particularly keen on the very early Disneys, the early Mickey Mouse cartoons. 'Those brilliant black-and-white, almost abstract, vigorous, graphic images.' When he did *In The Night Kitchen*, the inspiration was the movies and the things he loved as a child. 'I didn't love fine things. I didn't have fine things. I only loved what was at hand. What was at hand were comic books and movie books. *Night Kitchen* is based on comic-book art because it's a memory of childhood. In terms of subject, it's what I call my 'Vendetta Book'. It's about a boy who can actually stay up all night and see what is going on in the Night Kitchen – because usually you're sent to bed before the action begins. I remember an ad when I was a kid. It was from the Sunshine Bakers and it said, "We bake while you sleep." I thought that was just vicious. So this book was going to be about Mickey who stayed up and saw exactly what the baking was all about.'

Maurice Sendak's other great influence has been music. In fact, in his deepest self, he says that he wishes that he had been a composer. But he found that he wasn't gifted. So he says he pretends that he is because drawing is a kind of composing. What Schubert did to poems by Wilhelm Müller is what he tries to do to somebody's text. 'I was a colicky, tedious baby, and to shut me up there was the old gramophone, as my father was an opera lover. Caruso and all the rest were put on loud, I guess to wash me out, the sound of me. So if one believes that infants absorb all these things, as is the new view, and I'd like to believe it's true, then probably I was taking it in with my mother's milk, at a very early age. Caruso, opera, music.'

But Maurice Sendak has done stage designs for operas and adapted old stories. One of the best known adaptations is the picture book *Dear Milli*, where a little girl is sent off by her mother to escape the War and when she comes back, still as a girl, her mother is a very old woman.

From a personal, artistic point of view, Sendak saw *Dear Milli* as a follow-up to *Outside Over There*. 'It seemed to have the same Gestalt. It seemed to have the same thing emotionally going on. *Outside Over There* was such a knot of a problem and of my own books, is my personal favourite. *Dear Milli* was a kind of coda, to use musical terminology again, a kind of release of that knot, and a resolution of that book.'

In those days he thinks he wouldn't have chosen *Dear Milli* as he would probably have stayed away from a religious story. 'But oddly, as I've grown older, there is a different appeal to this story. What attracted me about it was the little girl. She's so much like my heroines.' Early on in the story the mother sends the little girl away saying, 'Go, run, run. If you live, come back to me in three days.' Sendak sees the girl as not understanding why her mother is saying this to her, though the mother knows precisely what it means. Men are about to invade the village. The child doesn't understand that but Sendak is moved that the child trusts the mother's intuition and does indeed, 'run, run, run, run, run'. And does indeed heroically, stolidly, faithfully, loyally, lovingly come back when she's told to. Even though, in fact, thirty years have gone by, which only seems three days to her. There's something very touching about children having faith in their parents and believing what they say, even though it's incomprehensible why they're saying it.'

There was a time when Maurice Sendak was regarded as the most important living children's illustrator but he seems, in recent years, to have devoted increasing amounts of time to his stage-design work, and treats children's books as a place to go for his smaller interests and obsessions. For people who admire the robust emotion and inventiveness of *Where The Wild Things Are* and *In The Night Kitchen* this always seems a pity.

Maurice Sendak

FAVOURITE TITLES

Where The Wild Things Are	**PB** Puffin £3.99
In The Night Kitchen	**PB** Puffin £3.50
Outside Over There	Bodley Head £9.99
I Saw Esau Verse selected by Iona and Peter Opie, Illustrated by Maurice Sendak.	Walker £9.99
Alligators All Around	**PB** Lion £1.50
Hector Protector	**PB** Lion £3.50
Higglety, Pigglety, Pop!	**PB** Bodley Head £2.99
The Sign on Rosie's Door	**PB** Puffin £3.50
Chicken Soup With Rice	**PB** Lion £1.50
One Was Johnny	**PB** Lion £1.50

ROSEMARY SUTCLIFF

'I love courage. Courage covers a multitude of sins, but I think basically that I only write one story which, in one form or another, is always the story of a boy growing up to be a man, finding himself in the process and usually paying a fairly heavy price for doing it.'

In the hands of Rosemary Sutcliff, the historical novel has become evocative and exhilarating. *Dawn Wind*, *Warrior Scarlet, The Eagle of the Ninth* and other books are powerful, haunting narratives which have been going strong for over thirty years and still remain as popular with children as they ever were. She continued to write until the day she died in June 1992, leaving two books, *Minstrel and the Dragon Pup* and *Chess Dream in a Garden* ready for publication.

Rosemary Sutcliff suffered as a child from a crippling disease which left her paralysed and she spent most of her life in a wheelchair. But the striking quality of her work is the level of action packed into each fast-moving plot; from riding and hunting to battles and hand-to-hand combat. These scenes are described in meticulous detail, conjuring up the sights and smells of another time; the withered flowers lying among the rushes on the floor of a medieval hall, the pungent flavour of a Bronze Age hearth.

Before she became a writer, Rosemary Sutcliff trained as an artist. She worked as a miniature painter and her power of observation, her trained eye was clearly an asset to her as a novelist. Even as a child, banished from the meal table for her bad behaviour, she took great delight in the world around her.

'I refused to eat the pale grey pudding which my aunt had cooked for us. It was pale grey, it tasted horrible and I said so. I was always a believer in speaking the truth. So I was put outside, not only the room, but outside the house, outside the garden, to sit in my wheelchair outside the garden gate on the Downs, which at that time, came right up to my aunt's gate. So, I sat on the Downs and looked about me and enjoyed the life going on in the grass, half an inch high all around me, a little tiny world.'

She has used a variety of places and periods for her work, writing about ordinary people and how they lived.

'I always try not to make my people, twentieth-century people wearing fancy-dress. I try to make them different, to make their attitudes to bloodsports, to cruelty, different from ours, but at the same time to make them understandable to people of our generation. I think I've always been able to put myself in the place of people who belong to, not only a different time, but who have different attitudes to things. I can think in terms of both the British and the Romans and I can switch from one to the other and feel them both with equal conviction.'

The Eagle of the Ninth is the first in a sequence of novels set in Roman Britain. Marcus Aquila, invalided out of the army, tries to find out what happened to his father's legion, which had marched far into the North of Britain, never to be seen again.

To Marcus, running with the rest, it seemed suddenly that there was no weight in his body, none at all. He was filled through and through with a piercing awareness of life and the sweetness of life held in his hollowed hand, to be tossed away like the shining balls that children played with in the gardens of Rome. At the last instant, when the charge was almost upon them, he swerved aside from his men, out and back on his tracks, and flinging aside his sword, stood tense to spring, full in the path of the oncoming chariots. In the breath of time that remained, his brain felt very cold and clear, and he seemed to have space to do quite a lot of thinking. If he sprang for the heads of the leading team, the odds were that he would merely be flung down and driven over without any check to the wild gallop. His best chance was to go for the charioteer. If he could bring him down, the whole team would be flung into confusion, and on that steep scarp the chariots coming behind would have difficulty in clearing the wreck. It was a slim chance, but if it came off it would gain for his men those few extra moments that might mean life or death. For himself, it was death. He was quite clear about that.

'That was written because I was faced with having an operation after a long gap and you can get out of practice with things, having an operation included. I was terrified and very lonely and very forlorn, and I needed somebody to go through this kind of thing with me. Marcus, the hero, was wounded and really did get out of the legions and he is also faced with having the healer with the knife, coming and digging bits out of him. And it was lovely writing the book. It was such company. I took him into hospital with me and wrote him about three days after I had the operation and I've always had this special feel for him, as you have for a friend who's been in a tight corner with you.'

Rosemary Sutcliff's heroes tend to be boys. Writing about girls, she admitted, was difficult for her. Perhaps because she felt she had a fairly masculine mind that could capture the atmosphere of the battle and manoevre army strategies into a story with a realism that avoided being bloodthirsty, but left the reader breathless at the end of the fray.

There are, of course, pitfalls with any historical novel. Nothing turns the reader off as much as the thought of a quick history lesson slipped in on the side. But this, Rosemary Sutcliff avoids, creating, through her research, a vision of the past into which you can step with conviction and ease, be it Roman Britain or, in *Dawn Wind*, Saxon times.

'I began with two very battered little books that I found in the local library. One was called *The Battle for Britain in the Fifth Century* and the other was called *The Rise of Wessex*. It was just at the end of the Second World War and these two books were written by one of those inspired crackpots, who really are pure gold to a writer. It remained with me forever afterwards and when I wanted to write *The Sword at Sunset*, I turned back to these books instantly, to see if they were still in the library, and they were and they were my basis. Then of course, from there I went on to, it sounds odd I know, just the encyclopedia, because there are always booklists and they lead on like a snowball. When I find things that nobody seems to know in books, I start writing to people. People who've bred horses for instance, I'll ask what colours mustn't I use if I want to breed a white horse? and things of that sort.'

Rosemary Sutcliff writes with passion and a commitment to reality. Her characters make mistakes, they do not always succeed and they have to accept the consequences, however bitter that might be. There are echoes of Kipling in her style and approach to writing.

'Kipling is my master. When I was five, I was introduced to Kipling and I've loved him ever since. My mother used to read to me. I couldn't see the point of reading because it was much easier and nicer to be read to. She read mostly historical novels, and some of them were quite dreadful, sort of Victorian historical novels, but somehow, they caught me and from then on it was always the historical stories that I loved.'

A prolific writer, Rosemary Sutcliff has written over fifty books. She was presented the Kate Greenaway Award in 1960 and the Other Award in 1978 for her book *Song for a Dark Queen* about the life of Boudicca, and in 1975 she received an OBE for her services to children literature. She has captured adults, as well as children, with her imagination and perception, and altered, to a significant degree, the way history is presented in fiction for children.

'I write for the little enquiring thing in myself which says, "Yes, this is right, this is what I like, this is what I want to hear." I think in a way, it is a pocket of unlived childhood which a lot of writers for children have. But it is not the same thing as writing for children at all.'

Rosemary Sutcliff

FAVOURITE TITLES

The Eagle of the Ninth	**PB** Puffin £3.99
The Silver Branch	**PB** Puffin £3.50
The Lantern Bearers	**PB** Puffin £3.99
Frontier Wolf	**PB** Puffin £3.99
Dawn Wind	**PB** Puffin £3.99
Warrior Scarlet	**PB** Puffin £3.99
Blood Feud	**PB** Puffin £2.99
Dragon Slayer: The Story of Beowulf	**PB** Red Fox £2.50
PLAY	
Song For a Dark Queen	Heinemann Ed. £3.50

ROBERT SWINDELLS

'My books tend to be about issues, and I think if you're going to write about an issue you've got to write about how it really is. I don't think that we're doing young people any favours if we don't tell them what it's really like out there. And that's one of my aims in writing my novels.'

Robert Swindells writes for a range of age-groups, producing short stories and novels. His short stories are inventive with plenty of tension as well as humour and his books for older children present tough choices and few cosy endings. They can be harrowing, they are certainly challenging but they are always compelling and imaginative. He won the Children's Book Award in 1990 for *Room 13* and the Other Award for *Brother in the Land*, a story set in the aftermath of a nuclear war.

He has explored the future in several novels. More recently, with *Daz 4 Zoe* which is set in a divided society where the two communities, those who have material well-being and those who have no such wealth or security, are totally segregated from one another. Families who are well-off and successful live in their fortified suburbs, with guards, wire and searchlights to protect them. Those who cannot aspire to such a lifestyle live in the city areas, which no longer have amenities or services provided. *Daz 4 Zoe* is a love story, a latter-day 'Romeo and Juliet', the story of Zoe who lives in the wealthy suburbs and Daz, a boy from the city. As their friendship develops, they contrive to see one another despite the barriers which make it illegal and dangerous for them to meet. To emphasize the affects of such segregation, Robert Swindells uses two narrators for the story, Daz and Zoe.

'One of these children is educated and the other is not educated and I wanted to show, with whatever impact I could, the consequences of not being educated and the fact that this chap can barely express himself, certainly not in writing or anything like that, because his education has been neglected.'

The repressive, divided and violent society depicted in this book presents a bleak outlook for the future, but Robert Swindells never shirks themes that are distasteful or harrowing. *Brother in the Land*, set in the North of England, is the story of a teenage boy who has to cope with living and adapting to the devastation, disease and disorder left in the wake of a full-scale nuclear attack. There is a total breakdown in society, hints of cannibalism and the descriptions are taut and sometimes horrifying. But Robert Swindells believes in being direct with his audience.

'I think that the more realistic you can make it for them, and the more you point out to them how horrific it would be in the aftermath of a full-scale nuclear bombardment, the better, because they are the people who can stop it from ever happening. They're the people who are going to be in charge of our planet when we've abdicated our responsibility. I've had letters from literally hundreds of children from various parts of the world and they have overwhelmingly been the sort of letters that say, "We must see that this never happens." It tends to be the adults who accuse me of writing a book with no hope in it and my answer to that, of course, is that there is no hope in my book because my book takes place after a nuclear war when there would be no hope. The hope is that it might never happen.'

Ben's out there under the snow, but he doesn't feel the cold.

He had a creeping dose. There was nothing we could do.... We kept him wrapped up and sat watching the life go out of him. He didn't make a fuss or anything, and then one night he slipped away.

We buried him in the garden. It was raining. We'd wrapped him in sacking and there wasn't quite enough and we could see a bit of his bald head glistening in the rain. I know you're supposed to say something over a grave, but I didn't know what, so I said what Branwell said once. I said, 'He who places his brother in the land is everywhere.' Just that. It's hard to talk when you're crying.

There was this book in the house. A ledger, with nothing in it. What I did was, I started to write down everything that happened after the nukes.... What I've tried to say is, it was horrible, too horrible to describe, though I've done my best. And so now I end it and it is for little Ben, my brother. In the land.

This is not to say that the story is overpowered by the message. Robert Swindells does indeed plead for tolerance, peace and kindness through his books, but the plot and the action are paramount and his style of writing compulsive.

'I believe that young people who are coming up now will probably make a better job of running society and running the world than we have, that's where my hope lies and that is why my work is directed towards young people.'

Robert Swindells turned to writing for children almost by accident. He went to college at the age of twenty-nine to learn to teach and part of the course involved reading children's fiction.

'I noticed that a lot of these children's books were a damn sight better than the children's books that were around when I was a kid and I really enjoyed them. I also thought, I bet I could write one of these, so when the Final year came along and it was time for us to choose a subject for our long study, I asked if I could do a children's novel. I had to do a sample chapter for the overseeing body which was Leeds University, and they saw this chapter and said yes, so I wrote my first novel which was *When Darkness Comes* and this was published, so they had to give me an "A" for it, and so it really started.'

Writing for a younger age group, Robert Swindells heads for pure entertainment, with a dash of tension. *Room 13*, for example, is a ghost story, which will appeal to most ten- to twelve-year-olds, especially if they've been away on their first school trip.

'*Room 13* is actually based on a real trip to Whitby with Class 2 from my wife's former school, Mandale Middle School in Bradford, and I went along as an extra adult. We stayed in an hotel where the daughter of the proprietor said to the children on the first day we arrived, "There's a special prize I'm giving at the end of the week for the first child who finds Room 13." Well, of course, it was a trick because there was no Room 13 for superstitious reasons. It was one of these hotels in a terrace, very tall, very narrow with about six floors and all week, these kids were up and down these stairs, looking for Room 13. They never found it of course, but what they did was to make up stories at night to frighten each other. One of them said something like, "I went to the toilet in the middle of the night and you know that cupboard on our landing? Well, it had a 13 on it." Then somebody improved on that the next night and said, "Yes, I saw that last night and I pushed the door open and there was a table with a coffin." And then somebody else says, "Yes, I did that and I looked in and there was Dracula lying in the coffin." It was the kids who had been away from home without their parents before, scaring the ones who hadn't.'

The dialogue is realistic and amusing and the characters will be readily identifiable in most Junior schools across the country. It is a book with spark and tension.

'What I'm really hoping to do is to help children to develop their imagination a little bit, because I think that the world needs people with imagination, and like everything else, it doesn't grow without stimulus. I think imagination and complete fantasy is as important as anything else in children's fiction.'

Robert Swindells

FAVOURITE TITLES

Dracula's Castle	**PB** Yearling £2.50
Room 13	**PB** Yearling £1.99
Ghost Messengers	**PB** Knight £2.99
Postbox Mystery	**PB** Yearling £2.50
Staying Up	**PB** Corgi £1.99
Brother in the Land	**PB** Puffin Plus £3.50
Daz 4 Zoe	**PB** Puffin Plus £3.99
A Serpent's Tooth	**PB** Puffin Plus £3.50
Hydra	Doubleday £8.99
Inside The Worm	Doubleday £8.99

GEOFFREY TREASE

One remarkable statistic about Geoffrey Trease is that he's been writing children's books for just about sixty years, producing them at the rate of over one a year. His first book, *Bows Against the Barons* came out in 1934. He has in his time, been a teacher, a soldier during the Second World War, a social worker and a journalist. Mostly he has written novels but over the years he has tackled various kinds of non-fiction too, biographies, information books and the like.

His contribution to fiction for children lies in two areas in particular. He was the first writer in Britain to write historical novels from the point of view of the underdog and the oppressed, as in *Bows Against the Barons*. He was also one of the first writers in Britain to write the modern school story, his first here being *No Boats on Bannermere* in 1949.

What set him writing school stories was a couple of girls who came up to him at a meeting in the Lake District. They said, 'We want to ask you something. Do you ever write school stories?' Geoffrey Trease said, 'Good heavens, haven't you got enough school stories?' He says he was thinking of school stories as they were then. 'Enid Blyton type of boarding schools, midnight feasts, secret passages and that kind of thing. I didn't want to be rude about it but I was very certain that I didn't want to write that sort of story. So they rebuked me gently, and they said, "No, that isn't what we mean at all. We mean school stories in which people go to school in the morning and go home at night as we do, and have the sort of happenings that happen in real life." ' So Geoffrey Trease went away and thought that this was quite a good idea. It hadn't been done before, as far as he could see. 'Five minutes conversation with the girls led in the end to five books about the same characters and something like three hundred thousand words.'

In recent years, he's turned to contemporary settings as with a book like *Shadow Under the Sea* where a teenage girl becomes embroiled in Soviet life at the time when perestroika was breaking the old system down. This was triggered off by Trease's long memory. He went to Russia in 1935, just as he was getting going with his writing and his books were being published there. He wanted to spend the money he had earned (he couldn't get the money out of the country), so spent a couple of months in Yalta. Over fifty years later, he thought he would like to write about the new Russia and use the setting he was familiar with, the 'lovely semi-Mediterranean setting of Yalta'. One of the problems writing the book was that history was changing while he was trying to create characters who were taking part in that change.

'Passport,' demanded the policeman curtly.

In Moscow no one had ever demanded her passport. Kate had heard that everything was freer now. All that official bullying belonged to the bad old days.

'I'm so sorry, but I . . .'

'Passport.' Her Russian had not brought the usual responsive smile. The sallow features were full of suspicion.

'I haven't got it with me, I'm afraid.'

. . . 'You will come with me. You will explain to my superior.'

She had no choice. They set off, his boots clumping on the pavement beside her softly pattering trainers . . . They walked for five minutes. Her wooden-faced escort ignored her protests. So much for the boasted new freedom, she thought bitterly. It didn't seem to have penetrated to the South.

When Geoffrey Trease was in his twenties and thirties he had been sympathetic to the Soviet Union, so to write this book was a way of showing how the dream had gone bad. 'As a young man in the Thirties, I was very idealistic, as many people were, about Russia. The way things turned out, like a lot of other things in modern history, has been very disappointing over the half-century. I have felt now things are taking a turn for the better. It was an opportunity to write about Russia, in a non-political way.'

Geoffrey Trease started writing in a time when there was a great deal of poverty and distress and yet neither this, nor people's hopes, were reflected very much in children's fiction. 'Children's books had hardly moved since the death of G.A. Henty, the boys' adventure story writer, in 1902. All the old clichés were still about in the 1930s: one Englishman equals two Frenchmen equals four Germans; girls can only be put into adventure stories as second-class citizens; in historical books, you can only show the mass of the population as the mob, or the faithful retainer. I was against the aristocratic, romantic bias.'

Bows Against the Barons tells the story of a young boy who joins with Robin Hood in a fight for an equal society. 'Being a Nottingham boy, I thought of Robin Hood and what being an outlaw must have been really like. Looking back at the first edition, I sometimes think that the campfire conferences of the outlaws only lack one thing: Friar Tuck coming home from Nottingham with a copy of the *Morning Star* under his habit – very anachronistic. I was trying to write sound history but I got some of the details emphatically wrong, though my heart was in the right place.'

Cue For Treason, another historical novel, came out at the beginning of the Second World War. It was spurred by two of Geoffrey Trease's passions: the Lake District and Elizabethan theatre. At the beginning of the book, though, the hero is busy with a movement against the enclosures whereby lords of the manor were enclosing common land, evicting peasant farmers and preventing them from grazing their animals. So the rebels were pulling down the stone fences to keep the land for the people.

The wall was so low I could no longer see it . . . So the dawn drew near and danger too, if I'd have only known it, and not been so occupied watching them scatter the last stones right and left in the long grass.

I felt, rather than heard, the coming of the horsemen . . . It was Sir Philip in front; I knew him by his grey mount. There were a dozen or more behind him, strung out head to tail, every rider with a sword or pistol, or both.

I gaped at them for a half-second, I was so dumbfounded. Then, as my big mouth was conveniently open, I stuck in two fingers and whistled . . . It was everyone for himself then. Luckily for me there were plenty of rocks heaped about on the steep hillside above the road, and once among these, I should be safe. I skipped into the shelter just before the cavalcade reached me. Then I was tempted by some devil I couldn't resist; I turned round with a piece of rock in my fist, and shied it straight at Sir Philip. I don't think it touched either man or horse. They were travelling too fast, but it made the horse shy and threw the men behind into temporary confusion.

'There's one of 'em, sir!' a man shouted, and flung up his pistol. The muzzle flamed in the twilight . . . I felt the bullet whizz through my hair . . .

Historical fiction is a difficult genre. Some people might say that it always carries with it the preoccupations of the present. Geoffrey Trease says, 'I like to make historical fiction relevant to the facts of modern life so children can draw their own conclusions. At the same time, you've got to beware of being unhistorical. You've got to strike a balance between the undoubted differences of people in past centuries and the eternal similarity of their relationships, political struggles and so on.'

It would be wrong to leave Geoffrey Trease's contribution to children's literature purely in the field of fiction. He devoted a great deal of time to raising people's awareness of children's literature through his critical work. 'Just after the War, in 1948, I did a lot of reviewing and I was still meeting books full of the old jingoistic values and attitudes. I thought it all ought to be changed, and children's literature deserved proper criticism, just like adult literature. It needed to be taken seriously.'

This interest in children's literature as a whole spanning sixty years puts him in a good position to see what changes have come about in that time. 'There's been a great increase in fantasy of the best kind for older children. Children's fiction has grown up, the characters have got more mature. You can mention almost anything you like now in a children's book. It's much more interesting to write because there aren't all the taboo subjects that there were when I was starting.' The reason for that, might be in part, the role that Geoffrey Trease has played.

Geoffrey Trease

FAVOURITE TITLES

Aunt Augusta's Elephant	**PB** Pan £2.99
Cue For Treason	**PB** Puffin £3.99
Shadow Under the Sea	**PB** Walker £2.99
Tomorrow is a Stranger	**PB** Pan £3.50
The Arpino Assignment	**PB** Walker £2.99
Calabrian Quest	**PB** Walker £2.99

MARTIN WADDELL

'I think you have to write from passion and I can truthfully say that everything I write is written from a passion.'

Few children's authors span every age range with their books, but Martin Waddell is a prolific writer producing memorable picture books for young children, stories about football and a series featuring Little Dracula for six-year-olds and upwards. He also writes for older children under the pseudonym of Catherine Sefton, creating ghostly tales as well as hard-hitting novels set against the political background of Northern Ireland. *Starry Night* won the Other Award in 1986 and two years later his picture book *Can't You Sleep, Little Bear?* won the Smarties Grand Prix. The following year came the Kurt Maschler *Emil* Award for *The Park in The Dark* and then in 1991, the Smarties Grand Prix again, for *Farmer Duck.*

Writing for young children, Martin Waddell's approach is gentle and quiet, exploring relationships within the family. He writes with that close moment in mind, when adult and child share a book together.

'It's a small intimate moment where all sorts of fears and worries can be ironed out. Therefore I think you take that situation and produce

Back where we've come through the park...
The Park in The Dark Illustrated by Barbara Firth

stories which have a tenderness, a quietness, a sweetness about them, and a little edge as well. I do believe, even for the very young, that fear plays a part, that you use fear, but you control it.'

There is an emotional core to most of Martin Waddell's picture books be it fear of the dark in *Can't You Sleep, Little Bear?* and in *The Park in The Dark* or the death of a pet in *We Love Them*. These are stories which help children to cope with their own fears and problems.

'I was lucky in that my wife went out to work and I was at home with a two-year-old, a four-year-old and a six-year-old, so I had an awful lot of wheeling people back home, making the meals and dealing with bloody noses. I had an intensive course in that, which at the time wearied me, but which I now think was one of the most valuable things that ever happened to me and I think that has spilled over into my books.'

In several picture books for the very young, Martin Waddell has looked at the idea of generations within the family, the cycle of life ending while another begins. *Once There Were Giants* and *The Hidden House* both explore these patterns which become apparent to young children as they grow up.

'I think that the pattern of life is one of the great mysteries for a small child. How did Daddy get to be Daddy? Was he ever a child? Will I be an old man like Grandpa? So therefore, if I can do a book, as for instance in *Great Grandpa* where a child looks at Grandpa and understands why Grandpa gets breathless, why he can't talk properly, why he dribbles a bit, this is a valuable thing to be doing.'

These themes are introduced in a simple and natural way, always viewed from the child's perspective and, as with his books for older readers, Martin Waddell captures the essence of ideas and emotions that face a child growing up today.

A passion for football induced Martin Waddell to write his series about Napper. As a youngster he wanted to be a professional footballer himself. He did actually play for Fulham, but after that finished, he turned to coaching a team of youngsters and started to look at some of the football stories which were around for young enthusiasts. Most of the books were high adventure and had little to do with the game of football.

'When I was a lad I read *The Wizard of Hotspur* and I used to skip the plot to get to the football. So I thought I'd write some books for kids which were totally football. I have a goalkeeper with asthma, full-backs who are too fat to run, a centre-forward who's bossy and somebody else who's too tough and I put those characters together. There's always a little boy who has to play the piano on the day of the big match and can't get to the game. That's what happens in junior football, so I wanted them to feel real. I think it's the only football series in which the team loses more games than they win. That I also felt to be important because most of the teams I've been mixed up with have lost, possibly because I was the goalkeeper!'

Martin Waddell also writes for older children: eleven- or twelve-year-olds and upwards. Many of the books under his other name, Catherine Sefton, are very different in content and style. They are set against the violent background of politics and religion in Northern Ireland, Martin Waddell's home territory. Catherine Sefton's books follow in the tradition of other novelists like Joan Lingard, whose book *Across the Barricades* reached out, speaking directly to teenagers in the Province. Visiting schools and talking to pupils, Catherine Sefton saw at first-hand the significance of these novels.

'Things have changed a lot since the Joan Lingard books were written. Things have got more bitter and blacker. Life is more difficult for children to understand. I'm sitting there, that's why I write about it. I don't propose solutions, what I'm trying to do is explain what's happening, the way the community is structured. That in fact was the way the trilogy was planned. With the first book *Starry Night*, the concept is to discuss what I call the acceptance community, which is based on the idea that you can be a mile and a half down the road, two different townlands, and you can have the same event reported in a completely different way according to the accepted beliefs within that community. Then in *Frankie's Story* and *Beat of the Drum* I wanted to show children involved with the actual groups within the community which are a danger.'

A Catholic woman had come out of the last of the four houses. . . . She stood there with her arms folded for the benefit of her Protestant neighbours. They were all at their doors, where they'd been watching the band.

'You'd think they'd move off somewhere,' Duggie said. 'Back to the Republic where they belong. The Catholics took over down below,' he said, meaning further down the Road, which is Provo land. 'They needn't think they're setting up their Republic here.'

The Catholic woman was kneeling down, inspecting her four foot of front garden. One of the kids following the band had tipped a flowerpot off her windowledge and it lay smashed up on the ground.

'Hey, Missus!' Duggie shouted. The woman looked up. 'No Pope here, Missus!' Duggie shouted and he gave her the fingers.

A big man came out of one of the nearest Protestant houses at the double. 'Get your bum out of here,' he shouted at Duggie.

'Bum yourself,' said Duggie.

'None of your lip, son.' he said. 'On your way.'

Duggie stood there looking at him.

'Come on, Duggie,' I said, 'Wise up.'

'We know who you are,' Duggie said to the big man. Then he turned away and started pushing me up the Road.

'I'm as good a Protestant as you are anyday,' the big man shouted after us. . . .

'He'll find a brick through his window one of these nights,' Duggie muttered . . .'

Catherine Sefton's trilogy reflects the pressures on young people growing up in Northern Ireland and the damage being wrought to families on a personal level.

'I've taken the books into Crossmaglen, I've taken them into East

Belfast. It can be uncomfortable to sit with thirty teenagers in a room and the teacher tells you later that a third of those boys have already been on charges. But in a way that's what I want to be doing because I'm saying very definitely to the children who're reading my books that death is not an answer and that death is the answer being given by the terrorists.'

Martin Waddell

FAVOURITE TITLES

The Park in The Dark	**PB** Walker £3.99
Can't You Sleep, Little Bear?	**PB** Walker £2.99
Once There Were Giants	**PB** Walker £3.99
Farmer Duck	Walker £8.99
Owl Babies	Walker £7.99
Napper Goes for Goal	**PB** Puffin £2.99
AS CATHERINE SEFTON	
Starry Night	**PB** Mammoth £2.99
Frankie's Story	**PB** Mammoth £2.50
Beat of the Drum	**PB** Mammoth £2.50
Along a Lonely Road	Hamish Hamilton £8.99

ROSEMARY WELLS

'I must say that it's more important, as a children's book writer, much more important than to have children, it is to have been a child.'

Rosemary Wells has a string of hilarious and wickedly observed picture books to her name. Best known are perhaps, *Stanley and Rhoda*, and *Morris's Disappearing Bag*. She was born in New York but went to school in Boston and her first book, written and illustrated by herself, came out in 1969.

Within most of her books her child characters, all clearly full of feeling and spirit, are drawn as animals. She says she does this because, 'You can make animals on a page in a picture do things that you can't have children do.' She gives the example of *Benjamin and Tulip* where Tulip waits in a tree and pounces on Benjamin and rolls him around in the dust. 'If you had a picture of children doing this, which of course is part of real life, it would look terribly violent. So I use animals because they can express things that children can't.'

It would be reasonable to think that these little sagas of home life were drawn from her own home, but Rosemary was an only child herself. They are closer to the lives of her own children. In fact, when she's doing a signing session, Victoria, her eldest daughter, will sign it as Stanley, Ruby, Timothy or any number of characters based on her. 'I like to say that my books are non-fiction because they're based on how my children get along with each other and how they get along with the world around them, from their particular point of view, and from the point of view of the writer who sees it all as being very universal and very funny.'

In *Max's Dragon Shirt*, Rosemary Wells runs several stories at the same time, representing the competing desires of a boy and his older sister: Ruby wants a new dress, Max wants a dragon shirt, and later, when Max gets lost in a department store, you have the need for Max and Ruby to find each other. She applied here, as always she says, the same rules as one would if one were writing a novel. 'You have to have character first, last and always. You have to have emotional content and then you string your plot or your idea along with that.'

She sees this as originating in childhood and if you remember your childhood very well then you can find the right voice. In fact, she likes to think of these ideas 'pre-existing'. 'They were there before I was even born and I just sort of found them.' So she feels that, in a Buddhist sense, the best way to write a children's book is not to make it happen but to let it happen. 'I just sit there and allow the books to come to me and it seems to work.'

Anyone looking at one of Rosemary Wells's books will see straight away that her superb dialogue catches the genuine emotions of children, sometimes encapsulated in one short interchange, as when Rhoda is so sure that she's in terrible pain (in fact she isn't) that she screams, 'Don't

'Dragon shirt, please!' Max asked Ruby.
Max's Dragon Shirt

touch it, don't look at it.' Rosemary Wells doesn't take notes, she eavesdrops, looking at everything, listening to everything. 'It's very difficult for me to tune anything out. Where other people can sit in a restaurant and not hear the lyrics the songs being played, I hear everything, the conversation at the next table, everything. And it's very tiring.'

In her *Bunny Planet* series, the animal-child starts off in the real world but then the child can escape to the Bunny Planet where everything is going to be wonderful. It isn't a paradise, Rosemary says, it's more a reflection on 'bad days'. Children have bad days, just as adults do. In the *Bunny Planet* books, each of these dreadful days involve little tragedies at school, or with illness and the like. So then the escape to the planet is a personal one. In fact, on the back of each of the *Bunny Planet* books there's a picture of the characters, Claire, Felix and Robert, in a huge chair that's upholstered with a globe of the world, and it says, 'Lean back in your easy chair, the Bunny Planet's waiting there.' So Rosemary wants the books to be an escape by the mind from the world.

Now this, Rosemary Wells is quite clear, means escaping from American materialist culture. She sees America's most successful export as being the culture of forcing children into buying things. Television and video screens make children buy. Books let children be,' she says, and so these books are ways of escaping that culture, and escaping the peer group pressures that begin very early in schools and amongst children. In fact, she sees that nowadays it's not so much 'authority' that children fear, as the approbation of the peer group.

In *Hazel's Amazing Mother*, Hazel is getting roughed up in the park, when 'Mother' appears, in a tree. It's almost as if she is the great goddess in the sky. This book came about when Rosemary's daughter had a favourite, very important bunny. It was so important that once, the family had to drive one hundred and fifty miles back to an airport to pick it up when it had been left in a locker. Once she took it into school for 'show and tell'. Halfway through the morning, Rosemary realized that the group of boys in her daughter's class who were famous for picking on kids and grabbing their toys would probably take Bunny apart in the playground and she would probably spend fifteen years on the psychiatrist's couch as a result. 'But there was nothing I could do. What has happened had probably already happened. So this is a book for mothers because I pictured myself literally flying across the town, into the school, and taking care of these bullies myself by throwing tomatoes at them from a tree, and making them sew up the bunny again, because I was afraid they had hurt her.' That said, it is also a very funny book.

'I try to make everything hysterically funny because you really must. If you look at life, it can sometimes be a bit grim for children, as well as ourselves and unless we have a terrific sense of humour ongoing, I don't think we can make it through.'

Parents often feature in the books, representing the way that Rosemary herself feels as a parent, 'kind of helpless on the outside of the children's world'. She does the best she can, smoothing children's lives out by trying to diminish the dimensions of disasters. Like every mother she hears herself saying to her daughter when she's upset about another girl at school, 'There, there, dear,' or 'Oh, she'll never do it again, it must have been a mistake – she can't get too much love at home if she talks to you that way.' But then once our children leave us at five or six, we're helpless to affect anything that happens at school, which is the dominant part of their life. 'We can't do anything.'

Anyone reading Rosemary Wells's books, or talking to her, picks up very quickly that childhood is a very important time for her. 'Childhood stays with us much longer than any other time. You can ask an eighty-five-year-old person what they remember best and they'll remember things very, very clearly from the time they were seven or ten or fourteen. I can remember everything that happened to me as a child. I think that's because your mind kind of prints up in three dimension everything that you feel and learn then.'

Rosemary says that she feels very fortunate in that she had a wonderful childhood, very happy – but not without pitfalls. 'My greatest pitfall was that I hated groups. I didn't like to sing in them, I didn't like to march in them, I didn't like to play in them. I wanted to be always looking on. If anything comes through in my books, I think it's the strength of the individual and the fact that often, the biggest bogeyman in a child's life is the peer group. It's that little bunch of girls who dominate the class and decide to throw out one of their own lot, each day, just to torture them. It's the group of boys on the baseball ground who decide continually to leave somebody out and not call them to join the team. If there's any force in my books it comes from playing around with that.'

Rosemary Wells

FAVOURITE TITLES

Stanley and Rhoda	**PB** Lion £3.99
Morris's Disappearing Bag	**PB** Puffin £3.50
Benjamin and Tulip	**PB** Puffin £3.50
Max's Dragon Shirt	**PB** Lion £3.50
Voyage To The Bunny Planet	Harper Collins £9.99
Hazel's Amazing Mother	**PB** Lion £3.99

Noisy Nora	**PB** Lion £3.99
Shy Charles	**PB** Lion £3.50
Fritz and the Mess Fairy	Harper Collins £7.99
Timothy Goes to School	**PB** Puffin £2.99

ROBERT WESTALL

'I like writing about war because, in peace-time, people can keep a surface, whereas war brings out the best and the worst, and that makes it, from the novelist's point of view, very exciting.'

Robert Westall won the Carnegie Medal twice – once in 1976 for his first novel, *The Machine-Gunners*, and again in 1982 for *Scarecrows*. He won the Smarties Award in 1989 for *Blitzcat* and the *Guardian* Children's Fiction Award in 1990 for *The Kingdom by the Sea*. In short, he was one of our best writers of fiction, often dealing with tough themes like the effects of war, as well as writing chilling ghost stories. He died in 1993.

He was brought up in Northumberland, went to university in Durham and, after doing National Service, went to the Slade School in London, where he studied Fine Art. He taught Art in various schools, dealt in antiques, worked as a journalist and critic on local newspapers and was a Samaritan.

The theme of war and its effect on ordinary people is a recurring theme in his books. In *Gulf* we witness the war through the eyes of an English boy who is mysteriously and frighteningly linked with an Iraqi boy who has been forced to fight in Saddam Hussein's army. The linking is really a kind of 'possession', the English boy is possessed by the Iraqi. As the war proceeds, this has a devastating effect first on the Iraqi boy but then on the English boy too.

Westall insists he is not, as some people have said, a pacifist. He wrote *Gulf* in response to the way the war was being treated in the media, turning the war into a video game on television, and refusing to acknowledge the Iraqi casualties. Westall felt we were being led along by our and the American governments into believing that the whole thing was a bloodless fantasy. This made him very angry. 'I don't normally write books out of anger, but this one just had to be written. I had no commercial thoughts about it. It was just something I had to say – that war is about people suffering, in the end.'

The doppelganger, twinning idea came to Westall through his interest in telepathy. The result is very frightening, because we, as readers, are drawn into believing that the English boy, Figgis, is going to go completely insane or possibly, even die. Westall admits that he likes frightening people in his books – but on the understanding that at the end they come back to being very much as they were in the beginning – only wiser. 'In a way, my novels are roller-coasters. You get on feeling quite calm. You're whirled round and round and over and over and wonder whether you're going to come out at the end. But my heroes and heroines usually do, just sadder and wiser.'

In fact, in *Gulf* it isn't the hero, Figgis, who comes out having learnt from the experience, it is the narrator, his brother. Westall sees that as the kind of burn-out that he experienced when he was a Telephone Samaritan. 'We all of us have so much compassion. If you use too much of it too quickly, you become quite burnt out and what Figgis suffered was the same kind of burn-out. It's quite frightening when you find that you can no longer care in the way you used to, and in a way, at the end of *Gulf* the whole family no longer cares the way it used to.'

Westall sees that in society as a whole we are in danger of using up too much compassion when we sit and watch newsreels of, say, a train crash in India, or a serious fire in New York. We are helpless to do anything about it, compassion is aroused only to be totally frustrated and this is the way the family in *Gulf* react.

The Machine-Gunners, Westall's celebrated first book, is, on the surface an action-packed thriller. It tells the story of a group of boys who are living in the North-east of England, who seize a real machine-gun from a German bomber plane that's been shot down. The children, young teens mostly, become a law unto themselves, doing what they want to, making up their own rules and codes of conduct. Westall lived through the same period at the same age as the boy characters in the book and he says that the book is three-quarters his experience. He didn't actually find a machine-gun but oddly enough, about five years after the book came out, someone wrote to him from Withernsea-on-Humberside, saying, very indignantly, 'How did you discover our secret?' It had actually happened, the whole plot, unknown to Westall on Humberside in the Second World War.

In real life, it was the Church Choir of Withernsea who had found the gun. A bomber had been shot down, the RAF had sent in a bomb-disposal team who couldn't do the job and headed off to the nearest farmhouse. The boys turned up on their bicycles and made off with a machine-gun and a cannon which they hid in the clock room of the church tower before trying them out on the beach. In other words, what Westall had made up in the book, was an accurate account of what actually happened. A kind of anarchy took over many young boys during the War.

Westall sees this continuing now with pre-adolescent gangs of boys who set up their own little societies. 'They build their camp, they furnish it, they nick from adult society mercilessly and set themselves up as a kind of secret tribe.' Most parents, he says, never even get to know about it. It's this world that *The Machine-Gunners* explores so powerfully.

Not only does the observation of this come from his own childhood but also from watching his son. On one occasion, his son's gang summoned Westall to advise on a roof to their den. He noticed that much of their activity was concerned with law-making. 'So, with my son having shown me how he was living at the age of twelve, I felt impelled to show him how I had been living when I was twelve. So all my wartime activities came out.'

'Look,' said the Sergeant desperately, jamming his foot in the door. 'They're up to something.'

'Take your foot out of my house,' said Mr McGill dangerously.

The Sergeant left, but Mr McGill was worried about Chas, for all his fighting words. He beckoned Chas to come into the cold front room with its big chiming clock. Chas trembled. He knew what was coming. He couldn't even pretend his father was some kind of Gestapo swine, like the Police Sergeant, or the Head flexing his cane. His father understood how kids really felt about things, more than most. Ever since he was little, Dad had meant safety. Large, solid, bristly-faced, smelling of tobacco. . . .

But could any grown-up keep you safe now? They couldn't stop the German bombers. They hadn't saved Poland or Norway or France.

. . . Their own air-raid shelter at home . . . was only covered with a foot of soil. Couldn't Dad have done better than that?

He looked at his father and saw a weary, helpless, middle-aged man. Dad wasn't any kind of God any more. Chas screwed himself up to lie . . .

Incidentally, Westall points out that though he is typified as a 'war novelist', war only features in eight or nine out of his forty books. Cats and ghosts feature in quite a few too, but he's also turned his attention to some other themes. In *Stormsearch*, he tells the story of Tim and Tracey who are able to follow clues and reconstruct something of the past. They find a model ship buried in the sand and this leads them, like archaeologists, to discover things about past times. But really, what they reconstruct is the nature of human relationships in the past.

Westall sees this past history of people's lives as very important for children because, he says, unless you have a history, you're not going anywhere. 'It's a bit like being on a ship. If you stand on the stern, and watch the wake, you can guess which way you're going next.' He's also troubled by the fact that he can no longer write a contemporary teenage character. When he started out writing, he was teaching children from eleven to eighteen, his house was full of adolescents, day in, day out. He was right in the mainstream. He says that the youngest person he knows now, is nineteen. He feels that this means that so much of what happens to today's adolescent children will never happen to him or people he knows.

'If I write truly about childhood, I can only write about my own childhood. Now this may seem valueless, except that it's a kind of near history. For a child to see how a child was fifty years ago does give a sense of proportion. He can compare that child with himself and see the way the world is going. And that I see now, as the main value of my books.'

Indeed, Robert Westall's great skill is in enabling the reader to experience emotions as the characters experience them. He seems to have a way of getting inside each and all of his characters' heads. As he tells the story, we feel directly the psychological responses and impact of any given action. And we feel it immediately in a child's head. This gives a certain dignity to child characters that is sometimes missing from children's literature.

For Westall, this entering into a character's feelings and motivations, is the secret of writing. 'Unless you're inside your narrator, or the person who is carrying the story, it doesn't work. I mean, if I'm writing Simon in

Scarecrows, then I am Simon.' Here, he tells the story of when writing ghost stories, his son discovered that he could creep up behind Robert in his stocking-feet, shout 'boo' and his father would literally go two foot in the air – 'because I'd be able to frighten most people because I can first frighten myself. I have this sense, in any novel, of writing myself right into it, so I can't distinguish myself from the character.'

Robert Westall

FAVOURITE TITLES

Rachel and the Angel and other stories	**PB** Pan £2.99
Blitzcat	**PB** Pan £3.50
Yaxley's Cat	**PB** Pan £2.99
The Kingdom by the Sea	**PB** Mammoth £2.99
Stormsearch	**PB** Puffin £2.99
Gulf	Methuen £9.99
The Machine-Gunners	**PB** Puffin Plus £2.99
The Scarecrows	**PB** Puffin Plus £3.50
The Wind Eye	**PB** Puffin Plus £2.99
The Haunting of Chas McGill and other stories	**PB** Puffin Plus £3.50

PAUL ZINDEL

'I have always tried to tap into what's classic about the teenager. So therefore, it's usually a rite of passage, a method of growing up. I think I'm in touch with life-giving issues and I never touch a story unless I can bring a sense of something beautiful and something that builds upon my past. Some of those events,

particularly the ones in my books, are the ones that you come across every day, every year, with every teenager, which is why, I think, the books have remained so popular over twenty years.'

Paul Zindel's career path took him into teaching rather than writing, but his pupils at the New York High School where he taught, have obviously been a rich source of material for his books. Although he began writing for the stage, he soon turned to books for teenagers, and in 1969 *The Pigman* was published. It was an instant success, setting him on the road to becoming America's leading writer for teenagers and earning him the Pulitzer Prize in 1971. The story concerns John and Lorraine who befriend a lonely old man, Mr Pignati. He is eager for their friendship, easily manipulated and conned by the two youngsters, who unwittingly, lead him towards disaster.

'Mr Pignati,' I said with an air of impatience, 'Miss Truman and I have many other stops to make today. I mean, where would the L & J Fund be if we simply sat around and drank wine all day and went to zoos?' . . .

'Oh, I'm sorry,' Mr Pignati said, and I couldn't help feeling sorry. His smile and bright eyes faded in front of us and he got awkwardly to his feet. 'Let me get the cheque,' he said, and his voice was so depressed, I thought he was really going to cry.

'You don't really have to,' Lorraine started. . . .

'Of course. That's what we came for,' I said, to make it look real at least. . . .

'Whom should I make it out to?' he asked.

'Cash will be fine. Make it out to cash,' I found myself saying. . . .

'Do you think you might like to go to the zoo with me some day?' Mr Pignati asked, just as I knew Lorraine was getting ready to flee out of the house. 'I always go to the zoo. I love animals. My wife and I both love animals. But I've been going to the zoo by myself lately. I always go. Every day.'

'I realized that when I wrote *The Pigman*, I tapped into something mythic that made kids cry a little at the end of it. I didn't know what it was until a boy sent me a cartoon and the cartoon was of two teenagers, as in my book, who are watching a sailing boat out on the ocean. The boat has a "pigman", this nice little old man, floating in it and the sail is billowing and it has innocence written on it and the boat is sailing away. So, I think the pigman is a mythic character that is the mentor that comes along in the hero's journey and gives to the young some lesson. But they sacrifice something, they have to give up something of their innocence in order to grow up.'

More about Paul Zindel's pigman emerges from his memoires, *The Pigman and Me*. Paul comes from what he calls a bizarre family background. At one point, as a teenager he and his mother moved in with an Italian family. The old grandfather took Paul under his wing, suddenly opening up to him mysteries and adventures that he had not known existed. He was the missing father who showed the boy how to plant tomatoes, where asparagus grows, how egg-plants are used. This was the pigman who gave him love and affection.

'I think with a true writer, whatever you write is coming from an obsession, so there is a part of me that's genuinely fifteen years old. When I'm talking with kids, I particularly stress the function of need in a story. Unless you have a very strong need, you don't have very much of a story.'

Zindel's books speak directly in the teenage idiom, but carefully skirt around any explicit sexuality.

'When it comes to sex, I thought that could be saved, perhaps, for the movies. I think that kids know what they do, and there are many levels, not everybody is tumbling in the hay at fifteen, some are eighteen and some are twenty-one. In other words, there's a maturation factor and I thought that stories should exist, calls to adventure should exist, that all kids could identify with and they can fill in other blanks as they wish.'

Paul Zindel has not shied away from controversial subjects. *My Darling My Hamburger* deals with teenage pregnancy and abortion and at the time it was published in 1970, it broke new ground. As a teacher, Paul Zindel knew that these problems existed and he wanted to explore them through fiction.

'I went to Chicago and was interviewed by a group of black students and I wanted to know which of my books they had read. To my surprise, they really loved *My Darling My Hamburger* and they instructed me that, in spite of pills and all the rest of it, some of them, because of their tradition, are going to have the "doll syndrome"; having their own baby because it gives them a sense of event and of ritual.'

Another theme, explored in Paul Zindel's books, is death. In *A Begonia for Miss Applebaum*, two teenagers seek out their much-loved teacher who is terminally ill with cancer and, befriending her, learn to experience the everyday pleasures of life with an intensity that foresees the end and comprehends the pattern of life and death. On occasions, the book overflows to become sentimental, but the basis of the story is real enough to overcome that failing.

'My mother was the kind of Shirley Valentine that didn't go to Greece. She was a woman scorned. She didn't like to go out in the outside world, so she would bring dying patients into our house to nurse them. I was surrounded by that and also the writer instinct in me knows that you're going to get more power, if you're taking on a piece of death, because it also happens to be a part of life.'

Parents may feel hard-done by with Paul Zindel, they are not depicted in a favourable light. They emerge as pushy, disinterested or bullies, even drunkards. But, bringing up his own two children has made him mellow his approach somewhat.

'My parents now are much better, they're nicer, because parents are very enlightened now, compared to when I was growing up. I think somehow we're all wiser. I find my daughter is much wiser about love and sex and dating and danger on the streets of New York and all those sorts of things, than I was. I find my son more rounded. I think everybody is smarter.'

Paul Zindel

FAVOURITE TITLES

The Pigman	**PB** Armada	£2.50
The Pigman and Me	**PB** Red Fox	£3.99
The Pigman's Legacy	**PB** Lion	£2.50
My Darling My Hamburger	**PB** Red Fox	£3.50
A Begonia for Miss Applebaum	**PB** Red Fox	£2.99
The Girl Who Wanted a Boy	**PB** Red Fox	£2.99
Pardon Me, You're Stepping on my Eyeball	**PB** Red Fox	£3.50
The Undertaker's Gone Bananas	**PB** Red Fox	£2.99

THE SHOESTRINGERS

Benjamin Trout, foreman of the K/K Ranch, has been cut loose for being too old — while Eddie 'Dink' Guest, a new hire, has been fired for being too young. With nowhere to go, both ride out together to seek work elsewhere. When they encounter widowed Beth Robinson and her daughter Minna in the wilderness, they are invited back to the women's ranch — and become the Robinsons' allies in the struggle to save their land from the predatory Cyrus Sullivan.

Books by C. J. Sommers
in the Linford Western Library:

GHOST RANCH
COMES A HORSEMAN
THE OUTLAW'S DAUGHTER
THE LONESOME DEATH OF JOE SAVAGE
CLIMAX
SKELETON HAND
WHITE WIND
LONGSHOT

SPECIAL MESSAGE TO READERS

THE ULVERSCROFT FOUNDATION
(registered UK charity number 264873)

was established in 1972 to provide funds for research, diagnosis and treatment of eye diseases. Examples of major projects funded by the Ulverscroft Foundation are:-

- The Children's Eye Unit at Moorfields Eye Hospital, London
- The Ulverscroft Children's Eye Unit at Great Ormond Street Hospital for Sick Children
- Funding research into eye diseases and treatment at the Department of Ophthalmology, University of Leicester
- The Ulverscroft Vision Research Group, Institute of Child Health
- Twin operating theatres at the Western Ophthalmic Hospital, London
- The Chair of Ophthalmology at the Royal Australian College of Ophthalmologists

You can help further the work of the Foundation by making a donation or leaving a legacy. Every contribution is gratefully received. If you would like to help support the Foundation or require further information, please contact:

THE ULVERSCROFT FOUNDATION
The Green, Bradgate Road, Anstey
Leicester LE7 7FU, England
Tel: (0116) 236 4325

website: www.foundation.ulverscroft.com

C. J. SOMMERS

THE SHOESTRINGERS

Complete and Unabridged

LINFORD
Leicester

First published in Great Britain in 2014 by
Robert Hale Limited
London

First Linford Edition
published 2017
by arrangement with
Robert Hale
an imprint of
The Crowood Press
Wiltshire

A catalogue record for this book is available from the British Library.

ISBN 978–1–4448–3452–9

Published by
F. A. Thorpe (Publishing)
Anstey, Leicestershire

Set by Words & Graphics Ltd.
Anstey, Leicestershire
Printed and bound in Great Britain by
T. J. International Ltd., Padstow, Cornwall

This book is printed on acid-free paper

1

Long in the war, long on the range. Now what, long in the rocking chair? Not for Benjamin Trout, called Mr Benjamin by the younger hands on the K/K Ranch out of Waco, Texas where Trout had ridden for twenty years for Ed Kramer. Kramer had replaced Trout as foreman with a younger man. Paul Elliott was engaged to marry Kramer's daughter, Candice, so Trout could sort of understand the move, although it was a little humiliating.

What was unfathomable was that less than a month later Trout had been called into Kramer's office and told that his services were no longer required on the ranch.

'I don't want you to worry, though, Trout. You can stay on around the ranch helping out here and there. We'll offer you shelter and meals same as always. It's just that I won't be able to pay you anymore.'

'I'm not yet forty years old,' Benjamin Trout said. Age was the only reason he could think of for his dismissal.

'No, and you're still a tall, strong, good-looking man. You'd be in your prime in any other sort of job. You ought to give that some thought — another line of work, that is.'

'Mr Kramer, I know cows, horses, knots and brands, water sources, prairie medicine, Indians and guns. What other sort of work would you say I was suited for?'

Of course there was no answer to that and Kramer had apparently spent all of the time he intended to on Ben Trout.

'You have your options, Ben,' the ranch owner said. 'It's not like I'm throwing you out to the wolves. Stay or go as you please.'

'Then if it's all the same to you, Mr Kramer,' Benjamin said, rising from his chair, 'I'll be getting along.'

The coming sun was low outside the

big house, the big oaks in the front yard still cast deep, cool shadows across the dusty earth.

The yardman, Connors, who was busy moving some rotted lumber from in front of the barn to a stack of discards, lifted his eyes and smiled as if to say something to Benjamin, but he must have seen something in Trout's eyes that stilled his greeting.

Trout walked on, hat tugged low against the rising sun, hearing the taunts and jeers, the familiar jokes of the crew as they saddled for their morning duties. These quieted a bit as Trout approached the bunkhouse. The word must have leaked out somehow. One of the men shouted out a 'Good morning, Mr Benjamin,' but Trout did not respond. He shuffled on, head down, toward the building he had called home for so many years on the K/K Ranch.

Inside the bunkhouse, someone was raising hell. Entering, Trout saw only two men. One was the camp cook, Frye, the other was a new-hire named

Eddie Guest whom the hands had nicknamed 'Dink'. It was Dink who was causing the uproar. As Frye, a huge man in a white apron, watched, leaning against the wall, Dink went the length of the building throwing bedding, slats, coffee pots and cards on the floor, at the walls, his wild hair flying.

'Tantrum,' the taciturn Frye told Benjamin.

'What's going on here?' Trout demanded, halting Dink's unruly display of temper.

'What?' a panting Dink, hair limp across his eyes, bent forward at the waist, asked. 'You mean you don't know, Mr Benjamin? I got fired this morning, that's what. Barely awake and they told me that I was fired, to pull my freight.'

'It happens. That's no reason to tear up the bunkhouse.'

'It's a reason,' Dink argued. He was no more than seventeen years old, just coming into his man's weight and strength. So far as Benjamin knew, his work was acceptable, although he made a few mistakes now and then. He had always seemed willing and content on the K/K.

'They didn't even give me a reason,' Dink went on complaining, as Benjamin walked to his own bunk to recover his few belongings. 'Folks call me 'kid', but I do my best and I'm learning fast. Is that it, Mr Benjamin? Did they fire me because I'm too young?'

'I wouldn't know,' Trout said honestly. 'No one discussed it with me.'

'But, you're the foreman — you must have been told,' Dink said in disbelief. He wiped back his hair, glanced at Frye, who was straightening the kitchen chairs and the table, and then turned almost pleading eyes back toward Ben Trout.

'Couldn't you maybe talk to the boss for me, Mr Benjamin? I really do like it here.'

Dink hadn't seemed to notice that Trout was gathering his own goods, packing his war bag, throwing his shaving gear together, fashioning his bed-roll. Ben Trout paused and looked directly at Dink. 'I can't help you, son. I'm sorry.'

'But where am I supposed to go?

What am I supposed to do now?' The bewildered Eddie Guest seemed suddenly to become aware that Trout was fixing his traveling gear.

'Where are you off to, Mr Benjamin?'

'I don't know. I can't say.'

'But . . . you're boss here, Mr Benjamin!'

'No more,' Trout said, shouldering his gear. 'I'm afraid I'm as footloose as you are. I've been fired, too, after a mere twenty years on the job. I don't know why; but it's so. I'm pulling my freight too, Dink.'

'But why?'

'I've quit asking myself that. The man owns the ranch. He can hire and fire as he sees fit.'

'It's not fair!'

'Maybe not, but it's the way things are, and so I'm drifting. Let me by, will you?'

Dink stepped aside for Trout, speechless. Then, suddenly the kid cried out, 'Mr Benjamin, can you wait a few minutes? I'd like to go along with you if you'll have me.'

'Makes me no never mind,' Trout answered. 'But I have no idea where I'm going.'

'Neither do I, but it would make me feel a whole lot better going there with a man like you.'

Trout considered for a minute. What did it matter to him? 'I'll be waiting in the barn, Dink.'

It was a silent, melancholy duo that rode out of the K/K later that morning. Sunrise was a watery orange glow at their backs; the long, dusty West Texas plains spread out before them.

'Well,' Dink said after the first mile had passed under their horses' hoofs, unable to hold his silence, 'where are we heading, Mr Benjamin?'

'I thought I told you. I haven't an idea in the world. My only thought is to make the tanks at Alamosa tonight so we'll have water for tomorrow's travels. After that I'm not real familiar with the lay of the land.'

Dink, who had placed all his trust in the older, wiser man he believed Ben

Trout to be, now appeared dismayed, as if he would melt under the high sun and puddle away in the saddle.

Trout, who had not asked for nor expected the kid's company, nevertheless decided to shine some mercy on the bleak outlook of Eddie Guest's world. Hell, he had been seventeen once, although it was hard to remember. And alone in the cold world — it had been no fun, he could remember that. Sleeping out, scrounging for any kind of meal with Indians wanting his scalp; Kiowas, mostly. All those dreary years ago. The K/K had been more than a refuge to Trout, more than a place to work. It was nearly the only home he had ever had. Did not Dink feel the same about the ranch, now lost to him?

'I've got some friends out in Arizona Territory,' Trout said, riding side by side with Dink as they traversed the long plains. 'Brothers named Wright. They inherited a few dollars and quit the K/K to go out there and start a freighting business. I got a letter from them about a year ago, asking me to come and join them. I never considered it before; now I am.'

'Tucson! That's one long way, Mr Benjamin.'

'It is,' Ben Trout agreed. 'But we're closer now than we were when we started. I figure to aim toward El Paso, rest up there for a while and then go on into the Territories.'

Dink said nothing, trying to assimilate this information. He supposed it didn't matter much just then. They still had five hundred miles of Texas land to travel over before they reached El Paso. They would be long on the trail, but at least there was a plan of some kind to cling to.

'We'll be all right,' Trout said, warming slightly to his position as mentor and guide. 'I've been saving some of my pay packet for nearly twenty years. I've no small fortune, but enough to serve me for a while in my poke.'

'I was only on the job for four months,' the young man on the dun pony muttered. 'Can't save much over that length of time. I think I have seven dollars and a nickel or two.'

'Don't worry about it,' Benjamin Trout said. 'We're saddle partners now.'

And they were, although he hadn't planned it that way. Two cowhands reduced to riding the line. One because he was too much under thirty, the other because he was too many years over it. It stank, but that was the way of the world, Ben knew. Because he had to, he began to think of his new life as a freight line driver, of meeting his old friends the Wrights again, maybe being introduced to new friends, and who knew, some level-headed widow lady.

You could know nothing of the world until you stepped out in it, he had told himself twenty years before, broke and dispirited. Maybe, despite the circumstances, it had been time to step out again, even if it was under force. That was the thing about life: it was unpredictable.

Trout lifted the head of his sorrel pony and let it stretch out its legs in a trot for the next mile. Dink was smiling now, urging his dun pony into a run. They were heading somewhere now, and more quickly, more eagerly. That was enough.

The land was a long, lonesome series of brushy hummocks and dry swales. No water ran in the depressions, no grass grew on the hills. It seemed that Trout's idea that they had to reach the Alamosa Tanks for water that evening was correct. They were still a long way from them, and they were not carrying enough water in their canteens to satisfy either themselves or the horses for long.

The sun rose higher and became fiercer on their backs as they crossed the long, barren miles. Twenty years in this country had left Ben Trout with only a sparse knowledge of the land this far west. Dink had never traveled this way before.

'My horse isn't used to this rough use,' Dink said in a miserable voice which indicated that he was not either.

Nor was Benjamin Trout. He had gotten spoiled. There was a reason Ed Kramer had never sought to expand the K/K ranch beyond the Tascosa Valley area. In Tascosa they had water, cottonwood trees along the creeks, good grass growing most of the year. There was little of value to be had farther west.

'I ain't seen so much as a coyote,' Dink said as Ben sided him on the empty land. 'Not so much as a sidewinder in ten miles. The only thing this country has over Hades is that it's above ground.'

Benjamin Trout nodded without answering. His mouth was too dry for speaking. The kid was right. They had seen no antelope, deer or even a jackrabbit. They were carrying little food and not enough water. Sun-stunned, they rode on toward the western lands where the now-almost-mythical Alamosa Tanks stood.

There was no help anywhere nearer, no hope of civilization. They had seen few other living things, and these were only swarming gnats and the occasional high-soaring black buzzard. It was a land utterly devoid of life.

Or so it seemed until they crested the next gravel-strewn ridge, and looking down into the sandy wash below, they saw the disabled wagon tended by two hectic-looking travelers in skirts.

2

Halted beside Trout on his dun horse, Dink muttered through dry, swollen lips, 'I must be seeing one of those mirages you hear about.'

'If you are, I'm seeing the same one, and one of the women in it is waving to us.'

They could both see a handsome woman, her green skirt tucked up in her waistband, and a younger girl, probably her daughter, trying to right a wagon which had failed on them. Even from that distance Trout could see that the spokes on the wheel had broken from jouncing over rough country, split and landed the wagon flat on its rear axle.

The women had been going about it right. They had collected stones and carried a levering bar with them. They also, fortunately, had a spare wheel to replace the broken one. The trouble was that the rocks they had gathered to use as they jacked the wagon up were too small and probably they didn't have the pure heft to lift the wagon with the lever.

'What are we going to do?' Dink asked.

'What folks do when somebody's in trouble,' Benjamin Trout answered. 'Give them a hand if we can.'

The older woman who had been waving to them met them as they dismounted from their horses at the wagon. She wore a grateful but concerned smile which Trout understood. Who were these men appearing off the plains?

'Hello,' she said. She seemed to be a notch on the far side of thirty years old, with a trim figure and finely etched features. Her blonde hair was wind-frazzled.

'Got a little trouble, I see,' Trout said.

'Yes. I know all about how to replace a broken wheel. In theory.'

'Theory is a good thing to have, but sometimes can be mighty hard to work with,' Trout answered.

'Can you help us?' she asked eagerly.

'I think so. Dink, why don't you work your way along the wash and find us a dozen or so head-sized rocks. Not round ones, though.'

'Sure,' Dink replied. He was trying to squeeze one last drop of water from his canteen.

The woman spoke up. 'Are you boys short on water? We've got a couple of barrels full on board. Help yourselves.'

'Grateful, ma'am,' Ben Trout said. 'We were hoping to make the tanks at Alamosa tonight, but it looks like we may come up a little short.'

'I'll say you will,' the woman said with a faint laugh. 'Those tanks — if there's any water in them this time of year — are another thirty miles ahead, and those are hard miles.' She stopped. 'You two aren't army deserters or some such, are you?'

'No, ma'am. We were ranch hands

until this morning. Now we're just drifters, I suppose.'

She looked at Trout's face carefully and nodded. 'Let's get on with this, shall we? By the way, my name is Beth Robinson. That over there,' she said, nodding toward the teenage girl who stood watching, hands folded in front of her, 'is my daughter, Minna.'

'Benjamin Trout,' Trout said with a nod. 'My friend's name is Eddie Guest.'

'You called him 'Dink',' Minna said, having come nearer.

'It's a nickname the boys at the ranch hung on him,' Ben explained. 'They're apt to do that.'

Even then Dink was struggling back out of the wash with a fair-sized yellow boulder.

'You've got a spare wheel; that's a real help.'

'Mr Robinson, my husband, was big on being prepared,' Beth Robinson said. 'He believed in the ounce of prevention. And the country's so rough around here, it was only a matter of time before something broke.'

'And it picked today,' Ben Trout said, rolling up his sleeves. 'How's the spindle, do you know?'

'It's fine; I've already checked it. All that has to be done is take the old wheel off and replace it.'

'Where are you people traveling?' Trout asked. Using the lever he had hoisted the wagon enough for Dink to lay a second layer of squarish rocks along the first. 'Should have been a mason,' Trout kidded. Dink, perspiring freely now, grinned and placed another stone down.

'We're just going home,' Beth Robinson said. A gust of hot wind rose from somewhere and swept over her, twisting her hair, pressing her skirt against her legs.

'Home?' Trout said, surprised. 'No one lives out here.'

'Oh, yes we do,' Beth told him. 'Along that road there.'

Ben Trout had to strain to see what she was pointing out, but finally he was able to make out a twin pair of ruts scoured into the rough earth leading off far on to the empty land.

'Out there?' he said before he could stop himself. He saw Beth Robinson stiffen a little.

'It suits us,' Beth said. Dink had returned with another flat stone which Trout helped him set.

'Almost got it,' Dink said, removing his hat to wipe his brow with his scarf. Sensing some sort of underlying, unhappy current between Trout and Beth Robinson, Dink scurried away again.

'Gerald, my husband,' Beth said, as they watched Dink sliding down the bank into the gully, 'bought the place sight unseen. Eighty acres on the West Texas plains with running water on the property. It was something to dream on. We didn't know how barren and isolated eighty acres could be out here where the nearest neighbor is miles away.

'But we made do, Mr Trout. It was never easy, but we always managed somehow.'

'The way you're talking . . . ' Trout asked, 'is Mr Robinson gone now?'

'Two years ago this May,' she answered after a minute.

'Sorry,' Trout said in a mumble men save for such occasions. Then his voice rose. 'All right, Dink. Let's get these ladies back on the road!'

Using a large leftover boulder and the lever, Trout formed a fulcrum to lift the back of the wagon. First he wanted to know, 'Can you get the broken wheel off, Beth?'

'I have the right wrench. I don't know if I can put enough weight on it.'

'Well, we've got Dink with us. He can put his young muscle to work.' Dink looked somewhat doubtful, but proud. The younger woman, Minna Robinson, looked at Dink with admiring eyes.

'Let's go,' Trout said. 'Don't leave me holding the fulcrum for longer than necessary once we get the wagon up.'

It was a project which took more time in the planning than in the actual execution. The lug nut on the wounded wheel was cracked — that did require Dink's muscle and Ben Trout hoisted the wagon and held it while the new wheel was placed on the spindle and bolted on. In five minutes the job had been done and Beth Robinson, who knew she and her daughter had been facing a terrifying night and a long walk, leaving their goods to the elements, was effusive in her praise.

'I can't thank you enough,' she repeated at least four times.

'It didn't take us long,' Trout said, the second time she thanked him. Then he quit responding. Too much gratitude always embarrassed him. 'Let's get those rocks out from in front of the wheel so these ladies can be moving on, Dink.'

That done, they helped the women up on to their wagon bench, Dink looking uncomfortable as Minna's skirt brushed against him.

Leaning forward and down on the wagon, Beth asked, 'What did you say your destination was, Mr Trout?'

'We were planning on making our

next stop in El Paso,' he said, tilting back his hat to look up at the lady.

'Oh, wonderful. You'll hardly be going out of your way at all,' Beth Robinson said, glancing at Minna.

'What do you mean?' Trout said cautiously.

'That was an invitation, Mr Trout,' Beth said. 'Come to the ranch and have a fried chicken dinner with us. We've the creek running with water for your horses. All of you will feel better for being fed and watered before you travel on.'

'They say Alamosa Tanks are still a long way off,' Dink spoke up. 'We might not even make it tonight. We're not carrying much food, Mr Benjamin.' It might have been the mention of a chicken dinner that had Dink's eyes so bright, but now and then Dink would shoot a hardly secretive glance in the direction of Minna Robinson, Trout noticed.

'I don't suppose we'd be losing much time,' Trout said finally. 'There's a chance the tanks are dry . . . All right, we'd be obliged to accept dinner from you, Mrs Robinson.'

'It's hardly a gift, Mr Trout. You boys got us out of a dire situation. Grab your ponies, boys — we're going home!'

The woman started the two-horse team along the little-traveled way, leaving Trout and Dink in their dust. Minna leaned far out of her seat to look back at them, her curls flying.

'Well,' Dink said, taking the reins to his horse, 'let's get going, Mr Benjamin. What are you waiting for?'

'I don't know,' Trout said honestly, as he watched the wagon gradually recede into the distance. 'Didn't the lady seem just a little too eager to you?'

'Eager?' Dink looked puzzled. 'Too eager to cook a good dinner for us to thank us for helping them, to offer us water for our horses? What's wrong with that, Mr Benjamin?'

'I don't know. Nothing, I suppose.' Dink had swung into leather; Ben still hesitated. 'I guess it's just that I don't like having my plans changed in mid-stride.'

'Your plan was pretty flat anyway, wasn't it? Mrs Robinson said the Alamosa Tanks were thirty miles farther on, and she ought to know, living out here. And if we're heading on toward El Paso, going this way is pretty much in a straight line as near as I can figure.'

'You're right,' Trout said, finally mounting his sorrel.

'You can't say we can't use the water and a dinner.'

'No,' Trout said. He still hadn't started his horse. He sat with his hands crossed on the pommel, still looking after the diminishing wagon. 'Are you sure that's why you want to go along, Dink? For a chicken dinner?'

'Why, what do you mean, Mr Benjamin? Why else?'

'Minna,' Trout said and Dink blushed to the roots of his hair.

'Ah, she's just a girl,' Dink said sullenly.

'And when's the last time you talked to one?'

'Maybe I do want to talk to her!

What's wrong with that?' Trout had started his horse forward. Dink rode in silence at his side for half a mile before saying, 'Are you sure there's not another reason you are against this ride, Mr Benjamin?'

'What would that be, Dink?'

'I don't know — but if I was a man of your age, I don't suppose I'd find the Widow Robinson unappealing.'

The two men glanced at one another as they continued on across the yellow grassland. Benjamin's jaw was set, his eyes narrowed; Dink was smiling happily.

The horses' hoofs kicked up white dust as they trailed across the featureless land toward the distant horizon. 'I still don't see a building,' Dink said, wiping his forehead. 'Did Mrs Robinson tell you how far their ranch was?'

'No, but it sure is a far piece from where they were coming from.'

'I wonder where that was,' Dink said.

'The wagon was filled with supplies. They must have been from the trading post down at Hinkley's Ridge. You know where that is, don't you?'

'Only heard of it. Someone said it was ten miles south of the K/K.'

'If not more. A mighty long way to have to go for a sack of flour.'

Half an hour on they still did not see any ranch structures, nor the glint of the sun off the water which was supposed to flow on the Robinson Ranch. They did pass four mixed-breed cattle standing in a group around a patch of greenish graze — the only new grass they had seen so far.

The cattle had slat sides and looked miserable with their lot in life. Round brown eyes watched their passing without concern and with little interest. Trout wondered if they should not be moved toward water, but it was none of his business. He did notice they were branded cattle, as did Dink.

The brand was a standing R with a U with irregular arms. 'Gerald Robinson had a sense of humor,' Trout said with a smile.

'What do you mean?'

'He chose the brand for whoever sold him the ranch.' Dink still didn't get it, so Trout correctly interpreted the brand for him: 'Are you crooked?'

Dink smiled faintly. He was more concerned with keeping up with the wagon, with feasting on a fried chicken dinner and talking some more to Minna Robinson, maybe even walking out with her in the evening. Trout, who had seen many of these cases, saw all the signs in the young man's expression. Oh, well, Dink's plan could cause him no problems, he decided. Or could it?

Rounding a low, brushy knoll now they saw ahead a stand of four scraggly, undernourished cottonwood trees and a small house which could have had no more than four or five rooms. The RU Crooked Ranch.

The women still sat on the wagon bench, resting before they clambered down to unload the wagon. It was a little cooler, the sun lowering itself toward the far hills. There was a faint breeze and Benjamin Trout could sense water on it. The creek, whatever it was worth, was nearby. Their ponies could use it, certainly. It had been a long, dusty trail that day.

And they could use the promised chicken dinner. Minna Robinson sat smiling in the direction of Dink as he swung down from the saddle. Beth Robinson looked all business. The question was — what sort of business did the woman have in mind?

3

They managed to get the wagon unloaded. Sacks of flour, beans, cornmeal, a side of bacon and a peck of potatoes among assorted tinned goods and a few womanly things Trout could not identify and tried not to look at.

With that done and the women in the kitchen putting their goods away and chattering happily, Trout and Dink led their horses to water. The little silver rill trickled prettily across the sparse grassland and the high, thin clouds were dusted with gold and stained a wispy pink.

Trout watched his horse drinking, but his thoughts were elsewhere. 'Dink, let's take a walk.' Dink, crouched beside his horse, looked up with surprise.

'Where would we want to walk to?'

'There's something not quite right about the way this river runs. You can see in the higher country that it flows a lot wider.'

'What are you thinking?'

'I just want to see what the problem is. There should be enough water flowing across the RU to spread and water a lot more grass than they have; instead it's being choked off somewhere.'

'Diverted, you mean?'

'That's what I mean. Not by a neighboring ranch, since as you can see there is none, but by a rock fall or landslide, something like that.'

And after half an hour's walk, that was exactly what they found. The face of a bluff had folded in on itself and choked off the natural course of the creek through the RU, sending a useless fork of water to the west where it died in the desert.

Crouching beside Trout on the twilit ridge, Dink commented thoughtfully, 'That could be dug out. It would give those ladies twice the water they have now.'

'It would be about a week's pick-and-shovel work for two men,' Trout observed. 'All we can do is tell them about it if they don't already know.'

'Maybe they can find a couple of men and hire them,' Dink said doubtfully. Rising he looked below them. 'That would be a pretty little grassy valley if they had enough water flowing.'

'It would be that,' Trout said. He had already started off, striding toward the spot where they had left their horses. They could see smoke rising from the house's iron pipe chimney and Dink swore that he could smell chicken frying even at that distance.

'You've got too much imagination,' Trout said at Dink's remark.

'It comes with being young, I guess,' Dink answered. 'You know, Mr Benjamin I . . . '

'No,' Trout said flatly. 'I know exactly what you are going to propose, and the answer's no. It's too much of a favor to ask, and I have to be traveling west to

Tucson, not practicing my pick-and-shovel work.'

'What's the hurry?' Dink asked out of the near-darkness. 'You haven't even seen the Wright brothers for years. It's not like they're sitting around waiting for you.'

'No,' Trout said again just as firmly. 'Besides, no one's asked us to do the job.'

'But if they did . . . We'd have meals for a week, help them at the same time . . . ' Dink's voice faded as they gathered up their ponies. It was obvious that he was disappointed in the older man. Ben Trout trudged on wordlessly, leading his sorrel horse.

They had taken the time to rinse off at the creek and wipe their hair back and so they were not totally unpresentable at the supper table despite their dusty clothes. The women were a wonder.

Beth Robinson, her hair brushed back and pinned, wore a dark skirt and a ruffled white blouse with a cameo on a velvet choker around her throat. Minna looked as if she had just emerged from a perfumed bath somewhere; her pink cheeks and bright smile would be the envy of any town girl. She swished about the room in her pale-blue dress serving while Dink tried to avoid staring at her.

Women were a constant amazement to Ben Trout. How had they found the time to fix themselves up at the same time as they worked away in a hot kitchen preparing chicken, biscuits and mashed potatoes? Both the front and rear doors to the small house stood open now, catching the sundown breeze which had begun to cool it off.

As they ate, Ben Trout, at a non-verbal nudge from Dink, mentioned what they had found along the creek to Beth.

'Yes, I've suspected something like that for a long time. Up until last year we had a nicely flowing river. Now . . . ' She shook her head as if the battle was becoming too much for her.

'We only had two steers to take to Hinkley's Ridge to sell this time,' Minna said, hovering around Dink with a plate filled with hot biscuits. 'Ones decent enough to sell, that is.'

'You drove two cattle that far?' Dirk said in disbelief.

'Yes, sir,' Minna told him. 'Tied them beyond the wagon and took them for a stroll.'

'Amazing,' Dink said, accepting two more buttered rolls from Minna.

'Well,' Beth Robinson told the men, 'Gerald, my husband, didn't have much to leave us. He had hoped that a ranch in the West would set us up nicely. We all have our dreams . . . ' Her words trailed off. 'The RU Crooked,' she went on, using the ranch's full name, 'wasn't anywhere close to what the realtor had promised, either in his brochures or in person. But here we were and the money had been spent, so we labored on as best we could.' She paused and then mused, 'I think that trying so hard is what killed Gerald in the end. So the few cattle we're running are nearly all we have outside of the gold.'

Gold? Trout's head came up from his plate. Beth Robinson, seeing his reaction, laughed.

'I'm sorry, Mr Benjamin, but that's the reaction people always have when they hear that word. In our case we have been able to pan a little dust now and then down along the creek. I don't think we've ever gathered more than twenty-five dollars' worth at a time. Still, it's been enough to help supply us with some provisions and a few small luxuries.'

'And that was hard come by,' Minna said. Trout had a vision of the women, skirts tucked up, wading in the cold water trying to pan a little color out of the shallow creek.

'But you survive,' Ben Trout said, folding his napkin and placing it on the table.

'We do survive. Of course I don't know what I'll do when Minna leaves home — '

' — I'll never leave you, Mother!' Minna protested.

'Of course you will,' Beth said. 'The time just hasn't come yet. You'll have to leave here or marry some big lummox with half a brain and bring him out here to live.'

'Mother . . . ' Minna moaned. Trout noticed that Dink was blushing again.

It did not sound like a good set-up to Trout, the more he listened. The ranch needed more care than the women could afford. A couple of hands might be able to whip the RU into shape. Then again, to take a job way out here on a broken-down patch of earth and work it for no pay, the man would indeed have to be a lummox with half a brain. Trout glanced at Dink, who did not seem to have the same view of things. But then, Dink was looking for a home and a family like he believed he had had on the K/K. Trout was looking for a reliable opportunity to see him through his later years.

'That gold!' Minna Robinson said

laughing as she finally sat at the table with them. She clasped her hands, rested her elbows on the table and smiled at each of them in turn. 'The time we did take twenty-five dollars' worth of dust into Hinkley's Ridge to purchase some supplies! Before we left town there was a rumor that there was a gold strike out our way, on a ranch that was just run by two little women. No one ever followed us, but for a while . . . '

'For a while,' Beth put in, 'we were hoping that someone would so that we could put him to work.' She was silent for a time, looking with fond eyes at her daughter, who had already suffered much, Trout guessed.

'That's the trouble with these shoe-string operations — they're born with such hopeful anticipation, but time wears them down until the wind, the cold, the loneliness just blows them and their dreams away to wait for the next hopeful, wide-eyed settler to be hoaxed into buying it.'

There was no humor in the woman's eyes now, and seemingly no hope. She rose abruptly from the table and stalked out of the room.

The young people rose and left the table as well, leaving Ben Trout to finish his coffee. The woman had herself a right little mess on the RU; that was so. In the morning Beth Robinson's troubles would mean nothing to Ben. He would be riding west, sorry for Beth Robinson and her daughter, but having no help to offer. She would have to succeed or fail on her own as all of these small ranchers did.

A faint click in the living room was followed by the rustling of garments. Trout's head turned that way. The lantern, too, had been doused in that room where he had seen Dink and Minna go. He sighed. It was none of his business what the two young people were up to, except that he was the one who had brought Dink to the RU. Pushing away from the table he rose and went that way.

What he saw was that the front door had been latched, the lantern extinguished, and Dink and Minna were crouched in front of the window. Dink had his pistol in his hand.

'Get down,' Dink hissed at Trout.

'What's happening?'

'There's someone prowling around,' Dink said.

'I saw him too,' Minna told him, keeping her grip on Dink's arm.

'Could be anybody,' Trout said, lowering himself beside the other window.

'That's just it — it could be anybody.'

'Nobody, I mean *nobody*, ever comes by way out here,' Minna whispered with excitement.

'Probably just a wanderer looking for water or a handout,' Ben Trout said. But he, too, had drawn his pistol and was searching the darkness with his eyes. He thought he saw some movement among the cottonwood trees caught by the starlight.

'Or looking for gold,' Minna said imaginatively.

'A place to sleep.'

'Women,' Dirk said anxiously.

'Or fresh horses,' Trout added.

'Anyway,' Minna said in a rapid whisper, 'a man who meant no harm would have hallooed the house, wouldn't he? Come up to the door and knocked?'

'Yes, you're right,' Ben Trout allowed. 'We'd better find out just who this is.'

They heard then a board on the swayed porch creak as it received some weight, and the soft, nearly silent sound of boot leather sliding stealthily over wooden planks. It was unsettling behavior for a visitor unless he thought the house was unoccupied, but their horses and the smoke from the chimney made that conclusion untenable.

Whoever the stranger was, he was not behaving naturally.

There was a sudden thud, a clang, a howl of pain which broke off even as it rose from someone's throat. And a pounding on the door.

'Let me in, somebody!' Beth Robinson's voice sounded.

Minna rushed that way, her eyes wide and frightened and flung open the heavy front door to the ranch house. Beth was not alone, nor was she unarmed. The door opened to allow a square-jawed man with a month's worth of whiskers to topple in to lie against the floor. Beth came after him, a heavy cast-iron skillet in her hand.

'That'll teach a body to come sneaking around,' Beth said, hugging her daughter tightly. The man on the floor was still out cold.

'You don't know this man?' Trout asked as he slipped the side arm from the man's holster.

'I never saw him; never care to again,' Beth said, walking to the kitchen where she put the heavy skillet back on the stove. 'I went out the back door when I heard you all talking. He's alone, that's all I can tell you. I looked around.'

'I think I know who he is,' Minna said, now standing close enough to Dink so that he could slip his arm around her waist. 'I saw a Wanted poster on an outlaw named Hiram Walsh in Hinkley's Ridge today. This man looks quite like the drawing on the poster, except he has a lot more whiskers.'

'You have a good imagination, Minna,' her mother told her.

'I don't think so, this time,' Trout, who had been going through the man's pockets, said. In his vest pocket, the man had been carrying a much-folded Wanted poster for Hiram Walsh. Trout handed it to Beth.

Beth examined the poster carefully, then crouched down beside the unconscious man, comparing the line drawing with his face. 'I'll be . . . I think it is him,' she said, handing the poster back to Trout, who let Dink examine it across his shoulder.

'Momma,' Minna said. 'It says here they're offering five hundred dollars for his capture.'

'I know, dear, but . . . ' Beth wiped back her hair and then stopped, her actions frozen by the realization of what she had done.

'You did capture him, Momma. You surely did.'

Walsh had begun to stir and Beth walked to a cupboard and returned with a ball of twine which she gave to Ben Trout.

'Five hundred dollars,' Beth said, seating herself on the sofa. 'Do you know what that much money would mean to us, what we could do?' Minna sat beside her, eyes glowing with anticipation. Trout continued to bind the outlaw's wrists, using figure-eight knots. Then he dragged him to the wall and propped him up there.

'It's just a matter of getting him into custody,' Dink commented. 'Where would that have to be? Hinkley's Ridge?'

'There's no jail, no law at Hinkley's Ridge. I can tell you've never been there. There's nothing there but a trading post and a saloon. No, it would have to be Riverton. If you started early in the morning, you'd be able to make it back by supper time.'

Beth's eyes were on Benjamin Trout

and Dink. The look in them started out as a kind of command and then softened to a pleading expression.

Dink shrugged. 'Well, I've never seen Riverton.'

Ben Trout snapped, 'And you're never going to! We're headed for El Paso, in case you've forgotten.'

Minna looked at Dink with damp eyes. Beth continued to gaze at Ben Trout. The outlaw, Hiram Walsh, muttered a single cuss word and fell over on to his face again.

4

Morning was bright. The morning birds had taken to wing. A flock of speckled brown chickens scratched at the dry earth in front of the house. The air was cool with a slight breeze rustling through the cottonwood trees. The men had been fed. It was a pretty morning — and Benjamin Trout was in a foul mood.

Well, he reflected, he had every right to be. The situation had been discussed and decided over his objections the night before. He and Dink were to take the outlaw, Hiram Walsh, to Riverton and deliver him to the county sheriff. The matter seemed almost to have been decided before Trout could voice his complaints.

He and Dink did not work for the RU Ranch; he was not heading in the direction of Riverton. It was plain none of his business. That should have been obvious to all of them, but was not.

'We can't send two women off with a known killer on such a long ride,' Dink, who seemed to have shifted loyalties, said. 'Who would watch the ranch while they were gone? Walsh might have friends in the area.'

'Who's going to watch the ranch if we do go?' Ben asked in a low growl.

Beth Robinson had an answer for that. 'I assume you know what this is, Mr Benjamin,' she said, bringing a long-barreled weapon from the closet to show him.

'Yes, I do, ma'am. It's a .50 caliber Sharps buffalo rifle. It'll take down a bull bison at 200 yards as it was designed to do.'

'Exactly,' Beth said, putting the old rifle away as if she had made her point. 'The next prowler I see around won't get a frying pan, he'll get a sample from the barrel of the buffalo gun.'

'With that five hundred dollars,' Dink put in, 'they could hire a couple of men to clean out the river bed. That would allow much more water to flow across the basin.'

'Yes,' Beth added, 'and we could also pay somebody to collect the stray cattle and drift them over closer to water. It wouldn't take a few good men more than a day or two to gather our strays and push them back toward better graze.'

'If they take the wagon,' Minna said to her mother, 'they could also bring back a few extra things we couldn't afford to get over at Hinkley's Ridge — Riverton is a bigger town by far. I'll make up a list!' Minna bounced up to do just that.

'They could even lead three or four cows and a bull back!' Beth said, catching the excitement. 'That shouldn't be too many to manage. By next spring we could have some new young blood on our range.'

Dink caught Trout's sour expression, sat on the sofa beside him and said in a low, reasonable voice, 'What's two days to us, Mr Benjamin? We could pick up some trail supplies for ourselves in Riverton — you know we're awful short. And we'd be helping two nice ladies save their ranch.'

Beth, who had overheard, put in, 'This man, Walsh, has to be put away where he can cause no more problems for society. It's our civic duty to see that he's delivered to the authorities.'

She gestured toward Hiram Walsh, who sat on the floor in the corner, his eyes blazing at times and at others clouding over with dull pain. His head was probably still ringing. He did speak once, asking, 'Don't one of you fine citizens have a dram of whiskey for a bad-hurt man?'

No one answered him; no one paid the bound outlaw a bit of attention. He might as well have not existed except as a piece of their plan.

As the night wore on and the others continued to talk, Benjamin Trout felt that he had as much existence as the outlaw — no one listened to a word of his arguments.

* * *

'Aw, Mr Benjamin, don't look so gloomy,' Dink said on that new morning. 'We're going a few days out of our way to be Good Samaritans. What's two days out of your life?'

'I don't like the way it's shaping up,' Ben answered, still glowering as they trudged toward the leaning gray barn where their horses were stabled. 'I have a feeling that the women are expecting more of us. Don't forget, Dink, I have a place to go, people to see.'

'If the Wrights even remember you or recall the invitation,' Dink said a little sharply.

'These men were good friends of mine,' Ben said defensively as he snatched up his saddle and threw it over the sorrel's back. 'They won't have forgotten their offer.' Correctly reading Dink's mood he paused and said seriously: 'Eddie, we were traveling together only because you did not know where else to go. If you think this might be a place you wish to light, do as you wish. As for me, I'm delivering that bad man to the law, seeing if we can hire a couple of men willing to work out here for a few days, trying to find four or five young cattle to bring along with us when we come back, and then I'm leaving. I have my future to think about and it doesn't involve shoestringing it on some dying ranch. There's better work to be had out there. When we finish what you've obliged us to do, I'm leaving for Tucson. You can do whatever you want.'

'You're right, Mr Benjamin. The same situation doesn't fit every man. I know this whole thing just kind of popped up on you. But what some might see as a roadblock, others might see as an opportunity. I may be traveling on with you, but right now I couldn't swear to it.'

No. Trout could understand that. Eddie Guest was a young man who had had his first introduction to romance. He had never wished to leave his home on the K/K in the first place, and now he thought he had found another home with two likeable women.

Dink could see the RU improving, growing until it was something rich and fertile. Ben Trout could only think of the situation the women might find themselves in when those five hundred providential dollars were gone — and they soon would be — and they were still stuck out here in this virtual wasteland, growing older.

For Ben Trout it was no choice. He wanted a steady job in a growing town and enough comfort to make his exit from this world as pleasant as possible.

Beth and Minna were both standing on the porch of the tiny house when they started the two-horse team out of the yard, Dink driving, his dun pony tied on behind, Trout straddling his sorrel. Hiram Walsh rode unhappily in the bed of the wagon, trussed like a captured boar hog.

Dink was looking back, and Trout glanced that way as well, knowing what he would see — Minna was waving a handkerchief enthusiastically, practically bouncing up and down. Dink lifted a hand to wave back.

What Trout had not expected to see and caught only briefly before the lady turned back toward the house was Beth's expression of hopefulness, and could it have been . . . fondness, which she allowed to linger ever-so-briefly on Benjamin Trout.

Trout shook his head. He had been without a woman for too long, and even as he frequently scolded Dink for his imagination, a stroke of the same emotion had gotten to him, it seemed.

Trout pulled the rough map Beth had sketched for them from his vest and pointed the way to Dink without saying anything.

Hiram Walsh had his own comment to put in. 'You can shorten the trip a mile or so if you take the Tehachapi cut-off.'

'You'll understand that we can't take any advice from you,' Ben Trout replied.

'Yeah, I do, but I'd like to make this ride as brief as possible. We're going the long way, this wagon bed is hard, and my head still hurts.'

'Sorry about all that, but a skillet is still better than a bullet.'

'Think so, do you? I've been shot more than once in my travels, friend, but that woman wields a wicked skillet.'

Drifting away from the wagon, so as not to hear any more of the outlaw's complaints, Ben followed the ranch wagon up the rocky trail into the low hills beyond. There the country was rife with purple sage and dotted with live oak trees. It was apparently waterless, but there were tracks of deer everywhere and cottontail rabbits scurried away from their horses' approaching hoofs. The sky held mostly clear although a few pennants of thin white clouds stretched out toward them from the far hills. The increased elevation did nothing to diminish the heat of the day. Trout dabbed at his eyes with his kerchief, keeping a watch on the country around and behind them. Dink had made one point — there was no way of knowing if Hiram Walsh had been riding alone, and the outlaw sure wasn't going to tell them the truth about that. It would be short work for a band of four or five men to take Walsh from them here in open country.

It was early afternoon with the sun still gliding high that they topped out a rocky ridge and, looking below them saw a small town spread out along the banks of a glittering river course.

'That must be it,' a weary Dink said, almost panting the words out.

'Has to be,' Ben said.

'Quit jabbering about it,' a red-faced Hiram Walsh hollered from the wagon bed, 'and get me down there. Any jail has to better than this!'

Ben Trout started to smile, found he did not have the strength. He nodded to Dink and they began making their slow, zigzag way down the trail leading to Riverton.

The county sheriff's office was not

difficult to find. It was one of only two or three painted buildings along the dusty main street of Riverton. The rest had already faded to the familiar weather-grayed color of a place that was not long for this earth.

The sheriff was in. A man of thirty or so, already turning to fat, he had small dark eyes that seemed to accuse everybody. The sign on his office door said his name was Charles Earl Stout. Charlie Stout looked up at the men escorting the prisoner into his office as if they were offending him somehow.

'What's this?' Sheriff Stout demanded, looking up at the two rough men who had entered his office, escorting the hard-looking, somehow familiar, bound man.

'This,' Ben Trout said, 'is a man you might recognize. His name is Hiram Walsh. There's paper out on him and we've come to claim the reward in the name of the woman who nabbed him, Beth Robinson.'

'Hold on a minute,' Stout said, lifting a hand, still not rising to his feet. 'This is a little too rapid for me to get a handle on. You say this is Hiram Walsh. Can you prove that?'

Trout unfolded the Wanted poster Walsh had been carrying as a souvenir and handed it to the sheriff. 'You can ask him who he is,' Trout said.

'I'm Hy Walsh — lock me up, please, Sheriff!' the outlaw begged.

'Been treating you rough, have they?'

'Rough enough,' Walsh believed.

'Well, that's what your kind deserves,' the sheriff said without sympathy. 'Now, then,' he said, tilting back in his chair and folding his hands on his belly, 'you boys say the Widow Robinson captured him. Is that the Beth Robinson who has the gold mine hidden out up north somewhere?'

'There's no gold mine,' Dink said. 'Those two women take about a teaspoon of dust out of their creek each day.'

'Is that so?' Sheriff Stout said dubiously. 'Rumor has it otherwise. What, then, was this man doing up there? What was he looking for if not gold?'

'You'd have to ask him,' Ben Trout said.

'Do you think he'd tell me anything?' the sheriff asked, drumming his thick fingers on his desk top. 'Now, you say the Widow Robinson captured this man by herself — you boys work for her, I take it?'

'That's right,' Dink said almost eagerly. He took a note from his pocket that Beth had written the night before and Trout had not seen, authorizing the sheriff to give Trout and Dink the reward money. The sheriff barely scanned it.

'How am I supposed to know that what you say is what happened?' Stout asked. 'Were there any witnesses?'

'We are the witnesses,' Trout said, his temperature starting to rise. He did not like Stout much, though maybe the man was just being cautious in his job according to his own lights, seeing that it involved money.

'Sheriff, I'm a witness!' the sullen Hiram Walsh spoke up. 'Give them the reward. The lady rattled my skull with an iron skillet. Now, can I find a peaceful place to sleep in your jail?'

Stout rose from behind his desk, his expression still far from cheerful. 'I'll grant your wish, Walsh,' the sheriff said. 'I know a little about your work in this county; it'll be a pleasure to send you off to the penitentiary.

'You boys,' he said, as he escorted Walsh to a cell, 'it'll take maybe two or three hours to get the paperwork done and for me to get the money for you.'

'All right,' Trout said, 'I guess we can wait that long.'

'You'll have to,' Stout grunted. He was busy sawing Ben Trout's knots free from Walsh's swollen wrists. Hiram Walsh, the scourge of the West, had thrown himself on to his bunk in the jail cell and was apparently asleep before Trout and Dink left the sheriff's office.

'He was still lucky,' Dink said as they stepped outside. 'Can you imagine if Beth had had that loaded buffalo gun with her?'

'Yes, and I have the feeling she would have used it. In defense of her daughter, she would have.'

'Now what do we do?' Dink asked as they stood on the plank walk in front of the sheriff's office, watching the passing men and horses.

'You can take the wagon over to the general store and start buying everything on the list the ladies gave you — I'll cover it with my own cash until Stout comes through with the reward money.' So saying Trout fumbled out fifty dollars of his own hard-earned, dearly saved money to give to Dink.

Dink whistled silently. 'I guess that twenty years of saving can leave a man in fair shape.'

'Fair,' Trout replied, 'but it wouldn't last me long if I had to plan to live off of it. You get a receipt from the man, Dink, because I will have repayment for that money.'

'I will do that, of course, Mr Benjamin. What are you planning on doing while I'm shopping?'

‘What the lady asked. I’m going to see what sort of cattle they are holding in the local pens and what their owner is asking. Then I’ll ask around and see if anyone has a bull for sale.’

‘That’ll be a lot for us to handle on the way back to the RU.’

‘It surely will; probably too much. But after finishing our shopping chores, we’ll look around for some likely men. Beth wanted us to find two pick-and-shovel men to clean out the stream bed. If we can find two likely-looking types, we’ll ask them if they’ve ever pushed cattle. In this country, they probably will have at some time or another.’

‘We can hire them on to help us with the cattle drive for now and to do the clean-out work on the creek later. Same pay, and an extra day of it. Should be able to find someone willing to drive cattle for that short a trip,’ Dink said. ‘If not, let ’em handle the wagon, and we can do it ourselves.’

‘That’s my thinking,’ Trout agreed. ‘So, let’s do our shopping, eat supper after that if we can find a decent place and then start hunting some likely looking help.'

Leaving Dink to his own devices, Trout walked out into the street, asking the first man he met where he could find the town's cow pens. A gnarled finger jabbed uptown and Trout followed the indicated direction.

Ben Trout pondered as he walked the dusty streets of Riverton. He was a long way from El Paso, a long way from Tucson, and not getting any closer. Instead he was in Riverton on a buying trip for a dry-earth widow, spending his own saved money on her behalf while he waited for some money from a sheriff of unknown character, and Dink and he tried to hire two strangers as ranch hands for the RU.

It was a situation Ben did not care for; certainly it was far away from his intended plan.

Why, then, was he doing it at all? Out of a sense of loyalty to Beth Robinson, to whom he owed none? Just because the two women were alone and needed someone to help them out? Their new-hired hands wouldn't stay around long after they had finished digging out the watercourse. Beth couldn't afford to pay them for long, not if she meant to keep the bulk of that five hundred dollars she was expecting to get. The women would find themselves right back where they had started from in no time. And if the river bluff caved in again? Ben had no idea that he was going to be able to hire qualified engineers to do the job. He would find two men with strong backs willing to work for a few days' whiskey money — it was all he could hope for.

He had already accepted as fact the notion that Dink was going to be remaining behind with the women. The kid could not see beyond those sparkling eyes of Minna Robinson. Well, that was the way of young men and of the world. But Dink was inexperienced. Could he alone help to stabilize the RU?

Ben Trout shook his head and found himself thinking of several improvements he could suggest to the women. Why? He had no time to spend on someone else's troubles.

What did he care about the fate of the RU?

He chased that thought from his mind as he approached the cattle pens south of town, but found himself still thinking of the last hopeful look Beth Robinson had given him as they left the ranch. Ben sighed loudly enough to turn the head of a man standing by. Things seemed to be proceeding well from everyone else's perspective, but they were not going well. Not at all.

5

Ben Trout bought one Holstein, two Jersey cows and one mixed, range-tough animal of indeterminate breed. He liked the look of this last one, a reddish beast still young, but with the look of an animal born to the range, one which would survive hard winters and baking hot summers and bear fine, strong, woolly calves.

Which brought him to the last point as he handed over much of his savings to the owner of the cattle, and asked for a receipt. 'I'm in the market for a bull; do you know someone who might have one?'

'That depends. I know some people who've got fat, sleek show bulls for sale — at a price. I also know a man who has a wild-eyed, untamed young bull just as full of himself as he probably is of calves. He's a handful, but can be had cheap because there's no way he can be contained or satisfied where he is now.'

'Where would that be?' Ben asked the corncob-pipe smoking old-timer.

'Right over there in that barn,' the man told him. 'I was speaking of myself. I got a young bull, but he's hell to handle.'

'I don't mean to saddle-break him,' Ben said with a faint smile and the old man nodded.

'I'll let you have a look, then. Come along.'

The old man moved with the hobbling gait of one who had once broken a leg and had it heal improperly. Seeming to be scurrying, he covered little ground as Ben strode alongside him toward the unpainted, somewhat dilapidated barn.

'He don't have a name. You wouldn't want to use the one that I call him when he starts acting up.'

'Kind of high-spirited, is he?' Trout commented as the old man swung the barn doors open.

'Yes, he is. Folks will tell you that's what you want in a bull — and they're right. But, mister, the last two times I let that creature out of the barn he broke free and stormed through the town. I'm telling you, I'm just a little too old for bull-dogging.'

'That's why you're selling him?' asked Ben as he strolled the dark barn beside the owner.

'That's it.' The old-timer smiled. 'That and the fact that I expect to get a good price for him.'

Ben winced a little. He was spending a lot of Beth's — his? — money, and he now had the feeling that he was in the clutches of a shrewd bargainer.

He was shown the young bull, which was placid on that morning. Still, its eyes held a gleam of devilry. Almost coal black it was, sleek and well defined. Ben looked it over as best he could without entering the pen, assuring himself that all the animal's body parts were in place and seemingly able to function. It might have been a risk, but he felt obligated to purchase the animal. That was the job he had been given, after all, and the price the owner quoted in the end was not that unreasonable.

'I'll be back after a while to collect the beeves,' Ben said. 'I do need a receipt for the bull too.' They started then toward the man's shanty office once again. Thinking ahead, Ben asked: 'I'm thinking that we'll drive the cows home, but the bull might not be so easy to handle. Do you think we should lash him to the back of a wagon and lead him?'

'I would,' the old man answered as they entered his stuffy office. 'Though he'd probably be content to follow the cows where they are going, he might get a little too eager for you and delay your trip.'

'We'll try leading him,' Ben said thoughtfully. 'That reminds me, I'd like to hire on a couple of cowhands for this little job. Do you have any idea where I might find some?'

'Mister, you couldn't have come through town without seeing the saloons.'

'I did,' Ben replied, realizing he had asked an unnecessary question.

Leaving the cattle for the time being, Ben went back uptown to find Dink. The dealer in livestock had recommended a small restaurant called 'Linda's' to him, and Ben was determined to give it a try; he was getting very hungry. Dink must also be by now.

He found Dink in the alley at the rear of the general store, the wagon bed nearly full. Ben eyed the collection of mixed goods uneasily, hoping that Dink had not gone over the allotted fifty dollars Ben had given him.

Dink was in the wagon, placing a crate of apples in a secure position. The young man was perspiring freely and must have been tired, but he greeted Ben Trout with a smile.

'Sure, show up now when I'm about done!' Dink gibed, standing to mop his face with his kerchief.

'How'd you do, money-wise?' Ben wanted to know.

'Forty-eight dollars and some change. The man's totaling the receipt for me right now.'

'Looks like enough food to feed an army through the winter,' Ben commented as Dink swung down from the wagon.

'You know how it is with food — always looks like a lot until you start in on it,' Dink said. 'And Beth's got more mouths to feed now.'

Ben didn't respond to that. He, himself, did not plan on being one of the extra mouths for long. He would deliver what they had agreed on to the RU, make sure that he was repaid for what he had personally spent and then be on his way to El Paso. Alone, the way it looked now.

Dink returned with the receipt from the storekeeper, slapped it in Ben's hand along with some change. In his hand Dink held a small bag.

'What's that?' Ben asked, nodding at the bag as he carefully folded the receipt and put it away with the others.

'This? Something the women didn't think of, but I did,' Dink said with some pride. 'Vegetable seeds. Do you like butternut squash?'

'I won't be here in the fall,' Ben said.

'I just asked. I've also got tomatoes, pole beans, cabbage, just about anything you can think of.'

'Trading in your spurs for a garden hoe, are you?' Ben said lightly.

'The earth is a bountiful provider,' Dink said, growing briefly philosophical. 'A handful of seeds can feed a family for months, years. What's the matter, Mr Benjamin, don't you like to eat?'

'I do, and that's what I intend to do now,' Ben said, swinging aboard the sorrel. He led the way toward Linda's Restaurant which he had already located on the main street, Dink following in the wagon with his dun horse tethered behind again.

'I suppose I'll have to lead the dun, or you'll lead my sorrel,' Ben told Dink as he tied up the wagon in front of the restaurant. 'We're taking along a tethered bull.'

'How big?' Dink asked. 'How old?'

'He doesn't have his size yet,' Ben told him. 'He's not yet three years old, but he's got a lot of spirit.'

'Well, I suppose between the two of us we can handle him for the four hours or so it'll take us to get him home.'

Home, he said, not 'to the RU'. Yes it was pretty obvious where Dink's head was, what he was hoping for.

They ate well if not sumptuously at Linda's Restaurant, and it was almost with shock that they emerged to find the sun still high in the sky. It seemed that they had already put in a full day's work. But they had only begun.

'Now we find some men?'

Ben nodded, 'Now we find some men to hire, but first we go back and talk to Sheriff Stout about the reward on Hiram Walsh. I haven't got enough money to carry on like this, and Beth Robinson won't have any at all to work with without that money.'

It turned out that it was not necessary to find the sheriff. Before Ben could swing into leather, the round, bustling form of Sheriff Charles Stout, sunlight glinting on his badge, could be seen approaching the restaurant.

'Are they serving those breaded pork chops with apple sauce today?' was what Stout asked Ben, at the same time handing him an official-looking manila envelope. 'I always did like those.'

'I saw them on the menu, but I didn't have them,' Ben said, opening the envelope to flip through the stack of bills it contained.

'You should have. I don't know what Linda does to them, but they're excellent. Goodbye, men; I doubt I'll be seeing you again.'

'I doubt it, too, Sheriff. Enjoy your lunch.' Ben tucked the envelope away in an inside pocket in his leather vest.

'Aren't you going to take out what you're owed?' Dink asked.

'I mean to sit down at the table with

Beth and do it together,' Benjamin Trout told his younger friend. 'That's a more respectable way to do business.'

'I can't see that it matters,' Dink said, unwrapping the reins from the brake handle, 'but seeing as you say it's so, Mr Benjamin, I'll keep that in mind for the future.'

Leaning forward on the bench seat, studying the town, Dink asked, 'Where now?'

'The nearest saloon will do,' Ben Trout said. Dink shrugged with his eyes and started the horses forward along the street.

Walking into the smoky, low-ceilinged saloon, Ben Trout knew what he was looking for: two broad-shouldered young men who had not been drinking enough to be in their cups, but had had a few to lift their spirits and make them bold enough to wish to try a new enterprise. They didn't have to be handsome, bright or especially law-abiding, just strong with young muscle and manageable for a few days.

While Dink waited outside with the wagonful of goods, Ben bought himself a mug of green beer and wandered about the room, dismissing the old and the frail-appearing, the sullen and the combative.

He thought he found his pair sitting at a corner table playing a desultory game of cards with an almost empty pitcher of beer on the table between them. Jim Hicks, although Ben had not yet learned his name, was a thick-chested, copper-haired man in his mid-twenties; his partner was Clarence 'Clare' Tillitson, who had the hands of a hardworking man and a likely grin. Ben approached them.

'You fellows cowhands?' Ben asked, perching on a nearby table.

'Have been,' Jim Hicks said, smiling pleasantly. 'At the present time, you might say we're fancy free.'

'How's your poke holding out?' Ben asked, seeing no sense in wasting time. The men could either be hired to work or they would decline and he could continue elsewhere with his search.

'You can see we're playing for matchsticks,' Clare Tillitson said, indicating the table stakes for their card game.

'Are you offering us a job?' Jim Hicks asked.

'I've got something that might appeal to you,' Ben said. 'It would only be for a few days, though.'

'What are you thinking of paying?' Clare Tillitson asked, looking at his cards, then at Ben's face again.

'Four dollars a day apiece,' Ben said. The wages were superior for that time and place, and the two men looked at each other questioningly.

'Did you say that this was cattle work?' Jim Hicks asked, sliding back from the table a little.

'Only about four hours of it,' Ben said with his own crooked smile. Clare Tillitson was perplexed. Ben told the younger man, 'The rest is pick-and-shovel work — I don't know if you boys would be willing to go at it.'

'Dangerous, is it?' Hicks asked with a squint. That was a lot of money for common labor. 'I mean, it's not down in a mine, is it?'

'No, nothing like that. It will take me a little time to explain it, men. I'll buy you a fresh pitcher of beer if you're willing to listen. Then we'll have to be trailing out while there's sunlight.'

'Planning on traveling far?' Hicks asked.

'Just those few hours. We should make it back to the RU by sunset. Let me get you that pitcher of beer.' As he leaned forward to rise, Hicks got a glimpse of the envelope in Ben's inside pocket and the sheaf of bills it held. Ben immediately secured the envelope that Sheriff Stout had given him for Hiram Walsh's capture, but Hicks had quick eyes. Right then he had quick, greedy eyes.

He asked Clare as Ben walked toward the bar, 'Who is that guy? It seems like I've seen him somewhere.'

'Sure you have. That's Benjamin Trout of the K/K,' Clare told his partner.

'What's he doing way out here, then?

And why did he say we were riding to the RU — wherever that is?'

'He must have got himself a new job he likes better.' Clare Tillitson shrugged, looking in Ben's direction.

'But he was foreman on the K/K . . . hold it a minute,' Hicks said in a low hiss, gripping his friend's forearm across the table. 'Now I remember hearing about the RU!'

'Well?' Clare prompted.

'Gold,' Hicks said, keeping his voice to a whisper. 'I heard some men saying that the RU was run by a widow woman and her daughter, and that they had a hidden gold mine out there.'

'Think it could be true?'

'Why else would the respectable foreman of a big ranch like the K/K leave? A widow lady with a gold mine could offer some inducements. Not only that,' Jim Hicks said, inching nearer, 'I got a glimpse of the wad of cash that Trout's carrying, and believe me it's fat.'

'When did you . . . how?'

'Just take my word for it,' Hicks said

as Trout started back toward the table. 'Ask yourself why the RU wants to hire pick-and-shovel men. Not to push cows. There's something going on out there, Clare, and I think if we go along with it, we're set for a big payday.'

6

The bull was still in a placid mood when it was led from the barn and into the bright sunlight to stand and blink. Hicks and Clare each had a rope around its neck, tugging from opposite sides, and they were trying now to position the animal behind the wagon to be tethered there.

Beside the wagon Ben sat loosely in the saddle while Dink stood beside him, watching the bull be tugged slowly forward.

'Shouldn't we give them a hand?' Dink asked.

'No,' Benjamin Trout said. 'You don't hire a man to do a job and then do it for him.'

'I guess not,' Dink said uncertainly. 'I haven't had much experience at being a boss.'

'You're about to get some,' Ben told

him. 'You're the boss now; I already told Hicks and Clare that.'

'Why me?' Dink asked with some uneasiness.

'Because you are the one who's going to stick around to see that they do their job. I won't be here, Dink. I'll probably spend the night at the RU, then I'm back on the trail to El Paso. I'm going to trade off with you and drive the wagon. You can lead this little drive of ours.'

Dink, looking vaguely discouraged, only nodded as the new-hires finished their job. The four heifers were then hied out of the pen by the man who had sold them to Ben, and Dink had to look to Ben for advice.

'Get them started ahead of us,' Ben advised. 'That'll keep the bull with his mind on what's ahead instead of trying to turn around to see what's behind him.'

Dink then led the way out, leading Ben's sorrel horse, the two cowboys and the heifers behind him. Ben followed in the wagon, leading the bull, which was still minding its manners. The first little stretch was four blocks through the center of town which surprised or startled no one along the way. Then it was out on to open country with Dink cutting trail for the new men to follow. Ben divided his time between watching the bull, studying the cowboys as they handled the docile heifers, and glancing at the western sky to judge how much light they had left to complete their journey.

He had hopes for a warm meal and a good night's sleep after settling the cattle and unloading the wagon. Then, come morning, he would leave the RU Crooked to the well-intentioned and wishful and proceed on his long journey west.

At one point along the way, the black bull suddenly became balky for no apparent reason and began to tug the wagon from side to side by its leads, but outside of that it gave Ben no problems en route.

With sundown casting a golden glow against the sky they came to the rise in the land which overlooked the long, dry valley below where the RU rested. Defiant little ranch that it was, there was something touching about it at this time of evening. Perhaps it was because it simply endured, still held the hopes of Beth and Minna, fragile though those might be.

Dink started the small group down the road to the RU. Ben leaned on the brake pole to slow the heavy wagon. Reaching the flat, they lined out directly toward the yard. There would be time to water the stock later. Dink obviously wanted to show the women how they had succeeded in their mission.

Home were the saviors of the ranch.

On the porch, drawn by the sounds of the cattle approaching, the whistles and shouts of the drovers, Beth and Minna stood close together watching the arrival. Ben drew up in front of the house as Dink let the cattle wander where they would. He was guessing, rightly, that they would find the creek, drink their fill and stay near it, having no idea where else to go.

'Did you get a look at the cattle?' Ben Trout called to Beth on the porch.

'Not much of one; I guess that will have to wait until morning. I see that, though!' she said, pointing at the big black bull tethered on behind. Minna moved nearer as if she would touch the bull.

'I wouldn't do that,' Ben said, swinging down. 'He's just play-acting. He's not really that calm.' Ben removed his hat, wiped his brow and placed one boot on the swaying step of the porch. 'Which brings this up, Beth: seeing that you're his owner now, do you want us to try to get him in the barn, stake him out, or just cut him free to roam?'

'What do you think is best?' she asked.

'I think we can just turn him loose. The cows are still here, and he'll find the water soon enough. Everything a healthy young bull could want.'

Ben didn't get the smile in return he was expecting from Beth Robinson. Maybe she just didn't have much of a sense of humor.

'What's his name?' Minna asked, her eyes bright even in the dim light of dusk.

'He hasn't one — that's one thing you can take care of.' Turning back to Beth, he said, 'How about getting a lantern out here and we can take the supplies in.'

'As soon as the bull is freed.'

'As soon as the bull is freed,' Ben agreed.

'I see you brought along two men to work on the bluff wash-out,' Beth said, lifting her chin toward the creek.

'Everything you asked for, and some extra,' Ben answered.

'Extra? What?' Beth enquired.

'Vegetable seeds,' Ben muttered before walking to the rear of the wagon to untie the bull.

It took less than half an hour, with everyone working, to get the supplies tucked away in the kitchen pantry. Beth stood back, looking at her cache with pride. They now had everything they needed to last them for months.

'Let's sit down and talk business,' Ben Trout suggested, going to the small kitchen table. He placed the envelope containing the reward money on the table and withdrew his stack of receipts from his own expenditures. 'Have you got a pencil?' he asked, and Beth went to a coffee mug on the counter which held a few miscellaneous items and removed the stub of a pencil from it.

She glanced once toward the kitchen door. Dink and Minna had retreated to the front room. The last time Ben had seen Hicks and Clare they were sitting on the front porch, having a smoke.

'This doesn't have to be done right now,' Beth said, seating herself opposite Ben.

'When is a better time?' Ben asked removing his hat, running his fingers through his dark hair. 'This is all a part of the same business; let's get it finished up and then you can go about whatever it is you want to do.' He paused for a moment, smiled at the handsome woman sitting there and added, 'It will make me feel better to have it finished.' They started with the large items and worked their way through them. 'I may have spent too much for the bull,' Ben apologized.

'Was there any other choice?' Beth asked.

'Not that I know of.'

'Well, then . . . we asked you to buy a bull and you did the best you could,' Beth answered. Her attitude seemed a little free and easy to Ben.

'Beth,' he said, 'you're going to have to be very careful with the remainder of your money.'

'I realize that,' she answered a little stiffly as if she had been insulted. Ben just looked at her for a moment longer, then nodded.

When the totaling had been completed and both pronounced themselves satisfied with the final tally, Ben returned his money to his scuffed wallet and Beth slowly gathered up what was left of the reward for Hiram Walsh, tucking it away in her apron pocket.

'Don't scowl, Mr Benjamin,' she said. 'I'm going to put it away in the strongbox in my room as soon as we get up from the table.'

'Was I scowling?' Ben asked. 'I'm sorry. I didn't mean for it to seem like I was nagging you. It's just that I was . . . ' He looked down at his big, weather-beaten hands and fell silent.

'What? Worried about us, Mr Benjamin?' Beth asked. She touched his hand lightly and there was a faint, warm smile on her lips. 'It's all right to say that. I know how it is; I've been worried about us for years.'

'Things will be better now,' Ben said uncomfortably. He was wriggling emotionally. He was afraid he would say something more to Beth, and his schedule did not allow for more conversation.

'Yes,' Beth said, placing her hands on her lap. 'That brings us to another point, doesn't it? These young men you brought out here — can they be trusted?'

'I don't know. Is there something bothering you about them?'

'Not really, except the way they have been looking at Minna.'

'The town was fresh out of young men who don't like to look at girls,' Ben said, again trying for a joke. Again it fell flat; Ben had about decided that humor was not his area.

'It's the way they look, Ben, do you understand? I saw them while we were unloading the wagon. They looked at her as if she were some saloon girl. I didn't care for it at all.'

'They should only be here for a couple of days, long enough to clean out the cave-in along the bluffs.' Ben paused, smiled and told her, 'Besides, Dink will be around to keep an eye on them.'

'Eddie Guest,' Beth said, reminding herself. To Ben she said, 'I'm trying to avoid calling him by his nickname. He can't like it much.'

'He never seemed to mind back on the K/K.'

'But that was among his fellow male workers, half of whom probably had their own nicknames like Red, Whitey, Tex and Smoky. It made him feel that he was accepted among equals. He can't want me to call him Dink . . . nor Minna.'

'I suppose not,' Ben admitted.

'How old is he, Ben?'

'Dink? I think he said that he was seventeen, going on eighteen. Why?'

'It's just that he seems little more than a boy next to those two hulking men you hired.'

'Maybe. But he was doing a man's work on the K/K,' Ben reminded her.

'Still . . . ' Beth said, looking down at the table now. It was obvious that she wanted to say something more. Finally with a sharp inhalation she lifted her eyes again to Trout and said, 'I'd feel a lot better about things, Ben, if you would stay around here just until those two are finished with their work.'

'I've got to be going on my way, Beth. You know that.'

'You said yourself that it would only take them a couple of days. Can't you wait that long?' She grew more emphatic. 'I'll pay you for it, Ben. Whatever wage you ask! Just for two days. Please . . . ? Please?'

* * *

Ben lay awake in the near silence of the desert night. Once he heard a nearby owl hoot and the howl of a far distant coyote. Beyond that there was not a sound to keep him awake. No one moved about the house. The two new hands had said they preferred to sleep outside, and it was a fine, warm night for it; besides, there was obviously no space for them in the small house. There was nothing to keep Ben Trout from sleeping; still he could not manage it.

Rolling over under his single blanket,

Ben found his mind continuing to turn about matters that should not have concerned him. Who were these two young hands that he had hired so hastily? Just men, no different from the dozens of unemployed, drifting cowhands that could be found in any Western town on any day. Beth seemed to have her suspicions of them, but that might have only been her motherly protectiveness.

All the same, Eddie Guest was in charge of them now; it was none of Ben's affair. Ben had not hired on to the RU, nor had he adopted Dink. He had his own thought-out plan summoning him back to the trail west. The women were struggling and would continue to struggle. Even with Ben's help they would have a hard time of it. That was the way things were in this country.

He had done all he could for them, all there was time to do. Let the two new-hires dig out the cave-in, let Dink manage the RU as best he could.

Benjamin Trout was on his way to Tucson to join the Wright brothers' freight company.

Rolling over again, he yawned and finally fell off to sleep.

* * *

Ben Trout was up with the first light he saw, which was that glinting uncertainly through a high slit window in his room. Dressing, he made his way to the kitchen where Beth bustled around the stove and Minna bustled around Dink, who looked well-satisfied with himself.

Clare Tillitson and Jim Hicks had eaten earlier, he was told, wanting to get a start on their digging while the desert was still cool.

'You laid the job out for them?' Ben asked Dink.

'I did, though anyone could see what the problem is and what has to be done.'

Ben frowned a little, realizing that he had been the last one up on that morning. It was a bad habit and one easily fallen into. Beth placed a cup of coffee on the table in front of him and surprisingly, almost casually, placed a hand on his shoulder. When he glanced up, he could see that she was smiling — tiredly, but she was smiling.

'The bull hasn't budged,' Dink told Ben. 'He's sniffing around the heifers like he's interested but doesn't know exactly what to do.'

'When it's their time, he'll know,' Ben muttered almost as if he were angry. He wasn't used to discussing such things in front of females. There was something else bothering him, and he knew it but did not want to admit it.

'Well,' Dink said, rising and dabbing at his lips with his napkin, 'I guess I'd better ride up to the gap and see how those two human dynamos are doing. There's some that only work hard when they're being watched.' He paused. 'I guess you'll be striking out before I get back, Ben. I just wanted to tell you thanks for everything.' He offered

Benjamin Trout his hand.

'Save that for a while,' Ben said with a scowl. 'Nobody around here, including the ranch manager, seems to be giving a thought to the RU's assets. I'm riding up to the eastern range to look for cattle and do a head count. If I find a few I can push toward the river without a lot of trouble, I'll bring them in.'

Dink murmured some words of thanks and Minna let out a few happy, girlish squeals. When the two youngsters had gone out of the room and left the house, Ben slammed down his empty coffee mug on the table and asked Beth Robinson in a growl:

'Are you happy now?'

'Why, Ben,' she answered, 'as long as you're happy, I'm happy.'

Then she went out the back door to do something in the yard and Benjamin Trout, still grumbling, went to saddle his sorrel horse and put in a day's work.

7

For most of the morning, Ben scoured the hills and brushy hollows, looking for strayed cattle. There were quite a few more RU branded steers than he would have imagined bunched in the small places where water seeped and grass greened the land. A gather could produce two or three dozen at a guess. And if they were driven to the flats below when the river returned to its normal course and volume, they along with the new stock might begin to thrive.

That prospect required many undertakings to bring to fruition. The cattle would have to be brought down out of the hills, of course, but first there would have to be a good source of water and graze provided. That meant, as Ben knew from long experience, the construction of feeder dams to spread the river flow out across the dry grasslands.

In his time he had done that many times, but usually with a full crew to help in the construction of the earthen dams.

Ben had seen at least two dozen cows among the wild beeves. That rogue of a black bull they had brought back to the RU should be able to make friends among them and repopulate the barren land, if he was all that Ben believed him to be.

There would be no more lashing two steers on behind the wagon and towing them to Hinkley's Ridge to sell for money to purchase a few necessities. Beth could afford to hire a crew at round-up time to drive the cattle to the best local market, whether that would be Hinkley's Ridge or Riverton. Assuming she didn't wish to spend the time on a long drive to one of the railheads.

Ben vowed to have a long talk with Dink that evening. Yes, the young man was inexperienced, but all of these operations should be within his capabilities.

Ben rode past a trio of sad-looking cows, angling upslope. The animals deserved better treatment than they had gotten since the river went nearly dry. There was a hot, dry wind gusting as Ben achieved the crest of the yellow hill. He paused, opened the front of his shirt to let the breeze dry his chest and looked down across the forlorn land.

The RU could have been something, he decided, with the proper management. Gerald Robinson had not been a cattleman, nor even a Westerner from what Beth had told them. Just another man with a dream of life in some wide open spaces. The cattle brand itself was a legacy to Robinson's own bitterness, though the land agent might not have deserved the blame he got. The land seemed to be as represented, but not necessarily as Robinson had envisioned it. Dreams and reality do not always mingle well.

Benjamin thought he would suggest to Beth Robinson that the new cattle and all future ones be branded differently. The ‘R’ for Robinson would stay, of course, and the ‘U’ if she was partial to it. But the prongs of the ‘U’ should be straightened out. Having the RU ranch should be a source of pride; the RU Crooked brand was a constant reminder of one man’s faded dreams.

Ben shook his head. What did any of that have to do with him? He would make his few suggestions to Beth and to Dink and then continue on his way. Between them they could figure out what they wanted to do with the exhausted ranch. He nudged the sorrel a little with his boot heels and moved farther along the ridge, intending to find a spot where he could look down along the collapsed bluff and make sure the pick-and-shovel men were making progress.

They were small in the distance when Ben finally could make out Jim Hicks and Clare. At the moment no picks were flashing silver in the air. The two were taking a break, apparently. Well, they were not prisoners, were not slaves. The sun was hot, the canyon airless. They could not toil constantly.

The two were young and very strong; Ben had no doubt they would finish the job. He only hoped that it could be done in the two days that Beth had asked him to remain and keep an eye on the working men. He turned his horse away as the men again lifted their tools and returned to their work.

* * *

'What are you thinking, Jim?' Clare Tillitson asked, resting on his pick. His shoulders bulged with muscle from years of such work. Neither man had on a shirt.

'Just what I thought before,' Hicks said, shoveling some of the loosened material away. 'They're planning on doing some serious mining up here. I've had some experience, as you know. Well, the way I see it is that they need an increased flow of water to go at it.'

'How's that?' Clare asked, interested.

'There's a bit of equipment called the long-tom, Clare. What it is is a kind of long sluice box for separating out the gold from the gravel, but it requires a lot of water to use. Four men usually operate one, and they can just work along it picking out gold nuggets like cherries.'

Jim Hicks wasn't finished with his specious reasoning yet. 'Look at this place. What do they need with more water — for four cows!' Hicks laughed. 'No, sir, there's gold here like everyone always said, and a lot of it if they're going to all this trouble. There's a fortune to be made here, and we are going to get our share. All we need,' Hicks said, stopping to mop his brow, 'is a little help.'

It was sundown of the following day, as Ben and Beth Robinson sat on the front porch watching the colors of the evening sky, when Dink rode his dun horse toward them, his teeth flashing a happy smile.

'Here it comes. You have to come and

see it!' His horse moved in a tight circle as he called to the two people on the porch.

'Come and see what?' Beth Robinson asked, standing from her porch chair.

'The river, ma'am! It's been freed of its bonds and it's flowing like a roaring tide.'

Ben stood, looked to the west, hands on his hips, and slowly smiled. Dink was right. Even from there he could see that the river was wider, moving more swiftly. The late sun shone on its face, silvering and staining it with the colors of sundown.

'Well, I guess we owe those two pick-and-shovel men our thanks. They seem to have done their job,' Beth said.

'And caused no harm,' Ben added. It made him feel better about hiring Hicks and Clare. They had bothered no one and gone about their work in an apparently praiseworthy fashion.

'And caused no harm,' Beth agreed, feeling a little foolish about her earlier doubts. 'I think they ought to be given a bonus, Ben,' she said.

'No,' Ben Trout said. 'That's money you don't have. They were hired to do a job, and they did it. They were paid well enough.'

'All right, boss. I suppose you're right,' Beth said with just a touch of sarcasm.

Minna had come out of the house, and from horseback Dink repeated his news, and his request that they all come and witness the rapidly flowing river. Minna rushed eagerly to Dink and was swung up beside him on his dun horse. Together the two started toward the river bottom.

'Aren't we going, Ben?' Beth asked.

'I've seen rivers run before,' Ben said, not sure why his mood had turned sour.

'So have I,' Beth said from out of the shadows. The lantern inside the house caught her profile and framed it appealingly. 'But I haven't seen this one running full for a very long time. It could mean new life for the land, new life for us, Ben. A chance to again try to make something of the RU.'

She was right, of course, and the way she said that made Ben feel ashamed of his manner. The river, restored to its old course and flow, held the promise of revival for the cattle, for those who occupied the land. As Dink had wanted them to rush that way and see what was happening, Beth wished to share her joy in a successfully completed, life-bringing project.

And here was Benjamin Trout grumping around.

'We'd better have our look, I suppose,' Ben said, 'before Dink bursts.'

She took his hand gently in hers which somehow did not surprise Ben and they went from the porch to view the new marvel. 'I know,' Beth told him as they walked across the dry grass, past the cattle, 'that you have been trying to tell me that I need to be more practical about things if I'm going to make a go of it.'

'I just . . . ' Ben began, but she held up a hand.

'You have been trying to get me to watch my money, and I appreciate it. I do need reminders to keep a better watch on my affairs.' She took in a deep breath, throwing her head back. 'Mr Gerald Robinson was a fine man, Ben. But he was what you might call a dreamer, giving little thought to tomorrow. I never really learned to be practical, though with a daughter and a ranch to run, you'd think that I would have.'

Ben gave her no answer. He was aware that Beth was still looking up at him. There was a question in those eyes, but he could not answer it now.

Ahead, the two young people stood near the bank of the rapidly flowing creek. Minna performed an impromptu jig, holding her skirts up while Dink just stood watching the river flow, a wide grin on his face.

'They can feel the rush of new life,' Beth said quietly.

'They're young,' Ben said, puzzling Beth, and perhaps stilling her own enthusiasm.

They watched the river stretch its limbs and take over its lost territory, shining in the late light. It was a living thing that had nearly been strangled and found its way back to life. 'It's all thanks to you, Ben,' Beth said, squeezing his hand.

'I don't know how you figure that,' Ben answered. 'You knew what had to be done, and you would have gotten it done. I'm not the one who did the digging. I'm not the one who banged Hiram Walsh's skull with a frying pan.'

'No, but you were the one who knew how to put everything together to make it work. I can tell that you are used to managing things — that must have been what you did on the K/K Ranch, manage the business affairs.'

'Not exactly,' Ben muttered, not wishing to discuss the K/K. The wound he felt from being fired off the ranch had still not developed any scar tissue.

'Look at it!' Beth exclaimed, with a fresh burst of enthusiasm. 'Why, this week we should be able to start pushing the lost cattle down from the open range, out of the hills.'

'I'd give it a while longer to let the grass recover. You might need to haul in some hay otherwise. Whatever you and Dink decide I'm sure will be fine. You can afford some patience now.'

'Everyone but you, Ben,' Beth said. She had turned to face him. He looked over her shoulder at the river, which now was slowing its initial surging rush across the flats. Beth would not be stilled. 'Everyone but you should practice a little patience. Meantime you're continuing your mad dash across the far lands, not even knowing where you're going or what you will find when you get there.'

'It's what I've set my mind to, Beth.'

'And you're going to stick to it whether it's for the best or not.'

'I'm going to stick to it,' he said, looking into those dark eyes of hers. He might have said more, but just then two muddy, soaked sandhogs appeared out of the darkness. They had their tools in their hands; Jim Hicks had his arm thrown around Clare's shoulder. Both men were smiling.

'It busted loose faster than we expected,' Hicks told them. 'We had to do some mighty scrambling to get out of the way.'

'It doesn't look like you quite made it,' Beth said, studying their filthy, sodden clothes.

'Good enough — we didn't get washed away,' Hicks said cheerfully.

'We can wash off in the river,' Clare said. 'There's plenty of water for that. Then we were thinking of striking out for Riverton.'

'Tonight?' Minna, who had been listening, asked.

'Yeah, tonight,' Jim Hicks said. 'It's still early and we mean to celebrate a little. As soon as we . . . '

'As soon as you get paid, yes of course,' Beth said. 'Whenever you boys are ready, just come up to the house — the back door to the kitchen — I'll have your money ready for you.'

'Thank you, ma'am,' Hicks said, nodding.

'You're welcome, boys. We'll be thanking you for a long time. The river is flowing freely again because of you.'

'We just did what we were told,' Clare said.

'You two come back and see us again sometime,' Minna said. Her eyes were on Jim Hicks. Dink, Ben noticed, had lost his smile.

'Oh, we will, you can count on that,' Hicks said.

'We surely will,' Clare Tillitson echoed.

Then the two well-muscled men strolled off toward where they had left their gear and their horses.

'Let's get up to the house if we're going to have supper tonight,' Beth said, taking Minna's hand.

Dink still stood frowning, looking after Hicks and Clare, who were chatting, laughing, no doubt discussing how they were going to spend their pay that night.

Dink turned, grabbed up the reins to

his dun and started off toward the house beside Ben Trout.

'What was that all about?' Dink asked Ben, meaning the conversation that had just gone on between the women and the pick-and-shovel men.

'Just polite talk,' Ben said, without looking at Dink, 'or what passes for it.'

'I didn't like it. I didn't like the way Minna was talking to that man at all.'

'Just polite conversation,' Ben said again. 'Besides, I guess she can talk to anyone she likes. You don't have that kind of claim on her.'

'I don't have any kind of claim on her,' Dink said. 'I just didn't like it, that's all. Is that all right with you, Mr Benjamin?'

'She'll never even see the man again,' Ben said as they approached the front of the house.

'I just don't like the man, that's all,' Dink muttered, and Ben only nodded. At seventeen-almost-eighteen Dink was feeling jealousy and frustration. It couldn't be helped. Ben didn't admit it, but he was slightly troubled himself about the way the two had assured them that they would be back. It seemed that there had been the barest shadow of a threat in their words, but probably he was imagining it.

While Dink and Minna were cleaning up for dinner, Ben again seated himself at the kitchen table with Beth, waiting for Hicks and Clare to call for their pay. Beth had counted their money carefully and put it into two identical packets. To Ben she looked a little nervous.

'What's the matter, Beth?' he asked her.

'Nothing. Just me being silly again, but I'll be happier when those two have their pay and leave. I'll lock the door after they ride away. I never liked having them on the ranch, and I still don't.'

'You and Dink.'

'What?'

'Dink doesn't like having them here either,' Ben told her.

'Well, in his position I can understand that,' Beth said with a small smile. She could hardly be unaware of Dink's infatuation with Minna. 'But I'm supposed to be a grown woman.'

'You are that,' Ben said without thinking. He had been admiring the graceful curves of her body. Beth lifted her eyes, seemed ready to snap out something and then just turned silently pink. They talked aimlessly of a few things then — Ben did bring up the subject of the RU brand which he felt diminished the ranch.

Ten minutes later Clare and Jim Hicks showed up at the back door and were given their pay. 'Well, that's that,' Beth said, turning back into the room. 'They've done their job and gone. It's all over. We've seen it through — that part of it.'

'Let's hope so,' Ben said, rising from the table. Beth looked up at him with some puzzlement.

'What do you mean, Ben?'

'Nothing.' He shrugged. 'Nothing at all. I suppose that some of your attitude and Dink's have rubbed off on me. I find that I don't trust those two either now.'

'But they're gone now, Ben. They won't be back. Why would they come out here again?'

'I don't know,' Ben said, although he had the barest glimmering of an idea why they might. 'All the same, maybe I'd better stay around a couple of more days to make sure they don't.'

Beth only nodded. Was Ben making some kind of excuse to stay around the ranch? She could have told him that he needed none. She sensed that he would not appreciate any comment she could make at that time, and remained silent as he went off to clean up for supper.

When he was gone, Beth got up again and quite deliberately locked the back door.

8

'You're crazy,' Cyrus Sullivan said, taking in both Jim Hicks and Clare Tillitson with his scathing glare. 'Do you know that? Both of you — you're crazy as loons.'

'Cyrus,' Jim Hicks said, leaning his arms on the poker table where they had gathered, 'we came to you because you're known as a man of vision. If you can't see the possibilities of this deal, maybe we should be talking to someone else.'

'Maybe you should,' Cyrus Sullivan, a hulking man with a drooping, grey-streaked red mustache told them. 'It sounds like a pipe dream to me,' he said, although avariciousness kept him from totally closing his mind to the proposition that Hicks and Clare had brought to him. Sullivan had taken a flyer on more than a few wild schemes.

Some of them had made him very wealthy. Others had left him with pennies in his pockets and sawdust in his mouth. The mention of gold had perked his ears as it always did, but how was he to trust the credibility of these two young roughnecks?

'Clare spoke up. 'We were out there only today finishing the run for long-tom mining,' he told Sullivan confidently.

'Yes,' Cyrus said, stretching and drawling out the word, 'and did either of you see any color?'

'No,' Hicks said with deliberate nonchalance, 'they wouldn't put us anywhere near the actual strike.'

'But you know those women have gold,' Clare put in, drinking from his beer mug. 'I mean, everyone from here to Hinkley's Ridge knows that those women do all their shopping with gold dust.'

'Yes, I've heard that,' Sullivan said, sipping from his own beer mug. 'But that doesn't mean much. You don't see a big house on that property, do you, or those women wearing finery and jewels?'

'They've just now decided, or had it suggested to them, that they open up their mining operation,' Hicks said, leaning forward across the table, careful to keep his voice down.

'By these new-hires they have on the ranch?' Sullivan asked, still meditating on the pluses and minuses of this idea.

'Sure, and where did they get the money to hire them? Or, where did they come up with a convincing idea for them to join forces?'

'There's new money going that way,' Clare Tillitson told Sullivan. 'A few days ago we drove some young cattle out that way, including Eric Finkle's bull.'

'And I saw the new honcho's wallet when he hired us — it was stuffed full of greenbacks, Mr Sullivan. Hundreds of dollars. Where'd he get it?'

Sullivan had heard another story about that money and where it might have come from, but it seemed totally ridiculous. The lady had supposedly hit a noted outlaw on the head with an iron skillet and claimed the bounty. Would a man like Hiram Walsh ever have let himself get that careless? It seemed very doubtful. The tale was circulating because it made a good story, that was all.

'These new-hires on the RU. What do we know about them?' Cyrus Sullivan asked, growing serious.

'One of them is a rangy old prairie wolf named Benjamin Trout. He used to ramrod the K/K. The question is, why did he quit? The other one is only a scrawny pup called Eddie. I had the idea he worked with Trout on the K/K Ranch.'

'Trout, huh?' Sullivan said. 'I've heard of him — he's supposed to be a tough man.'

'But he's pulling out,' Clarence Tillitson told the big man. 'He told us both that, didn't he, Jim? Said that he was only staying at the RU until the river was opened up. Maybe he's got some other deal working, I wouldn't know, but he said he was definitely leaving.'

Jim Hicks was nodding his head in eager agreement. 'That's what he told us, Mr Sullivan. So you see, that only leaves the two women and the sprout, this Eddie, out there to watch over the gold.'

'I see,' Sullivan said, pondering deeply. 'And your idea is that we just move in and take over the ranch and the gold strike for ourselves.' Sullivan was figuring risks and cost against possible profit. How much was there to lose, really, even if the report was utterly false?

But there could be much to be gained. Finishing his beer, he set it down on the table top and thought for a few minutes longer.

'How much would it take, Mr Hicks, for your plan to succeed?'

'Very little. Some lumber and screen material when we get to the point where we are ready to mine.' Hicks leaned forward again, hands cupped around his mug. 'For now all we require is two, maybe three, extra men who know how to use their guns and aren't shy about doing so.'

* * *

When Ben Trout made his way out on to the swayed front porch of the RU ranch house, coffee mug in his hand, Dink had already been long awake and out working. As Ben watched, the young cowhand hied three of the outlander cattle in to be nearer the free-flowing river. Weary, grinning, Dink rode his little dun toward the porch.

'That's three of 'em, Mr Benjamin!' he said with happy pride.

'It can't all be done in a matter of a few days,' Ben Trout said, chilling Dink's eagerness a little. 'The grass is going to need time to come back.'

'Mrs Robinson and I discussed it. I — we — decided that it was better to gather as many cattle as we can now and keep them bunched along the river, even if it meant having to haul in hay from Riverton for forage.'

Ben shrugged. That plan would mean buying an awful lot of hay over the course of a few months, and the cattle would still pick at the sprouts of new green grass, slowing its return. But it was not Ben's business. Beth owned this ranch and Dink was the property manager. Let them do as they wished. Trout knew that they were wasting money when a little patience would settle the situation.

He had spent too many years running the K/K Ranch and having his word taken as gospel, Trout decided. It was not his part to speak up now, as convinced as he was that these people were rushing ahead recklessly.

Hell, he considered, maybe they were right, and Trout's own ways were old ways.

It didn't matter; he was riding out and leaving them to their own conclusions, their own mistakes. He had nothing left to offer the RU.

'Where's the boss lady?' Dink asked with his horse performing its familiar walking-in-circles display of impatience. *Where was Beth?* Ben did not know.

'Abed, I suppose,' he answered. Both men glanced at the eastern sky, knowing it was late for Beth to be lazing about. That was not her custom.

'I'll get back to work,' Dink said, 'I spotted two more long-haired hideouts back along Snake Canyon.'

Snake Canyon? So the local hills and draws were starting to imprint names on Dink's mental geography. The kid was determined to be local, and he would be in no time at this rate.

Half-shrugging, half-sighing, Benjamin Trout went back into the house. He called out twice to Beth but got no response. Maybe that was for the best. He meant to offer his 'resignation' today. He could do no more here; nothing that Dink couldn't accomplish.

He wandered to his room, pulled his bed-roll from under his bunk and retrieved his kitbag from the shelf in the small closet. To reassure himself he opened his wallet and thumbed through the bills there. Pocketing that, he gathered his shaving gear from beside the washbasin. It was then that he heard the faint murmuring, almost like a child complaining in its sleep. Pausing, he lifted his head toward the sound. It came again, as faintly as before. Puzzled, he started in that direction.

Four steps down the short, dark hall, he could see that Beth's door stood ajar. A little light filtered through the crack. When the mewling sound came again, he could tell that it came from within.

Ben tapped on the door frame and entered. Beth lay in her bed, her dark hair disarranged so that part of it fell across her pale face as if it had trickled there. She was propped up on two pillows, wearing a sort of pale-blue chemise or bed gown — Ben had never learned the proper terminology for ladies' wear. It had no sleeves and her smooth arms looked pale and thin just then.

'Are you all right?' Ben asked foolishly, as people do at such times.

'I will be,' Beth answered with a short-lived smile. 'I'm tired, that's all. There's been a lot of stress around here, going back to our excursion to Hinkley's Ridge. At the time selling those two steers was the only thing that stood between us and starvation.'

Ben nodded his understanding. 'Do you want me to call Minna for you?'

'No. There's nothing she can do. Why ruin her day? She's out there chatting and laughing with Eddie. I'm glad that young man came over here. Minna's never had any friends, male or female, her own age to be with. Just sit and talk to me awhile, will you, Ben?'

'Sure,' he said. Looking around, he noticed there wasn't a chair in the room. Beth patted the bed near her head. She wiped back a few errant strands of hair and again tried a smile.

Ben removed his hat and sat near her. Beth made an effort to sit up straighter, failed and tilted over, her head coming to rest on Benjamin Trout's chest. Without conscious thought he looped his arms around her and held her upright against him. He was now aware of the soap and water, powder and perfume scent of the woman and it troubled him not a little.

Beth only sat with her back against him, saying nothing for a long time. He could feel the pulse in her body; having her there like that, holding her, was distantly comforting to him — and not so distantly a little disturbing.

The door to the bedroom swung open and standing in the doorway were Minna, in her riding togs, and a hatless Dink. Both were a little stunned to see Ben Trout sitting on the woman's bed holding Beth in her nightclothes.

'We were just wondering where . . . ' Dink began, but Ben Trout's growl cut him off.

'Get out of here!' he yelled, partly out of embarrassment.

Minna's face clouded. It seemed as if she were ready to cry. Dink looked a little shaken too. He took Minna's arm and tugged her away.

Beth was silent for a moment, then burst out laughing. 'Aren't you masterful?'

'It was an unexpected interruption at the wrong moment,' Ben said, feeling slightly foolish.

'That's all right. I'll talk to Minna later.'

Ben Trout felt suddenly that it was time to ride. Untangling himself gently, he got to his feet.

'I've gotten too used to you, Ben,' Beth told him as he reached for his hat. 'Too used to having you around in too short a time.'

There was no answer to that and so Ben said nothing. He stood in the middle of the room, just watching Beth, who now had her eyes closed. He knew pretty much what she was going to say next, and found that it did not bother him when she did.

'I shouldn't dare to ask you this, Ben . . . but is there any way you could see your way to staying around here for a little while longer — just until I'm feeling better and back on my feet again?'

'I wouldn't leave you while you're in bed and feeling poorly,' Ben said, and he felt an odd sense of relief as he said it.

'Thank you,' she answered in a faint murmur. 'Thank you, Mr Benjamin.'

There was a tap at the door and Ben turned angrily that way to find Dink again standing there. 'I thought . . . ' Ben said.

'I'm sorry, Mr Benjamin, Mrs Robinson, but this is something else. There's a man in the yard who's drifted in. He says he's looking for work.'

'Why didn't you just tell him that we've got no money to pay anybody any wages?' Ben asked.

'I didn't think it was my place to do that. The RU isn't my ranch.'

'No,' Ben said.

'I thought I should at least ask the boss,' he said, nodding at Beth, who had her blankets pulled up to her chin now.

'I'll go out and see him,' Ben said. 'What do you want me to tell him, Beth?'

'Whatever you think is right, Mr Benjamin,' Beth said. Was she smiling behind her blanket? 'We can afford a man for a few days. If you men plan to start gathering some of our stray cattle or building feeder dams, we could use some help. The man may even be willing to work for room and board. Maybe you can work out some kind of deal. You must use your own judgment, Mr Benjamin.'

Dink was looking from one of them to the other, wondering. Ben positioned his hat, and without smiling or looking at either of them again, he went out.

The man sitting in the shade on the porch, holding the reins to his old gray horse, was of a type usually seen sitting in saloons cadging drinks. He wore a reddish, narrow-brimmed hat with the crown pushed up to form a sort of uneven cone, run-down boots and a blue shirt torn out at one elbow. His jeans were badly sun-faded and Ben would have bet they were nearly out at the seat. He had the narrow, bony face of a New Englander and hopeful, watery-blue eyes.

'How do you do?' the scrawny man said, rising. Ben accepted his proffered hand, which was horny, gripping his firmly. 'My name is Robin Stoker. I've been dragging the line forever, looking for a place where I could find work. The young man, he said he didn't know if you were hiring or not.'

'What can you do, Mr Stoker?'

'I can work cattle or do about anything else you need done,' the man said, his eyes growing hopeful.

'Ever built a spreader dam?' Ben asked.

'Sure I have. Is that what you're planning on doing?'

'I was just asking,' Ben told him. 'Tell me this, what brought you out to the RU looking for a job?'

'It's just that I need work so bad.

Then there was these two young men in town who were saying they had worked out here for a few days and been treated right.'

Hicks and Tillitson. Ben told Robin Stoker, 'Here's the thing, Mr Stoker: we're pretty cash-poor just now, and I don't know if we can afford to take on a full-time hand.'

'Oh, no,' Stoker said unhappily. He almost pleaded as he said, 'I'll accept part-time wages, anything. Here's my situation, mister: I've got my wife, Cora, on her way out here from Fort Worth, and I've just got to have some kind of cash in my pockets to take care of her until I can find a real position. I'll do anything at all.' The man's eyes were begging. Ben felt sorry for him, but didn't know what they could do to help Stoker. He took a deep breath. 'Let me talk to the owner again.'

Ben went back into the house. He felt like he always had felt back on the K/K when they had had to turn away a man who was only looking for honest work.

Stoker did not look particularly strong, but he was eager for a chance, that was certain.

In Beth's room he found both Minna and Dink again. They had dragged in a couple of chairs from somewhere and sat looking up at Ben.

'Well?' Beth asked from under her bedclothes. 'What did you tell the man?'

'Nothing yet,' Ben said. 'I don't know what I'm supposed to do.' He looked at Dink and then back at Beth. 'The man says that the ranch manager didn't know what to say. And the owner doesn't know what to tell him. Who exactly is in charge of this ranch?'

'Why, Mr Benjamin,' Beth said in a small voice, 'I thought that was pretty obvious to everyone. It's you who are in charge of the RU, of course.'

9

His mood tangled, Ben Trout went back outside to deal with the stranger. It had seemed for a moment inside that all three of them were smiling as he went out of Beth's room. Was this what Beth Robinson had been angling for from the beginning, he wondered, or was it all just chance? He didn't want to attribute false conceptions which might have been all in his mind to Beth, but it did give him pause to wonder. Again.

With Beth's agreement he had come up with a plan the desperate Robin Stoker might be willing to accept. He put it to the man now.

'We just can't afford to hire a man full-time just now,' Ben told him, 'but here's what we're willing to do: room and board and half-pay, plus something we do have plenty of. You say your wife is coming out here without money and no place to stay. The owner of the ranch is willing to deed you a quarter of an acre of land anywhere you like on the property. Even at half-pay you should be able to earn enough to purchase building supplies and get started putting up some sort of shelter on the land.'

'Why, mister, that is generous of you,' Robin said, affected by the offer.

'It won't make you a rich man,' Ben said, 'but it should solve your basic problems for the time being. The boss-lady also said that if Cora should arrive before you've made progress on a place to live, she'll be welcome to stay in the big house for a while.'

Robin's dolorous face had brightened. He thanked Ben at least three more times and asked that his thanks be passed on to Beth. 'Mr Benjamin,' the narrow man said with what seemed to be deep sincerity, 'you'll never get less than my best effort and a full day's work, I promise you that. Yes, sir, the ranch has my gratitude. From now on I ride for the RU brand, and proudly.'

Jim Hicks was meeting again with the money man, Cyrus Sullivan. Clare had gotten himself too drunk the night before to attend.

'Is your friend, Clarence, always this unreliable?' Sullivan demanded.

'No, this is rare. We put in a few hard days out on the RU, Mr Sullivan. When it comes time, Clare will be there to be counted on.'

'What is it that prompted you to call me over here, Hicks? You know that I don't think it is a good idea for us to be seen together this much.'

'There have been a few developments,' Jim Hicks said, looking up as two cowboys pushed through the saloon door, letting a spray of afternoon sunlight into the room. 'So I was wondering if you had any luck getting a crew together yet.'

'I can get a crew together at any time, day or night, don't worry about that,' Sullivan told him. He leaned forward. 'What about these developments you're talking about? What exactly do you mean?'

'For one thing, Benjamin Trout is still on the RU. I was out looking the place over this morning, watching to see what was up.'

'You told me that Trout was riding out,' Sullivan said, unhappy with the news.

'That's what he told us. Maybe he changed his mind.'

'Or maybe he was lying to you,' Sullivan suggested.

'That could be, I suppose.'

'There's something else you have to tell me?'

'Yes, sir. While I was watching the RU house from the top of the ridge I saw another man arrive.'

'What man?' Sullivan demanded, now frowning.

'I can't tell you. I couldn't recognize him at that distance,' Hicks said. 'I saw the kid take him up to the house and after a while Ben Trout came out. Then Trout went back into the house. When he came back out he shook hands with the man. They talked for a minute more, then the new arrival tied up his horse and Trout led him along to the kitchen at the back of the house. Looked like they were going to feed him.'

Sullivan ignored this irrelevant deduction. He said, 'So it looks like they're bulking up their man-power.'

'That's the way it seemed to me, with Trout staying on and this new man arriving — and he might not be the last to trail in.'

'No.' Cyrus Sullivan was mulling it over. The front door to the saloon was nudged open again and the fleshy face of Sheriff Charlie Stout could be seen peering in, looking for any trouble-makers.

Sullivan rose hurriedly from his seat. He meant it when he had said that he did not want to be seen around Hicks or Clare Tillitson. Whatever he himself decided to do, Sullivan felt sure that the two younger men were going to get up to some devilry and he did not wish to be associated with it. He and Sheriff Stout had had some discussions in the past, most of them unpleasant. Cyrus Sullivan was comfortably well off, probably the wealthiest man in Riverton. At this time of life he did not wish to risk more trouble on what might have been a pipe dream.

On the other hand if there was a rich strike of gold on the RU and it could be taken over as easily as Hicks believed, Sullivan was not about to pass it up.

'It seems to me,' Hicks, who had now also risen, said, 'that the best thing for us to do is make our play as soon as possible. We don't know what Ben Trout has in mind. We can't have him gathering a crew and fortifying the place.'

'No,' was all Sullivan said, still glancing toward the door where the sheriff had been.

'I mean — it could be that Trout has it in mind to send for some of his old friends from the K/K. It wouldn't take them that long to ride to the RU.'

'No,' Sullivan said. He hated to admit it but Jim Hicks was probably right. If they were going to make their move it was better to do it sooner rather than later when something might change to tilt matters in the RU's favor.

There was always Aaron McCluskey, Sullivan was thinking as he stepped outside into the harsh sunlight. McCluskey was hardly Sullivan's favorite person to work with, but he and his crew did fit Hicks's description of the type of men they needed: men who knew guns and were not shy about using them.

Aaron McCluskey was hardly the shy type.

The only wonder was that the sly man from Utah hadn't been hanged yet or locked up in prison. Sheriff Stout would like to haul him in, certainly, but McCluskey was always careful to wear his best manners when he put his town suit on. Outside of town, as Sullivan had discovered after it was too late, the man was a butcher. But as long as he was paid . . . Yes, Sullivan thought as he started for home, McCluskey was his man. He would tell the bandit to have his men ready to ride.

* * *

There was no point in starting any major new projects with what was left of the day. Instead, Ben sent Dink and Robin out doing what he had already done: counting the stray cattle. Dink would be able to fill Robin in on the boundaries of the RU; at the same time Robin Stoker could be on the lookout for his promised home site. There really was no good spot for a house that Ben knew of away from the river, but perhaps Robin had privacy in mind.

'I can't believe that little man actually has a wife,' Minna said as she and Beth, who seemed to have recovered rapidly, darted about rearranging the kitchen while Ben watched.

'Or that he would bring her out with absolutely nothing prepared,' Beth said.

'Nothing is all he had,' Ben Trout reminded them.

Minna had stopped working to lean against the sink. 'What must she look like to have married a man like Robin

Stoker!' the pretty little blonde said.

Ben was growing tired of the unkind speculation. He said in a low voice, 'There's someone for everyone, Minna.'

'Yes,' Beth agreed instantly. 'That's what they say, Minna, and it seems to be true. There's someone for everybody.'

Beth was looking directly at Ben Trout when she said that, and reasonably or not it caused him to feel uncomfortable. He rose and left the kitchen.

Outside it was clear and very warm; a dry breeze stirred the cottonwood trees. In a sullen mood for no particular reason, Ben Trout walked out to take a look at what they had started to call 'the yard cows', meaning those which had not been driven in from the hills, but planted next to the river and left there to do as they liked. Prominent among them and of the most interest to Ben was the black bull. Minna called it 'Toro' which made sense but was a little unimaginative.

The bull, free to examine the cows closely now, was raising only contempt, or at best lethargy, from the heifers. The animals, placid though they were, could nevertheless display irritation with Toro, who was constantly snuffling at them. The truth was the cows were just too young; times would change for Toro.

None of the yard cows showed any wounds or signs of illness. They were spared the nicks and maladies common to open-range stock. Of the steers that Dink had overeagerly driven in, one had wounds on its shoulder of the type a cow got from barbed wire although there was no wire strung on the RU. Cactus, then, Ben guessed. The other two appeared to be in good shape; hopefully none carried parasites. They would have to be watched as would any other newcomers brought in from the hills. They could afford to have no parasite-borne illnesses on the ranch like the quick-spreading Texas fever. That would ruin the RU before it even had a chance to get started again.

Ben rose from examining a cow's hock, wiped his hands on his jeans and removed his hat. Taking a deep breath, he let his eyes scan the dark hills surrounding the basin. He paused.

Just for a moment he thought he had seen a man up there where none belonged, at the near end of the road to Riverton. And for just a moment he had thought he recognized the red-plaid shirt the man was wearing.

A shirt very like the one that Jim Hicks habitually wore.

Squinting into the glare of the sunlight, Ben found that he could no longer be sure that there was a man there. The shadows had combined to conceal him — if man it was. Perhaps he had been thinking of Hicks and his vow to return to the RU and provided his imaginary man with Hicks's shirt. The mind plays funny games.

If it were Hicks, Ben thought as he walked toward the barn and his sorrel horse, what did he want there, and why did he not just ride in? There was Minna, of course, and perhaps the man was waiting for a chance to see her when no one else would know. Hicks could be thinking like that. The human mind plays all sorts of games, sets up scenes which are never acted out except in imagination.

Ben did not think that his own theater of the mind was accurate. A girl of Minna's age could only cause trouble for a young buck like Hicks, and he undoubtedly knew that. He had been looking at Minna simply because she was there when he was.

He reached the barn and began to saddle his horse, still deep in thought. If it had been Hicks, what could he possibly want then? Four cows and an ornery young bull? Not likely. But what else had they?

A ridiculous-seeming notion that Ben had had before returned to him. It still made no sense to him, but it had sheltered in his chest and grown stronger over the past few days until it seemed almost logical.

Dropping the reins to his sorrel, Ben tramped back over to the house where he found Beth alone in the kitchen. Entering, he let the spring door slam behind him. She looked up at him from where she worked, pouring a bag of flour into a canister. Her face was wreathed in questions. The look on Ben Trout's face puzzled and alarmed her.

'What is it, Ben? What's the matter?'

'Mrs Robinson,' Ben said in a seldom-used gruff tone, 'there are some men who are after your gold mine.'

'Have you had too much sun, Ben? I have no gold mine, and you know it.'

'Yes, I know it,' he said, sitting on the corner of the kitchen table, 'but they don't.'

'This is . . . ' she stuttered and fumbled for a word, 'preposterous.'

'Yes,' he agreed.

'Absurd!'

'You are correct,' Ben told her. 'I've already had this conversation with myself.'

'Then why; then what . . . ?' Flustered, she spilled some flour on the floor.

'If enough people repeat a lie, it becomes the truth to some of them,' Ben said, shifting slightly. 'Look, there are people in Hinkley's Ridge who know that you have purchased supplies with gold dust. You even told me that there were rumors there about you having made a gold strike out here.'

'Yes, but . . . ' a frustrated Beth began. Ben Trout held up his hand.

'In Riverton you are known as the women with the gold mine. Sheriff Stout referred to you that way. The rumor must have gotten around all over that town. In fact when I hired those two men to work out here, one of them — Hicks — asked me if it involved dangerous work, like in a mine shaft.'

'Still!' Beth exclaimed. Now she was laughing.

'I know,' Ben said, 'I know — I told you I've already had this discussion with myself more than once.

'Don't you see,' he said, 'the next thing that happens is we go into Riverton to buy a ton of supplies and some cattle. If you are supposed to be so dirt poor, where did we get the money?'

'You know where, it was thanks to the bad man, Hiram Walsh.'

'Yes,' Ben said, holding up his hand for patience again, 'but then there is the river.'

'The river?'

'Unblocking it as we did. People won't believe that we did it for the benefit of the few scraggly cattle you are running on the RU. They may even believe that we purchased the new cows as a diversion, to keep people from thinking about what we really intended to use the increased water supply for.'

'Which would be?' Beth asked, no longer smiling.

'As you probably know there are certain types of gold mining which require large amounts of water. I think that's what Hicks and Clare thought we were working at. I think they jumped to a conclusion based on rumors and now the rumor has grown and spread.'

‘But it’s all so preposterous!’ Beth said again. ‘Ben, we must talk to these people and tell them that it’s all untrue.’

Ben rose and looked down at her, his face grim. ‘That’s the second thing we must do, you’re right.’

‘The second?’ Beth was again dismayed. ‘Then what is the first thing we must do? Tell me, Ben.’

‘We’d better fort up, because I have an idea we’re going to have a horde of gold-seekers overrunning the RU, and they’ll be chasing their dreams with wild eyes and guns, unwilling to listen to reason until it’s too late.’

10

'Can't we send for the county sheriff?' Minna asked as they all sat in a circle that evening in the living room discussing the situation.

'No,' Ben answered, 'we can't expect Sheriff Stout to ride out here on unfounded suspicion.'

'You're right,' Dink said. 'Whatever there is to take care of, we'll have to do it ourselves.'

'Yes, I think so,' Ben agreed 'Except for you, Robin,' he said, settling his gaze on the bulbous-nosed, scrawny man. 'You just arrived and you may have ridden into a hornets' nest, certainly not what you had in mind. You're free to leave and no one will think the less of you for it.'

'Not on your life!' Robin Stoker said stoutly. 'I didn't hire on with a promise that all would be sweetness and light. I ride for the brand. I'm an RU man now.'

'All right,' Ben Trout said with a smile. 'Here's what I think we should do. Dink, find a good lookout point in the hills behind the house. We'll have to keep a man up there day and night. And every man carry his Winchester at all times. It won't do to get caught unprepared.'

'What do we do in the meantime while we're waiting for the storm to break?' Robin asked. The older man now looked worried. Perhaps he was concerned about bringing his wife into a mess like this.

'What we can do. We meant to start on those spreader dams sooner or later. Now seems to be the time. Let's get this valley ready for a crop of spring grass.'

When the others were gone — Dink to search the hills for a good lookout spot, Minna to her room and Robin Stoker to collect shovels and picks for the work of the day — Beth asked Ben

Trout, 'Do you think we are really about to come under attack?'

'I just don't know,' Ben admitted. 'But it's better to be safe than sorry, don't you think? Men will do wild things for gold or the promise of it — I've seen it before.'

They stood in the doorway now, looking out at the dry yellow valley floor, holder of wishes, promises, rebirth and bloody war all at once. Beth must have been thinking of some of these things as well. She had been looking down, but now she raised her bright eyes to his.

'Do you think . . . ? Maybe someone should ride into Riverton and gauge the mood of the town. Even talk to Sheriff Stout and explain our concerns. I could do that.'

'No,' Ben said immediately and stiffly. 'We can't risk it. You could find yourself a hostage, and where would that leave us?'

Beth did not argue; she sighed. 'I didn't like the idea much myself, but I thought it was worth kicking around. Tell me, Ben, who are we really afraid of? The way you are thinking we only have the two men we hired to work out here, Hicks and Clare, who may have gotten the wrong idea of what we were up to.'

'And whoever they may have carried the tale to on some drunken night.'

'Even so — you're talking about a shiftless bunch of saloon rabble there. They'd be unwilling to leave their usual ways for something that required effort.'

'We don't know who they know in town. In Riverton, I only know three or four people,' Ben said. 'I have no idea what goes on there. Hicks and Clare may have other friends, men with more money, power and ambition.'

'They may,' Beth answered, 'but would men like that be willing to risk all on the word of two saddle tramps?'

'Gold rushes have started on less evidence,' Ben told her. 'The reason is clear — these men have no jobs or only poor jobs; gold holds a promise of wealth and ease — though the reality is usually far different.'

'I still say we have little to fear from two casual laborers,' Beth said as if trying to convince herself.

'What about Hiram Walsh?' Ben asked and Beth's voice stuttered to a stop.

'Why would you bring him up?' she asked.

'We never found out why Walsh was on the RU, what he wanted. He may have heard rumors of a gold strike back in Hinkley's Ridge and come out to have a look for himself. At the time, if you remember, we asked ourselves if the outlaw was riding alone. Maybe he was not, and by now the rest of his gang is wondering why he did not return.'

'Oh, dear,' Beth said with almost painful understanding. She turned and looked up at him again. Robin Stoker had pulled up in front of the house with the wagon and work tools. 'All of this is only speculation, is it not, Ben? We don't know if anyone is really interested in the poor RU.'

'No. No, we don't.'

She stared out the door in silence. 'Poor little patch of ground bringing so much sorrow to everyone.'

He did not want to let Beth worry so much that she might fall ill again, and so he told her that they were probably wrong, and anyway they had their defensive plans in place. Beth's face contained a trusting look and she stretched forward to lightly kiss Ben before walking away toward the kitchen. It was obvious that she didn't believe Ben's assurances.

Nor did Ben Trout trust them himself.

He scuffled across the porch to join an eager Robin Stoker on the wagon, only once allowing himself a look back at the house where a heavy-hearted woman on the brink of defeat waited.

It was nearly dusk when Benjamin Trout called a halt to the day's work on the spreader dam, which in his estimation was going well. The river water would be slowed and diverted to fan out and nourish the new grass when it came. The river still flowed strong and smoothly. In his mind Ben could still envision all of this paying off in the end: green grass, young cows, a healthy ranch.

If the destroyers did not come.

He rode off to find Dink, to relieve him. Robin had been assigned the late-night shift which the man did not object to. 'I'm the new-hire,' was his only comment about the situation. 'Got to expect that.'

Dink was in more of a complaining mood when Ben found him in a tight little rocky nook high on the near hills. 'About time. I come up here without so much as a sandwich.'

Ben avoided telling the kid that that was his own fault. Ben himself had two thick sandwiches, one of fried eggs, the other of ham, which Beth had made for him.

'You'll get your supper. Seen anyone around?'

'Not a soul.'

'Good, let's hope it stays that way.' It was going to be a long, endless night, Ben knew. There was a half-moon rising in an hour or so, but still the hours of staring into the empty canyons and across the long, dark land could produce night-ghosts, and Ben needed none of those.

'I don't think they'll come at night,' Ben said to Dink, but maybe he was only trying to reassure himself. 'But keep your rifle handy.'

'I mean to, Mr Benjamin, I surely mean to.'

It was a long, cold and dreary night for Ben Trout. He saw no one but a prowling coyote who seemed to be drawn by the scent of his sandwiches and was easily shooed away. Robin arrived promptly to relieve him, his face beaming, his own pockets stuffed with food. Ben told him about the scavenging coyote. There was nothing else to report, for which he was thankful.

* * *

At breakfast Robin and Trout discussed the spreader dams and a few other trivial matters. Dink had relieved Robin at his post just after dawn and was now standing watch on the hill.

'I made sure that Eddie took some food with him today,' Minna said with what seemed to be some pride.

Beth sat at the table with a cup of coffee. 'Ben,' she said, earnestly, 'as quiet as it has been, don't you think that there's a chance we both over-reacted to our fears?'

'Of course I do,' Ben said. 'In fact, I hope that's the case.'

'So do I,' Robin Stoker said, sipping coffee from his own cup. 'I'd really hate to have Cora land in the middle of this trouble.'

'Of course you would,' Beth said. 'Tell me, have you heard from your wife?'

'There ain't no way I could have,' Robin shrugged. 'I'll just have to wait and hope for her.'

'Have you found a home site yet?' Beth asked.

'If you don't mind, ma'am,' Robin told her, 'there's a little pocket valley not far north of where the river had to be widened out. There's three or four oak trees standing there, and good water of course. I thought it might do just fine.'

'You're welcome to it,' Beth said. 'It was part of our agreement.'

'When things settle down,' Ben offered, 'Dink and I can help you with the framing.'

'Assuming I can afford the lumber.'

'Maybe we can advance you a little on your wages,' Beth said, despite the look that she got from Ben telling her she still needed to watch her money. Actually neither believed it to be a great risk. A man who wants to build a house and settle in with his wife isn't going to fork his horse and ride off in the middle of the night.

Ben pushed his coffee cup away and the two men started off to work on the dam again. In the late afternoon Ben left Robin to it and took his sorrel to ride up to relieve Dink at lookout.

'How long are we going to keep this up?' Dink asked.

'The watching? Until we can feel fairly secure.'

'I don't care for it. It's like being under siege.'

'Isn't it? Well, Dink, I'm thinking that the longer it takes the better chance there is that cooler heads have prevailed and they've called off any plans they might have had.'

'Or maybe the cooler heads have just had the time by now to lay their plans more carefully,' Dink said dourly.

'That's why we're still here,' Ben said, unsaddling his horse. 'I don't like it any more than you do, but it only seems prudent.'

Dink swung aboard his dun pony with a grin. 'And to think, Mr Benjamin, you could have nearly been in Tucson by now.'

'It's an uncertain trail we all ride,' Ben said, settling into the shade, his eyes even now lifting to the far hills where he had previously seen the prowling man.

The sun was warm. Not a breath of air stirred in the rocky cleft they had chosen for their lookout point. The air smelled of sage and dust, nothing more. As the sun fell lower it was difficult not to grow sleepy with the warmth and inactivity. Ben tried playing mental games on himself. Most of these led him to Beth Robinson.

Ben did not fall asleep; he forced himself to remain as alert as he could, but by the time Robin Stoker arrived to relieve him, he had drifted into a dull lethargy and definitely needed to be relieved.

'Nothing, boss?' Robin asked.

'You didn't hear any shots, did you?' Ben asked, rising as the scrawny man swung down from his horse.

'No,' Robin answered with a smile.

'How's the dam coming?' Ben asked.

'I'd say we need another fifty feet or so. You tell me what you think tomorrow.'

Ben nodded and yawned, turning his horse's head toward the house. He was hungry and tired, and deserved to be both. Robin was in for another uncomfortable night, but Ben could do nothing about that. At least the little man had his wife to think about, that and the new house he was hoping to build. That was more than Ben had, he reflected as he rode along the narrow trail.

Robin would be safe in his hidden nook. As Ben had told Dink, it was unlikely that the raiders — if there were any — would come at night.

It took five more minutes along the trail to prove Ben Trout wrong.

11

Three gunshots racketed out in rapid succession from near the lookout post Ben had just quitted. His horse reared in fright at the report of the shots rising from out of the dark night and Ben tried to calm the sorrel and spin it on its heels at the same time as yet another near shot roared in the stillness of the darkening night.

Ben leaned low across the withers and flagged his horse with his hat uphill again, toward the thunder of the guns. At the same time he cursed himself. As the leader of these men, he should have been enough of a general to realize that they could not continue to use the exact same spot for their lookout post. It should have moved around, been varied enough to make any attacker uncertain of its location. Recriminations were of no use now. Ben continued his uphill charge, Colt in hand.

A man popped up from behind a screen of roadside sumac and Ben shot him dead without aiming, without thinking. The attacker stumbled back, slipped and fell on to his face to slide down the hill over the rough gravel.

From above, one final shot was fired, this one aimed at Ben Trout. Going to the side of his horse Ben fired back blindly but heard the grunt of a man as if he had been struck by flying lead. That was followed by hurried, stumbling footsteps as a man broke for the concealing brush.

Ben Trout burst into the cleft in the hill which served as their lookout post, surprised and pleased that Robin's old gray horse had stood its ground and not fled in the excitement. He would need the horse, because Robin Stoker had not been so fortunate.

The narrow man sat against the wall of the cave, rifle across his lap. He was holding his leg, which was bleeding freely. There was also blood showing on the shoulder of his shirt.

'Any more around, Robin?' Ben asked.

'I couldn't tell you, boss. All I seen was them two — they were enough to do the job on me.'

'Hold on. I'll get you back to the house. Can you sit on your horse?'

'I guess I'd better if I want to go along,' Robin said.

'I guess you'd better,' Ben said with an uneasy grin. There was no point in even trying any first aid with the house so near. Beth would have more available tools. With a deal of effort Ben managed to help Robin on to his horse's back and they started down the trail again, Ben's eyes shifting from point to shadowy point warily, Robin reeling in the saddle beside him.

The shots had alerted the house. Dink met them at the door in shirtsleeves, carrying his Winchester. He started to ask questions of Ben, but Trout told him: 'Give me a hand getting Robin into the house.'

Keeping a watch, Ben had still seen no other trespassers. No lurkers prowled in the shadows, no armed horsemen charged the house. The attack, if that was what it was, seemed strangely uncoordinated.

Together Ben and Dink got the badly wounded Robin Stoker from his horse's back and into the house where a frightened Minna and concerned Beth waited.

'Find some clean cloths, Minna,' Beth said, immediately taking charge of things. For the time being Robin was stretched out on the sofa and Beth began cutting away material from his pant leg and shirt with her scissors. Robin seemed to have already passed into unconsciousness. Minna had returned with strips of clean white muslin.

'Carbolic and hot water,' Beth ordered without looking up from her task.

'Is it bad?' Dink asked Ben.

'Pretty bad, I'd say.'

'What happened?' Dink asked in a lowered voice, turning toward the front door with Ben beside him.

'Two men jumped him up on the hill. I got one for sure; the other ran off into the brush, hit.'

'Did you recognize them?'

'I didn't have the time to try to identify them,' Ben told the kid.

Beth, who had paused briefly as she waited for Minna to return, had been listening. 'Was it our two, Ben?' she asked, meaning Jim Hicks and Clare Tillitson.

'I just don't know.' Ben had not even a recollection of how the two men had been built. The episode had just been a blurred flurry of night-shadowed action. 'It could have been, I suppose.'

'If it was them,' Beth continued, 'and you got both of them, that could mean our troubles are over, that it was just those two making trouble.'

'Maybe,' he said to appease Beth. He, himself, did not believe that the night's action had been the end to anything, but only the prelude for what was to come. Another minute proved him right.

'Riders coming in!' Dink said, closing

the front door. 'Three of them to the east, another two to the west.'

Ben Trout went to the window and knelt down, returning his attention to the world outside. He could now see the distant incoming riders in the hesitant moonlight. They had not fired yet, probably because the range was long. Beth was working on Robin's wounded leg, Minna assisting her. They were boxed in good and proper. The same thought had occurred to Dink.

'I can slip out there and take up a post in the shadows of the trees. They won't be able to see me if I go now and we douse the lantern.'

'I need that lantern light!' Beth complained.

'Then out the back door,' Dink said. 'We're all trapped here.'

'No,' Ben said, having made his decision. He stood and put his hand on Dink's shoulder. 'Stay here and keep your eye out the window.'

'Ben, where are you going to go?' Dink asked desolately.

'Why, out the back door,' Ben Trout answered with a grin. 'You had the right idea, Dink, but the wrong man.'

Beth's eyes looked up to follow him across the room as she continued to work on the pale Robin Stoker's wounds. She looked hopeful and fearful at once, as she had every right to be. Whatever either of them had thought of the night raid previously, it had not been a mad excursion by two deluded hired hands, but a frontal assault by an organized band. Who their leader was, how good a general he might prove to be, was the question. So far the assault had looked fairly uncoordinated, but who knew if the man had more tricks up his sleeve.

Fighting a last-ditch defensive battle with two women and a wounded man to consider was not Ben Trout's sort of war.

The sharp crack of a Winchester rifle sounded across the stillness of the night before Ben had reached his intended position of concealment among the cottonwood trees. The stab of flame he saw across the distances indicated that it was one of the incoming riders, perhaps jittery, overeager, who had fired first at great range. Ben had time to count to five, to wind his way toward the trees, before the snap of an answering shot from within the house indicated that Dink had been tracking the rider with his sights. From his position, Ben could see the bad man slap at his chest and then tumble from his saddle as his horse danced away.

The other outlaws would be more cautious.

Ben was braced beyond the large cottonwood tree he had reached, planning his next move. His targets, lost in the night, could not be easily tracked, whereas the night riders had the lighted house as their obvious target. The lantern within the house was dim, but still it was plain to see its outlines. With no light at all, those inside would not have been able to move around. Beth would have to abandon her attempt to save the badly injured Robin Stoker. That, he knew, she would not do.

At the sound of an approaching horse, Ben pressed his back more firmly against the trunk of the tree, holding his Winchester with the barrel pointed up. A bead of perspiration trickled into his eye, stinging it. Ben did not dare move even to wipe it away. The horse was nearly to him. Now he could see its shadow, dimly cast by the dying moon and the stars.

Something was wrong . . . and then he knew what it was. Ben hit the ground and rolled away as two shots were fired at him. The shadow he had seen had shown no horse's rider. The man had dismounted and sent his pony past Ben's hiding place to try to draw him out of shelter.

Now, positioned on one knee, Ben did see his target and he raised the rifle muzzle for a snap shot on the running man. The rifle cracked, bucked against his shoulder and his target crumpled up.

Looking around the yard, which seemed otherwise still, Ben moved in a crouch toward his victim. Lying on his back was a heavy man with eyes open to the night. He blinked at Ben Trout.

'Seen that trick before, have you?' the wounded raider asked. 'I learned it from the Indians. It'll generally fool a man.'

'Nothing works every time,' Ben said, crouching down to yank the man's revolver from his holster and hurl it away into the shadows.

'I wasn't planning on using that, mister,' the wounded man told Ben. 'I'm bad hit; I got no more fight left in me.'

'Who sent you out here?' Ben Trout wanted to know, not forgetting to keep his eyes on the darkness.

'Who?' the man said in a weak voice as if he was having trouble remembering or forming words.

'Who paid you for this job?' Ben demanded in a voice too loud for the situation.

'Paid me . . . ?' The man remained hesitant. Not out of loyalty, Ben thought, but only because he was working with a failing mind. 'It was Cyrus Sullivan who hired us,' the man said, barely moving his lips.

'Sullivan? I don't know him.'

'Then you don't know Riverton,' the bad man said feebly. 'Everyone knows who Mr Sullivan is . . . ' Then he said no more, could say no more. Ben got to his feet, waiting for a moment as he thought that here was another man who had died over nothing, the myth of a gold mine which did not exist.

He strode back toward the house, then ducked and scurried for its cover as two rifle shots sounded from the other end of the house and were answered by two timed shots from Dink's rifle within. Distantly another man's horse raced free across the valley. Had Dink gotten one of them? It seemed so. The outlaws' haphazard attack had been ill-conceived and ill-planned. Carried out by a group of men with no real heart for the job, possibly mostly drunk. It seemed a half-hearted affair, enough to earn them a night's pay when they returned . . .

To Riverton. *To Cyrus Sullivan*, who would now be convinced to give it up after the result of this raid, or possibly thinking that he had not sent enough men, enough of the experienced type he needed to pull off the attack, and send back a larger army. Ben had never met the man; he couldn't guess how Sullivan might react.

Ben called out softly before he entered the back door of the house. It was a good thing that he had. A shaky-looking Beth Robinson waited in the dark kitchen with that huge Sharps .50 buffalo gun of hers. Her face was ashen, her hands trembled a little.

'We heard a stray shot out there earlier. We didn't know . . . '

'I got lucky and took my man down,' Ben told her as she leaned up against him, rolling her head from side to side.

Beth looked up with damp eyes. 'But there will be other men, Ben. How many more? How long can we survive this? How long can it go on?'

'I'm going to put an end to it,' he said, holding both of her shoulders.

'How? How can you, Ben?'

'I'll tell you all in a little while. No one else got hit, did they?'

'No, everyone is all right for now. Except poor Robin, of course. He's in terrible shape, Ben. There was only so much we could do for him.'

They made their way to the front room where the dim lantern still glowed, Beth holding her rifle, Ben's arm around her. Dink glanced up from his position at the window.

'How many more are out there, boss?' he asked.

'It wasn't clear; I don't think many. Some of them may have taken to their heels already. Just keep a good watch and keep your rifle fully loaded.'

'Eddie got one of them a few minutes ago,' Minna said proudly. 'I saw him fall from his horse.' No one responded. Minna, young as she was, still did not seem to realize that men were actually dying out there. On the sofa Robin Stoker's lips fluttered audibly, but he remained blessedly asleep. Beth's bandaging was plain to see on his leg and shoulder.

'You said you were going to put an end to this, Ben,' Beth said, and Dink's eyes turned curiously toward them again. 'Tell us now — how do you intend to do that?'

'How I intend to try to do it,' Ben corrected. 'There's only one way to take care of a rattlesnake. They can bite even after you think they've been killed. You have to cut off the snake's head and bury it.'

'Yes, but . . . ' Beth said uncertainly, unsure of Ben's meaning.

'I know now where the snake's head is, who he is. Do you know a man named Cyrus Sullivan?' Both of the women wagged their heads negatively. 'Well, he seems to be some sort of big shot in Riverton, big enough to afford to launch this war against us. If he's that important, he shouldn't be too hard to find. I intend to go to Riverton and find the man — and cut off the snake's head.'

12

Riverton hadn't grown or prettified itself any since the last time Ben Trout had seen it. It was neither noisier nor quieter, cleaner nor dirtier than it had been. It simply clung to its tentative existence on the long desert flats as if its tilting buildings and sagging adobes had tenacious roots stretching into the desert soil.

Ben had decided that it was time to talk to Marshal Charles Stout. Now they had good evidence that the RU was under attack. What Stout could do about it was uncertain, but he had to be notified. First, Ben meant to find the one man who could do something about matters: Cyrus Sullivan. At the RU the dying man had indicated that Sullivan was well known in Riverton, perhaps chief among its citizens. He should not be hard to locate. Ben decided to avoid the saloons where some of the gathered men might be on Sullivan's payroll. He had not yet seen Hicks and Clare Tillitson on the ranch, though either or both of them could easily be among the dead men. At any rate he wished to avoid anyone who might recognize him. The general store was still open and Ben started the sorrel in that direction.

Inside the little man who was obviously ready to close down for the night looked up with a sort of expectant fear. Ben lifted a peaceful hand.

'I just dropped in to ask a question: where can I find Mr Cyrus Sullivan? We have a business deal pending.'

The mention of Sullivan seemed to draw the storekeeper's mouth into a tight, sour expression, but he answered readily, probably just to get Ben out of his store. The man walked forward, wiped a hand on his apron and pointed up the street to the west.

'Two-story white house about a quarter of a mile out. You can't miss it.'

'Do you think he'd be at home?' Ben asked. The storekeeper lost patience.

'Mister, I don't know and I couldn't care less where Cyrus Sullivan is.'

Ben touched his hat brim in a gesture of thanks and stepped out again. There was now a little bit of extra noise on the streets of Riverton. It seemed that the crowd had spilled out of one of the saloons on to the street. Ben didn't try to discover what had caused the ruckus — probably a fist fight — but rode past the knot of drinking men without showing his face clearly.

He had no time for their squabbles. He had only one objective on this night.

Stillness returned and the glare of the lanterns fell away as he proceeded up the road. Night birds sang in the oak trees along the way; the dying moon showed the way clearly.

The white house, when he came upon it, was truly impressive for this part of the country. Sitting on a low knoll, surrounded by live oak trees, it had colonnades in front supporting an upstairs portico flanked by two balconies. Behind one of these curved white balconies a lighted window showed, the lamplight shining through dark-green drapes. Sullivan's private office, his bedroom perhaps? There was no telling.

Were there guards around? That was of more concern to Ben just then. He saw no one, but he rode his horse as softly as he could into the shelter of the trees and sat there for long minutes, watching the shadows for any movement. Swinging down after a while, he began making his way toward the rear of the house, his senses still on high alert.

No one came forward or called out as he slipped through the shadows toward the back door of the house. It must be the kitchen, he thought, and his guess was reinforced as he passed a pile of slops intended for fertilizer or for hog food. Ben tensed as he stepped up on to the narrow back porch and reached for the doorknob, not knowing what alarm he might raise — a shout or, worse, a sudden blast of gunfire.

The knob turned beneath his hand. The door was open and he slipped into the kitchen, which still smelled of the evening meal. Which way? There was no point in hesitating now. He was committed to his course of action.

Ahead, then; he crossed the room beyond the kitchen and found himself at the foot of a curved stairway faintly illuminated by the burning lamp above. Ben had encountered no guards, meaning Cyrus Sullivan felt perfectly secure alone in his fortress. Sure — he had no reason to cringe and hide like two lonely, fearful women in the desert wilds.

Ben found the lighted upstairs room, and pistol in hand, he toed the door open. The room was all in white with gilt trimming and a high ceiling. The desk behind which Cyrus Sullivan sat was oak, topped with polished cedar. The eyes Sullivan lifted toward Ben were not startled, not angry, but only inquisitive.

'Who are you and what are you doing here?' he asked in an even voice.

'My name's Ben Trout. I've come from the RU to tell you to pull off your men before any more of them get killed.'

'My men?' Sullivan said innocently, spreading his hands.

'That's what I said. You can keep hiring them and having them waste their lives, or quit now. I'm telling you there's no gold on that property and never has been but for a little dust the women gathered in their spare time.'

'I am not going to argue with you,' Sullivan answered. 'I don't think I believe you, Mr Trout. I have my own sources . . . '

'You have the word of a couple of delusional roustabouts who wouldn't know a gold mine if they fell in one.'

Sullivan made that gesture with his spreading hands again and leaned back a little in his chair. 'Not that I'm admitting anything, Trout, but I haven't got the power to pull those men off the job. Those men you speak of aren't mine. They ride with a man named Aaron McCluskey; maybe you've heard of him.'

'I have,' Ben had to admit. 'He's that cheap little gunhand from down in the Brazos country.'

'Cheap little gunhand?' Sullivan laughed and sputtered. 'He'd take a man like you and spit you out again without even chewing.'

'Maybe. That remains to be seen. Meanwhile I'm telling you to get those men off the RU. We've killed a few, we'll quite likely kill a few more while they're trying to take over a mine that doesn't even exist.'

Sullivan's face turned thoughtful; too thoughtful, Ben decided. 'What I can do . . . ' Sullivan said, reaching for his desk drawer. That was as far as he got with his speech, as far as he meant to go.

From the desk drawer Sullivan pulled a Colt revolver. Ben flung himself to one side before the man had time to sight properly, and the bullet winged its way past him, shattering glass behind him. Braced against the wall, Ben Trout returned fire. His bullet tagged Sullivan just below the vest pocket on his left side, causing Sullivan to fold up, his pistol dropping from his hand to clatter against the floor.

Ben approached the dead man cautiously, his eyes shifting to the door behind him. Sullivan was dead, no doubt about it. Stupid of him. He had McCluskey, his hired gunny, out here ready to earn his wages by fighting it out with Ben or anyone else who got in their way, and yet he had chosen to try to do the job himself, quite clumsily.

'That wasn't smart,' Ben muttered to the dead Cyrus Sullivan. 'Let a man do the job he's hired to.'

Looking both ways, Ben briefly considered making his escape through the window, but he had still not seen another person since entering the house, and going out that way might draw more attention to him than simply walking back through the kitchen and exiting the way he had come in.

Slipping out into the night, which now had gone almost totally black with the moon disappearing beyond the western mountains and the stars covered with a veil of sheer clouds, Ben Trout returned hurriedly but warily to his horse, expecting to find men waiting for him lurking in every shadow, behind every tree.

He encountered none.

He rode back through the unconcerned town of Riverton. He saw no horses that had been hard-ridden in front of the saloons. Where, then, were the raiders who had fled the RU?

Ben Trout again considered trying to find the marshal and telling him what was going on, but balked at the idea of admitting that he had just killed Cyrus Sullivan. This was a small town and there could be some kind of connection between Sullivan and Marshal Stout for all he knew. He did not need to spend a night in jail, at any rate, but to make his way back to the RU as rapidly as possible and see what damage might have been done in his absence.

Turning north toward the ranch he was approached by three men and Ben breathed in deeply to slow his heart rate. These, judging by the direction they were travelling, had to be McCluskey men, raiders coming from the RU.

He decided to risk it — in the nearly coal-black night he drew his horse to the side of the road and waited for the approaching riders.

'Hold it,' he heard one of the men say and they all slowed their horses as they saw Ben on the side of the road, waiting. None of them could know him, and none could recognize him in the dark of night, but that gave him no sense of confidence.

'Who the hell are you?' their leader growled.

'Just a town-hire,' Trout said. 'I was riding out to find my friends when I got the news. Someone killed Cyrus Sullivan — there's no pay coming for this job.'

'What do you mean?' the outlaw demanded gruffly.

'Just what I said. There's nobody to pay the bills now. Any man fighting out there is fighting for nothing.'

'And dammit,' a second raider said, 'Darby got himself killed on this night.'

'Are you sure of this?' their leader demanded of Ben.

'You can ask anybody once you get back to town,' Ben assured the man. 'I was going out to call my friends off. They only hired on for the money.'

'Chet,' said the third man who had not spoken before, 'you know who's going to be on the boil.'

'Yeah, I know.'

'McCluskey don't like it when things don't go his way. He goes off his anchor and he shoots men, sometimes the wrong men. I've seen it before.'

'So have I,' the man called Chet said.

'So, what do we do?'

'First we go into town and ask around to see if this gent knows what he's talking about,' Chet said with a nod toward Ben Trout. 'If it's true about Sullivan being dead, I've an idea I wouldn't mind riding down to Nogales again just to look around.'

There was a little more conversation that Ben didn't understand, not being familiar with the places or people the raiders knew, but finally they trailed out toward Riverton with a few backward glances. Letting out his breath, Ben struck spurs to the sorrel and lined out toward the RU.

* * *

In the still of the night, with the stars now forming a silver blanket across the sky, Ben rode toward the ranch house door, calling out as he arrived. The door opened cautiously at first and then was flung wide as Beth rushed from the house, running toward Ben, who stepped down to greet her as she threw her arms around him and clung tightly to him. Over her shoulder Dink could be seen in the doorway, Minna, cowering slightly, beside him.

'Are they all gone?' Beth asked, looking around Ben. 'All of them?'

'I saw none riding in. I couldn't swear they're all gone. We'll have to continue to be watchful.'

'Of course, but things will be better now?'

'Things will be better,' Ben told her firmly, and they turned to walk back to the house.

* * *

In the morning Ben told them sketchily what had happened as they sat at the breakfast table. Robin Stoker was too ill to come to the table, but he had an appetite, and that was something.

'To work on the spreader dam this morning?' Dink asked.

'Yes. With our rifles near at hand,' Ben agreed.

Ben was pleased with what he saw of the dam. The catch basin was nearly full already. The little pond behind the dam was spilling out at either end, allowing the tamed river to irrigate the parched land and the new grass there.

'Looks like we may as well start the second dam, don't you think?' Dink asked. The young man stood beside Ben on the berm, holding his rifle with both hands. The rising breeze shifted his hair and tugged at his shirt. He looked somehow older, tougher on this morning.

Dink told him in a low voice, 'Today's my birthday, Ben. Eighteen at last.'

Ben Trout congratulated him. The two men shook hands and then got to work on the second dam they had planned. The day was long, very warm, the work hard, but they were beginning to see the results of their efforts. Once the black bull, Toro, wandered near to them, thinking unknown bull-thoughts, but they didn't bother to shoo him away. It would have been more trouble than it was worth, and eventually Toro decided that whatever the humans were up to was not worth his interest.

'How are you for a carpenter?' Dink asked as they rested on their tools.

'Me? I know up from down,' Ben answered with a self-disparaging laugh. 'Seriously, I can hang a joist, but I'm not sure I'd want to live in any house that I built.' He paused, squinting at Dink in the bright sunlight. 'Why do you ask?'

'It was Beth's thinking. Whenever you think it's safe to take the wagon into Riverton, she thought we should purchase some building materials, cement and lumber, and get started on Robin's house for him — seeing that he can't do it himself yet and his wife is on the way.

'Robin,' Dink continued, 'knows quite a bit about framing a house, as it turns out. He just can't swing a hammer himself yet. He could be kind of a supervisor while you and I did the rough work.'

'It'd be a break,' Ben shrugged. 'There's no hurry to finish this dam anyway as long as we've got the river managed.'

‘What are you going to tell Beth?’ Dink asked.

‘I’m going to tell her that she’s advancing her workers too much money, then do whatever the boss says.’

‘She says that you’re the boss, Ben.’

‘Well, then, I will politely ask her to inform the boss what she would prefer that he do.’

‘We’ll be framing the house,’ Dink said with a small grin.

‘We’ll be framing the house.’

13

Riverton was its same self two days later when Dink and Ben drove the wagon there to purchase building supplies with some more of Hiram Walsh's reward money, which Ben continually worried was getting eaten up at too rapid a pace. Five hundred dollars could dwindle away quickly if there was no income to replenish it.

They passed Marshal Charles Stout as they rolled toward the lumberyard, but the lawman did not hail them, although he did fix an uncertain look on Ben briefly. Halfway to the lumberyard, they passed the Overland Stage office. A small, uncertain woman stood in front of it, her trunks stacked beside her. She looked forlorn and lost.

'Dink! Slow this rig up. I think that woman is Cora Stoker.'

'I guess it could be. How many

women take a stagecoach to Riverton? I'll turn the wagon around, and we'll find out.'

Ben had guessed right. The woman turned out to be Cora Stoker. She was not what any of them had expected. Very small, almost tiny, she was nevertheless well proportioned and one of the most polite ladies Ben had met in his life. Soft-spoken, self-effacing, delicate in features and demeanor. She was a surprising contrast to the rugged Robin Stoker. And the little woman had braved the plains alone to come to her man! It was a lesson in the power of love.

They identified themselves as RU riders and offered her a ride to the ranch. It didn't seem the time to tell Cora that Robin was badly shot up. That could wait until they were back at the ranch. Ben saw no harm in telling her that they were in town to pick up some lumber for the house that Robin was building for them to live in; in fact it seemed to raise Cora's spirits a little. She waited silently on the wagon seat while Ben and Dink loaded lumber purchased according to Robin's order.

'It'll be enough to throw up something before Cora gets here,' Robin had said, 'so that she sees a promise for the future.'

Things hadn't worked out quite like that, but Cora seemed far from disappointed.

Following the rough ride across the flat, open country, Ben drew up the team on the crest of the hills surrounding the RU and Cora broke out in a wreath of smiles. Below, the river and the ponds behind the spreader dams glinted brightly in the sunlight. The yard cows and Toro stood along the river with the range cattle that had drifted in once the water was restored. By the house Minna could be seen tending to her new vegetable garden, which chore she took inordinate pride in. The new grass was only a dusting of color across the dry land, but you could see where it was coming up.

'It's lovely,' Cora said in a tone which no one would have ever used about the RU even a few weeks ago.

'We have hopes,' Dink said. Then he pointed out the spot along the upper river where the small oak grove stood and where the land had already been leveled for Cora and Robin's new house. She thought it was perfect.

Pulling up in front of the house Cora was greeted by Beth and Minna and then taken inside. Ben and Dink left the lumber for later and started unloading Cora's trunks. After a lot of kissing and cautious hugging with which Cora and the wounded Robin reintroduced themselves to each other, Beth whisked Cora away to the back of the house to wash and change. The woman had been long on the road.

Robin stood like a thunderstruck man in the middle of the room, leaning on his crutch.

'Boys,' he said to Dink and Ben, 'you plan for things, you wish for them, but somehow you never really believe they will come true. And when it does happen — Lord, it feels fine!'

They tried to briefly discuss the framing of the new house with Robin, but it was futile. He was still off on his own, walking among the stars. In the end they just withdrew and hauled the lumber up to the home site and unloaded it, figuring that tomorrow was soon enough to do any more.

* * *

He came in the middle of the afternoon on the following day.

Why he was afoot was anybody's guess, but he walked directly toward the house as Ben Trout, ready to return to work after a quick dinner, stepped down from the porch.

'Hold it right there!' the stranger with the crooked mouth shouted angrily. 'I'm looking for Ben Trout.'

'I'm Ben Trout,' Ben answered, squinting into the sun to try to make out the features of the man who stood, hands curled at his side, dark hat tugged low over his eyes.

'My name's Aaron McCluskey. Trout, you've caused me to lose out on a big payday. I had a contract with Cyrus Sullivan. You killed him. I've come for retribution.'

Looking at the man, knowing his reputation, Ben knew that he wasn't going to talk McCluskey out of it. He nodded and said, 'If you'll just let me get my gun . . . '

'You won't need one,' McCluskey said in a voice which had faded from bitterness to simple sarcasm. 'I'd beat you anyway — why waste all that time?'

'So that I'd have a chance,' Ben said uneasily. He didn't like the way things were shaping up. McCluskey was wearing a confident smile now. He wished that Dink had not stayed at the job site while Ben ate, but then again he was glad that Dink wouldn't be involved in this.

'I don't give chances,' McCluskey said. 'That's a stupid way of doing business. When I shoot, I plan to win.'

'You'd do murder, then?'

'Murder's just a word, Trout. Are you ready to take it?'

No, he was not ready, but apparently he was going to take it anyway. That was when the booming blast from the porch sounded and before McCluskey could draw his gun he was sent spinning around, arms windmilling before he flopped dead against the earth.

Ben turned to see Beth standing in front of the house, her big old Spencer .50-caliber buffalo gun leaking smoke from its muzzle.

'I had to . . . ' she said before she simply sat down on the porch, the rifle dropping free of her grip. 'He was going to . . . '

'Yes, he was,' Ben said, also sitting, putting his arm around her to brace and caress her. Dink could be seen coming on the run from the river. He looked at the two people sitting on the porch and then walked to where the dead body lay sprawled.

Dink joked nervously, 'Well, we were

wrong about that gun being enough to cut a man in half. He's still got a few threads holding him together.' Then Dink's false levity deserted him and he was forced to sit beside them on the porch. Minna had appeared from around the corner of the house in her gardening clothes, trowel in her hand. Her mouth opened to ask a question, but she looked at her mother's anguished face and simply went to sit down beside Dink to whisper to him.

Ben found that he was shaking only slightly less than Beth Robinson. 'That's as close as I ever want to come,' he said in a low voice. He managed to shake himself out of that dark mood and rise, calling to Dink, 'See that the tools are put away first, then go hitch the wagon and bring it around.'

'Are you going somewhere?' Beth asked.

'Have to,' Ben said, lifting his chin toward the dead man. 'We need to report this to Marshal Stout and deliver the body. There will be a reward coming, you know, Beth.'

'A reward?'

'Probably a quite large one. McCluskey was wanted in every county in West Texas.'

Beth nodded. There was no joy in her expression. 'What will Marshal Stout think of me?'

Dink had time for one more gibe before he left. 'He'll probably want to give you a badge and hire you on, the way you're cleaning up the outlaws in this part of the country.'

Beth couldn't even smile. Dink and Ben left the two women sitting on the porch close to one another for comfort and continued with disposing of Aaron McCluskey. Ben thought of McCluskey's words to him — 'Murder is just a word.' Now as he looked at the lifeless package of meat lying in the back of the wagon he couldn't help saying aloud: 'Dead is just a word. McCluskey.' Dink looked at him oddly, said nothing, and then started the wagon toward Riverton.

* * *

'How is the Stoker house coming along, Ben? I haven't had the chance to get up there.' Beth was walking with Ben Trout in the late afternoon coolness. They had chosen to make their way along the top of the recently completed second spreader dam. The pond water sparkled with rainbow colors.

'Robin told us to hold off. He said he'd rather finish the work himself. I don't know if that was pride or a comment on our carpentry. He'll have it finished in a week or ten days.'

'Did you know that Cora has already moved in there? She told me that was the only place of her own she has ever had, and she meant to stay. She told me that she could sweep up sawdust as fast as the men could make it, so that didn't concern her.'

'It seems that they're planning on staying around for a long time,' Ben said.

'It does . . . oh, look, Ben!' Beth said,

pointing. 'Can that be what I think it is?'

She was looking at a walnut-sized chunk of brightly glittering mineral mixed in with the material which formed the dam. They walked nearer. Ben narrowed his eyes a little and then kicked the stone off into the pond, where it rapidly sank.

'You must have been mistaken, Beth. I don't see anything.'

'Neither do I now. You're right, I must have been mistaken.'

Then, hand in hand, they walked back to the house in the light of dusk as the gold nugget was lost forever in the mud of the pond's bed.

We do hope that you have enjoyed reading this large print book.

Did you know that all of our titles are available for purchase?

We publish a wide range of high quality large print books including:
Romances, Mysteries, Classics
General Fiction
Non Fiction and Westerns

Special interest titles available in large print are:
The Little Oxford Dictionary
Music Book, Song Book
Hymn Book, Service Book

Also available from us courtesy of Oxford University Press:
Young Readers' Dictionary
(large print edition)
Young Readers' Thesaurus
(large print edition)

For further information or a free brochure, please contact us at:

Other titles in the Linford Western Library:

QUICK ON THE DRAW

Steve Hayes

Luke Chance has one claim to fame: he's real quick on the draw. Trying to outrun a reputation he doesn't want, he ends up in Rattlesnake Springs — where he meets the beautiful Teddy Austin. Teddy hires him to break horses on her father's ranch, but pretty soon Luke is locking horns with the Shadow Hills foreman, Thad McClory. As if that wasn't enough, the Austins are also having trouble with their neighbors. Though he doesn't want to get involved, it seems Luke can't help but do so . . .